RED RIVER GORGE SOUTH
A Rock Climbing Guidebook to Kentucky's Red River Gorge
5th Edition
Volume 2: Southern Regions

Authors: Ray Ellington and Blake Bowling.
Photographs by the authors unless otherwise credited.
Maps: Wolverine Publishing LLC and OutrageGIS.
Design: Wolverine Publishing LLC and McKenzie Long at Cardinal Innovative.
Published and distributed by Wolverine Publishing, LLC.

© 2017 Wolverine Publishing, LLC.
All rights reserved. This book or any part thereof may not be reproduced in any form without written permission from the publisher.

Cover photo:
Colette McInerney, *Kaleidoscope* (5.13c), Drive-By Crag. Photo: Javier Pérez López-Triviño.

Opening-page photo:
Josh Pugel on *BOHICA* (5.13b), the Motherlode. Photo: John Wesely.

International Standard Book Number: 978-1-938393-27-3

Library of Congress Catalog in Publication Data:
Library of Congress Control Number: 9781938393273

Wolverine Publishing is continually expanding its range of guidebooks. We collaborate with local climber/activists, authors, photographers, and small self-publishers to produce and distribute the finest guidebooks around. If you have an idea for a book, or would like to find out more about our company and publications, contact:

Wolverine Publishing
info@wolverinepublishing.com

www.wolverinepublishing.com   •   970.876.7100   •   PO Box 195 New Castle, CO 81647

Printed in Korea

Wolverine PUBLISHING

Reach for the best selection of guidebooks for the crags you love:

RED RIVER GORGE
BISHOP
JOSHUA TREE

NEW RIVER GORGE
CITY OF ROCKS
AND MANY MORE

www.wolverinepublishing.com

Photo: John Wesely.

WARNING

DO NOT USE THIS GUIDEBOOK UNLESS YOU READ AND AGREE TO THE FOLLOWING:

Rock climbing is a dangerous sport that can result in death, paralysis, or serious injury.

This book is intended as a reference tool for advanced/expert climbers. The activity and the terrain it describes can be or are extremely dangerous and require a high degree of ability and experience to negotiate. This book is not intended for inexperienced or novice climbers, nor is it intended as an instructional manual. If you are unsure of your ability to handle any circumstances that may arise, employ the services of a professional instructor or guide.

This book relies upon information and opinions provided by others that may not be accurate. Opinions concerning the technical difficulties, ratings of climbs, and protection or lack thereof are subjective and may differ from yours and others' opinions. Ratings may differ from area to area, holds may break, fixed protection may fail, fall out, or be missing, and weather may deteriorate; these and other factors, such as rock fall, inadequate or faulty protection, etc., may all increase the danger of a climbing route and may contribute to the climb being other than as described in the book. Furthermore, errors may be made during the editing, designing, proofing, and printing of this book. Thus, the information in this book is unverified, and the authors and publisher cannot guarantee its accuracy. Numerous hazards exist that are not described in this book. Climbing on any terrain described in this book, regardless of its description or rating, may result in your death, paralysis, or injury.

Do not use this book unless you are a skilled and experienced climber who understands and accepts the risks of rock climbing. If you choose to use any information in this book to plan, attempt, or climb a particular route, you do so at your own risk. Please take all precautions and use your own ability, evaluation, and judgment to assess the risks of your chosen climb, rather than relying on the information in this book.

THE AUTHORS AND PUBLISHER MAKE NO REPRESENTATIONS OR WARRANTIES, EXPRESSED OR IMPLIED, OF ANY KIND REGARDING THE CONTENTS OF THIS BOOK, AND EXPRESSLY DISCLAIM ANY AND ALL REPRESENTATIONS OR WARRANTIES REGARDING THE CONTENTS OF THIS BOOK, INCLUDING, WITHOUT LIMITATION, THE ACCURACY OR RELIABILITY OF INFORMATION CONTAINED HEREIN. WARRANTIES OF FITNESS FOR A PARTICULAR PURPOSE AND/OR MERCHANTABILITY ARE EXPRESSLY DISCLAIMED.

THE USER ASSUMES ALL RISKS ASSOCIATED WITH THE USE OF THIS BOOK INCLUDING, WITHOUT LIMITATION, ALL RISKS ASSOCIATED WITH ROCK CLIMBING.

FAILURE IS NOT AN OPTION

In November 2013 the Red River Gorge Fixed Gear Initiative (RRG FGI) started a campaign to subsidize the fixed gear used in the RRG. The goal was to have the community partner with the developers and share in the expense of purchasing the more expensive and sustainable stainless steel bolts. Since the first purchase at the end of 2013, the RRG FGI has continued to grow. In 2014 the RRG FGI secured Climbtech as our official partner. Climbtech was chosen for their exceptional product line, commitment to excellence and innovation in bringing sustainable hardware to market. The RRG FGI has now purchased over 4000 stainless steel bolts and raised over $30,000 in community donations and developer contributions to purchase subsidized stainless steel hardware.

The RRG FGI also recognized that many of the first-generation bolts placed in the past 10 to 20 years are corroding and supports their replacement. In partnership with the American Safe Climbing Association (ASCA), over 300 bolts have been placed by the hard work of developers who have volunteered their time and effort to benefit the climbing community.

- 116 PERMADRAWS
- 920 WAVE BOLT GLUE-INS
- 3280 HANGERS
- 3450 POWER-BOLTS

WITH YOUR HELP EVERY BOLT COUNTS

The RRG FGI continues to strive in its mission to subsidize all of the hardware placed on publicly accessible crags of the RRG so that the best materials can be used. If you love the Red and are enjoying climbing the classic routes, or the newer routes elsewhere, we ask that you support the RRG FGI. 100% of your donation goes toward the purchase of sustainable fixed gear that will be placed in the Red River Gorge.

You can learn more and donate at www.RRGFGI.com

CONTENTS

Foreword.. 10
Trip Beta 18
Natural History 26
Climbing History 28
Access.. 34

NATURAL BRIDGE 40

See Rocks. 44
Friction Slab. 44
Lady Slipper. 45
   Emerald City 45
   Global Village.. 48
Roadside Crag 52
The Zoo 59
Torrent Falls. 66
Beer Trailer Crag. 75

MUIR VALLEY 80

Slab City 88
The Arsenal. 90
Midnight Surf.. 92
The Boneyard.. 94
Animal Crackers. 98
Bibliothek. 99
Persepolis 102
The Solarium 104
The Great Arch 108
Sunbeam Buttress 110
The Great Wall .. .. .112
Shawnee Shelter 114
The Hideout 115
Indy Wall.. .. .. .118
The Sanctuary. 120
Inner Sanctum .. .. .124
The Stadium 126
Stronghold Wall 130
Ivory Tower.. .. .. .131
Tectonic and Johnny's Walls 133
Land Before Time Wall 138
Front Porch 139
Washboard Wall 140
Practice Wall .. .. .142
Guide Wall 145
Recess Rock 146
Bruise Brothers Wall 147
Sunnyside 150
Bowling Alley.. .. .. .152

PMRP .. .. .154

COAL BANK HOLLOW.. 157
   Gold Coast .. .. .167
   Solar Collector. 174
   Bright Side .. .. .177
   The Dark Side.. 182
   Far Side 188
FLAT HOLLOW 190
   Velo Crag.. .. .. .193
   The Shipyard 196
   The Getaway 201
   Throwback Crag 204
SORE HEEL HOLLOW 206
   Curbside 209
   The Gallery .. .. .212
   Volunteer Wall 220
   Left Field 223
   The Playground 224

Red River Gorge Retreats

Photos by Steph & Dave photography

606-663-3650
www.redrivergorgeretreats.com

Shady Grove	226
Megacave	228
Bronaugh Wall	230
Purgatory	232
What About Bob Wall	238
Rival Wall	242
Courtesy Wall	245
The Shire	248
North 40	250
BALD ROCK FORK	**253**
Chica Bonita Wall	254
Bob Marley Crag	262
Drive-By Crag	276

MOTHERLODE REGION 290

Bear's Den	292
The Motherlode	304
The Unlode	317
Chocolate Factory	318

SOUTHERN OUTLYING CLIFFS .. .. .336

Mount Olive Rock	336
The Oasis	337

GRADED LIST OF SPORT CLIMBS 339
GRADED LIST OF TRAD CLIMBS .. .. tk
INDEX .. .. tk

PEOPLE

Dave Hume	288
Bob Matheny	51
Shannon Stuart-Smith	247
Kipp Trummel	132
Miguel Ventura	38
Rick and Liz Weber	83

ADVERTISERS

Access Fund	17
Bad Bolts	349
Black Diamond	12-13
Climb Tech	208
Fixed Gear Initiative	5
J & H Lanmark	Back Flap, 33
Joshua Tree Skin Care	Front Flap
Lago Linda	20
Land of the Arches	23
Metolius	153
Miguels Pizza	Back Cover, 39
Petzl	207
Rakkup	15
RedRiverClimbing.com	11
Red River Outdoors	19
Red River Gorgeous Cabin Rental	22
Red River Gorge Retreats	7
Roads, Rivers, and Trails	9
RRGCC	35
Scarpa	200
Scenic Cabin Rentals	21
Torrent Falls Climbing Adventure	27
Trango	338
Wolfe County Search and Rescue	25
Wolverine Publishing	3

FOREWORD
By Bill Ramsey

It was an unusually hot day in late May of 1991. I was enjoying a rest day from climbing with some friends, swimming and jumping off bridges at the New River Gorge. This was during my one and only climbing trip of the year, and although I had started climbing 15 years earlier, I was being introduced to a new dimension of it — something called "sport climbing." My comrades were Steve Downes, a fellow climber/philosophy professor, and two local rock stars named Doug Reed and Porter Jarrard. As I grabbed another beer out of the cooler, the conversation turned to future plans. Porter casually stated that he was going to spend much of the following year bolting new routes at a major climbing area just outside Lexington, Kentucky. When I told him that I'd never heard of climbing in Kentucky, he turned and said with a classic Porter grin: "Trust me, you will."

No kidding. During the next few years, while I focused on writing and teaching at Notre Dame, reports would percolate up from Kentucky about wildly steep routes on good rock covered in pockets and edges. Eventually, I checked the map and saw

Bill Ramsey on *The Return of Darth Moll*, Dark Side. Photo: Hugh Loeffler.

that the Red River Gorge was "only" 400 miles away. I talked an ND graduate student into a three-day exploratory road trip to the Red. What we found would eventually change the direction of my life.

The climbing I discovered was so brilliant and fun that I started making a point of driving to the Red every other month. Soon this became a once- or twice-a-month affair. Before long, I found myself making the seven-hour drive every weekend — often connecting with partners from Chicago, Indianapolis, or with locals from Lexington. My eventual return to what can be characterized as full-blown "obsession-driven" climbing was partly the manifestation of something in my life-blood — having started at 17 with my father, I had experienced an emptiness since withdrawing from the sport to pursue an academic career. But I was also being pulled back by something external — something that had to do with the wonders of Corbin sandstone and people like Porter who knew how to turn it into a playground.

Religious philosophers often point to signs of "intelligent design" in the natural world as proof of God's existence — arguments that I generally scoff at. But the nature of the climbing at the Red sometimes makes me wonder. When one is desperately making a blind reach, it is not uncommon to find a natural pocket that is exactly where it needs to be and that perfectly fits the human hand, complete with a mini-pocket for the thumb. The overall quality of the rock, the diversity of the holds, the continuous steepness that makes for clean falls and athletic moves — all of these contribute to the sense that if one could actually construct an outdoor cliff with real rock, this is what it would be like. Climbs considered "bad" here would be four-star classics at most places.

Which is not to say everybody loves the Red. The most common complaint is that the routes are all mindless jug-hauls. This might have something to do with the fact that the first question most visitors ask upon arriving is, "Where are the mindless jug-hauls?" This is a bit like spending a week bouldering in Yosemite, and then whining that there are no long routes. The second criticism concerns the "down-home" culture of the folks that inhabit the surrounding countryside. While the local economy is indeed impoverished and there are a few bad apples, the people in this region are no less friendly than the ranchers around Rifle, or the farmers next to Smith Rock. Big surprise — the rural location of most rock-climbing areas tends to make the surrounding culture ... well, rural.

My rediscovered love of climbing wasn't due to just the geological aspects of the Red. The collection of dedicated and colorful characters who climb here offers kinship that is both welcome and welcoming. It is one of the few places where large factions of sport climbers and traditional climbers not only manage to coexist, but extend to one another a degree of mutual admiration. It is a place that spawned brilliant climbing prodigies like Katie Brown and David Hume, who set an example of grace and achievement, with no ego. The word that best describes the people here is "generous." This comes in many forms, including the hospitality of Miguel, who runs one of the friendliest climber campgrounds in the world. It includes the magnanimous efforts of route-developers like Porter, Hugh Loffler, Chris Martin, and Terry Kindred — folks who do all the hard work and often let others, like myself, receive the glory. It includes the energy Ray Ellington and others devote to maintaining an incredibly informative website that helps provide cohesion (and some useful friction) to those who climb here. And, of course, it includes the incredible devotion to access demonstrated by people like Shannon Stuart-Smith, the RRGCC, and Rick Weber — people who are responsible for the largest amount of climber-owned real estate in the country. The best way to thank these and others is by passing it on — by making an effort to give back as much to the land and the cliffs and your fellow climbers as you wind up taking. Considering just how much the Red has given me, I know I won't be able to fully reciprocate. But I am going to try.

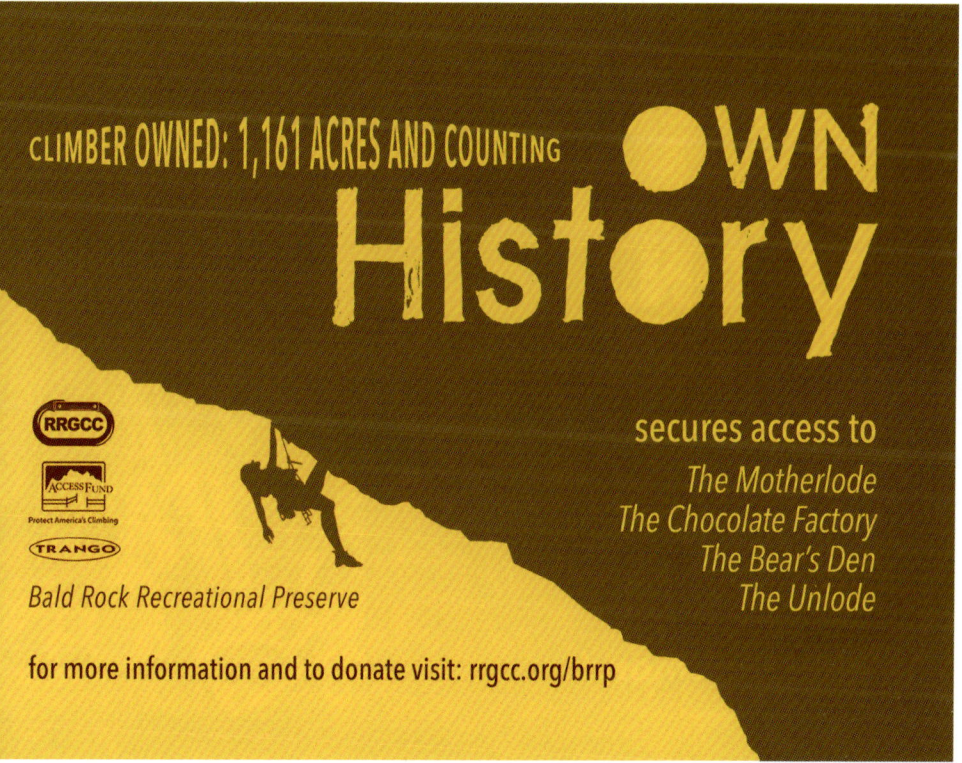

USE.
DESIGN.
ENGINEER.
BUILD.
REPEAT.

Black Diamond

Photographers: Sandra Salvas (l) and Andrew Burr (r)

INTRODUCTION TO THE 5TH EDITION

Blake Bowling

This fifth edition of the *Red River Gorge South* is the most extensive, complete, up-to-date guide to the rock climbing of the Red River Gorge, with more than 400 new routes, five new Pendergrass-Murray Recreational Preserve (PMRP) crags, six new Muir Valley crags, plus dozens of new routes at established crags. Sample one of the 20+ new routes at Bob Marley, or visit the "New Zoo," a quick-hit crag just up the road from Miguel's that has more than doubled its route count since last edition. The crags of Flat Hollow also make their debut in this guide, with a variety of climbs from 1998 Porter Jarrard sleepers to new-school classics. Maybe you heard the scream of a failed redpoint effort echo through the hollow beyond the Motherlode and wondered what was back there? That's the Bear's Den, another off-the-beaten path cliff that's previously been too undeveloped to include. Now with over 50 routes, this excellent wall finally earned its spot in the guidebook.

Photo: Jakob Skogheim.

Too often I see traveling climbers totally lost at the crag, trying to follow outdated info. Some parking areas have changed, new routes complicate previous guidebook descriptions, entire new trail systems throw off old directions — no wonder people get lost. Just the sheer number of new routes contained in this edition is enough reason to own it, not to mention new maps, updated trails and directions, and of course, great new photos from talented photographers. The Southern Region of the RRG has seen more new routes than anywhere else in Kentucky, and this guide gets you there. Icons, prominent features, and style, stories, historical/developer info, and relevant anecdotes give you a broad range of helpful and interesting information. We even utilized community input from RedRiverClimbing.com for grading and quality ratings.

As in previous versions, this edition contains short biographies, area histories, and often comical route descriptions. It is important to preserve this history; without it, we lose touch with our roots and some of the reasons we climb. Along with this edition's companion volume, *Red River Gorge North*, plus Ray Ellington's *Miller Fork Climbing*, you will have the complete listing of descriptions, directions, photos, and beta for several thousand rock climbs in the area — enough to keep you pumped for a lifetime.

I remember the moment I purchased my first John Bronaugh Red River Gorge guidebook, which set the tone for the RRG and for Ray Ellington's guidebooks that came after. I sat for hours at a time reading the descriptions, the grades, and approaches to every area in the book. Many of the witty descriptions have stayed with me to this day — even of routes I have yet to climb. This book builds on the foundation Bronaugh's book laid down in 1993, as well as the four previous editions that Ray has meticulously maintained. His online guide, RedRiverClimbing.com, shows the dedication he has to the area, the climbing, and its rich history.

I have tried to continue the Bronaugh/Ellington tradition, with jovial-yet-accurate route descriptions, while not giving too much away for your all-important onsight. I hope you enjoy this new guide to the premier sport climbing area in the nation, and that it has you reading for hours, as Bronaugh's first book did for me.

rakkup

Climbing Guidebooks. Reinvented.

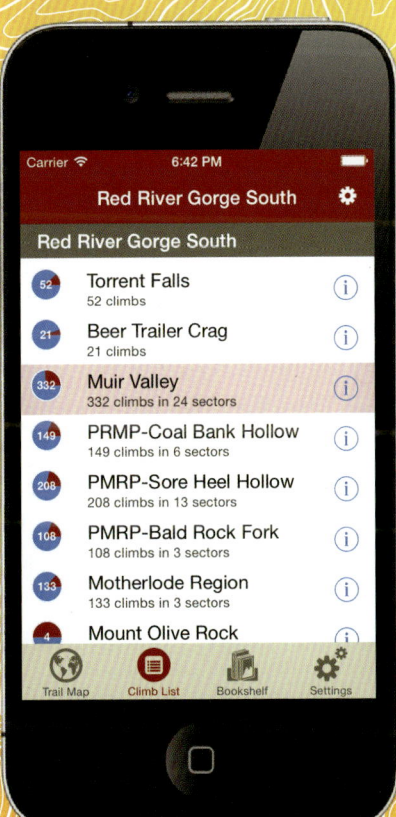
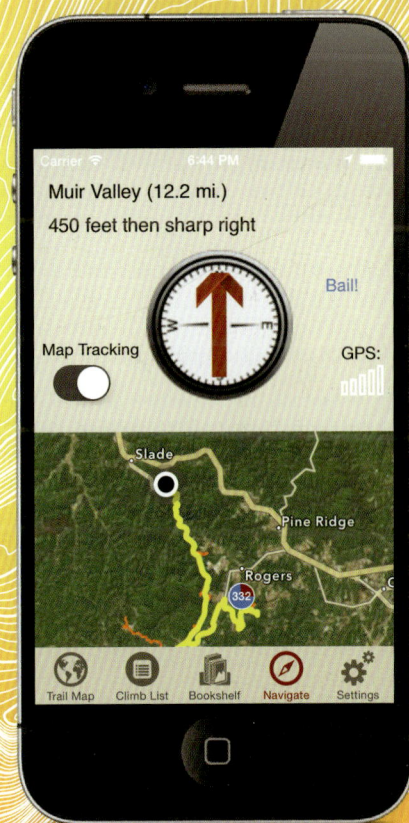

USING THIS BOOK

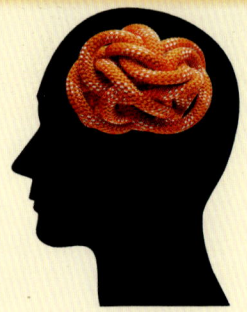

This book is one half of a two-volume guide to the rock climbing in the Red River Gorge, Kentucky. The cliffs in this volume are located in the "Southern Region," which means they are south of the Mountain Parkway (and Miguel's Pizza). This is a comprehensive guide to these cliffs, meaning all the roped climbing (sport and traditional) at press time is included. This is not a bouldering guide, although a few classic boulder problems are mentioned.

Routes are rated for difficulty using the Yosemite Decimal System, and for quality using a five-star scale (see below). The only convention that isn't standard is the use of **COLOR TO DIFFERENTIATE ROUTES**:

① **Blue denotes a sport climb.** Blue routes can be led with a rack of quickdraws only.

② **Red denotes a traditional climb.** It also denotes a mixed or aid climb. Red routes require the leader to carry and place natural protection devices.

③ **Green denotes a boulder problem.**

★★★★★ The **STAR RATINGS** in this guide are calculated not only by word of mouth and our own flawed opinions, but also, when available, from several years of community ratings taken from the online guidebook at www.redriverclimbing.com. As with anything involving taste of some sort, it is impossible to find a quality rating that matches everyone's opinion, so don't avoid a route just because it has a low number of stars. Routes clean up and change at the Red due to the nature of sandstone. On the other side, don't chase a route just for its five-star status. Five stars means classic, and as with anything labeled "classic," there may be other variables such as historical significance involved, which may not interest you. If you feel that a star rating is way off, go to www.redriverclimbing.com and vote in the online guidebook.

SYMBOLS are used to denote important beta about the cliffs in this book:

 Kid-friendly cliff. These cliffs are relatively close to the car, have straightforward approaches, and flat/safe bases, where momentarily unattended toddlers are unlikely to crawl to their deaths.

 Driving time from Miguel's Pizza to the trailhead.

 Hiking time

 Rain shelter. These cliffs have a good selection of routes that are overhanging enough to stay dry in the rain.

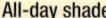 **GPS** in decimal degrees.

Sun/shade symbols: These indicate the general orientation and sun-aspect of cliffs. Take these symbols as a rough guide, bearing in mind that sun-aspect can change dramatically with the seasons.

 All-day sun

 All-day shade

 Morning sun

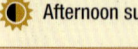 Sun-shade mix.
These cliffs have multiple orientations.

 Afternoon sun

DOGS are not allowed in Muir Valley, Graining Fork Nature Preserve, or Torrent Falls. Otherwise, the Red is a dog-friendly destination. Please keep your dog leashed in public areas, such as campgrounds and parking lots, and as courtesy demands elsewhere. Be a good dog owner and carry plastic bags to remove poop.

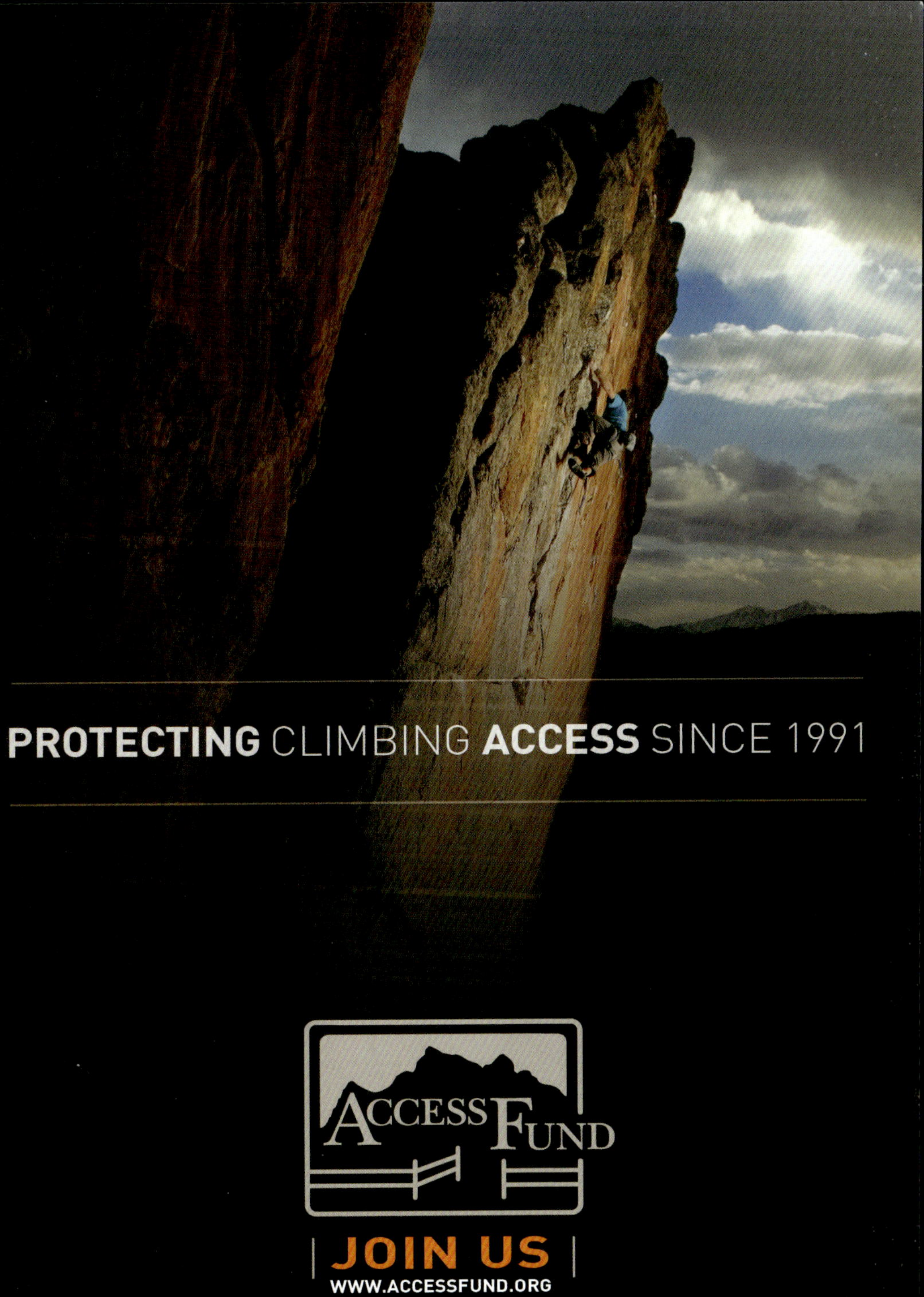
PROTECTING CLIMBING ACCESS SINCE 1991
ACCESS FUND
JOIN US
WWW.ACCESSFUND.ORG

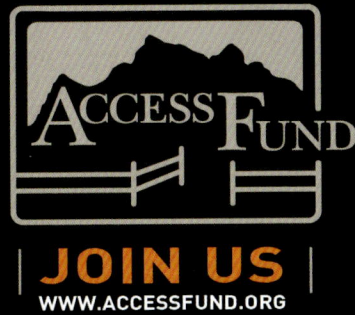

TRIP BETA

This section will help you plan your trip, and assist you in navigating the Red River Gorge and surrounding area.

Journey's end: Miguel's Pizza. Photo: Elodie Saracco.

DRIVING TIMES

Lexington, KY	1 hour
Louisville, KY	2 hours
Cincinnati, OH	2–2.5 hours
Knoxville, TN	3.5 hours
Indianapolis, IN	3.5–4 hours
New River Gorge, WV	4 hours
Asheville, NC	5 hours

GETTING THERE

The Red River Gorge is located in the state of Kentucky in the central/eastern US. The Red is in the eastern part of the state, about 60 miles southeast of Lexington. The closest airports are Lexington (one hour); Louisville, Kentucky (two hours); and Cincinnati/Northern Kentucky airport (two hours). To reach the Red from Interstate 64, take exit 98 onto the Bert T. Combs Mountain Parkway. Drive 33 miles on the parkway, then take exit 33 at Slade. Turn right onto KY 11 and head south 1.7 miles to reach Miguel's Pizza on the left. Miguel's Pizza is the starting point for directions to most climbing areas in this guide.

WHEN TO VISIT

The best time to climb in the Red is the fall (September through November), when the humidity is relatively low and the daytime temperatures range from the mid-50s to the high 70s. Spring (March through May) is also a great season for climbing at the Red, with temperatures similar to those in the fall, but the chance of rain is greater. It is possible to climb year-round in the Red, although the heat, humidity, and insects during the summer can be almost unbearable. Winters are normally relatively mild, with average highs in the 40s; unlike the western part of the country, however, the sun tends to remain behind the clouds. Snow and ice are common.

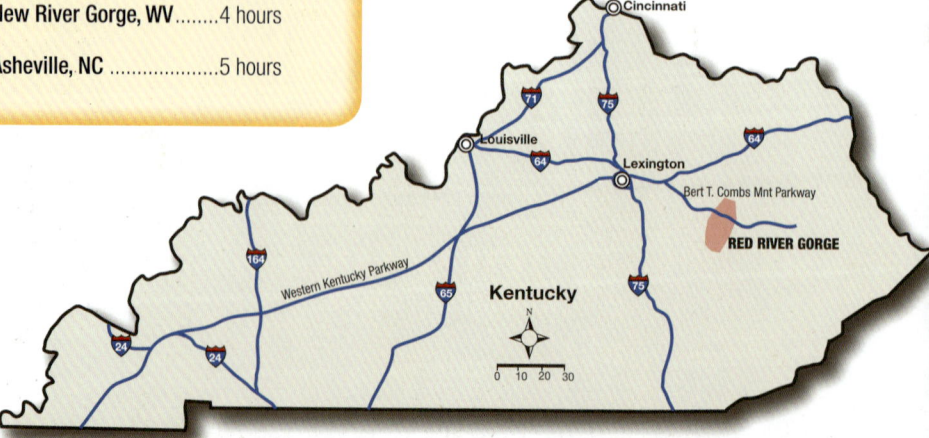

WHERE TO STAY

Campgrounds

Miguel's Pizza (606-663-1975). Rates are currently $3 per night per person. Showers are available for $1 per 4 minutes; laundry is $2 per load to wash and $2 to dry. Climbers can camp year-round (the restaurant itself is open March 1 until Thanksgiving). The parking lot and camping area can reach capacity during spring and fall, so try to get a spot early if you're coming on a weekend.

Lago Linda Hideaway (606-464-2876). Nestled in the Southern Region of the Red River Gorge, near the Motherlode and Pendergrass-Murray Recreation Preserve, Lago Linda offers a tranquil retreat and quiet surroundings. All campsites are graveled, with electric hook-ups, water, picnic table, and fire ring.

Land of the Arches Campground (606-668-7074) is another great option, located close to Muir Valley, with great indoor space and showers (but no dogs allowed).

Primitive camping with a permit is allowed almost anywhere in the Red on Forest Service land. Campsites must be at least 300 feet from roads and trails, and campers must have a permit. Permits can be purchased from the Shell station in Slade for $3–$5.

EMERGENCY INFO

The nearest hospitals are the Marcum Wallace Hospital in Irvine or Kentucky River Medical Center in Jackson, but the Urgent Treatment Center or University of Kentucky Hospital, both in Lexington, may be your better bets.

Useful numbers are:

Marcum Wallace Hospital: 606-723-2115

Kentucky River Medical Center: 606-666-6000

Urgent Treatment Center, Lexington: 859-233-4882

Lee County Dispatch: 606-464-4111

Wolfe County Dispatch: 911

Kentucky State Police: 606-784-4127

Cabin Rentals

Lago Linda (606-464-2876)

Miguel's (info@miguelspizza.com)

Red River Gorge Cabin Rentals/Cliffview Resort (888-596-0525)

Red River Gorgeous (606-663-9824; rrgcabin.com)

Red River Outdoors (606-663-ROCK)

Scenic Cabin Rentals (606-663-0000)

Motels

Lil Abner's Motel (606-663-5384, lilabnermotel.com). Located about a half mile south on the left from the rest area on KY 11.

- Offering 40 modern cabins with 1 to 6 bedrooms
- Will discount for long stays over one week
- Call for reservations: 606-663-0000
- www.sceniccabin.com

For fast pickup, order ahead at www.danielboonetradingpost.net

- Full service coffee shop and deli with local meats
- Groceries, fresh wraps and sandwiches to go
- Mountain Ranks T-Shirts
- Open 8:30-9pm weekdays, 7:30-9pm weekends

LAND OF THE ARCHES CAMPGROUND

- Hot Showers
- Private and Group Sites
- Within 5 minutes of Muir Valley
- 15 minutes from the Motherlode
- WiFi and Computer Area
- Gaming Area
- Running Water, Picnic Tables
- Great Cooking Location

Camping Starting At $5 A Night Per Person

Like us on Facebook!   606.668.7074

landofthearches.com

design by SpiderSavvy.com

EATS AND TREATS

Eating Out

Miguel's Pizza (606-663-1975). Miguel makes great pizza, pasta, salads, and breakfast. The price is impossible to beat and topping selections are unique — where else can you get black beans, pasta, mango salsa, roast pork, avocado, and rice on your pizza? You can also grab a pint of Ben and Jerry's or choose from a wide selection of non-alcoholic drinks.

Red River Rockhouse (606-668-6656). Climber-owned, serving burgers, burritos, salads, beer, and more, all with locally sourced ingredients. Open Thursday through Sunday during climbing season, with killer breakfast on Sunday. Located about a mile north of Torrent Falls on KY 11.

Sky Bridge Station (606-668-9927). Gourmet hot dogs, quesadillas, and the by far the biggest draft beer selection in the Red. Located in the town of Pine Ridge close to the Eastern Gorge.

Subway. Across from the Shell Station in Slade.

Sam's Hot Dog Stand. The name says it all... next to Thrillsville about a mile north of Miguel's.

VETS

Stanton Veterinary Clinic: 606-663-5866

Cundiff, Jim L, Beattyville: 606-464-2903

Minter Veterinary Services, Beattyville: 606-464-1155

Beattyville offers a perenially rotating cast of restaurants, including of course the ubiquitous **Dairy Queen**, as well as **Los Two Brothers** (606-208-8002) for serviceable Mexican, **Manna Cafe** (606-319-2233) for "upscale" Southern fare, **Billy's Place** (606-560-3333) for burgers and good milkshakes, and **Hilltop Pizza** (606-464-9990).

Stanton is seven miles west on Mountain Parkway and has several fast-food outlets including **Dairy Queen**, **McDonald's**, and **Taco Bell**. Also, don't miss **Bruen's** (606-663-4252) for some down-home Kentucky food that some might find a little "too authentic." **Mi Finca** (606-663-0980) also offers reasonable Mexican from the same owners as Los Two Brothers in Beattyville. Further west in Winchester, check out **El Camino Real** (859-737-9179) for the closest Mexican joint with good strong margaritas.

Campfire at Miguel's Pizza. Photo: Andrew Burr.

Groceries

The **Shell station** in Slade is pretty good about carrying supplies you might need during your visit. **Daniel Boone Coffee Shoppe and Deli**, on KY 11 about a half mile toward Slade from Miguel's, has an excellent selection of deli items, groceries, and supplies. The nearest grocery store is **Kroger** in Stanton. If you're driving west on Mountain Parkway, turn right off the Stanton exit, drive a few blocks, turn left onto KY 11/15, and Kroger will be on the left. There is a **Super Walmart** in Winchester: head back toward Lexington on the Mountain Parkway. Join I-64 west, take exit 94, and head left on Bypass Road for about a mile and a half. There is also an **IGA** grocery in Beattyville that is much closer to the Southern region and Lago Linda's, but the selection leaves a lot to be desired.

Climbing Gear

Miguel's Pizza. Harnesses, cams — you name it. **J&H Lanmark in Lexington** (859-278-0730).

Climbing Guide Services

Red River Outdoors (859-230-3567). **Sky Bridge Station** (606-668-9927). **Torrent Falls Climbing Adventure** (606-668-6613).

Internet Access

Miguel's Pizza. WiFi is free but spotty.

Lago Linda's and **Land of Arches.** WiFi included with camping fee.

Red River Rockhouse and **Skybridge Station.** Free WiFi.

Powell County Public Library in Stanton (606-663-4511). Located at 725 Breckenridge Street in the small town of Stanton, about seven miles west on Mountain Parkway from the rest area.

Wolfe County Public Library (606-668-6571). Located on the east side of KY 15 about an eighth of a mile north of Campton.

Rest-Day Fun

The Kentucky Reptile Zoo (606-663-9160) is a highly recommended rest-day activity. The owner is a world-renowned expert and regularly extracts venom for medical use. Be sure to make it by 1pm in time for venom extraction and feeding! Located just south of the rest area in Slade.

Rent a canoe or kayak from **Red River Adventure** (606-663-5258).

Tick the Via Ferrata at **Torrent Falls Climbing Adventure** (606-668-6613).

Wolfe County Search & Rescue (WCSAR) is an all-volunteer organization, chartered by Kentucky Emergency Management, specializing in technical rope rescue and search operations in and around the Red River Gorge. As the primary wilderness rescue squad for Wolfe County, the team provides its rescue services to the popular climbing areas of: Muir Valley, Roadside Crag (Graining Fork Nature Preserve), Lady Slipper, Emerald City, the Zoo, Torrent Falls, Sky Bridge, Funk Rock City, Princess Arch, Half Moon, and Chimney Top. WCSAR also works with other county teams in mutual aid SAR operations in Lee, Powell, Morgan, and Menifee Counties.

WCSAR typically responds between 30-40 rescues a year. And, although they never charge for their services, the team receives relatively little funding or equipment from the state and, instead, relies on the financial donations and moral support from local residents, businesses, and the climbing community.

Wolfe County Search and Rescue stands ready 24-7 to come to your aid in the event of a climbing accident. Donations are very much appreciated.

Wolfe County Search & Rescue
P.O. Box 822
Campton, Ky. 41301

TRIP BETA

Live like a local and hit up Lexington for an Indian buffet or some downtown nightlife. Don't miss the **Keeneland** horse-racing series during April and October (www.keeneland.com).

Lexington also has several movie theaters. Recommended is the **Kentucky Theatre** in downtown Lexington (859-231-6997). It shows first-run indie and vintage films, and serves beer!

The nearest large shopping area is Hamburg Place, just off I-75 at exit 108 in Lexington. Take Mountain Parkway west to I-64 west. Keep left when you reach the I-75 split to head south. After a couple of miles you'll reach the Man O' War exit (108). Turn right to get dumped directly into a wealth of places to drop money, including Barnes & Noble, Starbucks, Dick's Sporting Goods, Meijer, and Target, to name a few.

The Lee County Rec Center, on the left side of Hwy 11 just south of The Motherlode turnoff (498), has free pool tables, ping-pong, air hockey, cheap but pretty good pizza, and bowling for $5/hour.

For a taste of local life, check out the drive-in in Stanton. Just be careful not to get caught up in the ritualistic "circling of the cars" in town, unless you're into picking up local high-school chicks.

ALCOHOL

Beer and climbing go together like ... beer and climbing. However, don't get stuck jonesing for a brew on Sunday, because alcohol isn't sold on Sunday in some Kentucky counties. The laws are particularly strange around the Red because some of the counties are "dry," meaning no alcohol sales — ever. Rather than worrying about which counties are dry and which are wet, just remember that the nearest place to buy beer is C&S Carryout, aka "The Beer Trailer," located about a quarter mile south of Torrent Falls on KY 11. There is even great cragging in the backyard! If the Beer Trailer is closed, try One-Stop Liquor in downtown Campton, Beer King on 1036 in Zachariah, the Ashland gas station in Pine Ridge at the intersection of 715 and 15, and of course Red River Rockhouse and Sky Bridge Station (except on Sundays). A good rule of thumb while drinking in the Red is to be discreet and conceal your beverage wherever you are.

NATURAL HISTORY

Flora/Fauna

Much of the Red River Gorge is forested in oak, poplar, silver maple, beech, hemlock, and numerous pines. Beneath the canopy you will see the beautiful spring bloomer, the redbud dogwood, sassafras, magnolia, mountain laurel, and rhododendron. Many plants carpet the forest floor, including dozens of species of ferns, mosses, and lichens, and wild flowers including columbine, iris, trillium, orchids, and the endangered white-haired goldenrod. Watch out for poison ivy, which is widespread, both on the ground and at the anchors of certain climbs.

You can encounter a diverse collection of wildlife in the Red River Gorge, including deer, bobcats, raccoons, skunks, chipmunks, flying squirrels, and bats. Many bird species can be seen, such as turkey vultures, hawks, ruffed grouse, turkeys, owls, woodpeckers, and many songbirds. Reptiles and amphibians common to the area include newts, box turtles, fence lizards, skinks, copperheads, timber rattlesnakes, garter and green snakes, toads, spring peepers, and salamanders. Not to be taken lightly are the small but annoying insects of the Gorge. Climbers who brave the area in hot weather will become all too familiar with pesky mosquitoes, "no-see-ums," black flies, and deer flies. Wasps often build nests in pockets on rock faces, so use caution when climbing in the summer months.

Geology

The Red River Gorge has more than 100 natural arches and one of the finest collections of pinnacles and cliffs east of the Rocky Mountains. Whether you're new to the area or have spent years exploring it, its unique splendor cannot go unnoticed.

The stone of the Red River Gorge was formed about 300 million years ago as a deposit at the edge of a shallow inland sea that covered much of the middle part of North America. Over millions of years, the Red River and its tributaries eroded layer upon layer of rock, exposing clifflines up to 200 feet tall made of tough Corbin sandstone. The rusty-red appearance of the sandstone comes from limonite, which acts as a cement, holding together the pebbly and sandy layers. Striking iron-oxide bands, created from the limonite, can be seen at

Iron-oxide bands in the sandstone. Photo: Andrew Burr.

many climbing areas — a good example is the *Table of Colors* wall. Millions of years of erosion and weathering have sculpted the sandstone cliffs, creating arches, cracks, and heavily pocketed faces. The solidity of the rock and abundance of features are what make the Red River Gorge a world-class climbing destination.

Archaeology

About 13,000 years ago, when glaciers still covered much of North America, the first people are believed to have inhabited the Red River Gorge. Small bands of Ice Age hunters followed herds of mastodons and wooly mammoths to Kentucky, and stayed, utilizing the abundant natural resources of the area. The rock shelters common to the Red made ideal habitats for these people. They hunted and harvested many items such as acorns, nuts, wild fruit, fungi, and various plants.

The dry, nitrate-rich soils found in the rock shelters and throughout the Red River Gorge provide an excellent environment for studying these prehistoric people because they help preserve plant materials and other normally perishable artifacts. Excavations of inhabited rock shelters have revealed seeds that indicate the people living in the area started domesticating and cultivating wild plants at least 3,000 years ago.

The Red River Gorge has many recorded archaeological sites as well as many yet to be discovered. In 2003, the Clifty Wilderness and the Indian Creek area was designated a National Archaeological District and placed on the National Register of Historic Places. Please respect our archaeological heritage by not disturbing any sites you encounter.

Show your RRG Guide book for 10% off any Activity!

- AMGA Certified Instructors
- Guided Rock Climbing
- Guided Rappelling
- Climbing Clinics
- Multi-pitch Climbing
- 2 Hour Lessons
- Via Ferrata

Torrent Falls Climbing Adventure offers private guided classes and climbing clinics from certified instructors that are catered to your needs/level. Experience or no experience, you can learn **sport** or **traditional climbing**, from knowledgeable, helpful, and professional instructors. Torrent Falls Climbing Adventure is also home to the first Via Ferrata in the USA.

Reservations are _required_ please call us!
606-668-6613   www.torrentfalls.com
1617 N KY 11 Campton, KY 41301

CLIMBING HISTORY

Larry Day on *Dicey at Best* 5.8+ at Lower Small Wall, 1979. Photo: Larry Day collection.

The history of rock climbing in the Red River Gorge dates back to the 1950s when *Caver's Route* at Tower Rock is rumored to have been climbed. This route and others were established by local cavers, comfortable with the occasional chimney runout or even drilling a bolt here and there to reach the top of a pinnacle.

The Gorge started getting more attention in the late 1960s and early 1970s. D. Britz and Ron Stokely made some of the earliest recorded ascents, in 1969, when they climbed classics such as *Chimney's Chimney* and *Tunnel Route* on Chimney Top Rock. Soon, a group including Larry Day, Frank Becker, Tom Seibert, and Ellen Seibert started making regular visits. They came armed with Hexes, Stoppers, knotted slings, and Chouinard tube chocks. They found that Vietnam-War–style jungle boots, once the tread had worn off, provided decent friction on the Kentucky sandstone. These climbers were heavily influenced by the 1970s' clean-climbing ethic, advocating climbing with minimal bolts and without pitons, which were seen as "old school" by the younger generation. Thus, the cracks of the Red River Gorge never suffered the abuse of pin scars.

The focus during this era was making it to the top, and if a line did not run continuously from base to summit, it was ignored. The determined group probably spent more days looking for acceptable lines than they did actually climbing, although they did manage to bag around 40 documented ascents between 1970 and 1975, with grades as hard as 5.9. Notable routes include the still popular *Diamond in the Crack* on Jewel Pinnacle, *G.I.* at Military Wall, *Arachnid* and the perfect hand crack of *Africa* at Tower Rock, *Frenchburg Overhangs* at Dunkan Rock, *Buzzard's Roost North*, and the first pocketed-face route in the Red, *Face Farce* at Princess Arch.

1975 saw the area's first guidebook, *Red River Gorge Climber's Guide* by Frank Becker, which inspired more climbers to explore the area, and during the late 1970s the number of first ascents soared. More than 80 lines were established, some within the 5.10 range. Much of this development was documented in the 1978 guidebook *Rawk! A Climber's Guide to the Red River Gorge,* by Ed Benjamin and Ed Pearsall. Larry Day, Tom Seibert, and Ellen Seibert remained at the forefront, and Day and Ed Pearsall teamed up to apply their honed skills to some of the more difficult and bold lines, including *Tower of Power* (5.10c R) at Tower Rock and *Last Day* at Chimney Top. The duo came close to the first free ascent of probably the most challenging and definitely the best and longest 5.10 in the Red, *The Quest* (5.10c), but slipped out of the final 25-foot offwidth section and never went back to complete the line. They did manage to reach the summit, which was important to them. Anyone who has attempted *The Quest* will respect the efforts of these two men, who didn't have the security of the large camming devices available today. This period also saw the first 5.11s in the Red, with Bill Strachan's strenuous offwidth *Here Comes Batman* (5.11c) at Staircase Wall in 1978, followed one year later by Day's *Insanity Ceiling* (5.11a) at Tower Rock. 1980 saw a third guidebook to the Red, by Ed Pearsall, containing nearly 150 lines.

The early 1980s brought the total to more than 300 routes. A new generation stormed the Red with better gear, better shoes, bigger muscles, and wild tights. Two strong climbers from Cincinnati played cleanup, ticking off the proudest lines nobody had been able to do. Nicknamed the "Beene Brothers," om Souders and Jeff Koenig bagged modern-day testpieces such as *The Return of Geoff Beene* (5.10d) at Skybridge Ridge, *Pink Feat* (5.11d/5.12a) at Military Wall, and the five-star classic *Inhibitor* (5.11a) at Eastern Sky Bridge. Souders also teamed up with Bob Hayes to make the first free ascent of *The Quest*.

Another important contributor who made an appearance in the early '80s was John Bronaugh, who, with his partner Ron Snider, began what would become two decades of first ascents. The strong and bold Greg Smith established several difficult and poorly protected testpieces, some of which, like *Whimpering Insanity* at Tower Rock and *Invisible Barrier* at Bee Branch Rock, fell within the 5.11 X range. One of his safer and more popular routes, the finger crack of *Synchronicity* (5.11a), now stands out on the heavily bolted 5.10 Wall of Roadside Crag. The most prolific contributor, however, was Martin Hackworth, who managed to tick off about 70 lines between 1980 and 1985. His classics include the amazing finger crack *Finger Lickin' Good* (5.10c) at Hen's Nest and *Vector Trouble* (5.10a) at Long Wall. Much of this development was recorded in yet another guidebook, *Stones of Years*, by Hackworth and Grant Stephens, published in 1984.

Development plateaued from 1985 through 1990 as more climbers visited the area and the focus changed to repeating established climbs, but a few new lines were established. Although there were many people in the mix now, they had no idea of the madness that was about to consume their beloved sandstone. In the distance a faint sound could be heard — the sound of a power drill.

In 1990, with another edition of Hackworth's guide hot off the press detailing close to 400 routes, a young climber named Porter Jarrard stepped onto the scene. The Red already had a few rap-bolted face climbs, antique 5.10s like *Sundance* at Pebble Beach and *Captain One-Eye* at Purple Valley, but all had been established with a hand drill. Armed with a power drill, Jarrard took things to a different level. The once unclimbable, pocketed, overhanging sandstone walls of the Gorge became prime real estate as he began rap bolting at a furious pace. By the end of 1990, 30 sport lines had been established. Jarrard bolted 20 of them, and each became a classic: *Reliquary* and *Tissue Tiger* (5.12b), *Stay the Hand* (5.12a), *Wild Gift* (5.12c) ... the list goes on. Jarrard's *Table of Colors* in 1990, followed by *Revival* a year later, introduced 5.13 to the Red. He had an eye for a great line, and the quality of his routes quickly helped his tactics gain acceptance. It wasn't long before other climbers, including Jim Link, Jamie Baker, Hugh Loeffler, Neil Strickland, John Bronaugh, Jeff Moll, Chris Snyder, Stacy Temple, Mark Williams, and Charles Tabor, were lugging Bosch or Hilti drills to the crag.

In 1993, John Bronaugh published *Red River Gorge Climbs*. The guide contained nearly 700 routes, more than twice the number of lines published only three years earlier. It was clear that sport climbing was changing the face of rock climbing at the Red River Gorge, a fact made even clearer by the discovery in 1994 of the mother of all walls, the Motherlode. This crag solidified the grade of 5.13 and helped establish the Red as one of the best sport-climbing destinations in the country.

In 1995, with the sport-climbing craze gaining momentum, a quiet resurgence in traditional climbing was occurring at the Red. It became common to see climbers brushing cobwebs off old, abandoned trad lines. Kris Hampton and Ray Ellington started a campaign to tick the area's overlooked offwidths, previously dismissed as too wide, steep, or flaring, and with routes like *Country*

Ed Pearsall, 1979. Photo: Frank Becker.

The turn of the century saw a surge in development in what would become the Pendergrass-Murray Recreational Preserve. Top: Neal Strickland on his route *Buddha Hole*, 5.12a, the Solar Collector (2000). Bottom: Rob McFall on his route *Elephant Man*, 5.13b, the Dark Side (2002). Photos: Rob McFall collection.

Lovin' at Indian Creek and *Hidden Dragon* at Pistol Ridge brought the 5.12 grade to crack climbing at the Red. Around this time, the visiting finger-crack master Steve Petro sent the often-attempted *Nazi Bitch Crack* at Pebble Beach, renaming it *Welcome to Ol' Kentuck* and upping the ante for traditional lines to 5.13a.

Bolting slowed down dramatically between 1995 and 1999 as Porter left the scene and many people found a new home: camped out under their 5.13 projects at the Motherlode. Others started exploring the cliffs lining the roads owned by the oil companies, opening up a few new areas in the Southern Region. In 1998, John Bronaugh released the second edition of *Red River Gorge Climbs*. The book was almost twice the size of the first edition, containing nearly 1000 routes. In 1999, child prodigy Dave Hume pushed the boundaries of the possible even further, bringing 5.14 to the Gorge with his first ascent of *Thanatopsis* at the Motherlode.

With the Red quickly becoming known as one of the best sport-climbing destinations in the country, Miguel's Pizza began to run out of food on weekend nights as hundreds of climbers set up home in Miguel's backyard. It became common to stand in line for routes at Roadside Crag, Military Wall, and Left Flank. Climbing gyms opened in surrounding cities, bringing even more weekend warriors to the area to test their skills on real rock. It became close to impossible to find a camping spot at the once peaceful Roadside Crag camping area.

2000 marked a new explosion in route development. The oil fields in the Southern Region were still being explored, with remarkable walls such as the Dark Side and Gold Coast discovered, providing a place other than the Motherlode for elite climbers to play. Bill Ramsey, Dave Hume, and Ben Cassel solidified the 5.14 grade. John Bronaugh was still going strong, bolting just about anything he could rappel down at the (currently closed) Oil Crack Crag, while Terry Kindred was across the way developing the Arena. The back roads of the oil-company land became the new place to go. Although the land was privately owned, the oil company had the mining rights. Cars were getting stuck, and parking became a major issue as oil workers often found climbers' cars in their way. With relationships turning sour between oil workers and climbers, access was saved when the RRGCC stepped up and purchased most of the property, creating the Pendergrass-Murray Recreational Preserve (PMRP).

Several miles away, another private venture was being established. Rick and Liz Weber opened several hundred acres of land for route development, an area they named Muir Valley. In only a couple of years, between 2003 and 2005, Jared Hancock and his wife, Karla, along with Tim Powers, J.J., Mike Susko, Barry Brolley, and others, developed nearly 200 bolted lines on the property. Muir Valley became an overnight hit and contributed significantly to decreasing the crowds at vintage cliffs such as Roadside and Torrent Falls. In 2015, Muir was formally gifted to the climbing community by the Webers and the property is now managed by Friends of Muir Valley (www.friendsofmuirvalley.com), a non-profit organization.

In 2007, the RRGCC joined forces with Petzl to bring the Petzl RocTrip to the Red River Gorge. Nearly 35 professional climbers from all over the world made it to the backwoods of Kentucky to see what the Red had to offer. This proved to be a highly successful fundraising event, and also put the Red on the map with the professionals as having some of the best rock climbing in the world. Longstanding projects were quickly dispatched, and local testpieces were flashed and onsighted with ease. It was an exciting time for locals to see legends such as Chris Sharma, Dave Graham, and Lynn Hill rave about the excellent climbing.

That year marked the beginning of a new era at the Red. The word was out, and the area once known for its jug-haul endurance lines began seeing nearly featureless lines in the 5.14-and-up range go down on a regular basis. The number of routes within that elite range went from just a few to more than 20 within five years. On the forefront of the dispatching were locals Adam Taylor and Andrew Gearing, along with Colorado–based climber Jonathan Siegrist, who managed to routinely clean up abandoned projects such as *The Golden Ticket* (5.14c), *Pure Imagination* (5.14c), *The Death Star* (5.14b), and *Twenty-Four Karats* (5.14c). In 2011, Taylor fired the first ascent of *Southern Smoke Direct* and wavered between a grade of 5.14d and 5.15a. In 2012 the route was flashed by visiting Czech climber Adam Ondra, who confirmed the grade at 5.14d. During the same visit Ondra onsighted *The Golden Ticket* and *Pure Imagination* in a day (both originally rated 5.14d) and suggested a grade of 5.14c for both.

On the traditional front, Andrew Gearing took it to the next level by freeing the aid line *Right On, Solid, and Far Out* at Eastern Sky Bridge Ridge in 2012, making it the Red's first 5.14 traditional climb, *Silently Does the Sun Shine*. Only weeks before he had established *Sacred Geometry* (5.13b) at Long Wall, along with scads of other traditional 5.13s throughout the Red, including *Gingervitis* (5.13b), *Yamaraja's Abode* and *Cradle of Light* (both 5.13a). Over a five-year rampage, Andrew single-handedly tripled the number of 13a or harder trad routes in the Red.

In light of the continued prohibition on new sport routes in the Daniel Boone National Forest, private land purchases have been the go-to option for expanding climbing access in the Red over the last 15 years. In addition to the aforementioned generosity of Rick and Liz Weber in ensuring permanent access to Muir Valley, Roadside Crag

CLIMBING HISTORY

Bad Girls' Club

It all started in 1999 when a little kid named Katie Brown onsighted *Omaha Beach* (then 5.13d) to become the first female to onsight the grade. Since then, women have shown the Red no mercy, proving without a doubt that girls can climb just as hard as the boys on the area's steep sandstone. Surf through any online bro-fest forum about it and you'll find dozens of theories about why that is—maybe it's because the Red isn't "reachy" and there are lots of foot options for smaller frames, or maybe it's because they have smaller fingers that fit better in the pockets? **Wrong, guys!** It's because the girls are nasty strong and good at climbing and they've proven it time and again!

Sasha Digiulian thrust herself into the limelight in 2011 with her much-publicized ascent of *Pure Imagination* (5.14c) and a match of Katie Brown's onsight feat on *Omaha Beach*. The following year, 11-year-old Ashima Shiraishi took down *Southern Smoke* and *Lucifer* (both 5.14c) during her five-day fall break. Since then, 5.14 ascents by the ladies have become so commonplace that there are hardly any "first female ascents" left to be had. Perhaps the most coveted one, though, just fell to Michaela Kiersch in late 2016 with her ascent of the stout *Golden Ticket* (5.14c), probably the hardest female ascent at the Red so far.

Michaela Kiersch on the *Golden Ticket*, 5.14c, Chocolate Factory. Photo: Andy Wickstrom.

reopened in 2015 and is now managed by the landowners as the Graining Fork Nature Preserve (www.grainingfork.org). Climbing is allowed with a permit, and Muir Valley requires a signed waiver.

Dr. Bob Matheny continues to improve the grounds of the gorgeous Torrent Falls (www.torrentfallsclimbing.com). His solution of limited access is keeping crowds down, allowing climbers to experience the wonderful climbing in a peaceful environment. Please support these organizations when you climb on their property — maintaining climbing access to these amazing crags is not free!

Also, farther south, the Red River Gorge Climbers' Coalition officially took ownership of the Pendergrass-Murray Recreational Preserve (PMRP) during the 2012 Rocktoberfest, when they presented the Access Fund with a check for the final payment on the property. Since the 2014 purchase of the Miller Fork Recreational Preserve in the nearby Hell Creek drainage (again with support from Access Fund), route development has surged at a furious pace, bringing the count of published routes to more well over 3000. Several route developers remain consistent in their efforts, spending their free time doing the dirty work involved with bolting Corbin sandstone. These key individuals include Shadow Ayala, Blake Bowling, Scott Curran, Troy Davison, Ray Ellington, Andrew Gearing, Hugh Loeffler, Greg Martin, Rob McFall, Jeff Neal, Shannon Stuart-Smith, Dustin Stephens, Neal Strickland, Kipp Trummel, Dario Ventura, Andrew Wheatley and his dad, Mike Wheatley.

The Red has grown up to be the premier sport-climbing destination in the United States largely due to the continued development of the Southern region. This fifth-edition guidebook documents over 400 new routes that should help to disperse the crowds gathered at historically popular areas. Check out six new crags within Muir Valley, sample one of the 20+ new routes at Bob Marley, or visit the "New Zoo," which has more than doubled the route count at this quick-hit crag just up the road from Miguel's.

The recent development at the Red reflects the overall diversity of Corbin sandstone. One might wonder if the truly great routes have all been climbed, but we've seen that all it takes is the discovery of a new cliff, or sometimes just a new vision of a new line, to produce a classic anywhere on the spectrum of difficulty. Within one year, the RRG witnessed the establishment of *Child's Play* — a 25-foot, three-star 5.3 — and Alex Megos' first ascent of *Your Heaven, My Hell* — a 5.14d.

Countless crags remain tucked away behind rhododendrons just around the corner in the next holler, and a few dedicated individuals have bushwhacked through to keep the momentum alive. With hundreds of miles of crags hidden in the rocky ribbons of land stretching between Morehead and Corbin, there's still way too much perfect sandstone out there to sit back and be satisfied!

ACCESS

Unlike most climbing areas in the country, many Red River Gorge crags are on lands owned by non-profit organizations dedicated to climbing and conservation. Roadside Crag, on private land, is now open by permit through the Graining Fork Nature Preserve. Other much larger climbing-related preserves contain many other important crags.

Please help preserve access to climbing areas by joining the Access Fund and the Red River Gorge Climbers' Coalition. Photo: Elodie Saracco.

Pendergrass-Murray Recreational Preserve

The Red River Gorge Climbers' Coalition was founded in 1996 to address climbing access issues in the Daniel Boone National Forest, and continues to do so to this day, but much of the climbing in the Red occurs on private land. Knowing that access is always at the discretion of the owner, in 2004 the RRGCC directly purchased 750 acres, in two parcels, to create the Pendergrass-Murray Recreational Preserve (PMRP). This bold (and trend-setting) acquisition permanently protected access to the Coal Bank Hollow, Bald Rock Fork, Sore Heel Hollow, and Flat Hollow crags.

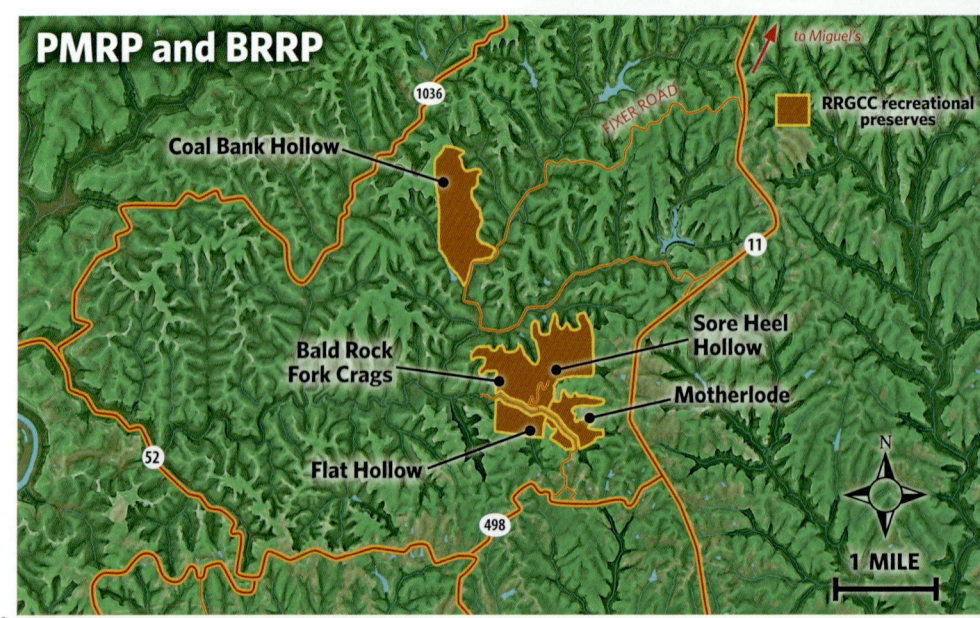

PRACTICE RESPONSIBLE CLIMBING
SECURE CLIMBING FOR EVERYONE

The Red River Gorge Climbers' Coalition is a nonprofit corporation started in 1996 by local climbers dedicated to securing and protecting open, public access to rock climbing in the Red River Gorge area of Kentucky and promoting conservation of the environment on the lands where we climb.

The world-class climbing at the Red is a national treasure that deserves everyone's best efforts to help keep it open and available for all climbers to enjoy, experience, and appreciate. Our community-based organization works hard to secure and preserve these unique climbing opportunities by working with private landowners, the US Forest Service, and direct ownership of over 1,000 acres. The RRGCC owns and manages the Pendergrass-Murray and Miller Fork Recreational Preserves. Donations to the RRGCC community helps keep this important work going and to keep our vision alive for the next generation of climbers.

Climb Responsibly at Red River Gorge

- **Pack Out or Bury Human Waste!** Pack out human waste using a bag system or bury in a 6-8" deep cat hole 200 feet from water, trails, cliffs, or camp.

- **Practice Leave No Trace Ethics:** Pack out all trash. Travel on established trails, roads, and durable surfaces.

- **Minimize Erosion:** Belay and place gear close to the base of the cliff on durable surfaces to prevent impact and soil erosion. Don't damage rock or vegetation.

- **Bolt Etiquette:** Hang your own draws at the anchors when working a route. Do NOT toprope through fixed gear or lower from glue-ins. Lowering or rappelling through the chains is acceptable.

- **Be Pet Conscious:** Only take pets to pet-friendly areas. Keep your dog under control at all times — no digging, disturbing wildlife, or acting aggressively.

- **Be a Steward of the Red:** Volunteer or donate to help maintain your favorite climbing areas. Join the RRGCC at www.rrgcc.org/join.

RED RIVER GORGE CLIMBERS' COALITION
Securing, Protecting, and Promoting Responsible Climbing
PO Box 22156
Lexington KY 40522-2156
www.rrgcc.org

Bald Rock Recreational Preserve

Just as this book went to press, with funding and loans from Trango Climbing Gear and Access Fund, the RRGCC secured access to the Motherlode, Chocolate Factory, Bear's Den, and Unlode crags. This is a huge success for Red River Gorge climbing access. In 2011, the Ventura Family (owner of Miguel's Pizza) purchased the land above the cliff line, and now the RRGCC's purchase of the land beneath the cliff line and the surrounding areas ensures that these iconic crags are climber-owned. Through the new Bald Rock Recreational Preserve (BRRP), the iconic Motherlode areas are now permanently preserved and secured for climbing. However, though the land is bought, it has yet to be paid for, and fund-raising efforts are now beginning. Visit rrgcc.org/brrp for more info — and, if you can, donate to the cause!

Muir Valley Nature Preserve

In 2003, Rick and Liz Weber purchased the 400-acre tract now known as Muir Valley. Over the next decade, the Webers and helpers would establish over 300 climbing routes, and the trails, parking lot, and facilities to go with them. In March of 2015, the Webers gifted Muir Valley Nature Preserve to the Friends of Muir Valley, a 501(c)3 non-profit corporation dedicated to managing the property and preserving the recreational area.

DANIEL BOONE NATIONAL FOREST

National Forest land is also important to Red River Gorge climbing, especially in the northern region, so know the rules!

Closures/Fenced-off Areas 🚫

Some cliffs have fenced-off areas. These protect archaeological sites or the endangered plant white-haired goldenrod (photo this page). Please obey the closures and stay out of fenced-off areas. The RRGCC posts current closure information on its website: www.rrgcc.org.

Trail Issues

Most climbing areas do not have USFS-designated trails going to them. Please use official trails wherever possible and do not cut switchbacks and cause erosion. Minimize your impacts when you travel off the official trails.

The endangered white-haired goldenrod grows nowhere else in the world except near rock shelters and cliffs in the Red River Gorge. Please do not disturb this threatened plant. Photo: US Forest Service.

KEY FOREST SERVICE RULES

- In order to protect sensitive archaeological and biological resources, no camping or fire-building is allowed within 100 feet of clifflines or the back of rock shelters.

- No camping within 300 feet of any developed road or trail.

- Please stay out of fenced-off areas. These areas contain sensitive archaeological or biological resources.

- Forest Service authorization is required prior to any of the following cliffline developments: permanent installation of protection devices such as bolts, slings, camming devices, or chocks. Construction of access trails. Clearing of vegetation. For several decades now, the installation of new fixed gear has not been permitted anywhere within Daniel Boone National Forest. However, the Red River Gorge Climber's Coalition continues to work with USFS officials on the development of a formal Climbing Management Plan, hopefully with provisions for new-route development so local and visiting climbers to eastern Kentucky can make the most of the seemingly limitless wealth of rock on the federal properties supported by our tax dollars.

In Clifty Wilderness, additional rules apply:

- Group size is limited to 10.

- No mechanical or motorized equipment or travel.

- No new rock-climbing routes with fixed anchors.

Respect Rockshelters

Rockshelters provide excellent preservation for plant remains, animal bones, and other objects used by ancient Native Americans and early pioneers. The earliest signs of prehistoric agriculture have been documented from botanical remains found in rockshelters in eastern Kentucky. Rockshelters also provide habitat for unique plant and animal species like the white-haired goldenrod (found only in the Red River Gorge) and the Virginia big-eared bat.

Threats: Camping, climbing, rappelling, burning, and digging in rockshelters can impact or even destroy these special resources.

Camping in rockshelters is prohibited forestwide. Camp at least 100 feet away from the base of any cliff, or the back of any rockshelter.

Building a fire is prohibited in rockshelters. Do not build a campfire or use a stove fire within 100 feet of the base of any cliff or the back of any rockshelter.

DO NOT CAMP OR BUILD FIRES IN ROCKSHELTERS

Leave rockshelters undisturbed by not digging in the soil, moving rocks, or trampling the ground.

All artifacts and cultural resources are protected by federal law. Report digging, looting or vandalism to the nearest District Office or law enforcement officer.

Daniel Boone National Forest
1700 Bypass Road
WInchester, KY 40391
859-745-3100

MIGUEL VENTURA
(a climbing tradition)

Climbers come to the Red to climb, camp, socialize, slackline, and to eat pizza in one of the most welcoming, climber-friendly places in the world, "Miguel's Pizza." Miguel Ventura is the owner and founder.

Born in Portugal, Miguel moved to Connecticut when he was seven. When Miguel was in his 30s, a friend offered him a chance to buy a share in some property in the beautiful green hills of eastern Kentucky. Without a second thought, Miguel and his wife, Susan — pregnant at the time — packed up the truck and headed straight out. The other shareholders had jobs that tied them to the city, but Miguel was able to move into an old building on the property and begin to fix it up.

After selling his house in Connecticut, Miguel opened an ice-cream shop, "The Rainbow Door." (Until only a few years ago, the shop's sign was still visible.) One day in 1985, Martin Hackworth and Tom Martin stopped by for ice cream. They asked Miguel if they could start selling climbing gear at his shop. Soon, climbers began to hang out at Miguel's and buy gear from Hackworth (proceeds from which helped put him through college), and Susan got the idea of selling pizzas. **Miguel had always loved to cook**, and, being a dedicated gardener, was soon serving unique and tasty pizzas to the small group of trad climbers who had become regulars at his shop.

In the early 1990s, after graduating college, Hackworth stopped selling gear and moved away. Nevertheless, **climbers had found their hangout**. Business really took off when Porter Jarrard moved to the Red and began establishing classic sport climbs, making the area hugely popular. "Porter brought in more climbers and basically made this place what it is today," says Miguel.

Those who have been to Miguel's on a crowded night can appreciate how hard he works. **Ten- to 12-hour days are common.** Throughout the years, Miguel has attracted dedicated workers to help him provide a consistently high-quality product. It's hard to get a complaint out of Miguel, always an incredibly friendly and giving man.

Off season, in winter, Miguel finds joy in woodcarving. You can see some of his beautiful work throughout the interior and exterior of the building. Winter also give him a chance to spend more time wi his parents, who live next door, as well a find peace in his passion for gardening.

When asked what he would purchas for his shop if he could have anythin in the world, regardless of price, Migu responded with two items. Althoug he's not one to take on technolog without a great need, first was dough-rolling machine that could hel save his tiring elbows and keep u with the growing demand for pizza an sandwiches. The other: a restoration o the 80-year-old historical building h currently occupies. In fact, this drear has been well underway over the pas few years as the Venturas continue t expand and improve Miguel's, althoug the old building and its familiar yellow facade still remain the centerpiece o this rock-climber's haven.

Pizza
Artisan pizza
40 Topping choices

Salads
Romaine or spinach
40 Topping choices

Bowls
Pasta, rice or bean
40 topping choices

Sandwiches
Hot roasted meat
Pizza combo

Breakfast
Traditional option
Omelets wraps
Bagel sandwich
French toast
Pancakes

Ice Cream
Ben & Jerrys
Nestles bars

Espresso bar

Dsl wireless

606-663-1975
miguelspizza.com

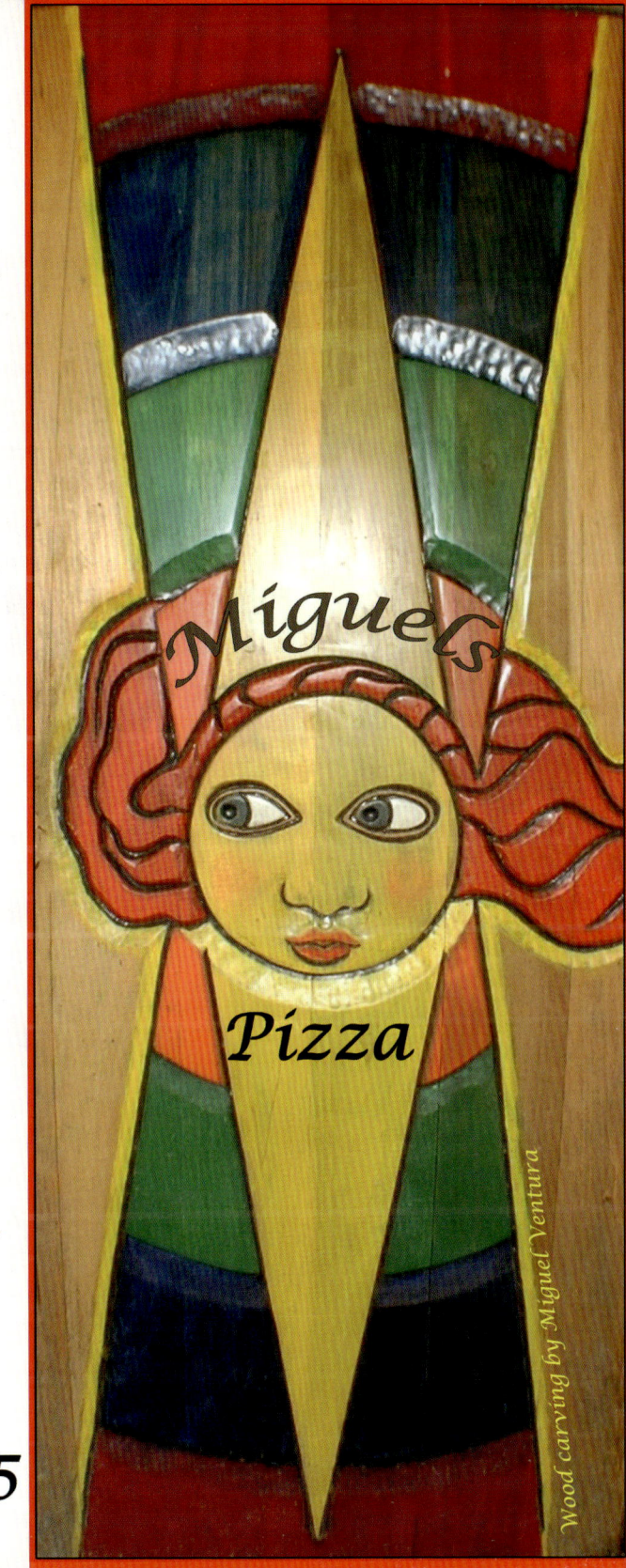

Wood carving by Miguel Ventura

Miguels Pizza

NATURAL BRIDGE

This area contains the extremely popular sport destinations Roadside Crag, Torrent Falls, and Lady Slipper. These cliffs also have some good traditional climbing. The overhanging walls of Roadside Crag and Torrent Falls provide good shelter on rainy days. Adding to the appeal of this area, most walls are only a short hike from KY 11.

Approach: Head left out of Miguel's and drive south on KY 11 a few miles. Most areas are accessed from pulloffs or parking areas along KY 11.

Access: Torrent Falls, Beer Trailer Crag, and Roadside Crag are located on private property, so respect the wishes of the landowners, which may include parking restrictions, donation boxes, leash laws, etc. Closed for several years, Roadside Crag is now open, with use by permit only. Visit grainingfork.org to get a permit. Registration is also necessary for climbing at Torrent Falls. Visit www.torrentfallsclimbing.com for more info. The Zoo remains open, and with dozens more good routes since the last guide. The remaining areas are located on Forest Service land; please respect signs and fences indicating closed routes or trails.

CLIFF	KIDS	RAIN	SUN	DRIVE	HIKE	ROUTES	GRADE RANGE	CLASSIC ROUTES
SEE ROCKS page 44			☼	5 min	10 min	3		
FRICTION SLAB page 44			☼	5 min	5 min	2		
EMERALD CITY page 45			☼	5 min	10 min	18		Yellow Brick Road 11b No Place Like Home 11c
GLOBAL VILLAGE page 48			☼	5 min	15 min	21		
ROADSIDE CRAG page 52	👶	☂	☼	5 min	10 min	50		Roadside Attraction 7 Mantel Route 10c Return of Chris Snyder 11d Ro Shampo 12a Wild Gift 12c
THE ZOO page 59		☂	☼	5 min	15 min	48		Barrel Full of Monkeys 11a Hippocrite 12a
TORRENT FALLS page 66	👶	☂	☼	10 min	10 min	52		Windy Corner 11b Bare Metal Teen 12a Steelworker 12c
BEER TRAILER CRAG page 75		☂	☼	10 min	5 min	30		Afternoon Buzz 12a Hang Over 12c Darkness Falls 12d Falls City 13b

NATURAL BRIDGE OVERVIEW

ROADSIDE AREA DETAIL

NATURAL BRIDGE

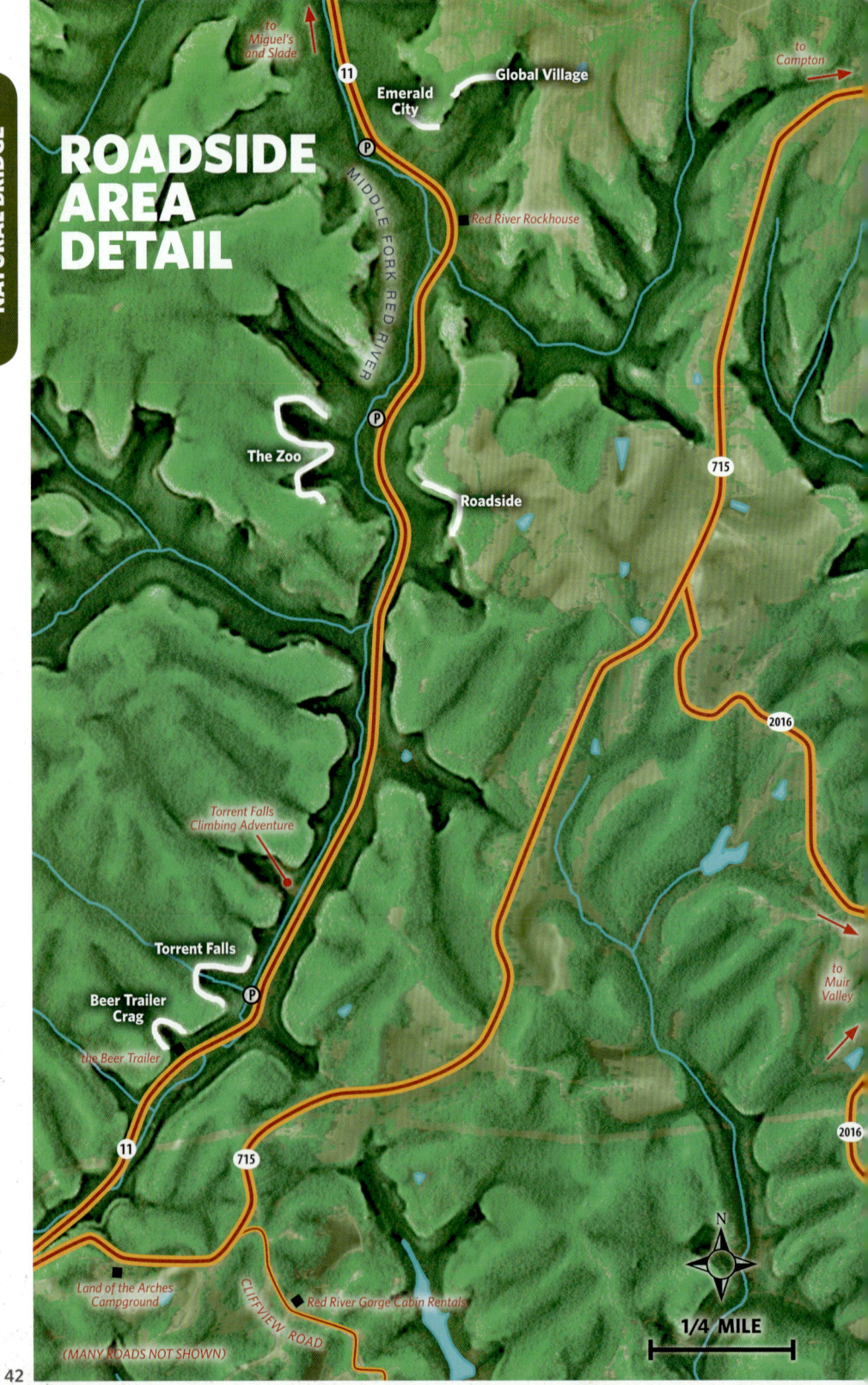

to Miguel's and Slade
11
Emerald City
Global Village
to Campton
MIDDLE FORK RED RIVER
Red River Rockhouse
The Zoo
Roadside
715
2016
Torrent Falls Climbing Adventure
Torrent Falls
Beer Trailer Crag
the Beer Trailer
to Muir Valley
2016
11
715
CLIFFVIEW ROAD
Land of the Arches Campground
Red River Gorge Cabin Rentals
(MANY ROADS NOT SHOWN)

N

1/4 MILE

Jamie Elizabeth on *Cordelia*, 5.8, Torrent Falls (page 35). Photo: Elodie Saracco.

SEE ROCKS

5 min | 10 min | 37.7885 / -83.746

3 routes
.14
.13
.12
.11
.10
.9
.8
.7
≤.6

These rock towers have only a few lines. The easiest approach involves crossing private property, but the crags are on Forest Service land and a less risky approach should be possible with a topographic map and a compass.

Approach: From the Shell Station near th highway in Slade, turn right out of the parkin lot and follow KY 15 about 4 miles. Turn left ont County Road 1639 and follow it about 2.5 mile while remaining left at a fork in the road. At th fork, you should be able to spot See Rocks on ridge in front of you. Park near the base of the hi and head up to the wall.

❶ **Nettles** 5.9+ ★
As you near the base of the wall, look to the rightmost tower to spot an arch. Just left of the arch is a right-facing dihedral, which this line ascends. Climb the hand crack to the top of the tower and rappel from a tree to descend.
45 ft. David Hume, Jack Hume, 1996.

❷ **Exit Stage Left** 5.10c ★★
Walk through the arch on the rightmost tower, turn right, and go around a corner to a large, chossy dihedral. Begin just left of the dihedral on the face. Climb to a 10-foot-high roof and pull over to a vertical face with a finger crack. Continue up the finger crack to a ledge and improvise a way down.
45 ft. David Hume, 1996.

❸ **South Fork Cemetery** 5.7
Locate a left-facing dihedral on the left side of an amphitheater just left of *Exit Stage Left*. Climb the face just left of the crack and move right into the crack when you are able to. Continue up a short slab to anchors on the ledge.
60 ft. James Newkum, Scott Hammon, 1998.

FRICTION SLAB

5 min | 5 min | 37.758 / -83.669

2 routes
.14
.13
.12
.11
.10
.9
.8
.7
≤.6

This large roadside boulder has always been popular for playing around on. The front side has been climbed since the 1980s; when the interest in bouldering took off, the back side provided potential for harder climbing.

Approach: From Miguel's, drive south on KY 1 toward Roadside Crag for 2.5 miles until you se a large boulder close to the road on the right Park in the pulloff in front of the boulder.

❶ **Bulldog** V8 ★★★★
This problem ascends the back side of the Friction Slab. Sit-start on pockets and slap up the formation using the arête on the right.
12 ft. Dave Hume, 2000.

❷ **Table Top** V3 ★★★
This problem ascends the right side of the face of Friction Slab facing you as you approach from Miguel's. Start near the arête (around the corner from *Bulldog*) and throw to a right-hand gaston. Top out and walk off.
9 ft. Unknown.

❸ **Friction Slab** 5.6 ★★
This problem ascends the right side of the front face of the Friction Slab. It is often soloed to access the bolt on top and set up a toprope. You can downclimb the dirty chimney.
20 ft. Unknown.

❹ **Critical Crystal** 5.11 ★★★
The face left of the groove on the front side of the Friction Slab. The problem can be toproped from a bolt at the top.
20 ft. Unknown.

LADY SLIPPER

Due to its length, Lady Slipper is broken into two sections: Emerald City and Global Village.

EMERALD CITY

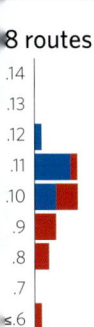

37.7426
-83.6571
5 min | 10 min

8 routes

Emerald City offers excellent sport routes, featuring vertical face climbing on solid, exposed rock, as well as some great traditional lines. The ledge routes (9-13) all begin 30 feet up, providing the added benefit of exposure, and are a bit more runout than the average Red sport line. Save the climbs here for cold days because the sun bakes this wall. A must-do is *No Place Like Home* — with well-spaced bolts, technical moves, and big exposure, it's one of the Red's most classic arêtes.

Approach: From Miguel's, drive 3.2 miles south on KY 11 and park in a muddy pulloff on the right, just across from mile marker 4. Cross the road to a trail, follow it straight uphill, and continue until it forks near a large boulder. Follow the left fork around the boulder and up the hill. The trail meets the wall directly beneath the 30-foot ledge with routes 1–5.

Conditions: Emerald City is exposed, faces south, and bakes in the sun. Due to the lack of overhanging rock, it's no good on rainy days. The approach is short and moderately steep. If you see lots of cars in the pulloff, don't despair — the parking is shared with Global Village, which is where most people end up.

The first seven routes are located left of the ledge area where the approach trail meets the wall, but for consistency are described from left to right (opposite to how you'll encounter them as you hike in from the right).

Pumped Puppies 5.10b
From *Father's Day*, head left to locate a thin crack in an overhanging face. Climb the face to a ledge, then move right to a rotten section of rock. Pull the lip with no protection.
50 ft. Jamie Baker, Rik Downs, 1989.

Father's Day 5.5 ★
This route ascends the next dihedral left of *Sharp*. Climb the dihedral to a flake and belay. Continue up the flake to the top of the wall. The first pitch is better than the second.
100 ft. Pete Huggybone, 2003.

Sharp 5.9 ★★★
Walk left and around the corner from *No Place Like Home* to locate a hand crack. Lower from anchors atop the crack.
45 ft. Jamie Baker, Chris Linderman, 1989.

❹ **No Place Like Home** 5.11c ★★★★★
Classic. This route ascends the obvious arête visible from the road, to the left of *Whiteout*. Begin by climbing *Whiteout*, then move to an alcove beneath an overhang. Step up and shake your way up the arête, making difficult clips along the way. Convince your partner to hang the draws for you! A #4 Camalot can protect the runout to the first bolt, although the climbing is fairly easy.
100 ft. 9 bolts. Jim Link, Jamie Baker, 1992.

❺ **The Man Behind the Curtain** 5.11a ★★★★
Reach this impressive dihedral by climbing *Whiteout*, but finish to the tree ledge out right instead of the anchors out left. From the big tree on the ledge, rap halfway down the wall to a small ledge. Crawl around the arête and end up at a small belay stance below this extremely steep, featureless acute dihedral.
40 ft. Kris Hampton, 2006.

❻ **Whiteout** 5.8 ★★★★
This multi-pitch line offers a fantastic view and great climbing. Head 100 feet left of *Friable* to a point just before the main corner of the wall. Climb up easy ground via a left-facing flake or a short line of bolts (5.7) and belay. Continue up the hand crack in a dihedral for the bulk of the route, then move left onto the face when the crack ends.
100 ft. John Bronaugh, Ron Snider, 1984.

45

NATURAL BRIDGE

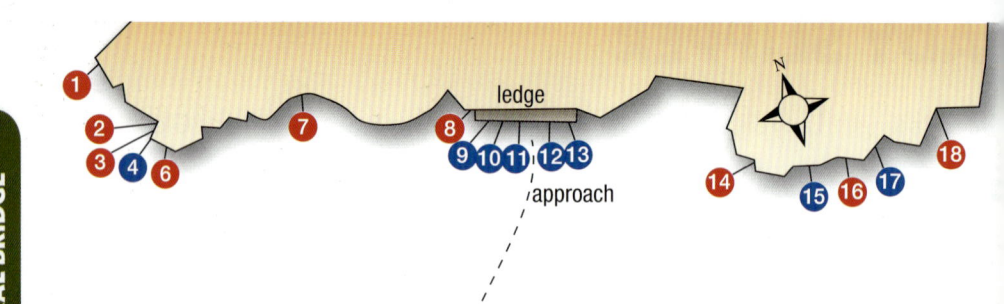

❼ Friable 5.9 ★★★
This route ascends the obvious arching crack visible from the road. From *Spiny Norman*, head left about 225 feet to locate two cracks about 15 feet apart. Begin by climbing the crack on the right, and take it to an overhang. Move left over chossy rock (5.6 R) to a belay near a corner. Continue up a crack and battle past an overhang. Belay when the crack forks to avoid rope drag, then continue up the arching right crack to the top. Rappel from the anchors on *Whiteout*.
120 ft. Ed Pearsall, Tom Seibert, 1980.

❽ Spiny Norman 5.9+ ★
Just left of the ledge with the sport routes #9-#13 is a hand crack splitting the wall. Scramble to the top of a boulder to gain the crack. Climb the crack, then move right at an overhang. Pull over the overhang into the flaring crack and take it to the top. Rappel from a tree to descend.
120 ft. Ron Snider, Bill Rieker, 1984.

❾ Flying Monkeys 5.11c ★★★
If your bouldering skills are up to par, expect success. Climb into the big hueco, then crank over the lip and locate hidden holds on the vertical face for the remainder of the route.
70 ft. 5 bolts. Tim Powers, Jamie Baker, 1991.

❿ Ruby Slippers 5.10d ★★★★
Left of *Diamond in the Rough* is a large hueco about six feet up. This route climbs up the right side of the hueco, then continues up the vertical face to the anchors.
70 ft. 9 bolts. Rob Turan, Jamie Baker, 1991.

⓫ Diamond in the Rough 5.10c ★★★★
Classic face climbing. Step left from *Oz* a few feet to the next bolted line. Climb straight up past nice finger ledges and well-spaced bolts to the anchors.
80 ft. 7 bolts. Jamie Baker, Rob Turan, 1991

⓬ Oz 5.11c ★★★
This is the next route left of *Lollipop Kids* and starts on the same ledge. Often wet.
70 ft. 6 bolts. Jamie Baker, Rob Butsch, 1991.

⓭ Lollipop Kids 5.11b ★★★★
At the end of the approach trail is a 30-foot-high ledge with gully approach. Scramble up the gully to access this and the next four routes. This is the rightmost line off the ledge. Crank through a bouldery start, then continue up the vertical face.
70 ft. 7 bolts. Jamie Baker, 1992.

The Ledge Routes

Yellow Brick Road

The Shining

The remaining routes are located to the right of where the approach trail meets the wall.

4 Scarecrow 5.10c ★★★ ☐

From the end of the approach trail (beneath *Diamond in the Rough*), head right about 400 feet to locate a section of rock containing a fat flake and two other cracks, which meet at a roof about 30 feet up. Climb the left crack to the roof, then move left to a corner. Arrange some gear near the corner, then move left to a finger crack and climb it to a belay ledge. Continue up easier ground to a ledge with a tree, then ascend a short face to the summit. Rappel from a tree to descend.
140 ft. John Bronaugh, Stacy Temple, 1993.

5 Yellow Brick Road 5.11b ★★★★★ ☐

Walk around the corner 100 feet from *Scarecrow* to a thin, detached boulder about 15 feet high. To the right of the boulder you will see a nice-looking line on lichen-streaked rock. Climb the slab, with long reaches and thought-provoking moves. Move right when you get stumped, then make a difficult move back left to gain better holds. Climb large ledges to the anchors.
50 ft. 5 bolts. Neal Strickland, Tim Powers, 1992.

16 The Shining 5.8+ ★★★★ ☐

Walk 50 feet right from *Yellow Brick Road* to locate this obvious, short finger crack in black rock. Tackle the awkward start, then lock your way up the granite-like finger crack to the anchors.
30 ft. Brent Lewis, Ron Snider, 1983.

17 The Bulge 5.12a ★★ ☐

From *The Shining*, walk right about 75 feet to locate a line of bolts near a section of rock with a 35-foot-tall flake. Crimp through a boulder problem and continue to the anchors.
45 ft. 5 bolts. Nick Cocciolone, Eric Szczukowski, 1992.

18 T N T 5.10b ★★★ ☐

This route is located in a short dihedral 50 feet right of *The Bulge*. Stem and lock up the interesting dihedral to a ledge. Lower from fixed webbing on the ledge or continue up the dirty crack to the top.
80 ft. Tim Powers, Tony Rooker, 1987.

GLOBAL VILLAGE

NATURAL BRIDGE

37.743
-83.655
5 min / 15 min

21 routes

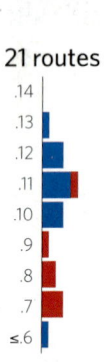

.14
.13
.12
.11
.10
.9
.8
.7
≤.6

Although the approach is twice as long as Emerald City, Global Village is Lady Slipper's more popular sector, with a mix of great trad and sport routes. Long, exposed, and only 5.6, *Eureka* is an incredible first sport lead if you can catch it in an "unchopped" state. (Trad activist "The Wolfman" first chopped the route in 2000. Since then, threats and rumors have surrounded the bolts. You can also lead the climb on gear.) For the neophyte crack climber, try *Father and Son*, which takes bomber gear and climbs a mostly juggy face with only a few crack moves.

Approach: Head up as for Global Village, bear fork right instead of left when the trail branches near the large boulder. Follow the trail for about 10 minutes, crossing over two ravines. After the second ravine, the trail heads uphill to the right. Follow the trail uphill to an outcropping where it forks. To reach routes 1–6, stay left and continue up the hill and over a sloping rock. For the remainder of the routes, bear right at the fork and continue another 100 feet.

Conditions: You'll have a little more luck with the rain at Global Village than at Emerald City. *Deep Six*, *Wreaking Havoc*, and *The Frayed End of Sanity* are steep enough to be sheltered from light rain. Still, this is not a destination rainy day crag. Global Village sees lots of sun.

❶ Unknown 12 5.12a ★★★
Unknown sport line, about 75 feet left of *Eureka*.
65 ft.

❷ Off With Batman 5.8 ★★★
This line takes on the wide crack left of *Eureka*. Begin on the ledge and use all the techniques you can't learn in a climbing gym to reach the top. Bring lots of big cams.
85 ft. *Jimmy Klaserner, Quincy Stang, 2010.*

❸ Eureka 5.6 ★★★★
This route is located near the obvious main arête on the wall as you near the end of the approach trail. Walk left from the arête about 100 feet to a plated face just left of an overhanging dihedral. Negotiate the tricky start, then continue up the face on positive holds.
85 ft. 8 bolts. *Unknown.*

❹ Howard Roark 5.9+ ★★
Ascends the obvious, wide, overhanging dihedral just right of *Eureka*. Rappel from a tree to descend.
100 ft. *Alexis Scott, 2001.*

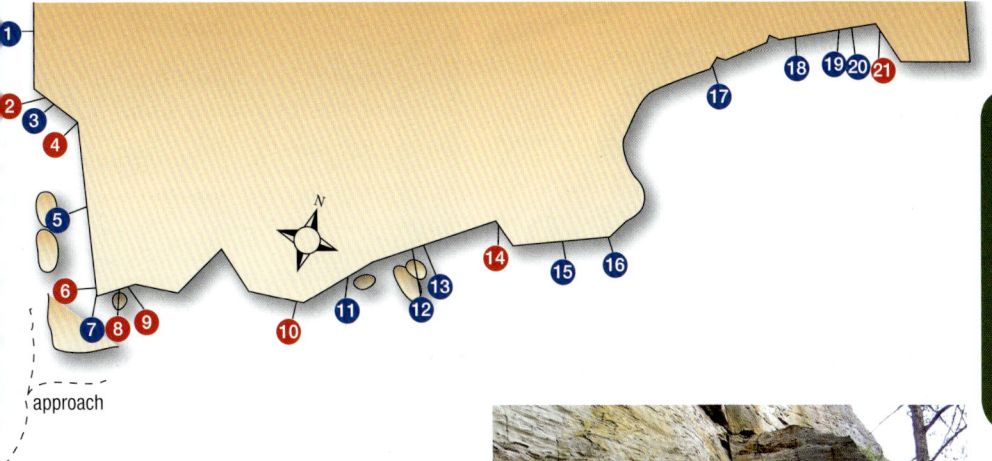

The Wheel of Time 5.13b ★★★

This line ascends the vertical-to-overhanging face about 30 feet right of *Howard Roark*. The route has recently had its "Porter hangers" replaced with modern hardware, so expect it to become more popular than in the past.
80 ft. 10 bolts. Dave Hume, 1996.

Father and Son 5.7 ★★★

John and Alex, father and son, spent many wonderful moments together. I'm sure this first ascent was one of their finest. This popular first trad lead climbs the left-facing dihedral about 30 feet right of *The Wheel of Time*. Climb the flake, making liberal use of face holds on the left wall. Pull a couple of crack moves at the top to reach a ledge with bolted anchors.
80 ft. John Bronaugh, Alex Yeakley, Dario Ventura, Miguel Ventura, 1993.

Kentucky Pinstripe 5.10a ★★★

Just right and around the corner from *Father and Son* is a line of bolts ascending an arête behind a tree. Climb up to a tricky little roof and balance your way over the lip. Continue up the slabby face to a good ledge. Rest your feet, then take on the remainder to the anchors.
80 ft. 9 bolts. Unknown.

Vision 5.7 ★★★

This line ascends the hand crack just right of *Kentucky Pinstripe*. Begin on top of a five-foot-high boulder and climb the splitter hand crack to a ledge with a tree. Continue up the flat flake past many good stances to the top.
80 ft. Scott Hammon, James Neukam, 1999.

Jake Flake 5.8 ★★★

The next thin flake right of *Vision*. Take the seam to a flake and continue on face holds to the top.
80 ft. Scott Hammon, 1999.

Father and Son

Kentucky Pinstripe

Chain Mail 5.11d ★★

Walk right about 75 feet from the main arête of the wall to locate a bolted face, which begins in some sandy rock. Climb past short cracks, placing protection in them if desired. Continue up through the line of bolts to chain anchors. The protection to reach the first bolt may be extremely sketchy, so be careful.
100 ft. 6 bolts. Porter Jarrard, 1992.

NATURAL BRIDGE

Disappearer

Casual Viewing

⓫ Deep Six 5.12b ★★★★
Move 20 feet right from *Chain Mail* to another line of bolts on an overhanging face. Battle up the bouldery face, with long moves separated by decent rests.
110 ft. 11 bolts. Porter Jarrard, Frank Waters, 1992.

⓬ Wreaking Havoc 5.11d ★★
From *Deep Six*, walk 30 feet right to locate this route. It shares its start with the following route. Boulder the beginning to gain an overhanging face above.
80 ft. 8 bolts. Jeff Moll, Porter Jarrard, 1992.

⓭ The Frayed Ends of Sanity 5.12a ★★
Begin by climbing the initial moves of *Wreaking Havoc*, then move right.
80 ft. 9 bolts. Porter Jarrard, Jake Slaney, 1992.

⓮ Pain Is a Spice 5.7 ★
This route ascends the thin finger crack in a dihedral to the right of *The Frayed Ends of Sanity*. Improvise a descent.
35 ft. Ethan Cumbler, Jane Kim, 1996.

⓯ Disappearer 5.11c ★★★★
Move right and around the corner a few feet from the previous line, to a vertical wall with many horizontal breaks. This is the first bolted line encountered. Climb up through easy ground for about 20 feet to reach a blank section. Locate the few holds it has to offer and figure out how to use them to reach the jug above. Continue through easier climbing to the anchors.
70 ft. 7 bolts. Porter Jarrard, Jeff Moll, 1992.

⓰ Loosen Up 5.10b ★★★
This bolted line ascends a slightly overhanging face 20 feet right from *Disappearer* and just before the wall turns a corner. Climb the face, making use of positive holds to reach a short roof. Step up and over the roof, then balance to the anchors.
50 ft. 6 bolts. Porter Jarrard, Jeff Moll, 1992.

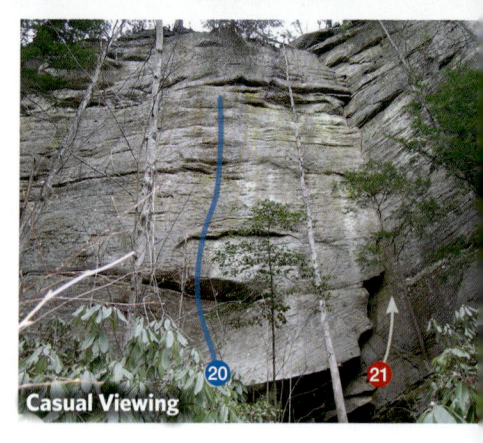

⓱ Seeker 5.12b ★★
Traverse the trail to the right and uphill from *Loosen Up* to an upper cliff band. Walk left past a slabby section of the wall containing a few bolted lines (see next routes) to a wide crack near a boulder. Ascend the blunt arête, then step onto the face to reach a ledge with anchors. Bring a brush.
50 ft. 7 bolts. Porter Jarrard, Jeff Moll, 1992.

⓲ Circa Man 5.10d ★★★
From *Seeker*, move back right to the slabby wall. This is the first route from the left corner and has a small roof. Climb up the face, making use of well-spaced bolts. Be careful clipping the fifth bolt or you may take a very long fall.
60 ft. 5 bolts. Unknown, 1994.

⓳ Out for Justice 5.11c ★★★★
This line begins about 25 feet right of *Circa Man*. A short, overhanging start leads to a horizontal break. Pull up and over the break and continue up the slabbier face to anchors. Tricky, technical, and hair-raising. You're lucky if the holds are chalked.
65 ft. 8 bolts. Porter Jarrard, Frank Waters, 1992.

⓴ Down by Law 5.11c ★★
A few feet right of *Out for Justice* is a line of bolts with a short roof about 10 feet up. Climb up to and over the roof to reach the slabby face above. Continue up through more short roofs to reach the anchors. Beware of a dead tree that may still be covering the final two bolts.
65 ft. 8 bolts. Porter Jarrard, Frank Waters, 1992.

㉑ Casual Viewing 5.7 ★★★★
Great line. Just right of *Down by Law* is this popular and sustained flake. Climb up to a pod, get some gear, then creep out and up into the flake. Stem and layback to the top. Lower from bolted anchors.
70 ft. Porter Jarrard, Jeff Moll, 1992.

50

BOB MATHENY
(saving climbing access)

You may have heard the name "Dr. Bob." More than likely, the words "saving climbing access" were mentioned in the same sentence. Although this humble man would never admit to such a thing, it is true. Dr. Bob Matheny has been a significant contributor to saving climbing access on the Pendergrass Murray Recreational Preserve (PMRP) as well as at Torrent Falls. How has he done it? A heart of gold and cold, hard cash. When the Red River Gorge Climber's Coalition (RRGCC) was trying to purchase the PMRP, Dr. Bob provided the entire 20 percent down payment, plus significant portions of the first year's mortgage on the property.

A few years later, when the owner of Torrent Falls shut the area down to climbers and put the property up for sale, **Dr. Bob stepped in and bought it,** thus preserving access to this outstanding cliff for climbers. You may never get a chance to meet Dr. Bob since he works a demanding job as an emergency room physician, frequently pulling 10–12 hour graveyard shifts for several days in a row, and also contributes a significant portion of his leftover spare time to the RRGCC as a board member. This doesn't leave him as much time for climbing these days as he would like, but hopefully one day he will have the time he deserves to appreciate the land he helped secure.

Dr. Bob Matheny, 51, has had a passion for the outdoors since he was a kid. When he was 15 years old he spent five and a half weeks alone on the Appalachian Trail, hiking as far as Virginia. Supporting his love of the outdoors, his parents bought him a bus ticket to the Tetons in Wyoming for the summer. He arrived back home in Kentucky and put together a rack from an old REI catalog. Armed with his shiny, new gear, young Dr. Bob got his feet wet on the cliffs of the Cumberland Falls area near the Kentucky/Tennessee border. In 1987, after completing medical school

Photo: Wes Allen.

at Tulane University in New Orleans, he decided on Lexington for his residency. During this time he made a few trips down to the Red, mostly to take on the man-eating offwidths at Muscle Beach. A few years later, after spending time out west, he decided to make Lexington his permanent home. Initially oblivious to the sport-climbing boom that had taken place while he was away, he partnered with Terry Kindred, who would slowly convert him to the ways of the stick-clip-carrying Red River sport climber.

Dr. Bob has a true passion for climbing, but also a deep appreciation for nature. When asked about his immediate plans for Torrent Falls, he said the area was "loved to death" and needs time to heal. He asks that no single climber feel entitled, and to remember that **climbing access is a community effort** that involves all of us who climb here. If you ever run into Dr. Bob Matheny, buy him a Guiness and tell him thanks for saving climbing access in the Red River Gorge ∎

ROADSIDE CRAG

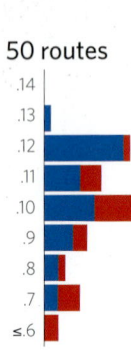

37.73
-83.65

5 min 10 min

50 routes

It doesn't get much better than this: A five-minute approach, amazing routes through the middle grades, and a big overhang to keep you dry! The slab on the right side hosts a slew of great beginner routes. The mega-pocketed 5.10 Wall cannot be surpassed, and is a great warm-up for the 5.12 wall just around the corner. 5.12 aspirants will love *Ro Shampo*, a route whose grade has been debated on the Internet as much as election-year politics!

After a period of indefinite closure in 2011, Roadside is now back open under a strictly enforced permit system. See "Access" at right for details.

Approach: From Miguel's, drive about 3.8 mil‹ south on KY 11 to a large parking area on the righ› Park, cross the road, and find the trailhead abo‹ 200 feet south. Follow the trail uphill about 30 feet. As the trail meets the wall, you will see t› obvious dihedral of *Roadside Attraction* direct› before you. During the past few years, a numb‹ of vehicles have been broken into at Roadside remove valuables from your car before climbin›

Access: Roadside Crag is privately owned a‹ was closed in May 2011 for a variety of reason› After much coordination between the RRGC and the Graining Fork Preserve, the area h‹ currently been reopened under a strictly enforce‹ permit system. Visit grainingfork.org for mo‹ information, or go directly to grainingfork.org› newpermit/ to obtain a permit. Abiding by t› regulations is crucial to keeping this area ope‹ All the rules are listed on the website, but kno‹ before-you-go rules include: no dogs, no beer, ‹ music, no soloing, no fires, and no camping. ‹ safe and leave no trace.

The wooded area behind the parking lot used ‹ be one of the Red's most popular camping spo‹ with climbers, but "No Camping" signs appeare‹ in 2003.

❶ Andromeda Strain 5.9+ ★★★★
Where the approach trail meets the cliff, walk left about 30‹ feet, rounding a corner, to a broad wall bordered on its left ‹ an incredible dihedral. You can't miss it. The climbing is as good as it looks. To begin, climb up the short slab to the ba‹ of the crack. Jam to the top, passing a couple of short roofs along the way. This route may be slimy and damp on humi‹ days. Catch it on a good day and you'll never forget it.
90 ft. Ron Snider, John Bronaugh, 1984.

❷ Wicked Games 5.12d ★★★★
This wickedly difficult line follows a line of bolts just right of *Andromeda Strain*. Notice the plethora of bail biners abandoned like wounded soldiers on the battlefield. Charge
85 ft. 9 bolts. Jamie Baker, Rob Butsch, 1992.

❸ Mantel Route 5.10c ★★★★★
Look for a line of bolts left of a conspicuous gray-and-orang‹ section of wall with a large hueco 50 feet up, and about 60 feet right of the *Andromeda* dihedral. Climb through some "nose to the wall" mantel moves, clipping bolts and placing gear in horizontals.
60 ft. 3 bolts. Ron Snider, Matt Flach, 1989.

Andromeda Strain

52

Headwall 5.12b ★★

...continuation of *Mantel Route*. From the anchors on *Mantel ...ute*, head straight up about 10 feet, make a toss, then ...rash through dirt to a big tree.
...0 ft. 5 bolts. *Matt Flach, Ron Snider, 1990.*

Home Is Where the Heart Is 5.12a ★★★★

...r is it "Home Is Where the Hueco Is"? Start directly beneath ...hueco about 50 feet up an impressive gray-and-orange ...all. Climb straight up to the hueco, past one bolt. Bring ...mall cams and stoppers for small cracks along the way.
...0 ft. 1 bolt. *Mark Williams, 1989.*

Hemisfear 5.11d ★★★★

...his short but excellent line ascends the line of bolts right ... *Home Is Where the Heart Is*, sharing that route's anchors. ...egin on a boulder and climb up the vertical face, crimping ... wicked eyebrow-like gashes. Gravitate left to the hueco ...r a spicy ending.
...0 ft. 3 bolts. *Matt Flach, Charles Tabor, 1989*

Hard Left 5.10a ★★★

...his route begins in an obvious left-angling crack that fades out ... the middle of the wall. Climb up a short slab to the base of the ...ack to begin. When the crack ends, traverse left and down to ...e large hueco and anchors shared with routes 5 and 6.
...0 ft. 3 bolts. *Charles Tabor, Mike Torbett, 1990.*

Science Friction 5.12c ★★★★

...bout 100 feet left of the split in the approach trail, find a ...0-foot-tall pyramid-shaped boulder. This bolted line begins ...om atop the boulder and climbs up through a blocky arête ...nd a low roof at the top.
...0 ft. 7 bolts. *Eric Greulich, 2005.*

Five-Finger Discount 5.8 ★★★★

...r *Fat-Finger Nightmare*! Just left of the obvious dihedral ...f *Roadside Attraction* is a cluster of climbs. This one is the ...rthest left, and ascends a flake with a finger crack. Traverse ...ght at the top on a ledge to anchors beneath *Runnin' Down ... Dream*.
...0 ft. *Tod Anderson, Martin Hackworth, 1984.*

Fadda 5.10a ★★★

...ocate a line of bolts just right of *Five-Finger*. Climb through ...ockets, crimps, and underclings to a delicate "blank" section ... the top. Step left to the anchors.
...0 ft. 5 bolts. *Chris Chaney, Brian Rogers, 2002.*

Motha 5.6 ★★★

...etween the bolted lines of *Fadda* and *Jump for Joy* is a ...ocketed face with some horizontal bands. Climb the face, ...aking use of pockets for protection. Lower from a set of ...nchors just below the ledge, or continue up to the ledge and ...p from the anchors beneath *Runnin' Down a Dream*. Bring

hand-sized cams for the horizontals, which are larger than they appear from the ground.
50 ft. *Grant Stephens, 1986.*

12 Jump for Joy 5.9+ ★★

Too short? Just jump to reach the first holds. Walk left from *Roadside Attraction* to a line of bolts above a boulder. Start atop the boulder and climb the face to bolted anchors.
50 ft. 4 bolts. *Tracy Crabtree, Jeff Ashley, 1993.*

13 Runnin' Down a Dream 5.10a ★★★

Or is it *Run It Out and Scream*? Climb either *Jump for Joy*, *Motha*, or *Five-Finger Discount* to the ledge on which they end. Move right along the ledge to a single bolt on the wall above. Climb the line, making use of this bolt and horizontals for gear. Head right for an alcove, then traverse left and over a bulge to the top. Keep your head. Rappel from anchors.
75 ft. 1 bolt. *Jim Link, John Whisman, 1989.*

14 Roadside Attraction 5.7 ★★★★★

This is the most classic line of its grade in the Red. Locate the obvious dihedral at the end of the approach trail when it reaches the wall. Scramble up to a ledge to begin. Climb the low-angle hand crack to a ledge with a tree. Continue up the hand crack past a couple of wide sections to another ledge and anchors. If you want to summit, belay from this ledge, then continue up to the top.
140 ft. *Greg Smith, Ron Snider, 1984.*

5.10 WALL

The following routes are located to the right of where the approach trail meets the wall.

15 Milkin' the Chicken 5.11d ★

From the end of the approach trail, make a right instead of heading up to *Roadside Attraction*. The trail will wind down through some trees and head back up to the section of cliff referred to as the 5.10 Wall. This route ascends the arête on the left side of the wall, making use of a couple of bolts and a slung chickenhead for protection.
50 ft. 3 bolts. *Mark Williams, 1990.*

NATURAL BRIDGE

16 A.W.O.L. 5.10a ★★★
This is the obvious, heavily chalked bolted line just right of the arête. Start at a low overhang and move up through pockets and bulges to a blank section. Circumvent this with a long move and a crimp, then pull past a small roof to reach the anchors.
50 ft. 5 bolts. Mark Williams, Porter Jarrard, 1990.

17 Battle of the Bulge 5.10a ★
Freak out your sport-climbing buddies and keep climbing above the anchors on *A.W.O.L.* via this crack system to the top of the wall. The first ascent of this route also included *A.W.O.L.*, before *A.W.O.L.* was bolted.
80 ft. Matt Flach, Ron Snider, 1989.

18 Dragonslayer 5.10d ★★★
Just right of *A.W.O.L.* is another popular line. Climb up and past deep mono pockets, then fight the pump to the anchors.
50 ft. 5 bolts. Mark Williams, Charles Tabor, 1990.

19 Crazyfingers 5.10c ★★★★
Move right from *Dragonslayer* to the next line of chalk. Crank through a sidepull crux at the bottom, then pace yourself the rest of the way to the anchors.
50 ft. 5 bolts. Rob Turan, Mark Williams, 1990.

20 Pulling Pockets 5.10d ★★★★
This is the next bolted route on the wall just right of *Crazyfingers*. Originally a mixed route, this was retrobolted for that amusement-park feeling. Nevertheless, it is an excellent route and can now be enjoyed by those without cams. Many variations exist from the last bolt to the anchors — including a hands-off dyno.
50 ft. Greg Smith, Tom Souders, 1987.

21 Synchronicity 5.11a ★★★★
This is the obvious diagonal crack splitting the face of the 5.10 Wall. Crank through the initial moves, then enjoy long reaches past good rests to the anchors. Protects great with stoppers.
50 ft. Greg Smith, Tom Souders, 1984.

22 Jersey Connection 5.12b ★★★★
This route and the next share the same start. Step right from *Synchronicity* a few feet to the next line of bolts. Crimp up the edge of a flake and pockets to a decent rest out right. When ready, move back left to a hideous crimp rail. Launch for a good hold, then relax on large jugs to the finish.
50 ft. 5 bolts. Matt Flach, Rob Turan, 1990.

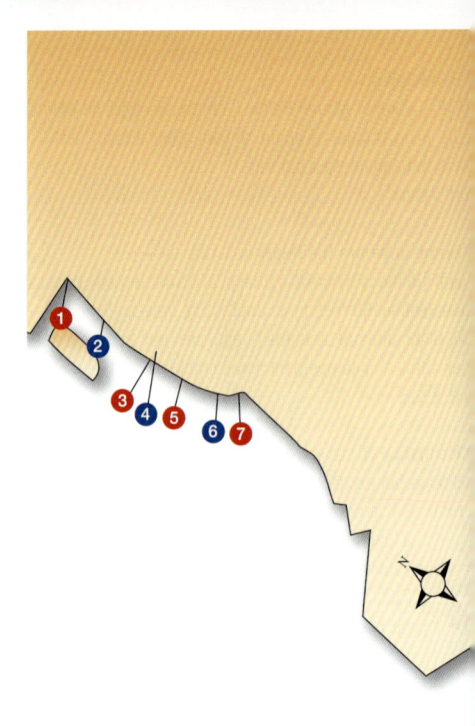

23 Stay the Hand 5.12a ★★★★
Start as for *Jersey Connection* but don't angle left. Instead, make a difficult move to reach a set of pockets, then angle right, pull another big move, then escape right to the juggy face. A more difficult direct start ascends the three bolts beneath the anchors (5.12c).
50 ft. 5 bolts. Porter Jarrard, Mark Schussler, 1990. Tim Steele.

24 Valor Over Discretion 5.8 ★★
Like *Pulling Pockets*, this route, originally a trad line, has fallen to the drill. Start by standing on the large boulder right of the 5.10 Wall. Climb the face a few feet right of the arête. Move left around the arête at a roof and continue to a ledge.
50 ft. 4 bolts. Roger Pearson, John Bronaugh, 1987.

25 Psycho Killer 5.10c ★
This route begins just right of *Valor Over Discretion*, on a large boulder. Climb up the face to a roof. Crank over the roof and continue up to the ledge.
50 ft. Greg Smith, 1984.

26 Harder Than Your Husband 5.11b ★★★
A few feet right of *Psycho Killer* is a roof with a finger crack. Traverse across the shelf, then make a long reach to a good hand jam at the lip. Power up to a fingerlock, then continue up the short dihedral to bolted anchors.
40 ft. Greg Smith, 1984.

54

ROADSIDE CRAG

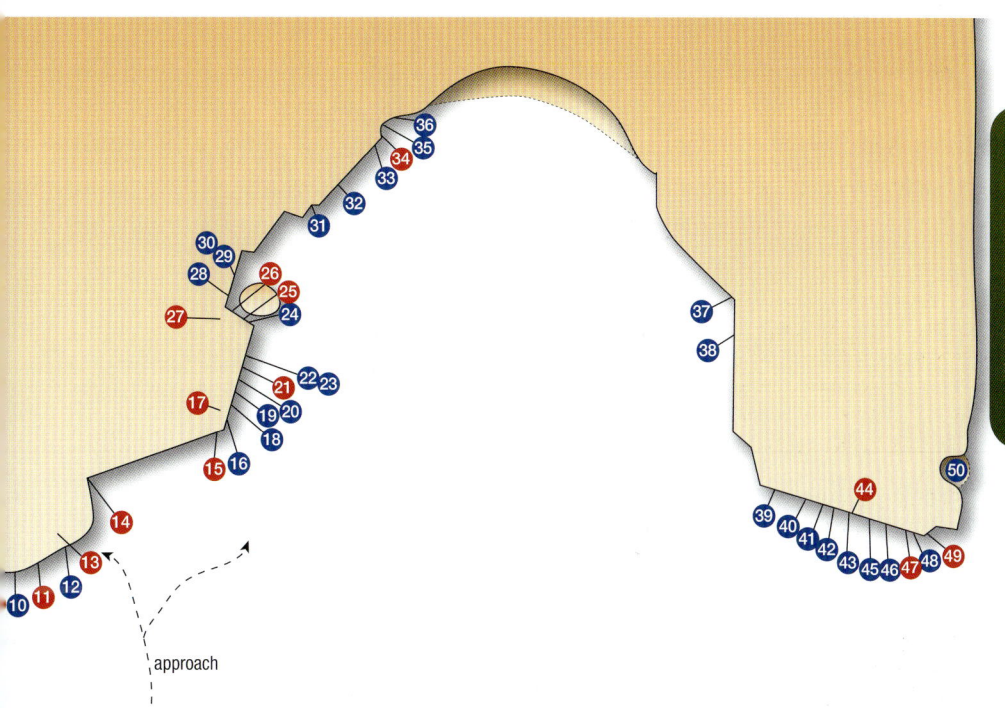

Jersey Connection

55

NATURAL BRIDGE

Ro Shampo

27 Holly Golightly 5.10b ★★
Located on the ledge above *Harder Than Your Husband* and *Valor Over Discretion*. Climb the face to an overhanging crack. Continue up the crack to anchors.
40 ft. Scott Hammon, Frank Waters, 2003.

5.12 WALL

28 Scissors 5.11d ★★★
Right of *Harder Than Your Husband* is a well-sheltered, overhanging, plated wall. This is the first line on the left side of the wall and has a very high first bolt. Stick-clip the bolt and jump up to a jug. Move left, then power up to a good pocket. Continue up the plated face past long moves and good heel hooks.
50 ft. 4 bolts. Porter Jarrard, Steve Cater, 1991.

29 Ro Shampo 5.12a ★★★★★
Is it 11d? Or is it 12a? I've even heard it called 11b! Either way, it's a classic so who really cares? Start in a sand pit about 25 feet right of *Scissors*. Step up onto a boulder to grab the first holds. Climb straight up over plated jugs, then kick out left. Crank the crux, then continue hauling on the steep, plated jugs. If you pitch trying to clip the anchors, you will join the majority.
60 ft. 6 bolts. Jamie Baker, Jim Link, 1992.

30 Tic-Tac-Toe 5.12b ★★★★
This often-overlooked line shares the start with *Ro Shampo*, but moves right after the first bolt. Move up the steep face through good horizontals separated by long reaches. Gain the occasional hand jam rest to prepare yourself for the boulder problem at the last bolt.
60 ft. 4 bolts. Brian McCray, 1993.

31 The Adventure 5.11d ★★
Locate a line of bolts near the second dihedral right of *Tic-Tac-Toe*. Climb up through a variety of movements to the anchors high above. Be careful not to knock loose rock onto passing climbers below.
100 ft. 11 bolts. Eric Anderson, Brian McCray, 1993.

32 Strevels Gets in Shape 5.12b ★★★
This bouldery line is located near an arête right of the previous line. Climb up an arching feature, then make an accuracy move to a wide pocket. Don't relax yet. Continue up the steep face to the first set of anchors. Take a good rest, then begin to make your way up to the overhanging wall above. Continue up the overhanging wall past long crosses and highsteps to the second set of anchors.
90 ft. 12 bolts. Porter Jarrard, Eric Anderson, 1990.

Wild Gift

The Return of Chris Snyder

Wild Gift 5.12c ★★★★★
Classic power endurance. Move right from *Strevels* about 20 feet to a steep, angling line just left of an arête. Jump up to the first hold, then angle right to begin the business. Crank through tough moves and difficult clips to a sick undercling move at the top. Rebolted in 2016.
45 ft. 5 bolts. Porter Jarrard, Mark Schussler, 1990.

Camel-Toe Jockey 5.9 ★
This dihedral is located just around the corner from *Wild Gift*. Inch your way up the dihedral, trying not to succumb to the tempting bolts of *Way Up Yonder*.
40 ft. Unknown.

Way Up Yonder 5.12a ★★★★
The line of bolts just right of *Camel-Toe Jockey*. Climb through sloping pockets up an overhanging wall to the first set of anchors. Continue up through the massive overhanging wall to the second set of anchors "way up yonder." Or you can stop at the first set of anchors for *Up Yonder*, a good 5.11b.
95 ft. 13 bolts. Porter Jarrard, 1993.

Sand 5.11d
Start by clipping the first bolt of *Way Up Yonder*, then angle right through an overhang. Not too popular for reasons made obvious by its name.
45 ft. 5 bolts. Porter Jarrard, Hassan Saab, 1993.

The Return of Chris Snyder 5.11d ★★★★★
Steep jug hauling at its best. Walk 250 feet right from *Sand*, past a wet amphitheater and around a corner, to a couple of bolted lines ascending a massive, pocketed face. Begin by climbing a flake up to a short roof. Crank over the roof to gain the overhanging face. Marathon-climb for about 65 more feet, past a couple of no-hands rests, to anchors 95 feet up.
95 ft. 11 bolts. Porter Jarrard, Mike Norman, 1992.

㊳ Pine 5.12a ★★★★
Similar to *The Return of Chris Snyder* but a bit more technical, with fewer rests. Begins a few feet right of the previous route.
95 ft. 10 bolts. Porter Jarrard, Jeff Moll, 1992.

㊴ Just Duet 5.10d ★★★
Walk around the corner and right from *Pine* about 150 feet to a slabby wall peppered with bolts. This is the first line encountered and begins on a five-foot-high ledge with a high first bolt. Climb the inital slab to a bulge with a good stance. Power over the bulge and continue through delicate moves to the anchors.
70 ft. 9 bolts. John Bronaugh, 2002.

㊵ Kampsight 5.9+ ★★★★
Named after a Bob Kamps sighting just after this route was bolted. He even managed to bag the second ascent! This route ascends the low-angle face 10 feet right of *Just Duet* and just left of a crack. Begin on a three-foot-high sloping ledge. Enjoyable and thought-provoking climbing topped off with a great view from the anchors.
80 ft. 8 bolts. Tina Bronaugh, John Bronaugh, 1992.

㊶ Trouble Clef 5.9 ★★★
This is the next bolted line 10 feet right of *Kampsight*. Begin on a three-foot-high sloping ledge just right of a crack.
80 ft. 9 bolts. John Bronaugh, 2002.

㊷ Altered Scale 5.9+ ★★
Begin on a three-foot-high sloping ledge, 10 feet right of *Trouble Clef*, and pull through a tough sequence to reach the first bolt. Climb through easier moves to reach a thin section toward the middle of the route. Relax again until the final bulge before the anchors.
80 ft. 7 bolts. John Bronaugh, 2002.

Trouble Clef

43 All Cows Eat Grass 5.8 ★★★
This is the next bolted line 20 feet right of *Altered Scale*. Begin just left of a crack with some bushes. Climb fun moves to an exciting finish.
80 ft. 9 bolts. John Bronaugh, 2002.

44 Strawberry Shortcake 5.7 ★
Start near *All Cows Eat Grass* and run it out to the first good gear. Move into the hand crack near *Ledger Line* and finish at that route's anchor. A second pitch goes left, up a short chimney, and left again to an alcove. It's reportedly loose and is not recommended.
60 ft. Aaron Jones.

45 Ledger Line 5.7 ★★★
Step right from the previous line to locate this route. Climb a thin start to reach the first bolt, then move up on large ledges to the vertical face. Sink a hand jam or two along the way while continuing up on smaller ledges to the anchors in a roof.
80 ft. 7 bolts. Ryan Adams, 2002.

46 C Sharp or B Flat 5.7 ★★★
Move right from *Ledger Line* to locate this classic beginner's route.
60 ft. 6 bolts. Tina Bronaugh, Jennifer Rannells, 1993.

47 Gumby Land 5.3 ★
Just right of *C Sharp or B Flat* is this thick flake. Climb the flake and face to the anchors on *C Sharp or B Flat*. Probably the only route in the guide first climbed top-down.
60 ft. Tim Powers, solo downclimb, 1994.

48 You Can Tune a Piano, but You Can't Tuna Fish 5.10b ★★★
This route begins just right of *C Sharp Or B Flat*. Climb 15 feet of slab to reach a high first bolt. Climb up through a series of crimps and underclings to reach a short, technical crux. Solve the crux, then continue up the fun face to the anchors. This route was stripped by the bolter soon after it was bolted so the hangers could be used for another route. The route was rebolted in 2004 by John Bronaugh.
60 ft. 7 bolts. Mike Woodhouse, 1997.

49 I Didn't Know This Was the End 5.7 ★★★
Named by Scott Brown in memory of the first ascentionist, Mason Allen. Mason passed away just days after he and Scott climbed this route together. Begin 15 feet right of the previous bolted line. Scramble to a ledge to gain a finger crack, then dive into an offwidth section. Follow the offwidth to a crumbly ledge to gain a hand crack. Run the unprotected slab to the barbed-wire fence at the top of the cliff or sneak left to a tree for a belay.
150 ft. Mason Allen, Scott Brown, 2006.

50 Chunnel 5.13a ★★★
Walk right from the main wall to locate this route, which climbs out the notorious "pee cave." Please don't pee in this cave, since it now hosts what has turned out to be a pretty decent roof climb. Boulder out the roof and turn the lip to be greeted by a somewhat blank face and the true crux. Starting at the back of the cave and bouldering to the first bolt ups the grade to 5.13c.
50 ft. 7 bolts. Lee Smith, March 2010. Equipper: Greg Martin.

THE ZOO

48 routes

.14
.13
.12
.11
.10
.9
.8
.7
≤.6

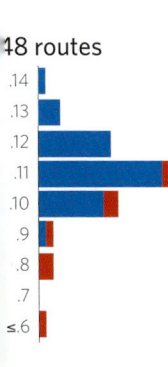

Once considered a sub-par crag, the Zoo has become more popular due to development on the north side, nearly doubling the number of routes. The original routes have cleaned up to become excellent overhanging moderate lines good for warm, early day climbing. The closure of Roadside Crag (now open by permit) has also added to the popularity of this cliff.

37.7335
-83.6616
5 min / 15 min

Approach: Park as for Roadside Crag but do not cross the road. Instead, hike back through the woods on the south side of the parking area toward the creek. Hike upstream a short ways and cross the creek at a tree-trunk bridge. Follow a trail steeply uphill about 10 minutes to the wall. You'll arrive near a low arch. Hike left around the arch to the area's original routes, or hike right for the "New Zoo."

Conditions: The Zoo has multiple sun and shade aspects for both cool- and warm-weather climbing. The right (north-facing) side of the crag stays shady all summer. The left side gets early sun except for *Hippocrite* and *Scar Tissue*, which stay in the shade. *Skin the Cat* through *Hippocrite* stay dry in the rain. The north-wall routes aren't quite as steep, so avoid them during a heavy rain.

Chimp

❷ **Armadillo** 5.10d ★★★
This is the bolted line directly left of *Put Me in the Zoo*. Begin just right of a tiny rockhouse.
70 ft. 6 bolts. John Bronaugh, Tina Bronaugh, 1998.

❸ **Jailbird** 5.10d ★★★
Walk about 30 feet left from the dirt ramp leading to the previous lines until you see a low-angle slab with a roof at the top. Begin on an easy slab, then gain a ledge and crimp up to better holds. Pull a small overhang, then follow larger holds to the anchors.
90 ft. 10 bolts. John Bronaugh, Ryan Adams, 2003.

❹ **Chimp** 5.10a ★★★
This route begins about 20 feet left of *Jailbird*. Begin on easy holds, then move over the lip of a small roof into the thin zone. Edge for a bit, then continue over some bulges to reach the anchors.
60 ft. 5 bolts. John Bronaugh, Tina Bronaugh, 1992.

❺ **Live Action** 5.9- ★★★
Follow the odd crack system just right of *Edgehog*. Shares the anchors with *Edgehog*.
75 ft. Will Sweeny, 2013.

❶ **Put Me in the Zoo** 5.10b ★★★
Walk through the small arch and around the corner to a dirt ramp that heads up to the right. Follow the dirt ramp to a ledge. This route is the bolted line on the right that heads up a vertical face.
70 ft. 7 bolts. John Bronaugh, Tina Bronaugh, 1998.

❻ **Edgehog** 5.11a ★★★
Move 60 feet left from the previous lines to another bolted line just before a large overhang. Edge up a thin slab, then pull a bulge to reach more-forgiving holds.
60 ft. 6 bolts. John Bronaugh, Alex Yeakley, 1998.

Susan Murphy on *Hippocrite*, 5.12a (page 62). Photo: Elodie Saracco.

THE ZOO

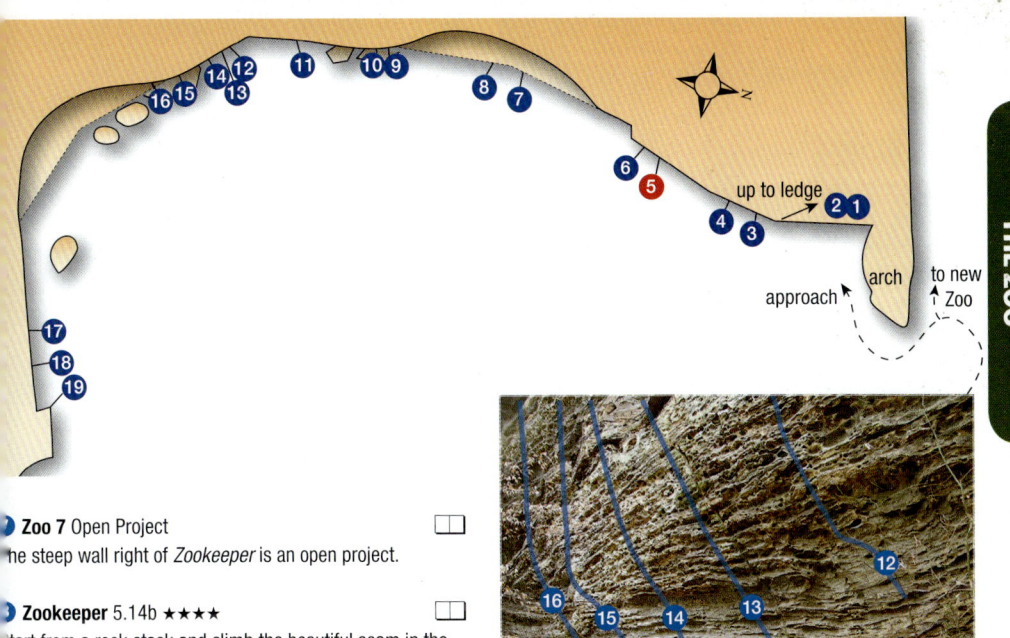

Zoo 7 Open Project
The steep wall right of *Zookeeper* is an open project.

Zookeeper 5.14b ★★★★
Start from a rock stack and climb the beautiful seam in the steep amphitheater.
50 ft. 5 bolts. *Andrew Gearing, 2016.*

Skin the Cat 5.11a ★★★
Hike past an amphitheater to a ledge with a boulder. This route starts on the boulder and begins with a low roof. Pull over the low roof, then angle right past hand jams and bulges to a finishing groove.
80 ft. 10 bolts. *John Bronaugh, Alex Yeakley, 1999.*

One Brick Shy 5.10c ★★★
Begin on the same boulder as *Skin the Cat*. Pull the roof and climb up left of a crack to a ledge. Move up and over some bulges to a vertical face. Pull on pockets to the anchors. Rebolted in 2015.
80 ft. 8 bolts. *John Bronaugh, Stacy Temple, 1992.*

Geezers Go Sport 5.11b ★★★★
This pumpy route is the next bolted line, 25 feet left of *One Brick Shy*. Bring a medium-sized cam for optional pro at the first ledge.
80 ft. 9 bolts. *John Bronaugh, Stacy Temple, 1992.*

Monkey in the Middle 5.11a ★★★★
Move another 25 feet left from the previous line to the next bolted route. Crank through the steep beginning section on pockets to a slightly overhanging headwall.
80 ft. 8 bolts. *Stacy Temple, John Bronaugh, 1992.*

Animal Husbandry 5.11b ★★★
Start from a boulder ten feet left of *Monkey in the Middle* and pump up the steep wall.
80 ft. 8 bolts. *Dustin Stephens, Dan Beck, 2014.*

Cannonball 5.11b ★★★
Walk 20 feet left from *Monkey in the Middle* to a point just before another amphitheater. Start on a boulder and climb through a short overhanging section to the second bolt. Continue up the pocketed face. This once-chossy line has cleaned up nicely, and was rebolted in 2016.
80 ft. 8 bolts. *Stacy Temple, John Bronaugh, 1992.*

On Beyond Zebra! 5.11b ★★★
This route begins to the left of *Cannonball* and atop a large boulder near the end of an amphitheater.
80 ft. 9 bolts. *John Bronaugh, Stacy Temple, 1993.*

Lynx Jinx 5.11c ★★★
This route ascends the steep face a few feet left of *On Beyond Zebra!*. Climb through a low overhang and continue up the face through some bulges.
50 ft. 7 bolts. *Jim Link, John Bronaugh, 1995.*

Scar Tissue 5.12a ★★★★
Although a little green at the start, this route serves as a great companion to *Hippocrite*. Steep and powerful. Walk left about 200 feet from *Lynx Jinx*, past an amphitheater, to a steep, pocketed section of the wall. This route begins on the left side of a low overhang. Climb through a very steep section to reach the hard moves on the not-so-steep section above. Crank through the final moves to reach the anchors.
45 ft. 5 bolts. *Phil Nemes, 2002.*

Hippocrite

Sidewinder

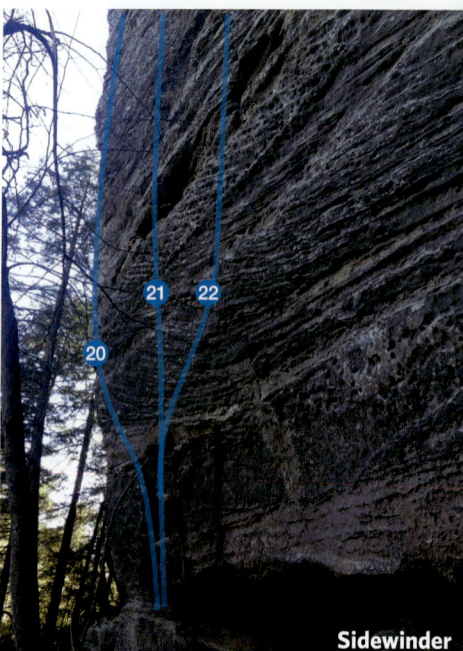

⑱ Hippocrite 5.12a ★★★★★
A short, classic route with incredibly cool moves. Crank up the obvious line of big huecos just left of *Scar Tissue*.
45 ft. 4 bolts. Eric Lowe, 1998.

⑲ Aviary 5.12b ★
Left of *Hippocrite* is an arête with a high first bolt. Begin on a large boulder and power up to a ledge at the second bolt. Get a shake, then make reachy moves on sandy holds to gain a roof. Traverse left to clip a stray bolt, then gun through more awkwardness to meet a good shake on an epoxied flake. Continue on thinning and disappearing holds to the anchors, which are way right from the last bolt. Use a 70-meter rope if you want to get down without any issues.
80 ft. 12 bolts. Doug Curth, 2007. Equipper: Mark Strevels.

NEW ZOO

The following routes are located to the right of the point where the trail meets the cliffline. Go right instead of walking through the arch that heads to the old Zoo.

⑳ Sidewinder 5.12b ★★★
This is the first of several routes located at the "New Zoo." When the trail meets the cliff line, head right instead of walking through the arch. *Sidewinder* and the next two routes begin on the same high, sandy ledge. From the ledge, traverse to a stance where you can stick clip the first bolt. Bouldery to a nice arête.
60 ft. 8 bolts. Blake Bowling, Jeff Neal 2012.

㉑ Speedy Gonzales 5.13b ★★★
The next route right of *Sidewinder* shares its first bolt. Begin on the same ledge in a dihedral. At the third bolt, climb straight up where the next route goes right.
60 ft. 8 bolts. Dylan Barks, 2013.

㉒ Irony of Twisted Fate 5.12c ★★★
Begin on the same ledge as the previous two climbs. Start as for *Speedy Gonzales*, but move right at the third bolt into steep pockets with decent rests.
60 ft. 9 bolts. Kipp Trummel, 2012.

㉓ Sparkling Jackass 5.12b ★★★★
Find this about 50 feet up the hill from the previous three climbs. Start on sparse pockets with cool moves to a obvious ledge, then continue through the headwall.
80 ft. 11 bolts. Ray Ellington, Jeff Neal, 2013.

㉔ Hippopotomoose 5.11b ★★★★
Just right of *Sparkling Jackass* is this excellent line that starts in the crack. Move up and left, passing a crux, then up the pumpy face.
70 ft. 8 bolts. Kipp Trummel, 2013.

㉕ Barrel Full of Monkeys 5.11a ★★★★
As the name suggest, this route is a lot of fun. Considered the warm-up of the wall, it begins just right of the crack start of *Hippopotomoose*.
80 ft. 11 bolts. Jeff Neal, 2012.

BabaBooey 5.11c ★★★

he next line right of *Barrel Full of Monkeys* begins with
everal tough moves on small pockets and edges. Good
dges await, along with some long runs on the headwall.
0 ft. 8 bolts. *Jeff Neal, 2012.*

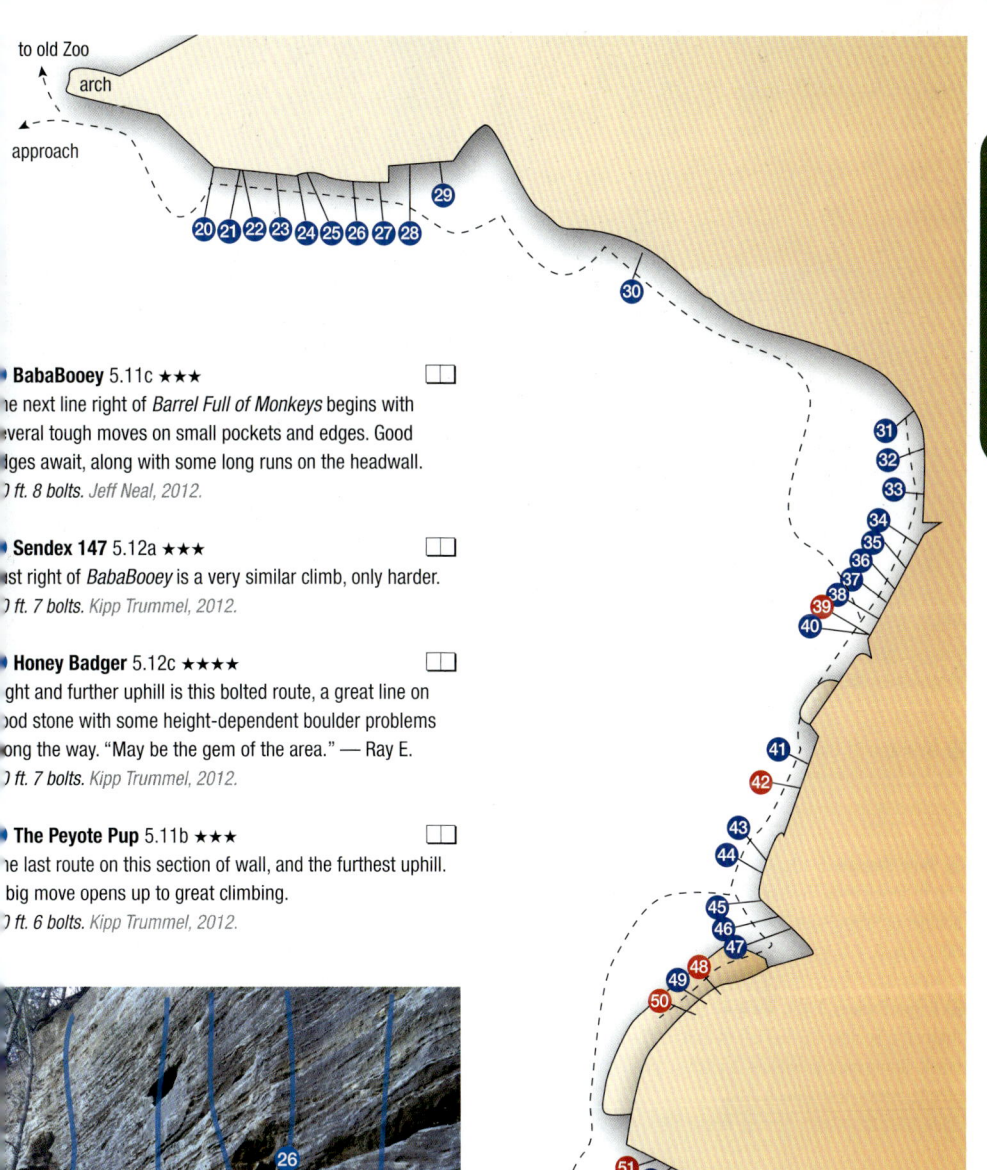

Sendex 147 5.12a ★★★

ist right of *BabaBooey* is a very similar climb, only harder.
0 ft. 7 bolts. *Kipp Trummel, 2012.*

Honey Badger 5.12c ★★★★

ight and further uphill is this bolted route, a great line on
ood stone with some height-dependent boulder problems
long the way. "May be the gem of the area." — Ray E.
0 ft. 7 bolts. *Kipp Trummel, 2012.*

The Peyote Pup 5.11b ★★★

he last route on this section of wall, and the furthest uphill.
big move opens up to great climbing.
0 ft. 6 bolts. *Kipp Trummel, 2012.*

BIRD CAGE

From the previous wall, continue right until you reach a large section of overhanging rock. This is the Bird Cage.

㉚ Sons of Perdition 5.12a ★★★

This is the first bolted line you come to. Twenty feet of easy climbing gains a high first bolt. Sequential bouldery sections and pockets lead to a sit-down rest, then a roof before the holds disappear. A long draw on the third bolt and back-cleaning the roof bolt is recommended.
80 ft. 12 bolts. *Kipp Trummel, 2013.*

NATURAL BRIDGE

The Peyote Pup — 28, 29

Sons of Perdition — 30

---

31 New Zoo 31 Closed Project
The leftmost line of bolts on the wall is a closed project.
Equipped by Andrew Gearing, 2014.

32 Slow Stepper 5.13c ★★★★
The middle line on the blocky wall left of *Hammerhead*. A low boulder problem leads to big moves on big holds.
80 ft. 9 bolts. Andrew Gearing, 2014.

33 Eager Beaver 5.12c ★★★★
Start off a boulder 25 feet left of *Hammerhead*, just left of a crack. Crimp hard down low to crazy jug haul above. A couple of long draws help reduce drag.
90 ft. 10 bolts. Andrew Gearing, Dustin Stevens, 2014.

34 Hammerhead Closed Project ★★★★
Walk right from *Sons of Perdition* down through a swampy section, or stay high and pass through some boulders to reach the right edge of the cave with bolted lines. This is the first line and has glue-in bolts.
65 ft. 7 bolts. Equipped by Kipp Trummel.

35 Jethro Bodean 5.13c ★★★★
Next route right of *Hammerhead*. Climb through big, steep moves on crimps and past a big dyno.
65 ft. 8 bolts. Andrew Gearing, 2014. Equipper: Kipp Trummel.

36 Slackjaw Willie Open Project ★★★
The third line out of the right edge of the cave.
6 bolts. Equipped by Kipp Trummel.

37 Reasonable Doubt Open Project ★★★
Currently the rightmost of the four steep climbs on the right side of the cave. Bouldery and steep.
65 ft. 6 bolts. Equipped by Kipp Trummel.

38 Botanical Gardens 5.10a ★★★
The long slab right of *Reasonable Doubt*. Start by stick-clipping the high first bolt and jumping off a cheater stack.
95 ft. 11 bolts. Dustin Stephens, Dan Beck, 2014.

39 Scantily Trad 5.11a ★★★
Starting on *Romance Explosion*, this mixed route pulls out le up the gaping crack — then things get messy.
90 ft. 5 bolts. Dustin Stephens, 2014.

40 Romance Explosion 5.11a ★★★
Fifty feet right of *Reasonable Doubt*, start with a jump off the boulder. New River Gorge-style crimping leads to wild move up the headwall.
90 ft. 10 bolts. Dustin Stephens, 2014.

41 Snake Charmer 5.11a ★★★
Around the corner from the previous route is this techy face starting with a flake and large hueco at about 20 feet.
65 ft. 7 bolts. Dustin Stephens, 2014.

42 Buried Alive 5.8+ ★★★
Start this traditional flake route just to the right of *Snake Charmer*. It's "a spicy hot lead" according to the FA, so be solid at the grade.
55 ft. Kipp Trummel, 2013.

Crimpin' Ain't Easy 5.11c ★★★★

ıis long, golden face route is just before you get to the rdcage Lab routes. Start on good crimps and pockets, rough larger holds, then back again to crimps. Perfect ange rock leads to the anchor.

5 ft. 9 bolts. Dustin Stephens, Marty Vogel, 2013.

Action Potential 5.11d ★★★★

art this spicy route in a hand/finger crack, then take a rest the ledge before finding the crux a bit higher. A harder rect start to the left is also possible.

0 ft. 8 bolts. Dustin Stephens, 2014.

Dirty Bird 5.10b ★★★

ırther right, you'll find a steep gully with three bolted lines the left side. This route is the first you reach, and climbs the wandering arête. It has cleaned up a lot since it was amed, but may not quite be classic.

5 ft. 6 bolts. Kipp Trummel, 2013.

Lone Coyote 5.10b ★★★

ıe next two routes right of *Dirty Bird* climb better than they ok. This one has high steps and small holds all the way to an vil runout to the anchors. Clean the draws on the anchors for our partner so they will have the same spicy experience!

5 ft. 9 bolts. Big E, Kipp Trummel, 2013.

Here Comes the Beep Beep 5.10b

ne next route right of *Lone Coyote* is quite similar.

0 ft. 10 bolts. Kipp Trummel, 2013.

㊽ **Harley** 5.8+ ★★★

Right of the previous set of lines, on the right side of the gully, is a ledge where this and the next two lines begin. This route ascends the face, making use of natural protection.

50 ft. Kipp Trummel, 2013.

㊾ **Gunner** 5.9 ★★★

Perfect warmup for the wall, or a nice beginner lead.

50 ft. 6 bolts. Kipp Trummel, 2013.

㊿ **Can of Biscuits** 5.4 ★★★

Climb the flake system just to the right of *Gunner.*

50 ft. Kipp Trummel, 2013.

(51) **Bumpin' With Bulldog** 5.10 ★★★

Continue right along the cliff until the trail meets back up with the wall. Look left and you can see this nice finger crack, with a few bolts midway up that protect a tricky section. Fun route.

60 ft. 3 bolts. Kipp Trummel, Jeff Neal, 2013.

(52) **Goblins in My Mind** 5.11d ★★★

Just right of *Bumpin* is this crimp ladder of a route. Be ready for the ending move.

60 ft. 7 bolts. Kipp Trummel, 2013.

(53) **The Fangs and the Furious** 5.10b ★★★

Climb the obvious finger crack that starts in the face, avoiding the death blocks in the cave.

65 ft. 3 bolts. Jeff Neal, Kipp Trummel, 2013.

TORRENT FALLS

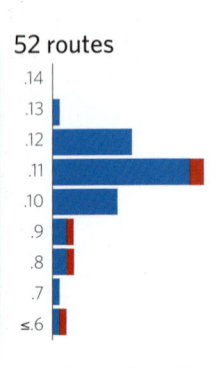

52 routes

Torrent Falls is a privately owned crag that offers some of the Red's finest sport climbing. The property changed hands in 2007 when Dr. Bob Matheny purchased it. Torrent is currently open to climbing, but you must register on the website (see the Access section for details). The routes here are, for the most part, grouped into their respective grades in different sectors — the 5.10 Wall, the 5.11 Wall, and the 5.12 Wall. The 5.12 wall hosts some of the longest and pumpiest 5.12s around, including the five-star classic *Steelworker* and the hardest 5.12a in the Red, *Bare Metal Teen*. You even get a five-star 5.11 overhanging hand crack, *Windy Corner*.

Approach: From Miguel's, drive south on K 11 5.3 miles until you see the sign for Torre Falls Bed and Breakfast on your right. Turn rig and park in the designated areas, paying clo attention to parking signs. To reach routes 1-1 hike straight back from the parking area ar cross a small creek. Head up a hill, which leads the base of the 5.10 Wall. To reach the rest of t routes, walk up the gravel road to a set of stai on the right. Follow the stairs to the base of t 5.11 Wall.

Conditions: Due to its horseshoe-shaped layou Torrent Falls offers good climbing in almost a conditions. The 5.11 and 5.12 Walls face south, expect excellent sun exposure. For shade, che out the 5.10 Wall, and for early morning su head to the east side. Most of the lines rema dry in a light rain, but the walls do seep duri periods of heavy rain.

Access: To climb at Torrent, you must regist at www.torrentfallsclimbing.com the day entry (not to be confused with Torrent Fa Climbing Adventure, a resort located in t next amphitheatre to the north). Parking ar registered climbing slots are limited. Ea registrant is valid for one vehicle only, and ea group is limited to no more than three climber All individuals must sign a waiver before enterir the property. Please throw some cash in th donation box just before heading up the stair Access to Torrent is often closed, but one way gain easy access is to rent a cabin through Re River Outdoors: www.redriveroutdoors.com.

❶ Windy Corner 5.11b ★★★★★
This classic overhanging hand crack is around the corner and left from *Smoke Screen*. Approach as for the 5.10 Wall, then go left. Climb the dihedral to a roof about 15 feet up. Pull the roof and pump through long reaches to decent jams. Follow the crack as it switches off right and take on a couple of fist jams to reach belay anchors at the ledge. Most people lower from here, for a classic and well-protected line.

  The second pitch continues up a thin seam leading to a long runout on the face to the top. Rappel from a tree or walk off right to descend.
100 ft. Tom Souders, 1983.

❷ Sam and Terry's Line 5.12a
Twenty feet right of *Windy Corner*, locate a line of bolts near a thin seam. Originally named *Sam's Line* because Sam Krieg bolted most of it, until a more doable start was added by Blake Bowling, making it *Terry's Line,* since Terry Kindred had the vision in 2007. Confused?
80 ft. 6 bolts. Blake Bowling, Sam Krieg.

❸ Smoke Screen 5.7 ★
Climb the obvious dihedral to rap anchors. The original line went to the top, but the rap anchors allow you to skip the mudslide.
90 ft. Dave Veldhaus, 1984.

❹ Impossible Choss 5.12c
The bolted line just right of the *Smoke Screen* dihedral. Climb a crack, then hand-traverse a ledge to reach the firs bolt. Continue up the face past large horizontals to reach the overhanging headwall. Pull a small roof at the top to cl the anchors.
60 ft. 6 bolts. Unknown.

Windy Corner

5.10 Wall

① Tourist Trap 5.9 ★★★
The arête. After a funky start, move left to reach the second bolt. Head right for the arête and fun climbing to a mantel before the anchors.
30 ft. 9 bolts. Terry Kindred, 2003.

② Last Resort 5.10c ★★
The next bolted line left of the 5.10 Wall. Originally the dirtiest line on the wall, this seems to be cleaning up nicely. Don't expect a bolt every time you want one, though. The crux is somewhat height dependent.
70 ft. 6 bolts. Terry Kindred, 2005.

5.10 WALL

③ Family Values 5.10d ★★★
This shares the start of *Rest Assured* and continues up the left bolt line. Climb the face using slopers and pinches to an obvious crux, then hang on to reach the anchors.
80 ft. 9 bolts. Terry Kindred, 2001.

④ Rest Assured 5.10a ★★★
Start as for *Family Values*, then bear right.
60 ft. 7 bolts. Terry Kindred, 2001.

⑨ About Five Ten 5.11b ★★
A reachy-start route right of the previous pair of lines. If you're about 5'10" you shouldn't have any issues.
70 ft. 8 bolts. Blake Bowling, 2008.

⑩ Reanimator 5.10b ★★★
This line and the next are the rightmost routes on the 5.10 Wall and share a start. Begin with or without cheater stones to grab the first jugs under the low roof. Pull the roof, traverse left to a stance, then go straight up the face on pockets and crimps.
55 ft. 8 bolts. Terry Kindred, 2001.

⑪ It's Alive 5.10d ★★★
Start as for *It's Alive*, but after the roof, follow the right-hand line of bolts to anchors.
70 ft. 7 bolts. Terry Kindred, 2001.

The next route sits by itself to the left of the falls.

⑫ Dark City 5.11c ★★
An extremely steep, bolted crack system. If you like them dirty but fun, this one's for you. Originally done on gear.
85 ft. 9 bolts. Terry Kindred, Blake Bowling, 2004.

⑬ Situational Awareness 5.11c ★★★
An extremely steep line that begins with an A0 move, or stick clip the first bolt and start back in the wettish dihedral, paying attention to the swing and bad landing if you fall from in there.
70 ft. 5 bolts. Blake Bowling, 2010.

Paranoia

⑭ Paranoia 5.13b ★★★
This difficult and rarely repeated line begins right of *Situational Awareness* and is marked by an intermediate set of anchors midway up. Climb the steep, thin face and pull over a roof for the heinous crux moves.
90 ft. 12 bolts. Dave Hume, 1996.

⑮ Hydro Shock 5.12c
An incomplete project right of *Paranoia*. Climb to the last bolt (5.12c) and lower, or finish this thing!
70 ft. 9 bolts. Unknown.

⑯ Into the Mystic 5.12c ★★★
Right of the previous routes and 40 feet left of the *Neither* dihedral is an intimidating line with fixed chain draws. Climb a pocketed face to a section of black, blobby rock and a severely overhanging finish.
85 ft. 11 bolts. Greg Martin, 2000.

⑰ Neither 5.11a ★★
The left-facing dihedral. Climb 25 feet of questionable rock to the clean dihedral above, where the rock improves. Layback and stem the dihedral and lower from chain anchors.
60 ft. Unknown.

⑱ Torrential 5.12c ★
On the wall right of *Neither* is a bolted line that moves through a series of overhangs down low and more overhang toward the top. Look for a fixed extended draw. This might be where you bail, due to choss or wet rock.
70 ft. 10 bolts. Bruce Adams, Dave Scott, 2000.

⑲ Burcham's Folly 5.8 ★★★
Ascend the left-leaning crack just left of the 5.12 Wall.
100 ft. John Burcham, 1993.

5.12 WALL

This small but stacked zone is about 100 feet left of the 5.11 Wall and is probably one of the best walls you'll see on your trip to the Red.

⑳ Big Money Grip 5.12b ★★★★
After *Bare Metal Teen*, this one may seem easy! Begin by climbing the dihedral on the left side of the 5.12 Wall to a high first bolt. Continue up through pockets and crimps to a slabby section, then fire to the anchors.
70 ft. 7 bolts. Porter Jarrard, Jeff Moll, 1993.

㉑ Bare Metal Teen 5.12a ★★★★★
Historically rated 5.12a, this is one of the cruelest jokes the Red has to offer. Begin near the center of the wall. Climb up to a horizontal, then, with the pump clock ticking, sprint up the sustained and overhanging face, taking full advantage of each jug you locate.
80 ft. 8 bolts. Porter Jarrard, Jeff Moll, 1993.

TORRENT FALLS

5.12 Wall

Centerfire

Steelworker 5.12c ★★★★★
Classic. One of the best lines of its grade in the Red. This route begins just right of *Bare Metal Teen* in a low overhanging section. Pull the low overhang, then race up a steep section on good holds, passing a couple of bouldery cruxes.
70 ft. 8 bolts. Porter Jarrard, Jeff Moll, 1993.

Racer X 5.12d ★★★★
The rightmost route on the wall. Begin by climbing through a low, steep section near the left side of an overhang 20 feet above the ground. Continue up the face on small edges to a big move toward the top, then shift right to the anchors.
80 ft. 8 bolts. Porter Jarrard, Jeff Moll, 1993.

5.11 WALL

Misfire 5.11c ★★★
The leftmost route on the wall. An easy introduction leads to a ledge where the business begins. Reach hard for the sloping right hand to mount the face, then race to the chains.
60 ft. 6 bolts. Blake Bowling, 2010.

Recoil 5.11d ★★★★
Climb a small dihedral to an overhanging face. Crank big moves on good holds and enjoy a nice run to the anchors.
55 ft. 5 bolts. Porter Jarrard, Jeff Moll, 1993.

Receiver 5.11b ★★★★
Begin just right of *Recoil*. Pace yourself through crimps and pockets to a high crux near the top. Slap left to a rail and try to get a rest, then continue through an interesting finish.
65 ft. 8 bolts. Porter Jarrard, Jeff Moll, 1993.

Centerfire 5.11c ★★★★
This goes up just left of a hole in the wall. Boulder through a starting section to a stance, take a breather, then continue up the sustained, pumpy face to the anchors.
75 ft. 8 bolts. Porter Jarrard, Jeff Moll, 1993.

Bandolier 5.11a ★★★★
The rightmost 5.11 on the 5.11 Wall is a great introduction to pumpy Red River Gorge sandstone at the grade. Climb up the slightly overhanging face past a couple of cruxes to a no-hands rest out left if desired. Pump out on the final overhanging flake to the chains.
70 ft. 7 bolts. Porter Jarrard, Jeff Moll, 1993.

NATURAL BRIDGE

29 Wadcutter 5.9+ ★★★
This more vertical line becomes slightly overhanging and heavily pocketed toward the top. Climb up and left to dodge an overhang. Move back right and head up the pumpy face to the anchors.
50 ft. 5 bolts. Porter Jarrard, Jeff Moll, 1993.

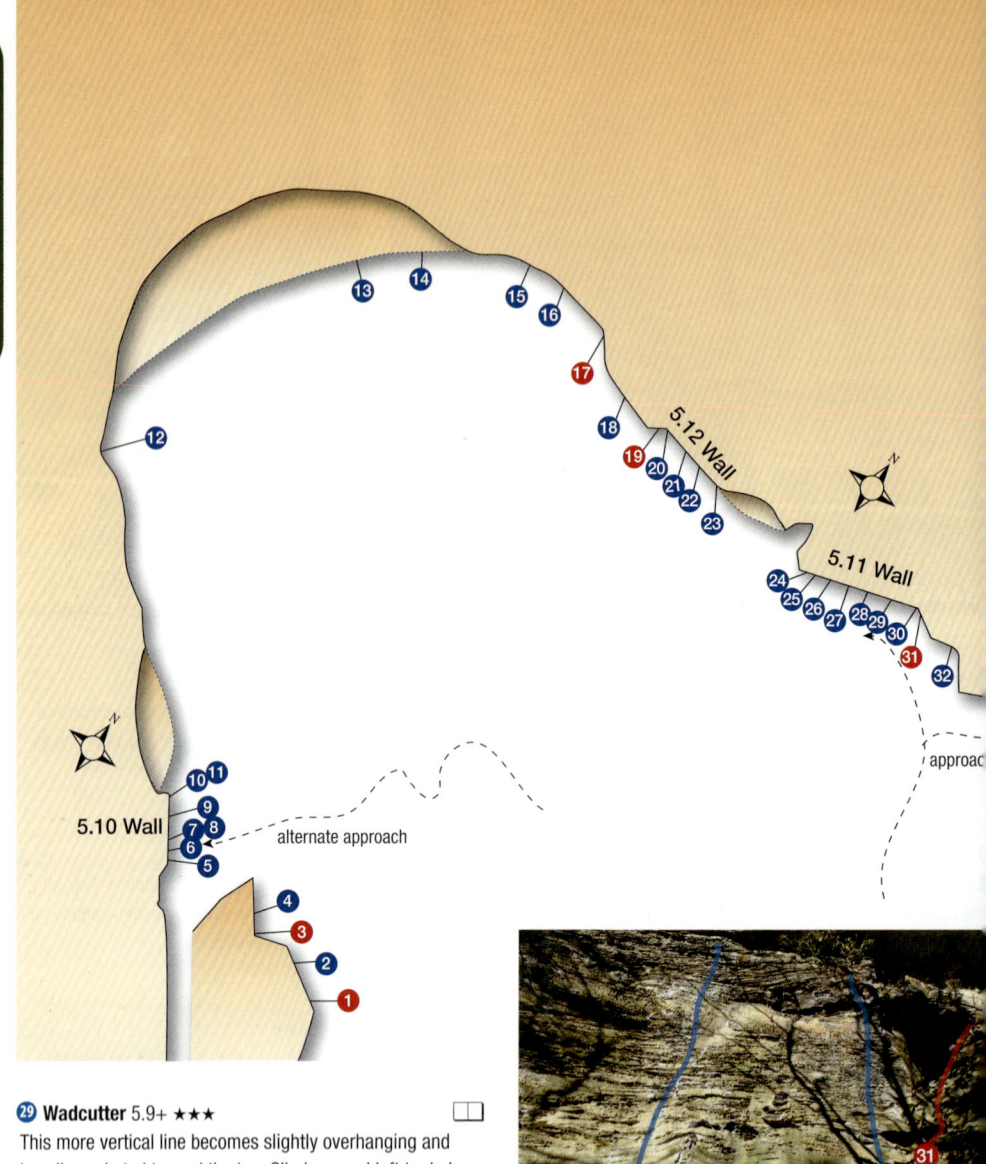

30 Dream of a Bee 5.8 ★★
This ascends the face just left of the *Hmmm* dihedral.
45 ft. 6 bolts. Unknown, 2002.

31 Hmmm 5.2 ★
Fifty feet left of the top of the approach stairs is a short, thin dihedral. Climb it to the ledge, then move right to rappel from the anchors on *Cordelia*.
50 ft. Joe Finney, 1992.

TORRENT FALLS

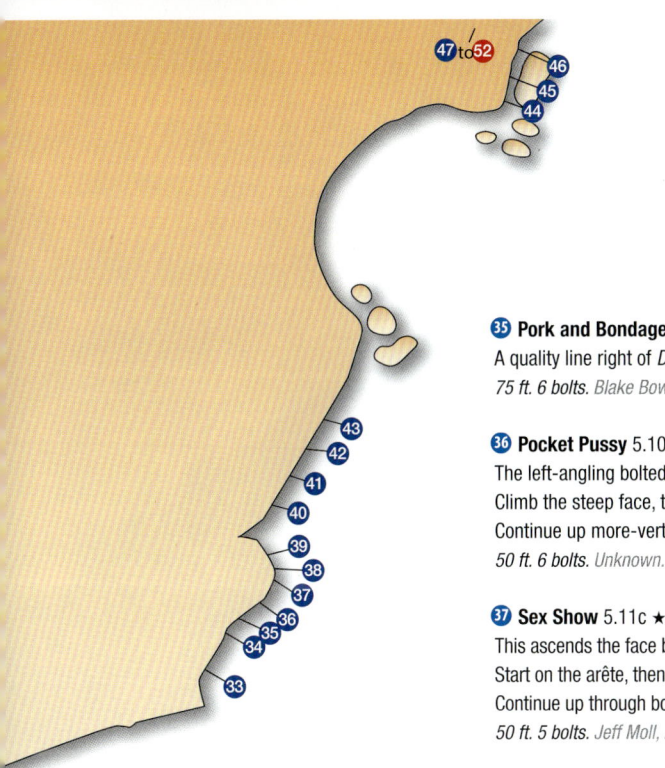

㉟ Pork and Bondage 5.10d ★★★
A quality line right of *Del Boy*.
75 ft. 6 bolts. Blake Bowling, 2011.

㊱ Pocket Pussy 5.10d ★★★
The left-angling bolted line 10 feet right of *Pork and Bondage*. Climb the steep face, then step out left to a small ledge. Continue up more-vertical terrain to the anchors.
50 ft. 6 bolts. Unknown.

㊲ Sex Show 5.11c ★★★
This ascends the face between *Pocket Pussy* and the arête. Start on the arête, then follow the bolts left onto the face. Continue up through bouldery moves to a long reach at the top.
50 ft. 5 bolts. Jeff Moll, Porter Jarrard, 1993.

Cordelia 5.8 ★★
t the top of the stairs used for the approach, walk to the all directly in front of you and locate this route on a slabby ection right of the taller 5.11 Wall. Balance up the well- olted slab to the anchors.
0 ft. 9 bolts.

Us and Them 5.12a ★★★★
om the top of the stairs, hike 300 feet right to a ledge atop flat boulder. This is the leftmost bolted line that starts from e ledge. Climb through solid rock and flowing moves to eet up with a smackdown crux that may thwart anyone not miliar with the fine art of sloping on dah slopah.
0 ft. 7 bolts. Greg Martin, 2002.

Del Boy 5.11b ★★★
his route is just right of *Us and Them* and is marked by small roof about 15 feet up. Climb the steep face to the of, pull the roof, then wander through interesting moves to nother roof. Sidestep the roof and finish on a steep face.
5 ft. 9 bolts. Jeff Moll, Porter Jarrard, 1993.

Sex Show

71

Craig DeMartino on *Poopie Head,* 5.10c (opposite). Photo: Mike Wilkinson.

Seek the Truth 5.11d ★★★★ ☐

This mega-steep line climbs the severely overhanging face just right of *Sex Show*. Begin on the arête, then move right to take on the steepness. Use big moves and heel hooks, passing a well-defined crux just before the anchors.
70 ft. 4 bolts. *Jeff Moll, Porter Jarrard, 1993.*

Sport for Brains 5.11d ★★★ ☐

Step about 10 feet right from *Seek the Truth* to another extremely steep route. Relatively easy climbing on a vertical face gains the high first bolt, then continue through the steepness to a decent rest on a small ledge. Climb a few more feet to clip the anchors.
70 ft. 6 bolts. *Steve Grossman, 1996.*

Ode to Poopie Head 5.11b ★★ ☐

Walk right of *Sport for Brains*, past a wide crack, to the first route on a short wall. Climb through small pockets and potholds to reach better holds. Continue up the pumpy face to a roof, mantel the lip, and clip the anchors.
70 ft. 4 bolts. *Steve Grossman, 1996.*

Poopie Head 5.10c ★★★ ☐

This is the next line just right of *Ode to Poopie Head*.
70 ft. 4 bolts. *Neal Strickland, Chris Snyder, 1995.*

Stool Sample 5.10c ★★★ ☐

This is the next bolted line right of *Poopie Head*.
70 ft. 4 bolts. *Tony Reynaldo, 1996.*

Rectal Exorcism 5.11a ★★ ☐

This route begins on a short slab to an overhang just right of *Stool Sample*.
75 ft. 5 bolts. *Tony Reynaldo, 1996.*

The following routes are closed and included strictly for historical purposes. They reside on a separate private parcel, owned by Torrent Falls Climbing Adventure, and are accessible for guided climbing only. Contact: nicole@torrentfalls.com; 606-668-6613.

G'sUs 5.11c ☐

Walk right of *Rectal Exorcism*, past a waterfall and up a steep, sandy section of trail littered with loose boulders. At the top of the steep hill, near a large boulder, are two bolted lines. This is the leftmost line.
80 ft. 7 bolts. *Greg Martin, Gregg Purnell, 2003.*

Onaconaronni 5.11d ☐

Ten feet right of *G'sUs*, climb through the overhang near the bottom and move up a vertical rib for a few bolts. Continue on larger holds to the top.
85 ft. 8 bolts. *Greg Purnell, 2001.*

Seek the Truth

Poopie Head

TORRENT FALLS

Photo: Elodie Saracco

46 Hoosier Buddies 5.11d
The bolted line 20 feet right of *Onaconaronni*.
65 ft. 7 bolts. Greg Martin, Greg Purnell, Tim Powers, 2001.

47 Hired Guns 5.7
Walk right about 20 feet and head up a short, steep hill to reach the next group of very short "kid routes." These were put in place at the request of the landowner for Boy Scout Troops. Begin with a ladder-step made of rebar.
20 ft. 5 bolts. Tim Powers, Jared Hancock, Mike Susko, 2002.

48 Physically Strong, Mentally Awake, and Morally Straight 5.5
This is the slabby, blunt arête with big, easy ledges 20 feet right of the previous route.
30 ft. 4 bolts. Jared Hancock, Mike Susko, Tim Powers, 2002.

49 Livin' in the UK 5.11c
Walk downhill and around the corner 50 feet right of the previous lines to the next group of routes. This one begins 20 feet right of an arête and climbs to a horizontal ledge 25 feet up. From the ledge, move over a small roof and continue up the pocketed face to the anchors.
65 ft. 5 bolts. Jeff Moll, 1992.

50 Mad Porter's Disease 5.12d
Move 35 feet right from the previous line to a blank-looking section of wall. Climb up to a flat, triangular roof at midheight and crank a series of difficult moves around the lip. Continue past a stopper crux to a much easier finish.
70 ft. 6 bolts. Jeff Moll, 1992.

51 My How Things Have Changed 5.11d
Thirty feet right of *Mad Porter's Disease* is another great line on a vague arête. Climb thin holds to fun moves up high.
60 ft. 6 bolts. Jeff Moll, 1992.

52 Retroflex 5.9
This route ascends a crack 20 feet right of the previous sport lines. An easy start gains a rest, then continue up a dihedral to chain anchors.
75 ft. J. Bronaugh, R. Snider, B. Lewis, G. Robinson, 1984.

BEER TRAILER CRAG

37.7150 / -83.6667
☂ ☀ 🚗 10 min 🚶 5 min

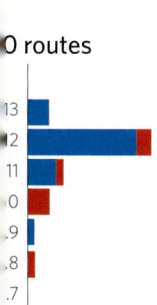

If you like beer, powerful climbing, and short approaches, then this is your crag! The wall's right side gets great sun and also stays dry in a downpour.

Approach: For the first 10 routes (*Magic Medicine* to *Beer Trailer*), walk around to the right of the beer trailer, and head uphill to the left. For the remaining routes, locate a trail near the road, on the right when facing the beer trailer. Hike up the short trail to end up beneath *Darkness Falls*.

Access: The landowners are OK with people climbing on their property, but ask that you do not block business parking. If you see more than a couple of climber cars (look for climbing stickers, out-of-state license plates, or evidence of road-trip grunge), then head to another crag. If it's Sunday, the beer trailer is closed, so you're OK.

Magic Medicine 5.9 ★★
the far left of the crag, around the corner from *Falls City*, cate this overhanging dihedral to an undercling roof.
ft. *Dru Mack, Josh O'Bryan, 2010.*

Two Cups of Silly 5.12c ★★★
the far left, on an arête, find this line of glue-ins. A boulder oblem leads to a ledge, then an obliviously techy face.
ft. 6 bolts. *Steve Andrew, Scott Curran 2013.*

Falls City 5.13b ★★★★
cated just right of the *Two Cups of Silly* arête. Punch rough a series of difficult boulder problems on the first half, en ease up to the chains.
ft. 5 bolts. *Frank Byron, 2009. Equipper: John Cioci.*

Tie One On 5.12d ★★★
st right of *Falls City* is another tough boulder problem, this e more of a height-dependent, one-move-wonder. Shorter lks do have options though.
ft. 5 bolts. *Ben Cassel, 2010. Equipper: Frank Byron.*

Evening Wood 5.12a ★★★
is route was partially completed when the crag's first lines ere established, and finally finished 13 years later. Begin on *orning Wood* and break left at the third bolt.
ft. 5 bolts. *John Cioci, Frank Byron, 2009.*

Morning Wood 5.12a ★★★★
is route may give you just that! Boulder up through quential pocket moves to the overhanging, more-featured ce above. After the third bolt, continue angling right to the xt bolt.
ft. 4 bolts. *Chris Snyder, 1996.*

Falls City

❼ **Sluts Are Cool** 5.12a ★★★
Begin 10 feet left of a green dihedral. Crank through a tough start, then continue up the sustained, steep face to anchors.
40 ft. 4 bolts. *Todd Burlier, 1996.*

❽ **Fake ID** 5.11b ★★★
Balance up the vert/slab on cool holds.
50 ft. 5 bolts. *Johnny Murch, Dru Mack, 2013.*

❾ **Mini Keg** 5.8 ★★★
Start 100 feet right of *Sluts Are Cool*. Climb obvious finger and hand dihedral crack to ring anchors.
40 ft. *Josh O'Bryan, Nick Hellmich, 2010.*

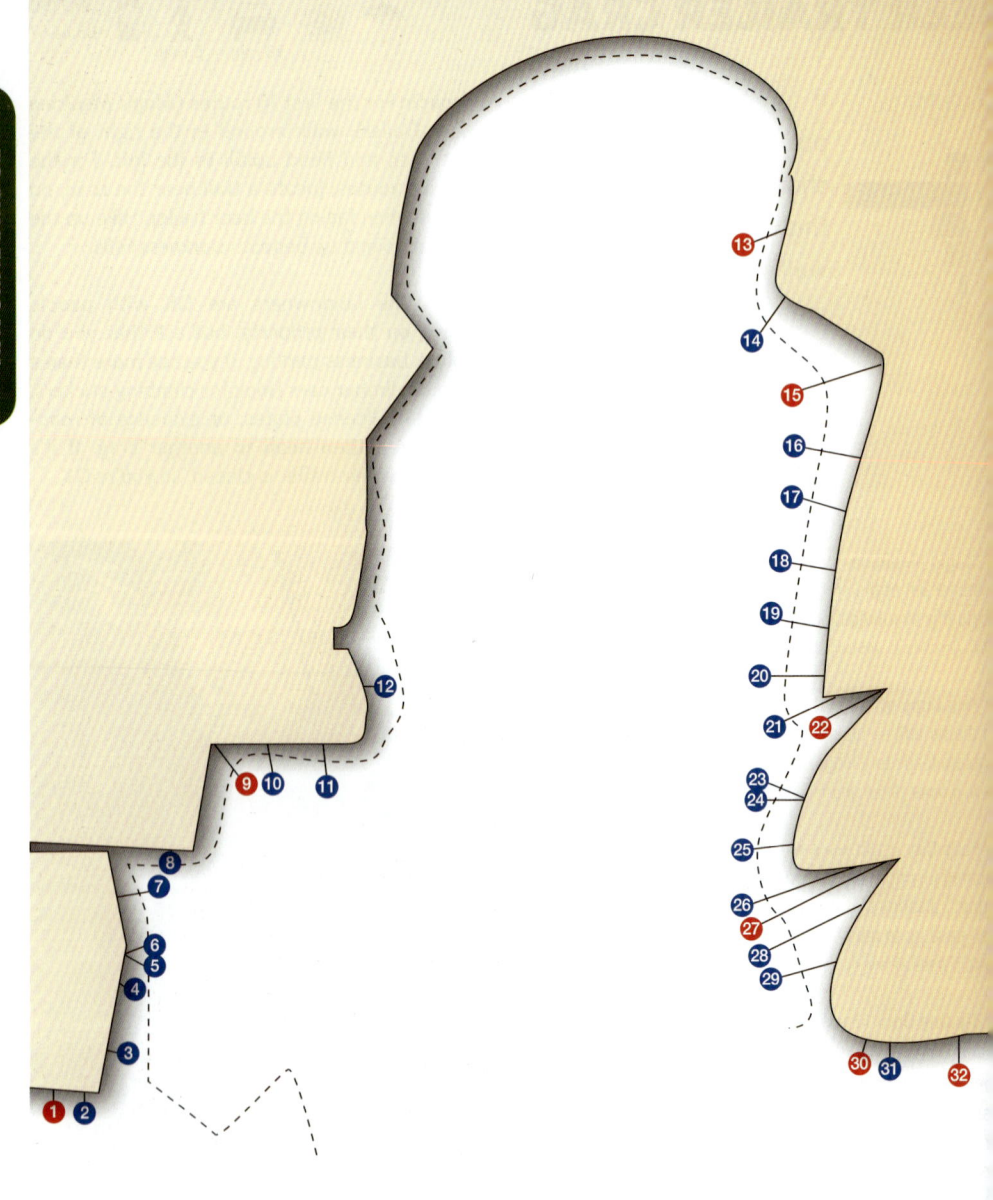

NATURAL BRIDGE

10 Specific Gravity 5.12a ★★★★
This is the next sport route about 25 feet right of *Mini Keg*. A bouldery start to the right of the bolt line leads to a flake midway up. Continue up the technical face to a right-leaning ramp at the top.
45 ft. 4 bolts. Josh O'Bryan, Nick Heilmich, 2010.

11 Bottles Up Open Project ★★★
The next bolted line right of *Specific Gravity*. Currently an open project. Expect extremely long moves if you're tall, and shut-down moves if you're not. Grade estimated to be between 5.12d and 5.13b.
50 ft. 5 bolts. Equipped by Jason Forrester.

12 Beer Trailer 5.12b ★
Move right and around two corners from the previous route to locate this line, which ascends an ivy-choked blank face.
40 ft. 4 bolts. Unknown.

The following routes are on the wall opposite the previous routes. From the parking lot, look for a trail near the road that leads shortly up to the cliff and meets the wall just right of *Darkness Falls*. Continue walking left, past several bolted lines, to reach the main overhanging gold wall.

BEER TRAILER CRAG

Specific Gravity

Bourbon Barrel Shot Gun

Hang Over

Summer Shandy 5.10d ★★★
...mb a flared hand crack to another hand crack system. Finish
...more flared jams and crimps on the face.
... ft. Scott Curran, 2013.

Bourbon Barrel Shot Gun 5.13b ★★
...is route is located on an outcropping of sorts on the left
...de. It follows a left-leaning flake to a blank section of
...rtical rock where a V8 boulder problem awaits.
... ft. 7 bolts. Adam Taylor, 2010. Equipper: Dario Ventura.

Imperial Stout 5.10d ★★★
...the dihedral between the main wall and *Bourbon Barrel*
...otgun is this often-damp, left-leaning crack. An improbable
...art with a couple of good finger-sized cams leads to fun,
...f-balance jamming and liebacking. Save a .5 Camalot for
...e Horsepens topout slopers. Well worth doing if you catch it
...y (late summer or fall).
... ft. Dave Rowlands, Jeff Jenkins, 2013.

Drunken Master 5.13b ★★★★
...ft of *Better Than Homemade*. Follow a seam up the
...autiful wall.
... ft. Shadow Ayala, Rachel Stewart, Daniel Spollen, 2014.

Better Than Homemade 5.12d ★★★
...egin with a tough move right off the mud castle and crimp
... to a decent ledge. From the ledge, choose your path
...rough the crux based on your ape index to reach another
...ecent ledge. Crawl up on more sloping pockets to the next
...olt, then pinch increasingly better holds to the chains.
... ft. 7 bolts. Adam Taylor, 2009. Equipper: Dario Ventura.

NATURAL BRIDGE

Wet Your Whistle — 23, 24

PBR — 26

The Fray Train — 28

⑱ Hang Over 5.12c ★★★★
Right of *Better Than Homemade*. Start with a jug, then bust through a tough start and gun for the ledge. Scum out of the ledge on small crimps and slap hard at chalk spots to reach the next bolt. A few more moves get you a reward ledge and easier climbing to the chains.
55 ft. 7 bolts. Dario Ventura, 2009.

⑲ High Life 5.12b ★★★
Next route right of *Hang Over*, sharing a start with the next route. Begin on a ledge and pull long moves on good edges to a lie-down rest in a horizontal. When rested, crawl out of your coffin and take on a crimpy groove to another comfy shake before the final haul to the chains.
55 ft. 5 bolts. John Roark, 2009.

⑳ Liquid Courage 5.12b ★★★
Begin with the first bolt of *High Life*, but continue straight up on decent edges to reach the main coffin horizontal. If you're desperate, crawl in. Continue up through groove, crimping to reach a final jug, from which you can contemplate how you'll reach the distant chalk spot near the chains.
50 ft. 4 bolts. Shadow Ayala, 2009.

㉑ Korsakoff Syndrome 5.11c ★★★
Begin right of *Liquid Courage* on jugs and climb to a blunt arête which ends with a tricky slab to an anchor. The extension to upper anchor is an open project with an estimated V5/6 move.
60 ft. Dustin Stephens, 2012.

㉒ Delirium Tremens 5.10b ★★★
Start in the chimney between *Wet Your Whistle* and *Korsakoff Syndrome*. Liebacking, underclinging, and jamming gets you to the top. Lower from the upper anchors of *Korsakoff*, top out and rap, or walk off left for full trad value.
75 ft. Scott Curran, Dustin Stephens, 2012.

㉓ Wet Your Whistle 5.12a ★★★★
Share the start with *Afternoon Buzz*, then move up and left past a seasonal wet spot.
70 ft. 6 bolts. Lena Bakanova, Dustin Stephens, 2012.

㉔ Afternoon Buzz 5.12a ★★★★
Start as for the previous route, but take the right-hand bolt line. Easy climbing to a ledge, followed by a boulder problem and long reaches between good holds.
60 ft. 5 bolts. Lena Bakanova, Dustin Stephens, 2012.

㉕ Beer-Thirty 5.11d ★★★
Just right of *Afternoon Buzz* is this steep line with cool, sustained movement. Generally considered the warmup of the wall. The top holds the final thin crux moves.
65 ft. 7 bolts. Dustin Stephens, 2013.

㉖ PBR Street Gang 5.11c ★★★
An excellent face climb around right of *Beer-Thirty*. Great movement with crimps and flakes make way for a smackdown move to a sloper from itsy-bitsy crimpsies.
60 ft. 6 bolts. Shadow Ayala, 2012.

Xach Millbern on *Sluts Are Cool*, 5.12a (page 75). Photo: John Wesely.

Trailer Trashed 5.11- ★★★
...e wide, overhanging dihedral just right of *PBR Street Gang*. ...escend from the anchors of *PBR*.
...0 ft. *Jon Kulikowski, 2013.*

The Fray Train 5.12a ★★★
...ust right of *PBR Street Gang*, on the opposing wall, is this ...e, which begins with tough opening moves. Chug up ...rough the midsection to reach the final few bolts, which ...ake the ride worth it. CHOO! CHOO!
...0 ft. 6 bolts. *Troy Davison, Rob Frayer, Chris Frayer, 2010.*

Darkness Falls 5.12d ★★★★
...ext route right of *Fray Train*. Boulder up to a series of roof ...orizontals, which lead to a difficult lip move to gain the face.
...0 ft. 9 bolts. *Dave Linz, 2012.*

Four Out the Door 5.12a ★★★
...ust right of the large beech tree is this mixed line, a fun, ...chnical face with horizontals.
...0 ft. 2 bolts. *Scott Curran, 2014.*

Quaffed Up Open Project
...e slab line following a series of eyebrow-like features to ...e right and around the corner from *Darkness Falls*. Probably ... the 5.12 range.
... bolts.

Four Out the Door

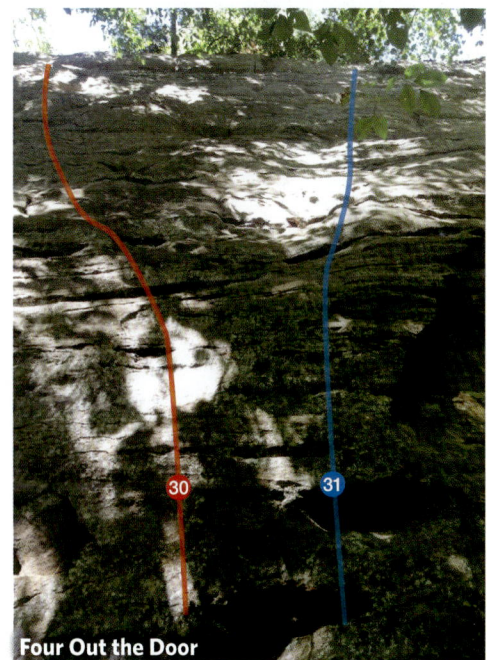

㉜ 12-Ounce Curl 5.12a ★★★
Climb a hand and finger crack to a good rest. Get it all back, then tackle a boulder problem that guards the chains.
60 ft. 2 bolts. *Scott Curran, 2015.*

79

MUIR VALLEY

MUIR VALLEY

The 360-acre Muir Valley Nature Preserve is a private preserve walled in by seven miles of fine Corbin sandstone. Waterfalls and caves abound, as do arches and stone-bottomed creeks. Mountain laurel, rhododendron, and many other plants grace the slopes and bottomlands. Muir was purchased in 2004 by Rick and Liz Weber, who developed, managed, and financed it until March 2015, when they gifted it to the 501(c)3 corp **Friends of Muir Valley**. MVNP may be freely enjoyed by hikers, and climbers alike. Note, however, that **dogs are not allowed!**

Muir is known for its large concentratio of easy climbing — you'll find mor 5.8s here than anywhere else in th gorge — and amenable infrastructur Well-maintained trails, bridges, stair national-park-like signs, route badge toilets, practice walls, and helpful sta make this a popular destination fo those new to the sport. More seasone rock-climbers will enjoy the steep, har routes found at crags like Midnight Su and the Sanctuary, both home to som of the area's most classic 5.12s.

Elena Bakanova on *Jesus Wept*, 5.12d (page 121). Photo: Dan Brayack.

MUIR OVERVIEW

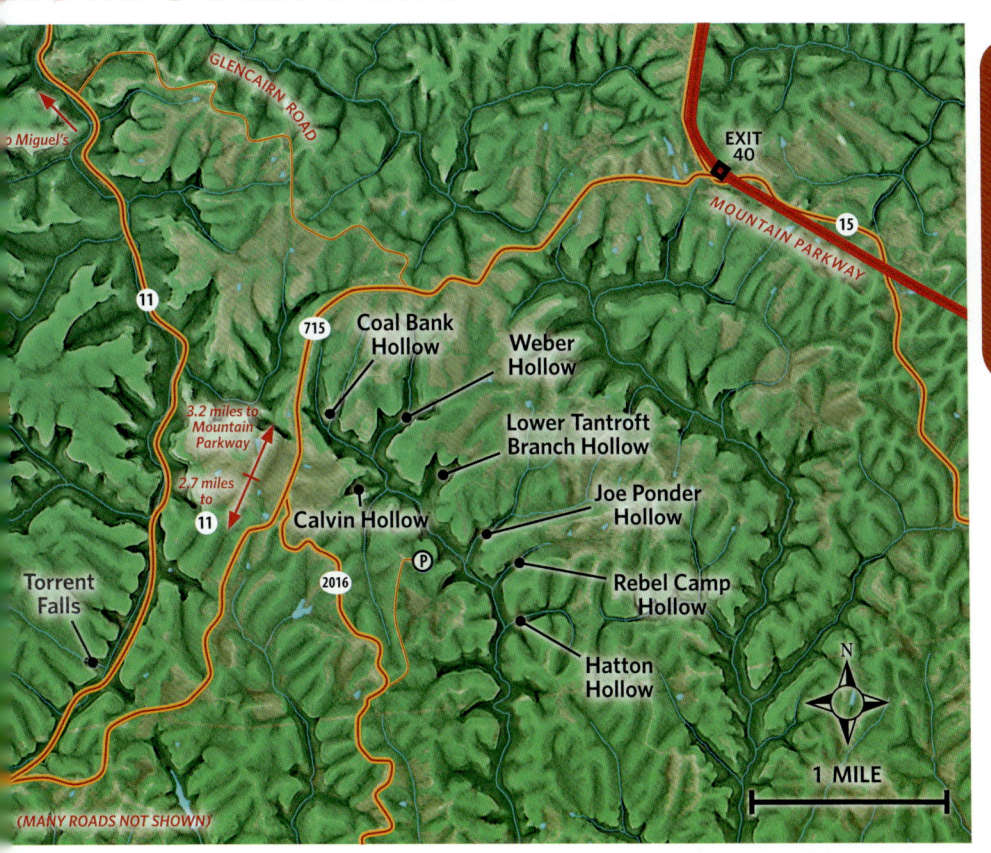

Approach: From Miguel's Pizza, drive south on KY for 6.3 miles and turn left onto KY 715. Follow KY 715 for 2.7 miles and turn right onto road 2016. Drive 1.4 miles until you see an old carpet store on your right. Just after the carpet store, when the road curves downhill, take the first gravel road on the left. After about 100 feet, turn left. Follow the gravel road 0.7 miles, bearing left at each fork, until you see a road on the right (just before an overflow parking lot) that heads down to a large parking area with a maintenance building and shelter.

Crags are described generally northwest (upstream) to southeast. Two main trails lead to the climbing, both beginning between the maintenance building and shelter: The North Main Trail forks left and leads to Coalbank Hollow, Weber Hollow, Main Valley North and Central, and Lower Tantroft Hollow. The South Main Trail, heading due east, leads to Joe Ponder Hollow, Rebel Camp Hollow, and Hatton Hollow. See map on page 82 for specific crag locations.

Access: Please respect the privacy of MVNP's neighbors by driving slowly on the graveled access road. If the parking lot is full, DO NOT park on adjoining property or grassed and landscaped areas around the parking lot. Please carpool whenever possible — especially on weekends and holidays. On busy days, the parking lot often reaches capacity.

Parking Fee: Muir Valley is now one of the most popular climbing destinations in North America with over 40,000 visitors each year, and the previous donation-based revenue stream is no longer sufficient to maintain the area.

Admission to the Valley is still free, but as of March, 2016, there is a **parking fee of $10 per car**. Pay at the kiosk near the entrance to the parking lot. Staff will occasionally be available to accept credit/debit cards, but don't count on it. When staff isn't present, an honor-system drop box for **cash** will be the only payment method available. Alternatively, purchase an annual parking pass for $120 on the Muir Valley website. To purchase a pass, find the online waiver, or learn more about Muir Valley, visit www.muirvalley.com.

81

MUIR DETAIL

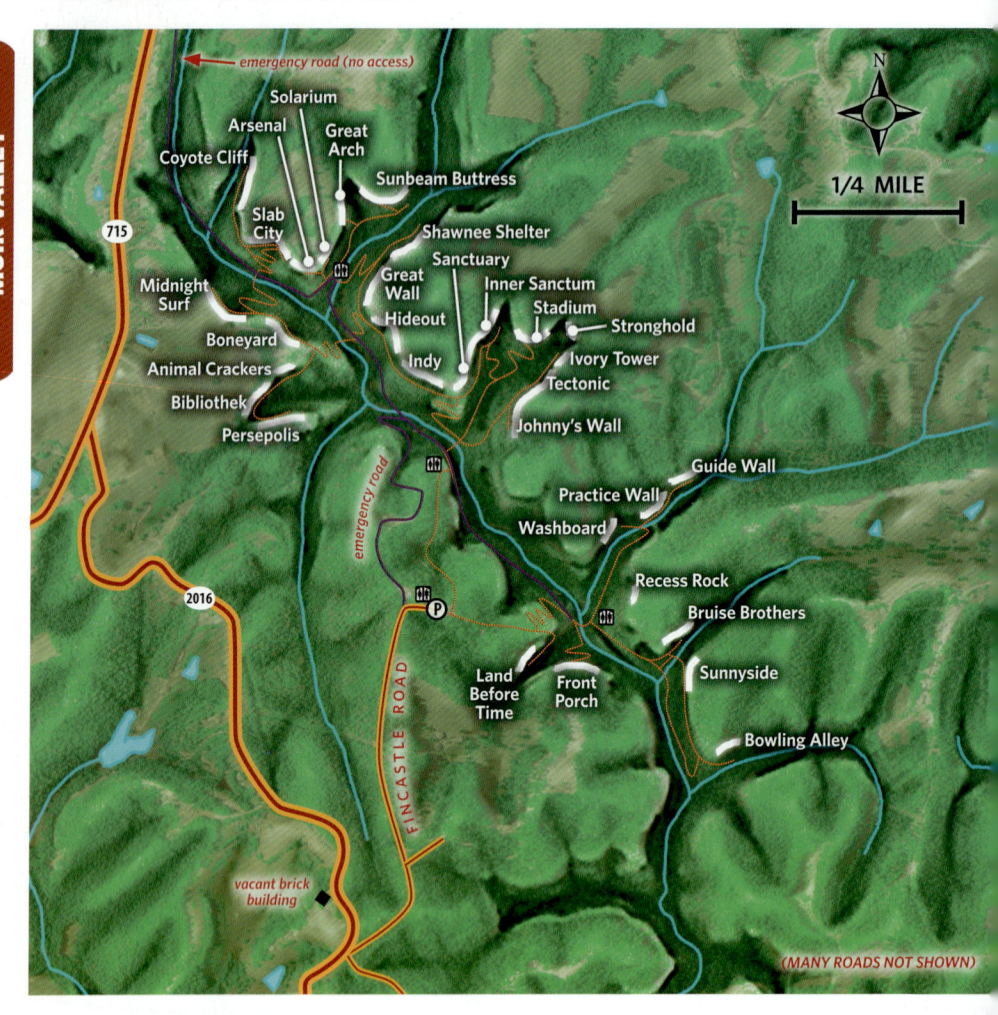

Enjoying Muir: Some of the most popular crags in Muir Valley are Bruise Brothers, Solarium, and Johnny/Tectonic walls, all of which host a variety of fun routes, heavy in the 5.9-10 range. If you are just learning or looking for even easier routes, try the short climbs at Animal Crackers Wall, Practice Wall, Guide Wall, and Recess Rock.

If you're looking for a crag that packs a little more punch, Sanctuary and Midnight Surf feature some of the best steep climbing around. There you'll find classic, overhanging 5.12s like *Cell Block Six* and *Tapeworm*.

All of these popular crags can get very crowded, but with 30-plus crags to choose from you can usually find a way to beat the crowds. The Stronghold, Front Porch, Ivory Tower, and Bowling Alley are a few crags that rarely see a huge gathering of people.

The climbing season in MVNP is the same as for the rest of the gorge, but for the best Muir Valley fantasyland experience, be sure to visit in the spring when the wildflowers come into bloom — they are truly a wonder.

Rules of Muir Valley Nature Preserve: Visitors may climb, hike, and enjoy the natural beauty as guests, but at their own risk. Rock climbers are required to fill out a legal release form prior to climbing. This can be done online at www.muirvalley.com. The website also includes a set of rules and guidelines that all visitors must agree to follow, as does the MVNP kiosk in the main parking lot. Dogs are not allowed in Muir Valley. Visitors who are not willing to accept full responsibility for their presence in Muir Valley should not enter the property.

Rick and Liz Weber
(in John Muir's footsteps)

For two of the Red's most well-known climbers, Rick and Liz Weber sure did start late in life. In their fifties, still enjoying careers in engineering, and with their best years ahead of them, the adventurous duo decided to try out rock climbing. A trip to Hoosier Heights climbing gym in Bloomington, Indiana, changed the course of their lives forever — they were hooked.

Their first trip to the Red River Gorge was in 2000 where they were introduced to the area by local climbing guide Blake Bowling. Rick and Liz fell in love with the area and the climbing, and returned frequently over the next three years. In 2003, a friend showed them a little forested valley with nearly impenetrable undergrowth and lined with beautiful **unclimbed rock walls**. The Webers recall their first impression as, "virgin wilderness with no structures and none of the thousands of feet of cliff line that ringed the valley having any developed climbing routes. It was resplendent with cliffs, waterfalls, caves, rock shelters, and spectacular flora and fauna. In addition to the rock climbing possibilities, **this place was a nature-lover's paradise ...**"

Smitten, and determined to preserve this unique place for climbing and public enjoyment, that very day the Webers negotiated a deal with the land owner and purchased the property, which they later augmented by subsequent purchases of adjacent land, to form what is now Muir Valley. It took vision to see the potential for a wilderness preserve beneath the hundreds of tons of trash initially on the property, but after a generous grant and extensive volunteer effort, the valley was returned to its pristine state.

Over the next decade, the Webers and fellow developers would establish over 300 climbing routes in the valley, and the trails, parking lot, and facilities to go with them. The quality of the rock, abundance of moderates, and overall feel of a recreational sanctuary have now turned Muir Valley into what is arguably America's most popular crag.

Through the years, the Webers developed the methodology and infrastructure for managing and supporting the ever-growing numbers of visitors — which reached 40,000 in 2014. In March of 2015, the Webers made a gift to the public by deeding Muir Valley to the Friends of Muir Valley, a 501(c)3 non-profit corporation dedicated to managing the property and preserving the recreational area in perpetuity.

Muir Valley is now preserved for the public as the Webers envisioned it just over a decade ago and an apt reflection of **the valley's namesake, John Muir** — a man they admire as "a great American" and the "Father of the National Parks," a conservationist widely regarded as the greatest American climber of his time.

Muir's preservationist efforts helped lead to the establishment of Yosemite National Park and, on a much smaller scale, the Webers see parallels with the beautiful little valley they took under their wing. "We believe, as John Muir did, that responsible rock climbing in places of natural beauty is altogether fitting and proper," they say now. The Webers hold hopes that their little Kentucky valley, with its waterfalls, caves, and breathtaking cliffs will grow into a place that old Muir would have enjoyed climbing in and sauntering through. ∎

Photo: Friends of Muir Valley.

MUIR VALLEY

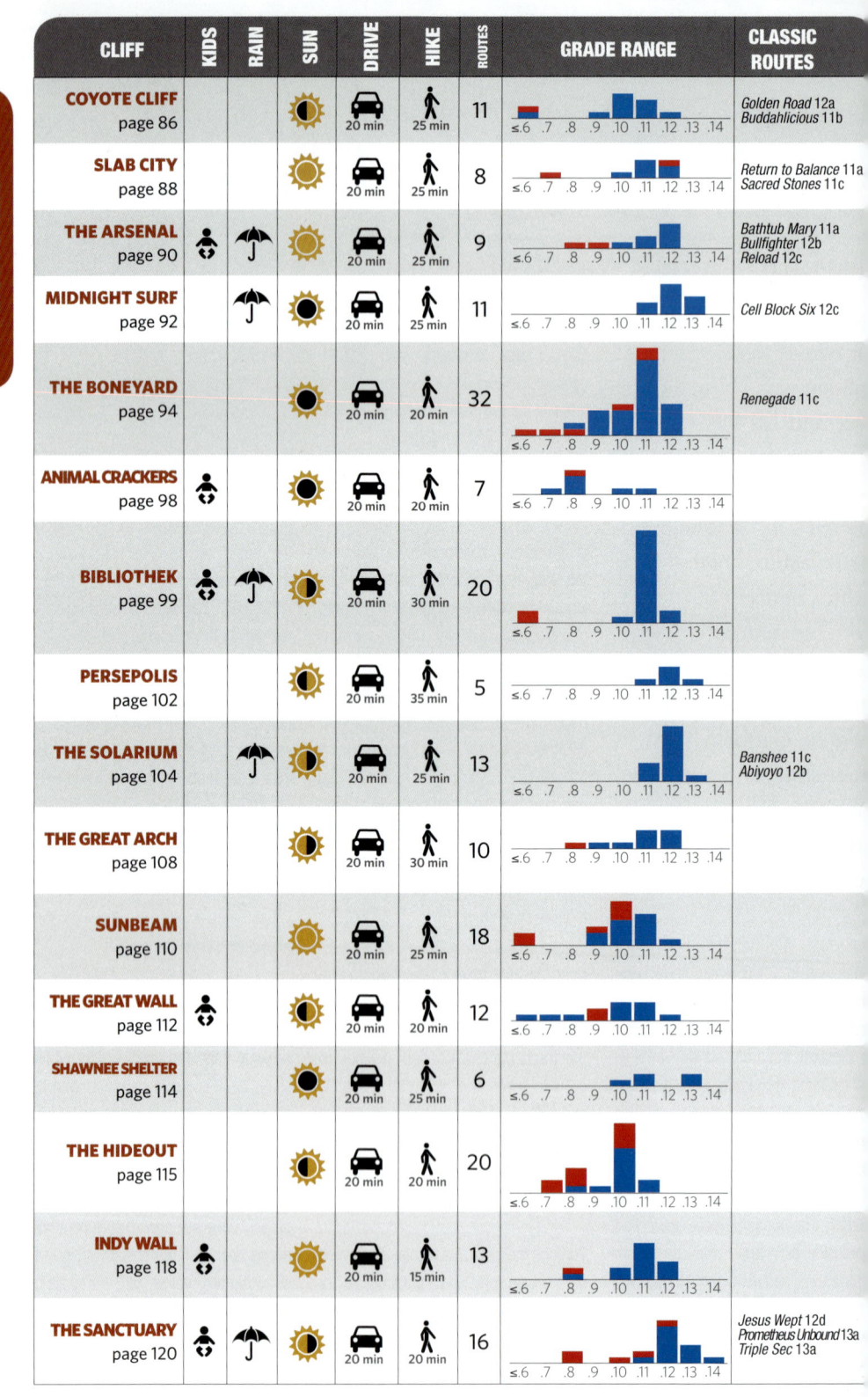

CLIFF	KIDS	RAIN	SUN	DRIVE	HIKE	ROUTES	GRADE RANGE	CLASSIC ROUTES
COYOTE CLIFF page 86			◐	20 min	25 min	11	≤.6 .7 .8 .9 .10 .11 .12 .13 .14	*Golden Road* 12a *Buddahlicious* 11b
SLAB CITY page 88			☀	20 min	25 min	8	≤.6 .7 .8 .9 .10 .11 .12 .13 .14	*Return to Balance* 11a *Sacred Stones* 11c
THE ARSENAL page 90	👶	☂	☀	20 min	25 min	9	≤.6 .7 .8 .9 .10 .11 .12 .13 .14	*Bathtub Mary* 11a *Bullfighter* 12b *Reload* 12c
MIDNIGHT SURF page 92		☂	◐	20 min	25 min	11	≤.6 .7 .8 .9 .10 .11 .12 .13 .14	*Cell Block Six* 12c
THE BONEYARD page 94			◐	20 min	20 min	32	≤.6 .7 .8 .9 .10 .11 .12 .13 .14	*Renegade* 11c
ANIMAL CRACKERS page 98	👶		☀	20 min	20 min	7	≤.6 .7 .8 .9 .10 .11 .12 .13 .14	
BIBLIOTHEK page 99	👶	☂	◐	20 min	30 min	20	≤.6 .7 .8 .9 .10 .11 .12 .13 .14	
PERSEPOLIS page 102			◐	20 min	35 min	5	≤.6 .7 .8 .9 .10 .11 .12 .13 .14	
THE SOLARIUM page 104		☂	◐	20 min	25 min	13	≤.6 .7 .8 .9 .10 .11 .12 .13 .14	*Banshee* 11c *Abiyoyo* 12b
THE GREAT ARCH page 108			☀	20 min	30 min	10	≤.6 .7 .8 .9 .10 .11 .12 .13 .14	
SUNBEAM page 110			☀	20 min	25 min	18	≤.6 .7 .8 .9 .10 .11 .12 .13 .14	
THE GREAT WALL page 112	👶		◐	20 min	20 min	12	≤.6 .7 .8 .9 .10 .11 .12 .13 .14	
SHAWNEE SHELTER page 114			☀	20 min	25 min	6	≤.6 .7 .8 .9 .10 .11 .12 .13 .14	
THE HIDEOUT page 115			☀	20 min	20 min	20	≤.6 .7 .8 .9 .10 .11 .12 .13 .14	
INDY WALL page 118	👶		☀	20 min	15 min	13	≤.6 .7 .8 .9 .10 .11 .12 .13 .14	
THE SANCTUARY page 120	👶	☂	◐	20 min	20 min	16	≤.6 .7 .8 .9 .10 .11 .12 .13 .14	*Jesus Wept* 12d *Prometheus Unbound* 13a *Triple Sec* 13a

CLIFF	KIDS	RAIN	SUN	DRIVE	HIKE	ROUTES	GRADE RANGE	CLASSIC ROUTES
INNER SANCTUM page 124			◐	20 min	15 min	13		
THE STADIUM page 126			☀	20 min	20 min	25		
STRONGHOLD page 130		☂	◐	20 min	30 min	2		
IVORY TOWER page 131			◐	20 min	20 min	4		
TECTONIC/JOHNNY'S page 133			◐	20 min	20 min	25		
LAND BEFORE TIME page 138	👶		◐	20 min	15 min	7		
FRONT PORCH page 139			●	20 min	20 min	9		
WASHBOARD WALL page 140	👶		◐	20 min	20 min	9		
PRACTICE WALL page 142	👶		☀	20 min	20 min	24		
GUIDE WALL page 145	👶		☀	20 min	20 min	6		
RECESS ROCK page 146	👶		◐	20 min	30 min	4		
BRUISE BROTHERS page 147	👶		☀	20 min	20 min	28		
SUNNYSIDE page 150			◐	20 min	20 min	15		
BOWLING ALLEY page 152			☀	20 min	30 min	4		

MUIR VALLEY

85

COYOTE CLIFF

MUIR VALLEY

37.73
-83.64
20 min | 25 min

11 routes

This tall, impressive cliff is just around the corner from Slab City. It has a few existing gems and room for a few more. The two popular lines, *Golden Road* and *Buddhalicious*, stand side by side, yet climb completely differently. They, along with *Thunderclinger*, are definitely worth the trip.

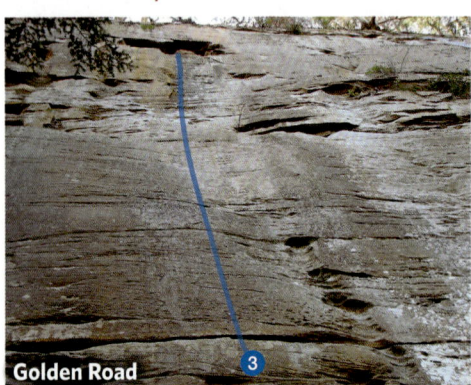

Approach: Walk left from Slab City (page 8) but as you approach the cliffline take the trail the left. In a few minutes you'll reach a large led from which it's possible to descend a 3rd-Cla gully on your left, or continue another 50 feet a short slot and make a 4th-Class move ont wide, 15-foot-high ledge. You will soon reach aesthetic cliff line and mossy rock garden. T first bolted route left of the mossy rock garden *Golden Road*. Routes described right to left.

Conditions: Coyote Cliff faces west to northwe so expect afternoon sun and some shade. T area's many pines also shade the wall fairly we

Golden Road ③

Buddhalicious ④

❶ Primortal Nonsence 5.4
Toprope. This and the next route are difficult to access, but offer great exposure above the valley. They are located approximately 100 feet above the sidewalk-sized traverse ledge mentioned in the approach directions to Coyote Cliff. To reach these routes, backtrack past the 3rd-Class gully area and find a faint trail leading up to another exposed ledge above. Make a sketchy traverse high above the lower traverse ledge to reach a giant balcony above that contains more rock. This route is a few feet left of an obvious left-leaning flake, used to access the bolted anchors.
40 ft. Jared Hancock, Pete Hogaboam, 2005.

❷ Hiking Boot Highway 5.5 ★
This is the obvious left-leaning flake mentioned in the previous route description.
40 ft. Pete Hogaboam, Jared Hancock, 2005.

❸ Golden Road 5.12a ★★★★
This is the first bolted line on the main wall after the mossy-rock area. A tough start leads to fun moves before a blank section up higher. Stand in the giant hueco for a great view and some solid chain anchors.
90 ft. 9 bolts. Jared Hancock, Tim Powers, 2005.

❹ Buddhalicious 5.11b ★★★
This line follows the left edge of an obvious groove about 20 feet left of *Golden Road*. Finesse the first groove to a desperate crux just before a large ledge. From the ledge, s and squeeze the striking golden Buddha bellies all the way to the chains. Be careful of the potential to hit the ledge if a wrongly timed fall occurs.
60 ft. 7 bolts. Karla Hancock, Jared Hancock, 2006.

❺ MumMum 5.11a ★★
Begins on a flake 30 feet left of *Golden Road*. Climb up to a small roof and smack over it to reach a ledge. Continue up decent sidepulls and edges to end with a nice, sloping fina.
70 ft. 9 bolts
Brad Combs, 2009. Equipped by Skip Wolfe, Jared Hancock.

❻ Manteleer 5.9 ★★★
Move left a few feet to reach this flared, obtuse dihedral. A reachy start on good jugs takes you to a ledge. Step left an cruise the crack above. First line put up at Coyote Cliff. The bottom tends to stay wet.
70 ft. 7 bolts. Mark Ryan, Skip Wolfe, Jared Hancock, 2005.

Thunderclinger 5.10c ★★★★
This tricky line begins on a vertical face left of a large hemlock. If you're at a loss, remember this: fingers pointing down and palms against the rock. Sit back and watch your buddy try to onsight this one.
30 ft. 6 bolts. Tom and Ines Truesdale, Jared Hancock, Karla Carandang, 2005.

Bombardier 5.10b ★★
Bombs away! Don't kill your belayer. This is the next line left of *Thunderclinger*. Climb at your own risk and beware of the lob. This route has reportedly cleaned up quite a bit and the bombs have gotten much smaller.
30 ft. 5 bolts. Jared Hancock, Pete Hogaboam, 2005.

Trundling Trolls 5.11a
Continuing left along the cliff you will soon reach a small amphitheater with a short, overhanging sport line. Blast through the steep lower section to reach a dramatic change in angle and grade.
30 ft. 4 bolts. Karla Carandang, Ines Truesdale, Jared Hancock, Tom Truesdale, 2005.

Retirement Day 5.10b ★★
This slightly overhanging line is 15 feet left of *Trundling Trolls*.
25 ft. 4 bolts. Jeff Colombo, Skip Wolfe, 2011.

The Golden Box 5.10d ★
Another short, overhanging route, beginning 10 feet left of *Retirement Day*.
25 ft. 4 bolts. Jeff Colombo, Skip Wolfe, 2011.

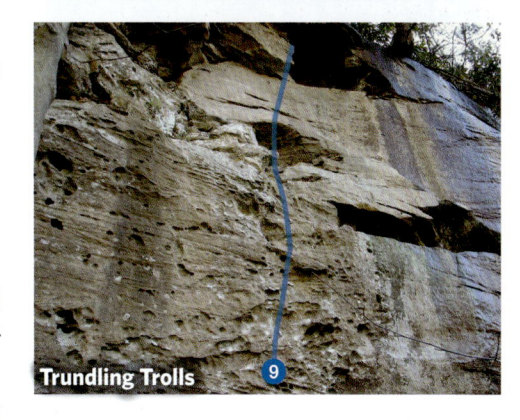

SLAB CITY

20 min   25 min   37.73 / -83.640

8 routes

.14
.13
.12
.11
.10
.9
.8
.7
≤.6

MUIR VALLEY

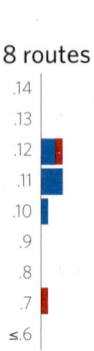

The name says it all: If you don't like climbing on your toes and cranking on minimal edges, then avoid Slab City. However, if you do, this vert-style RRG "slab" offers some of Muir Valley's best lines. For the traddies, *Flash Point* is a superb thin crack. More slightly overhanging than slabby, *Iron Lung*, with its smackdown boulder problem and solid edges, will make your visit worthwhile. And for anyone who enjoyed *Boltergeist* at the Hideout, *Thrillbillies* is the definite sequel.

Approach: Take the Main Trail North valley floor, where the stairs/trail meets the maintenance road. Walk left on the lower, main valley road for about 1/2 mile, passing a pit toilet at the hairpin turn. Continue on the road, up the hill and down the other side. As you bottom the hill, look for the signs on the right to Slab City and Coyote walls.

Conditions: Faces primarily south, so expect to bake in the sun, especially on *Strip the Willows* and *Thrillbillies*.

❶ Return to Balance 5.11a ★★★★
From the top of the trail, head left past several bolted lines to a vertical section of wall with several large flakes. This line is located on the left side of the wall near an arête. Begin by climbing up to a flake, then continue to a wide water-groove like feature. Reach left around the arête for a sloper and a hidden pocket or crimp, then edge straight up the groove to bigger and better holds.
50 ft. 5 bolts. Jared Hancock, Skip Wolfe, Mark Ryan, 2005.

❷ Child of the Earth 5.12a ★★★★
Move right a few feet from the previous line to the middle of the three sport routes on this section of the wall. Reach through a thin and techy crux to gain the reward of jugs in the pocketed orange rock above.
60 ft. 6 bolts. Jared Hancock, Karla Carandang, 2005.

❸ Sacred Stones 5.11c ★★★★
This is the third bolted line from the left on this section of wall. Begin just left of the dihedral *Go West*. Balance, precise footwork, and flexibility are required to reach the first bolt, then enjoy easier but long moves to the anchors.
65 ft. 7 bolts. Jared Hancock, Rob Copeland, James Case, 2005.

❹ Go West 5.7 ★★★
The right-facing dihedral to the right of the previous bolted lines. Fun the whole way.
70 ft. Joel Bruhn, Jared Hancock, Rob Copeland, 2004.

❺ Strip the Willows 5.11b ★★★
This is the first bolted route right of the dihedral *Go West*, on the wall's slabby section. It's called Slab City for a reason.
80 ft. 8 bolts. Karen Clark, Kipp Trummel, 2006.

Return to Balance

Strip the Willows

Photo: Elodie Saracco.

Thrillbillies 5.10b ★★★★
egin just right of *Strip the Willows* on a small pedestal,
en trend up and left to thin water grooves, sidepulls,
eep horizontals, and plates. Find your way up the featured
ab and finish on a large ledge. Take your shoes off at the
nchors to relieve your toes. Check out the view, too!
0 ft. *9 bolts*. Karla Carandang, Jared Hancock, 2005.

Flash Point 5.12a ★★★★
his is the obvious thin and slightly overhanging crack at the
p of the trail. Excellent, powerful, and technical climbing.
5 ft. Josh Thurston, 2006.

Iron Lung 5.12c ★★★★
ead right from *Flash Point* to locate this impressive face
imb. Begin just right of a large black hueco. Ride the right
dge of the hueco, then contemplate the blank face from the
st point of comfort. When ready, tiptoe out onto the face,
ack a loogie, and crank hard on edges to the anchors. A
ore direct line has been bolted that merges with *Iron Lung*
t the top. It is currently an open project.
0 ft. *6 bolts*. Ray Ellington, Kipp Trummel, 2006.

Flash Point 7

Iron Lung 8

THE ARSENAL

37.73
-83.63
20 min 25 min

MUIR VALLEY

9 routes
.14
.13
.12
.11
.10
.9
.8
.7
≤.6

This wall has a small collection of high-quality lines. *Bathtub Mary* is classic for its grade and will challenge the 5.11 leader with tricky moves and a fierce pump. Side by side, *Bullfighter* and *Reload* deliver great, tough moves on quality stone.

Approach: Take the Main Trail North to valley floor, where the stairs/trail meets the maintenance road. Walk left on the lower, main valley road for about 1/2 mile, past the pit toilet and up the hill to the top. Take the trail on the right, and follow the signs toward several crags. The Arsenal trail exits rather early, and follow the cliffline left around the corner for about 15 yards to the crag. The wall can also be accessed from the Solarium by hiking left and around the corner for about 300 feet from near *Air Ride Equipped*. Routes listed left to right.

Conditions: The Arsenal soaks up sun, so is great during winter. The routes are usually dry during heavy rain, except for the top of *Reload*.

❸ **Bathtub Mary** 5.11a ★★★★
Move 15 feet right from *Sacriledge* to the next bolted line. Climb pockets to a slabby section with interesting moves, then attack the pumpy headwall.
70 ft. 9 bolts. *Kipp Trummel, Karen Clark, 2005.*

❹ **Picador** 5.11c ★★★
After a thin beginning, mantel into a hueco. Crawl out of you hole to less stressful climbing to the chains. Use the cleaning draw on the last bolt to avoid swinging into the tree.
55 ft. 8 bolts. *Dustin Stephens, 2010.*

❺ **Flesh Wound** 5.12b ★★★
Begin on *Picador*, but veer right after the fourth bolt up into and over the roof.
55 ft. 8 bolts. *Dustin Stephens, Jimmy Farrell, 2011.*

❻ **Bullfighter** 5.12b ★★★★
Right of *Flesh Wound* is a ferocious opponent. Begin with a launch to a good hold, then remain graceful and confident while acting masterful over the cruxes. Duck into a large hueco for a breather, then emerge as a brave matador to battle again. Clip the chains for victory. ¡Ole!
65 ft. 6 bolts. *Kipp Trummel, Rob Hunter, Jared Hancock, 2005.*

❶ **Quicksilver** 5.8 ★★★
The obvious dihedral just left and around the corner from *Sacriledge*. Lower from chain anchors.
70 ft. *Josh Thurston, Brian Boyd, DRC, 2006.*

❼ **Reload** 5.12c ★★★★★
Just right of *Bullfighter*. Climb increasingly harder moves to a roof. Reload the forearms, fight through it, and continue on less overhanging rock to the anchors.
70 ft. 7 bolts. *Brad Weaver, Eric Heuermann, 2006.*

❷ **Sacriledge** 5.10d ★★★
At the top of the approach trail are several bolted lines on a heavily pocketed wall with large huecos mid-height. This is the leftmost line. Climb pockets to a sometimes-damp ledge to reach better rock on the slightly overhanging face above.
60 ft. 8 bolts. *Jared Hancock, Rob Copeland, James Case, 2005.*

Étienne Seppecher, *Bullfighter*, 5.12b (opposite). Photo: Elodie Saracco.

8 Freakin' Deacon 5.12a ★★★

Just right of *Reload*. Climb through large slots that grow increasingly farther apart and smaller. Tougher than it looks from the ground.
55 ft. *6 bolts*. Andrew Wheatley, 2009.

9 Chicken Little Loves Abubu 5.9 ★★

The obvious left-leaning dihedral right of the previous bolted lines. Climb a few easy ledges, follow the crack, then launch around the arête and onto an exposed alcove below the anchors.
50 ft. Loren Wood, J.J., 2005.

MIDNIGHT SURF

37.731
-83.642
20 min 25 min

11 routes

.14
.13
.12
.11
.10
.9
.8
.7
≤.6

Midnight Surf is one of Muir Valley's best walls for tough sport climbing. It's big and intimidating, with most routes involving big throws to square incuts. The geometry of the wall's right half is unique for the area; you'll barely believe it's the Red River Gorge. Be prepared to use your fast-twitch muscles and get dynamic, especially if you're short! Side by side on the far right side, *Cell Block Six* and *Iniquity* are two of the Red's most coveted 5.12s. These routes, along with *Shiva* and *Tapeworm*, are must-dos. The left half of the wall is more typically pocketed and featured, yet still offers excellent steep pumpers such as *Vortex* and *The Crucible*.

Approach: For the fastest approach, take the Main Trail North to the valley floor, where the stairs/trail meets the maintenance road. Walk left for about 1/2 mile, past the pit toilet, up the hill and down the other side, passing the trail to Slab City. Look for the sign and trail on the left that takes you to a long set of stairs. At the top of the stairs take a right, passing a few Boneyard routes, to the main Midnight Surf amphitheater. For the "warm-up approach," hike in as for the Boneyard (page 94). Warm up here, then head right along the cliff line (down and then up the upper stairways) to Midnight Surf.

Conditions: Midnight Surf faces north and is a good warm-weather destination. The wall stays dry in a downpour, but can sweat after many days of rain.

❶ **Babyface** 5.12b ★★★
Midway between the Boneyard and the first route at the main Midnight Surf wall is this long jug haul with a high, sloping crux. A 60-meter rope will barely get you back to the starting ledge — be sure to knot the end of your rope.
100 ft. 10 bolts. Scott Curran, Dustin Stephens, 2012.

❷ **Starfish and Coffee** 5.13a ★★
This is the first route encountered to the right of the amphitheater and waterfall. Begin on a large ramp/ledge feature and trend up and left on the severely overhanging pocketed face toward a giant hueco near the top.
80 ft. Greg Kerzhner, 2009.

❸ **A Farewell to Arms** 5.13a ★★★
Begin just right of *Starfish and Coffee*. Climb a right-leaning flake to reach a hand ledge at the first bolt. Continue up on large holds to just before the body-length roof, where the hammer drops and things get serious. Bust over the roof to a ledge, then race up the severely overhanging wall on pockets and pinches to a big-move crux near the top.
80 ft. 12 bolts. Ray Ellington, Kipp Trummel, 2007.

❹ **The Crucible** 5.12c ★★★★
Move about 20 feet right to the next line, which begins on a stack of boulders. Climb easy moves up to a three-foot roof. Make a big move to an edge, then slap for another good ledge. Take advantage of the rest, then move up the overhanging face through a series of pockets and sidepulls to a pump crux near the top.
80 ft. 9 bolts. Ray Ellington, Kipp Trummel, 2007.

The Crucible

MIDNIGHT SURF

Tree Hugger 5.11d ★★★★
Wild jug-hauling with just a couple of tricky moves. Get an attentive belay and watch out for the tree down low. A two-bolt extension up the black streak above the first anchor adds some vert crimping with no change in difficulty.
30 ft. 9 bolts. Dustin Stephens, Lena Bakanova, 2015.

Vortex 5.12c ★★★★
Begin a few feet right of *Tree Hugger*. Climb easy moves up to a large roof. Reach over the roof to good holds, then continue up the overhanging face on pockets and underclings to a good rest. Recover, then finish up the second half of the route, saving some juice for the brutal finger-cramming pocket crux just before the chains.
30 ft. 8 bolts. John Cioci, Kipp Trummel, 2007.

Shiva 5.13b ★★★★
Move right from *Vortex* about 40 feet to the next bolted line. Begin 15 feet right of a tree. Boulder through the initial blank face to reach a series of long moves to large ledges. Power through a long undercling move to reach a decent edge. Take the easy road out to the left or contrive straight up for a fun boulder problem.
30 ft. 8 bolts. Brad Weaver, 2007.

Tapeworm 5.12d ★★★★
Begin by climbing a flake 15 feet right of *Shiva*. Continue up the vertical face, passing some big moves, until the wall kicks out. Take a lay-down rest out left (if nobody's at the wall to see you), then move up to a good ledge and head into the business — a full-on dyno if you can't use the bad sloper. Consider another chump rest out left near the top, then crank down on a pair of very bad holds and gun for a big hold just before the chains.
80 ft. 8 bolts. Brad Weaver, Kipp Trummel, 2007.

Cell Block Six 5.12c ★★★★★
It doesn't get much better than this! *Cell Block Six* begins 20 feet right of *Tapeworm*. Begin by climbing a short dihedral to reach the first bolt, then attack the overhanging gray stone with gorilla-swinging style. Take advantage of every rest you get, because you will need them for the redpoint-crux run to the chains.
80 ft. 9 bolts. Brad Weaver, Kipp Trummel, 2007.

Iniquity 5.12b ★★★★
An excellent companion to *Cell Block Six*. Boulder out the start to reach a good horn. Edge and throw to perfect ledges and hang on as the wall steepens dramatically near the middle. Take a squat rest on a ramp, then get dynamic again as you make the final push to the chains. If you can't do the crux boulder problem, just yard through (or start on *Cell Block Six*) to experience the route minus a letter grade or two.
90 ft. 8 bolts. Brad Weaver, Kipp Trummel, 2007.

Mellow Yellow 5.11b ★★★
The last bolted line on the right side of the wall. This route is sometimes referred to as "caked mud." Nevertheless, talk it up to your friends who don't climb 5.12 so they'll head up to the Surf with you. Take on the arête, then move right at the roof near mid-height to reach the caked mud. Claw to the chains.
80 ft. 8 bolts. Andrew Wheatley, Kipp Trummel, 2007.

THE BONEYARD

37.731
-83.640
20 min 20 min

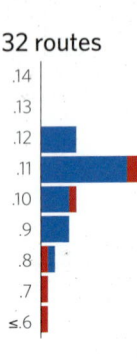

32 routes

This wall contains a few mossy lines on not-so-great rock, but also a few excellent lines on solid rock. The striking zigzag hand crack of *Renegade* sits high above the valley and offers a remarkable long ride. Named by the late Craig Luebben in remembrance of his buddy the late Todd Skinner, it would not disappoint Skinner were he alive today. If you lugged your rack for *Renegade*, hike around to the left side and do the two mixed lines *The First Fast Draw* and *Son of a Wanted Man*. Also check out *Glide*, an excellent 5.12a face climb with a powerful crux.

Approach: Take the Main Trail North to the valley floor, where the stairs/trail meets the maintenance road. Walk left on the lower, main valley road for about 1/4 mile and into the meadow. Here you will see a single trail and signs on the left to Boneyard, Animal Crackers etc. Take this trail to near the cliff and follow the signs and trail to the right to the "Boneyard South" area. This trail winds uphill to meet up the cliff between Animal Crackers Wall and Boneyard. For the Boneyard, hike right. The first routes you encounter will be *Lula Mae* and *Stealing Melinda*. Continue hiking right along the wall for the rest of the routes.

Alternately, from the valley floor directly across from Slab City, follow the marked trail across the creek and uphill to an impressive wooden staircase. Bail left atop the first set of stairs for routes #1-24, and continue to the top of the second set of stairs and walk right to reach the remaining routes and eventually Midnight Surf.

Conditions: The Boneyard faces primarily north to northeast, so expect a bit of early morning sun and good shade for the rest of the day. A few of the steeper lines stay dry in the rain, but head elsewhere if you're looking for a true rainy-day crag.

❶ **Lula Mae** 5.6 ★
This route takes the twin flakes just left of *Stealing Melinda*.
25 ft. Eric Cox, 2007.

❷ **Stealing Melinda** 5.9 ★★
A short, bolted line, the leftmost on the wall. Surprisingly fun for its length. Pull a difficult start, then reach and step to the chains.
25 ft. 3 bolts.
Jeff Colombo, Mark Ryan, Skip Wolfe, Rick Weber, 2008.

❸ **Unknown Road** 5.11b ★★★
Second bolted route you encounter on the left side of the sector, this slabfest will keep you working till the top.
60 ft. 5 bolts. Unknown

Glide

Hot Fudge Sunday 5.11a

...he new route with glue-in bolts left of *Glide* has bad rock ...nd is poorly bolted. Skip it unless you're into that sort of ...ing. Climb into the hueco about 20 feet off the ground, then ...eander through sandy, soft rock, with a few solid holds ...ong the way. Use longer-than-standard quickdraws, as ...any of the bolts force the carabiner over edges or pinch ...e rope.
...5 ft. 7 bolts. Craig "I did not bolt this" Smith, 2016.

Glide 5.12a ★★★★

...ocate a vertical wall hosting three bolted lines. This is the ...ftmost. Climb easy moves to an undercling before the third ...olt. Get powered up, then crank hard on edges to reach a ...nob up and left. Grab a quick shake, then dance up the face ...solid edges interspersed with the occasional iron-oxide ...g. Some folks prefer to stick-clip the third bolt, or pre-hang ...long sling, to prevent a fall onto the slab.
...5 ft. 6 bolts. Kipp Trummel, 2008.

Gorilla 5.12c ★★★

...imb up to a large pocket and make a big move left to a ...ecent set of holds. Dive into two bolts' worth of insanity, ...en try not to blow it for the remainder of this superb ...impfest.
...5 ft. 6 bolts. Ray Ellington, Kipp Trummel, 2009.

Three-Toed Sloth Open Project ★★

...his is the rightmost line of the three on the vertical wall. If ...eco's *Black Mamba* was a cakewalk for you, then give this ...shot.
...5 ft. 6 bolts. Equipped by Kipp Trummel.

Surfin' the Whale's Back 5.10b ★★

...imb a chimney for the first three bolts, make an awkward ...ird clip, then step left onto the face for interesting pocket ...imbing.
...5 ft. 7 bolts. Jeff Colombo, Mark Ryan, 2008.

Oink! Oink! 5.8 ★★★

...his line follows the thin finger crack beneath a roof.
...0 ft. Karen Clark, 2007.

Winona 5.7

...ocate a crack with a pod. Follow the crack to a cave with ...me strange formations. Squeeze through a hole at top of ...ve, then continue to a set of chains.
...5 ft. Skip Wolfe, 2007.

The Last Slow Draw

⓫ **Hijacked Project** 5.9 ★
This is the short, bolted line left of *Jeff's Boneyard Project*. Pull through a six-foot-high roof to begin, then continue on crimps and plates to a slightly steeper finish to chains that come quicker than you'd like.
50 ft. 6 bolts.
Mark Ryan, Jenny Ryan, Jeff Colombo, Ashley Coll, 2007.

⓬ **Jeff's Boneyard Project** 5.12a ★
This bolted line begins 15 feet left of *Son of a Wanted Man*. Grab high crimps to start and pull up to a ledge.
70 ft. Equipped by Jeff Colombo.

⓭ **Son of a Wanted Man** 5.10a ★★
A mixed line that begins with a knobby face and leads to a horizontal where the crack begins.
75 ft. 1 bolt. Craig Luebben, Kris Hampton, 2006.

⓮ **The First Fast Draw** 5.11c ★
Move 10 feet left to a mixed line, which begins as an obvious crack but continues up a bolted face for the second half.
75 ft. 4 bolts. Craig Luebben, Kris Hampton, 2006.

⓯ **The Last Slow Draw** 5.11d ★★
Five feet left of *Gym Jones* is another line with a roof near the bottom. Pull over the small roof and continue up a pocketed face past a few bulges.
70 ft. 9 bolts. Craig Luebben, 2006.

⓰ **Gym Jones Approved** 5.11b ★
Following the trail left, eventually you will reach an impressive wall containing this and the next few lines. This is the rightmost route on the wall. Pull up to a five-foot-high ledge, then tackle a roof to gain another ledge near the first bolt. Continue on pockets to the chains.
70 ft. 11 bolts. Barry Brolley, Craig Lubben, Mark Ryan, Jeff Colombo, 2007.

Richard Strange on *Cell Block Six*, 5.12c, Midnight Surf (page 93). Photo: Elodie Saracco.

17 Van der Waals Goo Open Project ★★★
Find a nice-looking wall with a gold streak. This route takes the line of bolts right of the streak. Climb through moderate terrain, then make a big move to a hueco. Move straight up out of the hueco, then trend left on small edges to reach a heinous and extremely difficult move on minuscule holds. Stretch and tiptoe the remainder to the chains.
50 ft. 7 bolts. Equipped by Kipp Trummel.

18 Hoosierheights.com 5.11c
This route could possibly be closed at some point due to a large loose block near the beginning. Proceed with caution if you choose to climb it. Begin 30 feet left of *Captain Blondie Sinks the Ship*. Traverse in on a hand ledge from the left to start, then climb through large ledges to reach a no-hands rest. Once recovered, tackle the slightly overhanging but positive finish.
75 ft. 10 bolts. Greg Martin, Josh Thurston, 2006.

19 Flavor of the Week 5.11b ★★
AKA *McMooseKnuckle*. Start on a cool arête feature and climb massive ledges to an airy roof move. Pull the lip and cruise to the anchors. Take care with the anchors as their position makes for bad carabiner placement and rope drag.
75 ft. 10 bolts. Unknown

20 Captain Blondie Sinks the Ship 5.11a ★★★
Begin just left of the arête with an easy vertical section, which quickly leads to a left-angling, pumpy, overhanging face. Dig for heel-toes when you need them to recover.
75 ft. 11 bolts. Craig Luebben, Kris Hampton, Sarah Gross, 2006.

21 One-Armed Bandit 5.9 ★★★
The obvious arête.
80 ft. 12 bolts. Sarah Gross, 2006.

22 Lucy Goosey 5.10b ★★
Climb to a dirty ledge and continue up a dirty face to chain anchors.
80 ft. 11 bolts. Barry Brolley, 2007.

23 Cindarella 5.9 ★★★
This is the second route left of the wooden stairs, 15 feet le of *Armed Insurrection*. Begin on a flake and pull a difficult move to get started. Continue up a low-angle pocketed face to a steeper finish.
80 ft. 9 bolts. Cinda Norton, J.J., 2005.

24 Armed Insurrection 5.10d ★★★
This is the first sport route encountered left of where the original approach trail meets the cliff atop the first set of stairs. Bouldery start to short roof to dirty, vertical face. Rap don't lower, from the anchors to avoid twisting your rope.
80 ft. 9 bolts. Jared Hancock, Rob Copeland, 2005.

The following routes are located climber's right of the approach stairs.

25 Abby Gabby Doo 5.8
This is the first bolted line about 100 feet right of the top of the second set of stairs.
30 ft. 5 bolts. Mike Susko, Stacia Susko, 2006.

Flying Serpents 5.12a ★★★

the next overhanging wall, find three bolted lines. This is
leftmost line and is worth doing for the final moves alone.
ft. 6 bolts. *Jared Hancock, Tim Powers, Karla Carandang, 2005.*

Tanduay Time 5.10d ★★★

s is the middle of the three sport routes up the slightly
erhanging pocketed face. Fun!
ft. 5 bolts.
ed Hancock, Tim Powers, Karla Carandang, J.J., 2005.

Tao Bato 5.11a ★★

s is the right of the three lines on the pocketed face. Not
fun as *Tanduay Time,* but worth jumping on.
ft. 7 bolts. *Jared Hancock, J.J., 2005.*

Renegade 5.11c ★★★★

lk right about 40 feet to this obvious zigzag crack. Start
an alcove under a bolt about 20 feet up. Take fingers-to-
ds pro, with extra off-fingers and thin-hands sizes. Bolt
chors.
ft. 1 bolt. *Craig Luebben, 2006.*

Bangers and Mash 5.11c ★★★★

is and the next two routes begin right of *Renegade* and can
approached by traversing along the ledge near the base of
e wall. For this line, keep a careful belay going to the third
lt. After the ledge rest at midheight, watch your forearms
n to mash as you throttle for the chains.
ft. 9 bolts. *Kipp Trummel, Karen Clark, 2007.*

Sweet Tater 5.11d ★★★

st right of *Bangers and Mash.* Named in honor of "Sweet
ter" Creech, a matriarch of the area. Casual climbing to a
ackdown crux.
ft. 8 bolts. *Kipp Trummel, 2007.*

Flying Serpents

Trouble in Paradise

㉜ Hagis, Neeps and Tatties 5.11c ★★

Traverse the ledge to the righmost line. Climb to a roof, then
pull over on large holds to encounter a line of edges and
slopers with some way-right-of-the-bolts excitement.
85 ft. 9 bolts. *Kipp Trummel, 2007.*

㉝ Trouble in Paradise 5.12a ★★★★

Thrutch through two low cruxes to gain good rests, followed
by crazy jug hauling through the roof and engaging face
climbing above. Perma-draws down low, but take seven or
eight draws for the upper section of the route.
95 ft. 11 bolts. *Dustin Stephens, 2014.*

㉞ Hematopoiesis 5.11b ★★★

Stick clip and traverse hard right to gain this long, water-
streaked arête. Back-clean or extend the first draw after
clipping the second to reduce rope drag.
100 ft. 12 bolts. *Dustin Stephens, 2014.*

THE BONEYARD

97

ANIMAL CRACKERS

7 routes

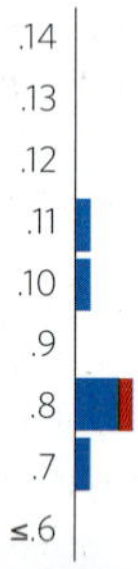

Animal Crackers Wall is just as it sounds: fun for the kids. It's a short section of slabby wall with a few fun climbs. If you're en route to Bibliothek, stop and do *Sam* as a warm-up.

Photo: Elodie Saracco

Approach: Take the Main Trail North to valley floor, where the stairs/trail meets maintenance road. Walk left on the lower, m valley road for about 1/4 mile and into meadow. Here you will see a single trail a signs on the left to Boneyard, Animal Cracke etc. Take this trail to near the cliff and foll the signs and trail to the right to the "Boneya South" area. This trail winds uphill to meet up cliff between Animal Crackers and Boneyard. He left until you reach a small, slabby wall w several bolted lines. To reach *24-Hour Bug* a *Much Ado About Nothing*, continue walking pa the main wall. If you reach an overhanging w with several bolted lines, you've walked too and ended up at Bibliothek.

Conditions: Wet when it rains; sun fr midmorning until early afternoon.

❶ Panda Bear 5.8 ★★
This is the rightmost route, and the first encountered, on the slabby Animal Crackers Wall. Crimps on a slab.
45 ft. 4 bolts. Natasha Fischer, 2007.

❷ Sam 5.10b ★★★
Next route left of *Panda Bear*. If you approach this route with the mindset that nothing at a wall named Animal Crackers could quite possibly be difficult, then you may get smacked down by this tough little slab. Best route on the wall.
45 ft. 6 bolts. Brett Stark, 2007.

❸ Rikki Tikki Tavi 5.8 ★★★
Next line left of *Sam* and the third route from the right. It is what it looks like.
50 ft. 5 bolts. Reese Nelson, 2007.

❹ Harvey 5.7 ★★
Next route left of *Rikki Tikki Tavi*. Stop at first anchors at 45 feet (six bolts) or continue past four more bolts to the second set of anchors for extended fun.
80 ft. 10 bolts. Rick Weber, 2007.

❺ Casey 5.8 ★★★
This is the leftmost bolted route on the main Animal Cracke Wall. Crimpy for 45 feet, then pure friction and balance for the next 30 feet to the top.
75 ft. 11 bolts. Rick Weber, 2007.

❻ 24-Hour Bug 5.8 ★★
To locate this crack, continue past the main Animal Cracke Wall a couple hundred feet until just before the trail heads down a steep ravine beneath a large ampitheater. Begin jamming 10 feet off the deck and continue to the chains.
45 ft. Josh Thurston, Rick Weber, 2007.

❼ Much Ado About Nothing 5.11c ★★★
This left-angling bolted line begins 10 feet left of *24-Hour Bu* Climb through easy moves to a stopper crux at the fourth bo Continue on good handholds and bad feet to the chains.
45 ft. 5 bolts. Josh Thurston, Ron Bateman, 2009.

BIBLIOTHEK

37.7302
-83.6408

If 5.11 is your grade, then check out Bibliothek, with its 15 decent-quality overhanging 5.11s, all close to each other. Most of the main wall's lines climb similarly and feel about the same grade, so s tempting to give them all 5.11b/c. A ouple do stand out, however, including *erything That Rises Must Converge*, the est and most difficult climb. Oh, and e names? They're book titles. If you an't remember any of them, you're not one.

Approach: Follow the approach for Animal Crackers Wall (opposite page) but continue past Animal Crackers a few hundred feet until you reach a steep ravine near a large amphitheater. Walk down the sandy ravine and cross a small stream near the bottom. Hike a short distance up and around the corner to reach an overhanging wall with several bolted lines. The routes *100 Years of Solitude* through *Tea at the Palaz of Hoon* are located on this main wall, from right to left. To reach *A Confederacy of Dunces* through *American Psycho*, continue walking past the main wall for 100 feet.

Conditions: Most of the lines overhang, thus are climbable in a decent rain. They're a bit tough on the skin due to the rock's texture, but you'll like it when you're trying to hang the sloping holds. The wall gets sun from morning until early afternoon.

99

MUIR VALLEY

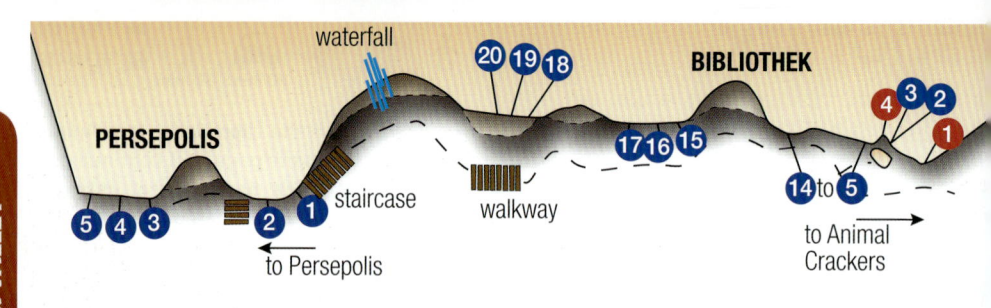

PERSEPOLIS — waterfall — BIBLIOTHEK
staircase — walkway
to Persepolis — to Animal Crackers

① A Prayer for Owen Meany 5.6 ★★
Past Animal Crackers Wall and down a steep ravine is this short, right-angling handcrack, located about 35 feet before rounding the corner to reach the main Bibliothek wall.
30 ft. Ron Bateman, Josh Thurston, 2009.

② 100 Years of Solitude 5.11a ★★★
Rightmost line on the main wall. Climb the aesthetic face just right of a large scoop in the cliff. A bouldery start leads to comfortable stances and fun moves to a thinner finish.
55 ft. 5 bolts. Ron Bateman, Josh Thurston, 2007.

③ Who Pooped in the Park? 5.11c ★★★
The second bolted line from the right. Begin by either climbing the crack, if it's dry, or the face to the left. Leave the comfort of large holds and move right onto the face to make the second clip. Continue up to a rest, then bust through single-pad edges up the short but pumpy headwall. Sucker your partner into hanging the draws.
55 ft. 6 bolts. Andrew Wheatley, Brad Combs, 2009.

④ The Giver 5.6 ★
Climb the flake left of *Who Pooped in the Park?*. Reach for the first hold and continue up the left-angling flake, using hand-sized gear. Shares anchors with *The Short Happy Life of Francis Macomber*.
45 ft. Cleveland Wilson, Brad Combs, 2008.

⑤ The Short, Happy Life of Francis Macomber 5.10b ★★
Short but sweet. Just left of the crack climb *The Giver* and the first route left of the large scoop. A steep, technical start leads to enjoyable climbing above.
45 ft. 4 bolts. Ron Bateman, Josh Thurston, 2007.

⑥ The Stranger 5.11d ★★★
Next route left of *The Short, Happy Life*. Boulder through a short section of slopey, textured rock to reach a set of good sidepulls. Clip the second bolt, then bust through pockets and pinches to reach the easier upper section.
55 ft. 5 bolts. Josh LaMar (L.J.), Josh Thurston, 2009.

⑦ Everything That Rises Must Converge 5.11d ★★★★
With excellent movement, this is likely the best route on the wall. Begin just left of *The Stranger*. Grab high pinches on textured orange rock to start. Pump up through a sequential series of protruding edges and finger pockets while keeping an eye out for the occasional hidden hold.
60 ft. 6 bolts. Josh Thurston, Ron Bateman, Josh LaMar, 2009.

⑧ Resuscitation of a Hanged Man 5.11b ★★★
Ten feet left of the previous line. A little sharp, but should dull out over the years. Medium-sized holds and no big resting ju
65 ft. 7 bolts. Josh Thurston, Ron Bateman, 2008.

⑨ All the Pretty Horses 5.11c ★★★
Take on the sustained and pumpy face just a few feet left o the previous line.
70 ft. 8 bolts. Josh Thurston, Ron Bateman, TJ Halls, 2007.

⑩ No Country for Old Men 5.11b ★★★
Start just left of *All the Pretty Horses*. Move through the pump lower section to a rest, then crank through a tough finish.
65 ft. 7 bolts. Josh Thurston, Ron Bateman, 2008.

⑪ The Unbearable Lightness of Being 5.11c ★★★★
Next bolted line left of *No Country for Old Men*. Move up the overhanging face, taking advantage of the occasional gargantuan jug rest. Scoot left near the top and make a big move before the chains. Be aware of the tree if going big near the end.
70 ft. 7 bolts. Josh Thurston, Ron Bateman, 2007.

⑫ A Portrait of the Artist as a Young Man 5.11b ★★★
Twenty feet left of *The Unbearable Lightness*. Pinch and crimp up the overhanging face. Don't waste time searching for huge double-handed ledge jugs — the route to the right stole them all.
70 ft. 7 bolts. Ron Bateman, Josh Thurston, Betsey Adams, 200

The Love Song of J. Alfred Prufrock 5.11c ★★★ ☐
...cond bolted line on the left side of the main Bibliothek
...ll, just before the trail heads down into a large
...phitheater. Begin 10 feet left of the previous line.
...stained, technical climbing.
... ft. 7 bolts. *Josh Thurston, Ron Bateman, 2008.*

Tea at the Palaz of Hoon 5.11b ★★ ☐
...rthest left route on the main Bib wal — shares the start
...th *Alfred Prufrock*, then angles left. Pull the entrance moves
... *Alfred Prufrock*, then move left to a large undercling near
... second bolt.
... ft. 5 bolts. *Josh Thurston, Ron Bateman, 2009.*

A Confederacy of Dunces 5.11c ★★ ☐
...om the main Bibliothek wall, head left down a ravine for 50
...rds to reach another section of the wall with a few bolted
...es. This is the rightmost line on this sector. If you can make
...through the first three bolts of dirty and fragile rock, you'll
... rewarded with slightly better climbing the rest of the way.
... ft. 7 bolts. *Joel Handley, Kipp Trummel, Ron Bateman, 2008.*

The Fury 5.11c ★★★ ☐
...st left of *A Confederacy of Dunces* and much cleaner.
...gin in a swampy mess to gain the face, then watch your
...rearms swell as you take on this overhanging monster of a
...ute. If you're desperate for a rest, think kneebars.
... ft. 8 bolts. *Kipp Trummel, 2008.*

The Sound 5.11c ★★ ☐
...st left of *The Fury*. If you climbed *A Confederacy of Dunces*
...d enjoyed it, then you've proved that your standards are
...w enough to have a good time on this route as well. Similar
... its neighbors on the right.
... ft. 8 bolts. *Kipp Trummel, 2008.*

East of Eden 5.11d ★★★ ☐
...alk left from the previous lines about 50 feet. Locate three
...ort lines up on a ledge; this is the far right one. Crank
... hard pocket problem to start and gain a good jug ledge.
...unch onto the sustained face and bicep-curl your way to
...e chains.
... ft. 5 bolts. *Kipp Trummel, 2008.*

Lolita 5.12a ★★★ ☐
...st left of *East of Eden*. This spicy route will keep your
...tention. Have your belayer on his A game while you clip the
...ird bolt.
... ft. 4 bolts. *Kipp Trummel, 2008.*

American Psycho 5.11a ★★ ☐
...ove left of *Lolita* a few feet for this one. It's longer than
...olita and *East of Eden*, but don't expect the same quality.
... ft. 6 bolts. *Ron Bateman, 2008.*

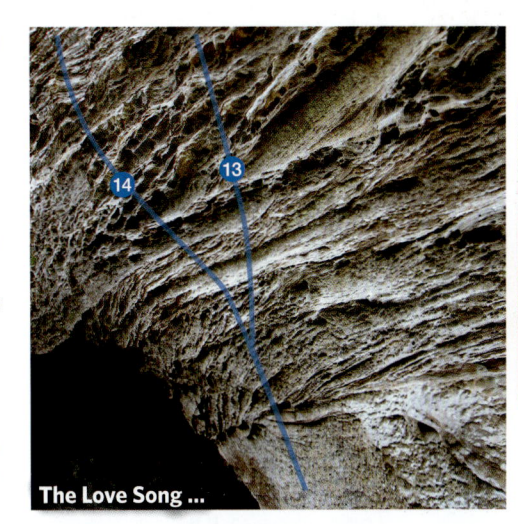

PERSEPOLIS

37.729
-83.640
20 min | 35 min

5 routes

.14
.13
.12
.11
.10
.9
.8
.7
≤.6

The routes at this small sector have strange names and strange moves. *Zendebad* is well worth the extra hike from Biblitothek, as is *Rostam*, the line just left of it, with its 50 feet of relentless slapping and sliding. The lines here are hard and conditions-dependent! See topo on page 100.

Approach: Head as for Animal Crackers Wall b continue past Animal Crackers a few hundre feet until you reach a steep ravine near a larg amphitheater. Walk down the sandy ravine an cross a small stream near the bottom. Hike short distance up and around the corner to reac an overhanging wall with several bolted line — Bibliothek. Continue hiking until you reach wooden bridge. Cross the bridge and head dow to a waterfall and a set of wooden stairs. Walk u the stairs to end up just beneath *Zendebad*. Se topo on page 100.

Conditions: The sun hits in late afternoon, b you'll probably want the shade for higher frictio Not a good candidate for a rainy day.

❶ Zendebad 5.13a ★★★★
This is the first route encountered after the top of the wooden stairs. Begin left of a blunt arête. Make a difficult move to start, then continue through a series of bizarre and powerful moves on slopers, small crimps, and knobs to a more overhanging and pumpy finish on sidepulls and pinches.
55 ft. 7 bolts. *Ray Ellington, Kipp Trummel, 2007.*

❷ Rostam 5.12c ★★★
This is the next line, 15 feet left of *Zendebad*. Bust through sloping holds and sequential moves, taking advantage of an occasional shake along the way. If you do this in the summer, give yourself a couple extra letter grades.
55 ft. 5 bolts. *Kipp Trummel, 2007.*

❸ Ferdowsi 5.11b
Not recommended. Per the FA, "Man, this makes my list of chop-able lines." Climb down a wooden ladder from the ledge that the previous two routes begin on, then head left about 50 feet to a taller wall with three lines. This is the first line from the right. Climb to a horizontal break midway, then take on the more overhanging second half of the route. Be careful making the next clip after leaving the midway ledge.
65 ft. 6 bolts. *Kipp Trummel, 2007.*

❹ Paladine 5.12a ★★
Next route left of *Ferdowsi*. Climbs slanting, sloping crimps (yes, "slimpers") to a spicy run for a jug.
65 ft. 6 bolts. *Kipp Trummel, 2007.*

❺ Apadana 5.12a ★★★
This is the last route on the wall and begins near a low crac Start with a difficult opening move, then climb to a bulge beneath the second bolt. Make a tough move to reach a dee pocket near the bolt, then continue up the face on sequentia limestone-like finger pockets. If you aren't afraid of a little moss, this route is actually pretty cool.
65 ft. 6 bolts. *Kipp Trummel, 2007.*

Zendebad ❶

Heath Rowland on *Ascentuality* 5.11a, the Stadium (page 129). Photo: Mike Wilkinson.

THE SOLARIUM

12 routes

.14
.13
.12
.11
.10
.9
.8
.7
≤.6

37.73
-83.63
20 min | 25 min

This gold-striped wall seen from the main trail is as good as it looks. Most lines are within the 5.12 range and have hard moves near the bottom, leading to huge incuts on the upper "baked-mud" section. Although it has a couple of epoxy-reinforced holds, *Banshee* still ranks as one of the valley's most enjoyable and exposed 5.11s. If the glue bothers you, branch left onto *Abiyoyo* for an epoxy-free and more difficult variation. It's hard to go wrong with any route here.

Approach: Take the Main Trail North valley floor, where the stairs/trail meets the maintenance road. Walk left on the lower, ma valley road for about 1/2 mile, past the pit toil and up the hill to the top. Take the trail on the right, following the signs toward several crag The Solarium is directly above, between the Arsenal and Great Arch.

Conditions: The Solarium gets sun early in the day and offers a great escape from the rain. Eve if the upper section is getting sprinkled on, i mostly incut jugs up there so you should be ab to tag the chains.

❶ **Air-Ride Equipped** 5.11a ★★★★
The leftmost bolted line on the wall, just left of where the trail meets the cliff. Climb a tricky start up to a severely overhanging section with a number of tiered roofs. Heel-ho and swing out the roofs, pulling a crux move just before the angle kicks back to vertical.
65 ft. 7 bolts. Barry Broley, J.J., 2004.

❷ **Manifest Destiny** 5.11d ★★★★
This excellent line is just right of *Air-Ride Equipped* and marked by a short roof midway. Crank on crimps with poor feet to start, then fight the pump to reach the roof. Pull this with burly moves and keep it together to the chains.
70 ft. 8 bolts. Jared Hancock, Tim Powers, J.J., 2004.

❸ **So Long Mr. Petey** 5.12c ★★★
Next route right of *Manifest Destiny*. Bouldery, with a powerful section and a much thinner finish.
70 ft. 8 bolts. Tim Powers, 2005.

❹ **Magnum Opus** 5.12a ★★★★
Next sport route to the right. Fun and fingery pocket climbin passing a couple of large huecos along the way.
90 ft. 10 bolts. Jared Hancock, Tim Powers, Mike Susko, 2005.

❺ **Urban Voodoo** 5.12d ★★★
Nice boulder problem to the third bolt. Deceptive roof crux, then mostly good holds to the anchors. This route currently has fixed draws on the first five bolts.
95 ft. 10 bolts. Greg Martin, Brian Boyd, Andrew Gearing, 2005.

Manifest Destiny

Becksta Johnson on *Super Best Friends*, 5.12b (this page).
Photo: Elodie Saracco.

Summer Sunshine

Abiyoyo

Delicatessen 5.12a ★★★★

This route climbs through the huge roof right of *Urban Voodoo*. A smorgasbord of movement leads to a few well-paced jugs in the steepness. Sharpen up the heel spurs for success.

90 ft. 8 bolts. Dru Mack, Dustin Stephens, 2014.

❼ Super Best Friends 5.12b ★★★★

Begin left of a stack of large boulders on good holds. Climb to a large roof, passing a few big moves along the way. Take advantage of some good heel-hooks, then bust over the lip to reach the fun and easy juggy headwall.

95 ft. 10 bolts. Brian Boyd, Greg Martin, 2005.

105

⑧ **Summer Sunshine** 5.12b ★★★
Begin right of *Super Best Friends*, on the left side of a short arête. Trend right on good holds, then dig for power to sneak around the arête and reach the relaxing headwall.
95 ft. 10 bolts. Greg Martin, Josh Thurston, Greg Purnell, 2005.

⑨ **Galunlati** 5.12b ★★★★
This is the overhanging face that begins on the short arête feature right of the enormous roof. Make thin, reachy moves past the second and third bolts, then fight your way through a few more cruxes to gigantic jugs at the top.
95 ft. 10 bolts. Jared Hancock, Tim Powers, Josh Thurston, 2005.

⑩ **Mirage** 5.12c ★★★★
This is the next route right on the gorgeous, overhanging orange face. Climb up between two huecos and enter into ultra-sustained crimping for 30–40 feet. As with most lines at the Solarium, relax on the comfortable incut jugs of the upper headwall.
95 ft. 10 bolts. Chris Martin, 2005.

⑪ **Bundle of Joy** 5.13a ★★★★
This project has finally been fully equipped and sent. Most of the routes at the Solarium mellow out toward the top, but this one just pours it on. Begin right of *Mirage* and start tryin hard as soon as you step off the ground. A big flake that

Let it rain! Zach Ruswick on *Delicatessan* 5.12a, (page 105). Photo: John Wesely.

...ooks sketchy from the ground is actually very solid and will become a good friend when you need to shake out the pump. ...ave a stick clip or leaver biner ready if you can't pull the ...oulder problem guarding the chains!
...0 ft. 7 bolts. Andrew Wheatley, 2009.

⓬ Abiyoyo 5.12b ★★★★★

...t the right edge of the Solarium wall, look for two gray bolt ...angers on a ledge above a 25-foot cliff, at the base of the ...ark-orange overhanging wall. Once the belayer is anchored, ...tick-clip the first bolt. Climb up and to the right, past four ...olts, to a well-deserved sit-down rest in the leftmost of ...wo large huecos. Exit the left side of the hueco. Moderate face climbing leads to an obvious crux, followed by 30 feet of pumpy face climbing. The crux may be more difficult for climbers under 5'8". 60-meter rope recommended.
95 ft. 10 bolts. Eric Anderson, Mark Strevels, 2005.

⓭ Banshee 5.11c ★★★★★

Same start as *Abiyoyo*, but head up and right from the hueco rest after the fourth bolt. A tricky crux move leads to a second sit-down rest in a large hueco. Follow large jugs to the top. 60-meter rope recommended.
100 ft. 11 bolts. Eric Anderson, 2005.

THE GREAT ARCH

MUIR VALLEY

10 routes

.14
.13
.12
.11
.10
.9
.8
.7
≤.6

37.734
-83.638
20 min / 30 min

The Great Arch is small, but has one absolute must-do route, *Lip Service*. While you're there, check out the 5.11 pumpers *Night Moves* and *Battery Life*, and then cool down on *Black Powder*.

Approach: Follow the approach to the Solarium (page 104), but continue down the trail another 100 yards. Look for a sign and trail on the left leading up to the base of the crag, between *Lip Service* and *Black Powder*. If you look directly left at the opposing wall, you'll see *Double Stuff*.

Conditions: The Great Arch receives morning sun, so if you want good friction for *Lip Service* visit in the afternoon. Most routes are good candidates for rainy days.

❶ Double Stuff 5.12a ★★
Ascends the left face of the dihedral *Ear Drops*, on the left side of the wall. It is recommended to bring the belayer up to the first ledge and climb this route in multi-pitch style to avoid rope drag. Climb large ledges on steep stone to reach the first set of anchors. From the ledge, move left to tackle the airy second pitch via sidepulls and underclings.
90 ft. 11 bolts. Josh Thurston, Jordan Garvey, 2006.

❷ Ear Drops 5.8+ ★★★
Climb the wide dihedral in the left side of the Great Arch and continue to a set of anchors.
85 ft. Jason Haas, Sarah Maclean, 2005.

❸ Ear Infection 5.9 ★★★
This two-bolt variation start avoids the slimy, often-wet start of *Ear Drops*. Climb the slab to the right of *Ear Drops* for 20 feet, then join with the crack. Finish on *Ear Drops*.
50 ft. 2 bolts. Erik Kloeker, 2016.

❹ Dyn-o-mite 5.9 ★★★
This is the leftmost sport route under the giant arch. It often appears wet, but can still be climbed. Fun movement with interesting features.
85 ft. 10 bolts. Rick Weber, J.J., Tom Kwasny, 2005.

The *Banshee*, 5.11c, Solarium (page 107). Photo: Mike Wilkinson.

Black Powder 5.10a ★★★
ore great climbing on fantastic features. Begin 15–20 feet
ght of *Dyn-o-mite* and angle up and right. Most climbers
nd the beginning moves fairly tough.
5 ft. 10 bolts.
ick Weber, Jared Hancock, Karla Carandang, J.J., 2005.

Lip Service 5.11c ★★★★
his varied and unusual route starts as juggy roofs and
ecomes a technical face with big slopers. Excellent!
0 ft. 9 bolts. *J.J., Josh Thurston, 2005.*

Beef Stick 5.12a ★★★
he obvious black streak 20 feet right of *Lip Service*. Mantel
o on sloping holds to the chains. It looks like *Lip Service* but
ıst isn't the same.
0 ft. 5 bolts. *Josh Thurston, Mike Uchman, 2006.*

Night Moves 5.11b ★★★
tick-clip the first bolt, then start on boulders left of the first
olt. Casual moves on big holds to a lay-down rest. Soak it up
efore the bouldery finish.
0 ft. *Josh Thurston, Danny Rice, Mike Thurston, 2005.*

Battery Life 5.11c ★★★★
hare the first bolt of *Night Moves*, then move right into a
ugh move. Crank it out, then fight the pump on hand-
ver-hand sidepulls up the overhanging face. If you have an
ppetite for grungy cracks, you may feel this line is contrived.
0 ft. 7 bolts. *Josh Thurston, Max Rodatz, 2005.*

Night Moves

⑩ The Hunt for Red's October 5.12c ★★★★
A couple hundred feet right of the main wall. Three distinctive
boulder problems separated by good rests lead to a tall, steep
face with good holds.
90 ft. *Steve Sandman, 2015. Equipped by Erik Kloeker.*

SUNBEAM BUTTRESS

37.735
-83.637
20 min / 25 min

18 routes

This sun-soaked wall has an abundance of short, enjoyable lines and a few longer pumpers. The 5.11 climber can easily knock out every route here in a day and have a great time doing it. The shorter lines begin on an exposed ledge, so don't have that "quickie" feel, and their powerful starts have been known to send climbers home crying.

Approach: This wall is just a few minutes up from the Great Arch. Continue along the main road accessing Solarium and Great Arch. Pass through a grassy area, then look for an obvious trail to the left just as the road begins to head uphill.

❸ Stems and Seeds 5.11+ ★★★
Toprope. This difficult toprope problem ascends the clean, short dihedral that ends beneath *Predator*. Use friction, tension smearing, and all the other techniques you don't learn in the Red. Bolted anchors on the *Predator* ledge.
30 ft. *Jared Hancock, J.J., 2005.*

❹ Mossy Mayhem 5.1
This line ascends the dirty gully on the left side of the pinnacle near the main wall. It can be used to access the ledge routes.
30 ft. *Jared Hancock (free solo), 2005.*

❺ Trekker of the Treacherous 5.4
This line ascends the right side of the pinnacle, opposite *Mossy Mayhem*.
40 ft. *Jared Hancock (free solo), 2005.*

❻ Sunbeam 5.10c ★★★
When the approach trail meets the cliff, there will be a ledge to the left with a steel rebar ladder for access. This route is the first line that starts on the ground to the right of the ledge. Scramble to a fixed draw, tackle a difficult section near the second bolt, then continue on big holds to a set of anchors below the cave.
65 ft. 7 bolts. *J.J., Jared Hancock, Bram Bell, 2005.*

❼ Moonshine 5.10a ★★★
Fifteen feet right of *Sunbeam*. Climb to a large ledge beneath an intimidating roof. From the ledge, find the holds you want to use, then muscle over. Larger holds lead to an interesting finish.
60 ft. 5 bolts. *Jared Hancock, J.J., Bram Bell, 2005.*

❽ Out of the Dark 5.10c ★★★★
The overhanging arête above the ledge right of *Moonshine*. Start as for *Moonshine*, then traverse right along the ledge to the high first bolt. Negotiate the roof, Tarzan up the overhanging arête, then get your focus back for the finish.
65 ft. 6 bolts. *Jared Hancock, J.J., 2005.*

❶ Where's My Chisel? 5.9
For this and the next four lines, walk left from the rebar ladder used to access the ledge routes. One way to generate controversy in the Red is to bolt on an artificial hold. That was done on this route, but the hold has long since been removed.
35 ft. 4 bolts. *Rizzo, 2005.*

❷ Directed Panspermia 5.12 ★★
Toprope. Access the anchors from the left end of the ledge, below *Predator*. Power and finesse up a thin face and flake just left of *Stems and Seeds*.
30 ft. *Jared Hancock, 2005.*

SUNBEAM BUTTRESS

Ledge

Rebar Ladder

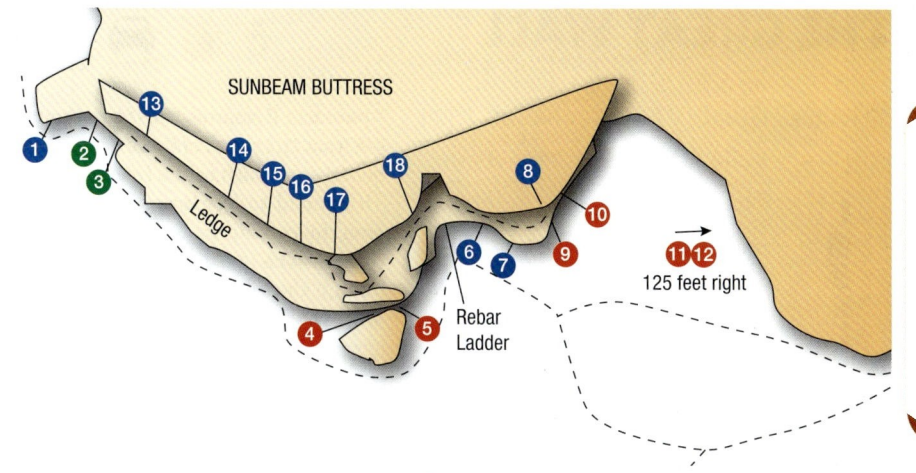

125 feet right

⑨ Revenge of the Sith 5.10 ★★
This is the short, overhanging hand crack directly beneath *Out of the Dark*. Boulder it, or stick-clip the first bolt of *Out of the Dark* and do it as a direct start for that route.
20 ft. Tom Kwasny, 2005.

⑩ One-Cheek Wonder 5.10a ★★
Climb the dihedral 10 feet right of *Out of Darkness*. From the same ledge, clip the bolt, figure out a tricky crux, then enjoy casual climbing up the dihedral.
55 ft. 1 bolt. Al Edwards, Skip Wolfe, 2014

⑪ Three Amigos 5.9+ ★★
This hand crack is found by following the cliff right for about 100 feet. As soon as you reach a small clearing with a tiny creek, look to your left and you will see this crack with a steep start. Bolted anchors.
70 ft. Tim Powers, Tom Kwasny, Mike Susko, 2005.

⑫ Primordial Dissonance 5.10 ★★★
This route begins 20 feet right of the previous route. Climb up to the bolt and fight to reach a right-arching crack ending on a ledge. Clip another bolt, then pull over a roof to reach a crack leading to another ledge with anchors.
80 ft. 2 bolts. Jared Hancock, 2005.

Ledge Routes: Lines #13-18 begin on the ledge left of Sunbeam. Approach via a rebar ladder. Routes described left to right.

⑬ Predator 5.11b★★★
This excellent line is the leftmost route on the ledge, which is accessed via a short scramble up the steel rebar ladder, just left of where the trail meets the cliff. Start with a reachy move, then continue up the vertical face with what few holds it has to offer. End with a mantel.
45 ft. 5 bolts. Jared Hancock, J.J., Karla Carandang, 2005.

⑭ Prey 5.11b ★★★
Ten feet right of *Predator*. Dig into your bag of tricks to solve the roof at the start and be rewarded with less burly moves. Tape up if you plan to use the old hand-jam trick.
55 ft. 6 bolts. Jared Hancock, J.J., 2005.

⑮ Universal Gravitation 5.10d ★★
The next route right follows the theme of tough starts. Fiddle around for holds, then commit and crank through the desperate beginning. Take a breather, then edge to the chains.
40 ft. 3 bolts. J.J., Barry Brolley, 2005.

⑯ Backstabber 5.9 ★★★
The arête right of *Universal Gravitation*. Beware of the tree when cleaning.
40 ft. 4 bolts. J.J., Karla Carandang, Jared Hancock, 2005.

⑰ Radical Evolution 5.11a ★★★
The next overhanging route right of *Backstabber*. Fun, steep climbing through several roofs.
45 ft. 4 bolts. J.J., Jared Hancock, 2005.

⑱ Morning Sun 5.11a ★★★
This is the farthest route right on the ledge. No tough start here, but instead a longer, pumpy ride.
50 ft. 5 bolts. J.J., Jared Hancock, 2005.

THE GREAT WALL

37.732
-83.637
20 min | 25 min

12 routes
.14
.13
.12
.11
.10
.9
.8
.7
≤.6

Great Wall is one of Muir Valley's more popular venues. The routes are relatively short and very well protected, making it ideal for those wanting to bag their first 5.10 or 5.11. The climbing tends to be more technical than burly, with plenty of rests. Rock quality is high, and the routes are all great, if a bit crammed — expect a crowded feeling on good-weather days.

Approach: If approaching from the Hideout, wa[lk] left from *International Route of Pancakes* to the nex[t] bolted line, which will be *La Escalada* (route #12).

If headed to the Great Wall from the parkin[g] area, follow the road to the right, located nea[r] the entrance to the parking area, and find a sho[rt] trail on the left that leads to another road. Thi[s] road winds downhill to reach the valley floo[r] near a stream. Take the first left on the road a[s] it doglegs back left and immediately crosse[s] the stream. Within a few minutes there wi[ll] be a sign indicating Calvin Hollow/Boneyard/ Midnight Surf on the left. Continue past this sig[n] and stay on the road, passing the approach fo[r] the Hideout, until the road turns sharply righ[t] just after crossing the stream again. Follow th[e] road a few minutes longer and look for a woode[n] sign on the right pointing to the Great Wall, jus[t] before the road hairpins left and uphill towar[d] the Solarium. Turn right on the trail, cross [the] creek, and continue through a marshy sectio[n.] After a couple hundred feet, the trail will win[d] uphill to meet the left side of the Great Wall.

Conditions: The lines are slightly overhangin[g] and broken up by small roofs, so it is possible t[o] continue climbing during a light rain. However, [it] is not a recommended rainy-day destination.

❶ Weapons of Mass Deception 5.9 ★★★
Follow an aesthetic, angling finger crack on the right side of a dihedral to a leftward roof traverse. Continue up the hand crack and arête feature to a large ledge with a roof. Enjoy th[e] view from the top!
85 ft. J.J., Jared Hancock, 2004.

❷ Ledgends of Limonite 5.8 ★★
The leftmost sport route on the Great Wall. Shares the start with *Glory...*, then traverses left along an easy ledge to a slab[by] face loaded with limonite ledges. The direct start is 5.10.
55 ft. 6 bolts. Jared Hancock, Mike Susko, 2004.

❸ Glory and Consequence 5.7 ★★★
Very juggy face with many rests along the way.
50 ft. 5 bolts. Jared Hancock, Toby Hamilton, 2004.

❹ Touch of Grey 5.10d ★★★
Aesthetic and slightly pumpy climbing with a few small edge[s] and a long move or two.
60 ft. 7 bolts. Jared Hancock, Karla Carandang, 2004.

Touch of Grey

Bitter Ray of Sunshine 5.10a ★★★★ ☐
...eat climbing! Start with a delicate mantel onto a ledge right
...*Touch of Grey*. Follow the rib to a series of surprisingly
...od jugs and two-finger pockets. Pull through the tricky roof
...d jug up the left water groove.
... ft. 8 bolts. *Karla Carandang, Jared Hancock, 2004.*

Dynabolt Gold 5.10a ★★★ ☐
...ure out the tough start and reap the reward of giant plates
... rest of the way.
... ft. 7 bolts. *Jared Hancock, Karla Carandang, 2004.*

Little T-Bone 5.9 ★★★ ☐
...gin under the obvious hand crack splitting the Great Wall.
...ulder out the initial roof to an alcove with a bolt. Plug a
...ece, make the mental move, protect in the crack, and enjoy
...ge plates all the way to the end of the crack and another
...lt on the juggy face above.
... ft. 2 bolts. *Tim Powers, Mike Susko, Jared Hancock, 2004.*

Momma Cindy 5.11a ★★★★ ☐
...chnical and sustained. Pull the bouldery start with a two-
...ger pocket, some edges, and a few crimps, then enjoy
...veral balancey and reachy sections with a few fun slopers,
...ges, and sidepulls.
... ft. 8 bolts. *Tim Powers, Mike Susko, Jared Hancock, 2004.*

Edge-a-Sketch 5.11a ★★★★ ☐
...st line on the wall. Begin left of a ramp on the far right side
... the wall. Solve the bottom boulder problem, only to be
...nfronted with a series of moves that will keep you guessing to
...e chains. The extension is listed as the next route.
... ft. 8 bolts. *J.J., 2004.*

Ohio Arts 5.12a ★★★ ☐
...e extension of *Edge-a-Sketch*. Continue past the anchors
...d three more bolts up a black slab and overhang to another
...ab. Be careful of the fall onto the slab when clipping the
...econd bolt on this extension.
...0 ft. 11 bolts. *John Thurston, J.J., 2004.*

Buccaneer 5.11b ★★★ ☐
...ext route right of *Edge-a-Sketch*. Sharp crimps up a slightly
...verhanging face.
... ft. 6 bolts. *Tim Powers, 2006.*

La Escalada 5.6 ★★ ☐
...ep up some easy ledges to a right-leaning ramp. Continue
... the well-protected plated face to the anchors.
... ft. 9 bolts. *J.J., Jane Maurer, 2004.*

THE GREAT WALL

6 Dynabolt Gold

9 Edge-a-Sketch

SHAWNEE SHELTER

37.73
-83.63
20 min | 25 min

6 routes

.14
.13
.12
.11
.10
.9
.8
.7
≤.6

This wall still has some potential. For developers, expect to do some cleaning: the wall orients north, and its uncleaned portions are coated with the infamous powder moss found on most north-facing sectors at the Red. Fortunately, a couple of guys have scrubbed away some excellent lines, including *Kya* 5.13a and *Noo-tha* 5.11c. At around 100 feet tall, the only thing small here is the holds. Be prepared to try hard.

Approach: Follow the approach for the Gre Wall (page 112), but continue along the cl about 200 yards until you reach an enormo section of wall hosting these lines. Routes a listed from right to left.

Conditions: Although not extremely overhangin these routes usually stay somewhat dry. The w is north facing, so don't expect much sun.

❸ Black Hoof Open Project
This tall route has a short but very difficult crux section. Bo may need to be moved depending on which direction is tak through the hardness.
110 ft. 9 bolts. Equipped by Andrew Wheatley

❹ Tecumseh's Curse 5.11d ★★★★
This gorgeous arête contains a stack of difficult moves culminating with a spicy crux move through a small roof midway up the route. Originally sandbagged at 5.11b.
60 ft. 9 bolts. Andrew Wheatley, Brad Combs, 2009.

❶ Kya 5.13a ★★★★
Climb through somewhat sustained, powerful moves to reach a decent shake. Boulder some more, then enjoy a great finish. This ain't no jug haul.
90 ft. 10 bolts. Andrew Wheatley, 2009.

❺ Waterfall Ballet 5.10a ★★★
If you can overlook the spiders and large, sketchy flakes, th route is actually great due to the gymnastic moves and fun cruxes. It's not often you get this much fun out of a 5.10a.
50 ft. 6 bolts. Mark Ryan, Jeff Columbo, 2009.

❷ Blue Jacket 5.13a ★★
Pockets to a large roof, then finish on a fun upper headwall. Awkward bolt placements reduce the quality of the line.
90 ft. 10 bolts. Thomas Cunningham, 2009.

❻ Noo-tha 5.11c ★★★★
Fun and wandering adventure climbing with a nice little surprise after the hueco.
90 ft. 10 bolts. Brad Combs, 2009.

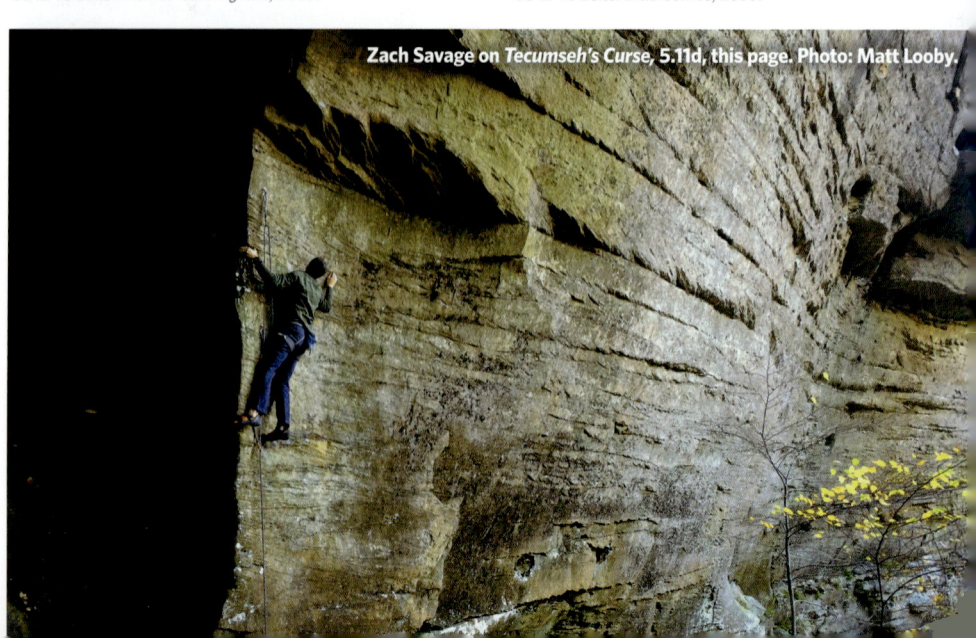

Zach Savage on *Tecumseh's Curse*, 5.11d, this page. Photo: Matt Looby.

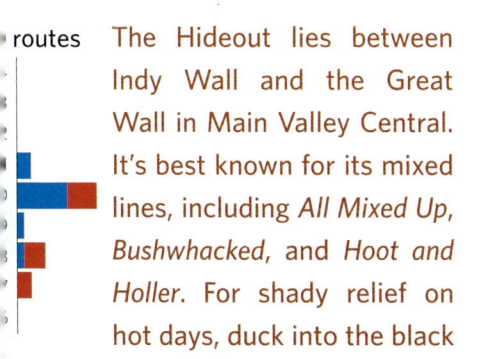

THE HIDEOUT

37.7318
-83.6365
20 min / 20 min

The Hideout lies between Indy Wall and the Great Wall in Main Valley Central. It's best known for its mixed lines, including *All Mixed Up*, *Bushwhacked*, and *Hoot and Holler*. For shady relief on hot days, duck into the black corridor and climb *Old School*, *Special K*, and *Beware the Bear*. Also do *Boltergeist* (.10b); at 100 feet long with 13 bolts, it's a classic for 5.10 aspirants.

Approach: If approaching from Indy Wall, walk left a couple hundred feet from *Parasite* to the next bolted line, which should be *Apothesis Denied*. If approaching from Great Wall, head right and around the corner, where you'll see the short, three-bolt arête *International Route of Pancakes*. If headed to the Hideout from the parking area, follow the road to the right, located near the entrance to the parking area, and find a short trail on the left that leads to another road. This road winds downhill to reach the valley floor near a stream. Take the first left on the road as it doglegs back left and immediately crosses the stream. Within a few minutes there will be a sign indicating Calvin Hollow/Boneyard/Midnight Surf on the left. Continue past this sign a few hundred feet and you will see the sign for the Hideout on the right. The trail winds uphill to end up near *International Route of Pancakes*.

Conditions: The majority of this wall faces south to southwest, so expect a lot of sun, especially in the evening. There are no severely overhanging lines, so don't expect dryness in a downpour.

International Route of Pancakes 5.8 ★
This is the first route on the left at the Hideout, and can be found by walking right from the Great Wall to the next sport line. It follows three bolts up an arête with large holds.
ft. 3 bolts. *Karla Carandang, Carol Yates, 2004.*

Roof Crack 5.8
Walk right from the previous line to locate this unappetizing chimney and roof crack beginning in the back of a narrowing corridor. Find tricky pro and a chimney-traverse out and through the roof.
ft. *Bill Hebb, Loren Wood, 2004.*

Earthsurfer 5.11d ★★★
Continue walking right from *Roof Crack* to locate a section of wall with several bolted lines. This is the leftmost route on the wall. Begin on large pockets, then fight through some edges to reach a crimpy crux just before the relaxing water above and slab run to the chains.
0 ft. 11 bolts. *Karla Carandang, Jared Hancock, 2005.*

Cruisin' for a Bruisin' 5.10d ★★★
Just right of *Earthsurfer*. Climb incut crimps up the gorgeous, vertical orange face. A short crux at a perplexing bulge can be surmounted several different ways. May feel harder for the short climber.
ft. 7 bolts. *Jared Hancock, David Fromke, 2004.*

Moots Madness 5.10a ★★★
Next bolted line right of *Cruisin' for a Bruisin'*. Begin with a reachy move below the first bolt and relax the rest of the way to the final overhanging section.
ft. 4 bolts. *Jared Hancock, Neal Schlatter, 2004.*

Earthsurfer

MUIR VALLEY

6 Preemptive Strike 5.10c ★★★★

Start 15 feet right of *Moots Madness*. A thin, crimpy face leads to a technical slab and a finish on large, overhanging plates. This route has it all.

90 ft. 11 bolts. Mark Ryan, Jenny Wagner, JJ., Jared Hancock, Rick Weber, 2005.

7 Shock and Awe 5.7 ★★★

A magnificent bright-orange crack between *Preemptive Strike* and *Boltergeist*.

95 ft. J.J., 2004.

8 Boltergeist 5.10b ★★★★

This long route offers fun climbing and plentiful protection. Great for the beginning 5.10 leader. Start on positive crimps and follow large ledges up the never-ending slab with plenty of rests and enjoyable moves. Be sure to enjoy the great view of the valley from the chains.

100 ft. 13 bolts. Jared Hancock, Tim Yates, Rick Weber, 2004.

9 All Mixed Up 5.10c ★★★

Twenty feet right of *Boltergeist* is a wall with some low roofs which ends just before the trail heads uphill to a narrow corridor. This mixed line is the first route on the left side of this wall. Bring a large piece or two for the exposed wide crack near the top.

85 ft. 4 bolts. J.J., 2004.

10 Bushwhacked 5.10c ★★★

This mixed line takes on the next path of least resistance right of *All Mixed Up*. Monkey through the low roof to reach sporty face above, which eases up toward the chains.

60 ft. 4 bolts. J.J., Jared Hancock, Tom Kwasny, 2004.

11 Hoot and Holler 5.10c ★★★

This is the final mixed route on this section of the wall. Begin 15 feet right of *Bushwhacked*. Stick-clip the high first bolt, then angle up toward a challenging bulge split by a handcrack. Jam through, then continue past a few long reaches on jugs to the chains.

60 ft. 4 bolts. Jared Hancock, J.J., Tom Kwasny, 2004.

12 Born Again Christian 5.8 ★★

Walk right and uphill from *Hoot and Holler* to a cool black corridor that provides good air conditioning in the summer. This line takes on the crack system in back of the corridor. Climb past a chockstone and up into the squeeze chimney above. If you don't count your calories, then don't go too deep in the beginning! The chimney gets less green after the start.

50 ft. Loren Wood, Bill Hebb, 2004.

Old School 5.8+ ★★

 fist-to-offwidth starts just right of *Born Again Christian*
the corridor. Be wary of the infamous 5.8+ grade. Bring a
 uple of large pieces and rap from anchors just before the
 t green section.
 ft. *Loren Wood, Bill Hebb, 2004.*

Special K 5.10c ★★

 the corridor there are two sport lines. This is the one just
 ht of *Old School*. Begin with a bouldery start, which leads
 several sustained, sloping pockets.
 ft. 6 bolts. *Karla Carandang, Jared Hancock, 2004.*

Beware the Bear 5.10b ★★★

 s fun corridor route takes on the line of bolts just right
 Special K. Positioning yourself appropriately on the holds
 uld make the difference between sending or falling. Be
 epared for a tricky anchor clip.
 ft. 5 bolts. *Jared Hancock, Tim Yates, 2004.*

Mantel Peace 5.10d ★

 st left of the right-arching crack of *Bourbon and Bluegrass*,
 a line of bolts. Climb the arete to a stance, clip a couple
 bolts, then enter a no-fall zone while doing the crux. The
 e is not on. Mantel again, step 15 feet right to more bolts,
 d go through a headwall. Mantel again and clip the chains.
 oect horrible rope drag.
 ft. 9 bolts. *Unknown*

Bourbon and Bluegrass 5.10c ★★★

 ve right from the corridor to locate this right-arching crack
 at widens to a chimney after 30 feet. Ascend the crack
 til it is possible to escape out of the chimney onto the
 etty, pocketed orange face to the left. Continue past a short
 ulder problem and three bolts to the top.
 ft. 5 bolts. *Jared Hancock, 2005.*

Call of the Wild 5.7 ★★★★

 me start as *Bourbon and Bluegrass*. Climb the bolt-
 otected chimney, then stay in the arching crack. You can
 p the anchors on *Dance of the Druids*, or answer the call
 d journey upward past an easy overhang to the top where
 u will find another set of belay/rappel anchors above the
 al ledge.
 ft. 2 bolts. *Jared Hancock, Karla Carandang, Andy Moore,*
 nny Wagner, 2005.

Dance of the Druids 5.9 ★★

 e slabby face right of the arching crack. Follow big holds to
 grassy ledge, then dance up the thinning but well-protected
 b above.
 ft. 7 bolts. *Jared Hancock, Skip Wolfe, Mark Ryan, Karla*
 randang, 2005.

Mantel Peace

Call of the Wild

20 Apotheosis Denied 5.11c ★★★

Begins 30–40 feet right of *Dance of the Druids*. Crimp off
the ground, then cruise moderate terrain to a bouldery blunt
arête. Slap, squeeze, and smear up this mildly desperate
section and finish up the heavily featured slab above.
80 ft. 9 bolts. *Jared Hancock, 2005.*

THE HIDEOUT

117

INDY WALL

37.73
-83.63

20 min 15 min

13 routes

.14
.13
.12
.11
.10
.9
.8
.7
≤.6

Indy Wall, situated between the Sanctuary and the Hideout, is a short, squared-off wall with lots of great lines and a nice flat base. The routes are vertical to slightly overhanging, and each offers a unique experience. *Annie the Annihilator* is an area-favorite 5.10 and serves as a good warm-up for the other climbs. For something hard, try the starting moves of *Stretcherous*. It is guaranteed to test the vertically challenged.

Parasite

Approach: Follow the approach to the Sanctuary (page 120), but continue left and around the corner when the trail meets up with the cliff.

Conditions: Indy Wall faces southwest and gets sun in the later hours — hit it early if you want shade. The routes are slightly overhanging, so a light drizzle won't force you away.

❷ Social Stigma 5.11b ★★★
Locate a line of bolts up a dark orange stain just right of *Parasite*. Pull a difficult start to reach sustained crimping on a steepening face. Make a couple of big moves on positive holds near the top. Bail at the first set of chains, or continue to the second set for a great view. The three-bolt extension is 5.10b.
60 ft. 9 bolts. *Karla Carandang, Jared Hancock, 2004.*

❸ Posse Whipped 5.12a ★★★
Begin 15 feet right of *Social Stigma*. Edge through a few bolts of nothing, passing a tough clip or two, to reach a short overhang up high. As with *Social Stigma*, you can stop at the first set of chains or continue on for three more bolts of average 5.10a climbing. Use a 60-meter rope for the extension.
60 ft. 9 bolts. *Karla Carandang, Jared Hancock, 2005.*

❹ Drop the Hammer 5.12c ★★★
A crimpfest on the orange face right of *Posse Whipped*.
80 ft. *Tim Powers, Mike Susko, 2004. Equipped by Justin Ridder*

❺ Owgli Mowgli 5.8 ★
Find this green and dirty crack system about 30 feet right of the previous route. Begins as an offwidth and ends as a hand crack. Shares anchors with the next route, or the crack can be climbed out the roof and taken to the top of the cliff.
40 ft. *Jared Hancock, Mike Susko, 2004.*

❻ Face Up to That Arête 5.8 ★★
This short route begins as a slab and climbs the left side of the arête to an anchor below the roof.
35 ft. 4 bolts. *Jared Hancock, Karla Carandang, 2004.*

❼ Makin' Bacon 5.10d ★★★
Next sport route right of *Face Up to That Arête* and the leftmost route on the main short, squared-off wall hosting the remaining lines. Bouldery start to positive crimps and rails, with one long, thin move along the way. Harder than it looks.
40 ft. 5 bolts.
Jared Hancock, Karla Carandang, Tim Powers, 2004.

❶ Parasite 5.11c ★★★
This is the leftmost line at Indy Wall, located just left of a tree with a sign pointing toward the Hideout. To reach it, walk left about 50 feet past the obvious squared-off main wall of the crag to a taller wall containing several sport lines. Edge and crimp up to a difficult move, then dart left into a recovery zone before the final push toward the chains.
60 ft. 6 bolts. *Kipp Trummel, 2006.*

MUIR VALLEY

the Hammer

The Happy Fisherman 5.11d ★★★

egin on a slab 10 feet right of *Makin' Bacon*. Follow five
olts up the thinning face to a bouldery pocket section. Enjoy
urprisingly good holds on the overhanging finish.
0 ft. 5 bolts. *Tim Powers, Karla Carandang, Jared Hancock, 2004.*

Midlife Crisis 5.11c ★★★

reat climbing with crimps, edges, pinches, and an exciting
nish. Begins as a steep slab, finishes as an overhang.
0 ft. 4 bolts. *Tim Powers, Mike Susko, 2004.*

Stretcherous 5.12b ★★★

rank through a height-dependent boulder-problem start,
en enjoy reachy, technical 5.11 to the anchor.
0 ft. 4 bolts. *Jared Hancock, Mark McGarvey, 2004.*

Annie the Annihilator 5.10c ★★★

his slightly overhanging jug haul is a great warm-up. Reachy
art to pumpy climbing with a short, technical crux. This was
e first sport route in Muir Valley.
0 ft. 4 bolts. *Jared Hancock, Karla Carandang, 2004.*

Mentor Powers 5.11b ★★★

egin left of the beech tree. Technical, thin face up a mildly
verhanging orange wall, with a couple of cruxes and some
gs mixed in just when you want them. This route can be
imbed to the left or right of the bolts in places. You decide.
0 ft. 4 bolts. *Jared Hancock, Tim Powers, 2005.*

The Muir the Merrier 5.11b ★★

ightmost bolted route on Indy Wall. Harder than it looks.
ustained, with back-to-back cruxes.
0 ft. 4 bolts. *Jared Hancock, Dave Hoyne, 2004.*

Owgli Mowgli

The Happy Fisherman

INDY WALL

THE SANCTUARY

37.731
-83.633
20 min 20 min

16 routes

.14
.13
.12
.11
.10
.9
.8
.7
≤.6

This is one of Muir Valley's best and toughest walls. The wall is beautiful, the rock is solid, ranging from slightly to severely overhanging, and the routes are stellar. Keeping the climbing consistent, the holds usually get smaller as the angle decreases. *Jesus Wept* and *Triple Sec* are two extremely popular lines, which are far from the average Red River jug haul; bring your pocket-pulling power and crank them out.

Approach: From the parking area, follow the road to the right, located near the entrance to the parking area, and find a short trail on the left that leads to another road. This road winds downhill to reach the valley floor near a stream. Skip the first left on the road as it doglegs back left and immediately crosses the stream and instead continue along the road until you reach a field on the left. Walk through the field to reach a stream crossing. Cross the stream, then take the first left trail, which winds uphill, ascends some stairs, and eventually meets the cliff between the Sanctuary and Indy Wall. Head to the right to be greeted by the stellar overhanging stone of the Sanctuary. The first bolted route you'll encounter is *Cherry Red*.

❷ **Cherry Red** 5.14a ★★★★
This prominent red streak is the leftmost line on the main wall. Being rarely climbed it may be slightly dirty, but after a good brushing it transforms into an excellent technical face climb. Begin by climbing through a series of sharp crimps to meet up with a tough boulder problem on very shallow pockets. Wish you had those crimps back now, huh?
80 ft. 7 bolts. Andrew Gearing, Greg Martin, 2005.

❸ **Name Dropper** 5.13a ★★★★
Fifteen feet right of *Cherry Red*. Begin on a low ledge, then traverse left to reach the start. Launch up the overhanging face through bulges, big moves, and shrinking rest holds.
70 ft. 7 bolts. Kenny Barker, 2007.

❹ **Blue Sunday** 5.13a ★★
An obvious mix of ledges and steep, switching dihedral/arêtes that splits the Sanctuary cave in the middle and shares the last few bolts of *Peace Frog*. Originally, the start was extremely chossy, but has cleaned up over time.
70 ft. 8 bolts. Jason Forrester, 2008. Equipped by Kenny Barker.

❺ **Peace Frog** 5.12d ★★★★
Begin just right of *Blue Sunday*. Climb up to a ledge, then move out a low roof to gain the overhanging, well-featured face. Make several large moves to a decent rest before the final steep run to the chains.
80 ft. 8 bolts. Brian Boyd, Greg Martin, 2005.

❻ **Hoosier Boys** 5.12d ★
Begin just right of *Peace Frog*. Climb up and over a roof to gain the steep face. Sharp pockets lead to a big sidepull move, then more pockets to a suspect flake. Carefully pass the flake and continue the chains.
80 ft. 9 bolts. Mike Kerzhner, Greg Martin, 2005.

Cherry Red

❶ **Perfidious Deciduous** 5.11b ★★
This overhanging crack is on the left side of the main wall just before you turn the corner to Indy Wall. Boulder up the initial overhanging crux to a good rest on a ledge. Layback and face climb on good holds to the chains.
55 ft. Jason Haas, Sarah Maclean, 2004.

THE SANCTUARY

Peace Frog to Jesus Wept

Prometheus Unbound 5.13a ★★★★★
Boulder up and mantel the initial face right of *Hoosier Boys*, then pull on crimps to reach the steeper section. Continue to the steep face, passing a pocket crux near the middle of the line. Grab a shake, then continue through more sustained climbing and pull a small roof to reach the chains.
75 ft. 10 bolts.
Greg Martin, Brian Boyd, Jeremy Stitch, Tommy Wilson, 2004.

Jesus Wept 5.12d ★★★★★
Begin beneath the amphitheater. Boulder through the initial section, trending right, to reach a steep pocketed face that quickly becomes more vertical with fewer holds. Aesthetic climbing with several cruxes along the way. Requires a 70-meter rope. A two-bolt direct start climbs the arête and chedral to the right, meeting up with the normal route at the fourth bolt. Dubbed *Atlas Shrugged* (5.12d) — FA Kris Hampton, 2008.
75 ft. 11 bolts. Tim Powers, Mike Susko, 2004.

❾ **Triple Sec** 5.12d ★★★★★
AKA *50 Bucks*. In between *Jesus Wept* and *Immaculate Deception* is a beautiful, blank, yellow-and-black face with small pockets and a few visible crimps. A no-hands rest breaks up the climb after a bouldery crux. Good face climbing leads to a deceptive crux near the top.
95 ft. 9 bolts.
Andrew McDonald, Peter Maroni, Greg Martin, Brian Boyd, 2004.

Photo: Andrew Burr.

Zach Ruswick on *Jesus Wept*, 5.12d, (previous page). Photo: John Wesely

Triple Sec

Blue Collar

⓿ Buddha Slept 5.12a ★★★★
Climb the first three bolts of *Immaculate Deception*, then continue up and left to a good stance below a gorgeous left-leaning crack. Enjoy fine finger-locking and laybacking until you reach a thin dihedral below the chimney. Crank on up and clip the anchors on *Triple Sec*, or continue up the chimney to an exposed ledge with bolted anchors on the right.
100 ft. 3 bolts. Jared Hancock, 2005.

❶ Immaculate Deception 5.11d ★★★
Start from the ground or a ledge 10 feet up. Begin on two undercling crimps and make a long move to a two-finger pocket. Hang on through the thin crux, then relax on the ledge before beginning the balancey, technical arête. Ride the arête, then step left to finish via a sensational overhanging jug haul to an anchor under the roof.
90 ft. 9 bolts. Jared Hancock, Tim Powers, Mike Susko, 2004.

❷ Dirty Old Men 5.8+ ★★★
The right-facing dihedral right around the corner and uphill from *Immaculate Deception*. Climb a wide hand crack to a slot. Layback and jam to an offwidth. Slither up the offwidth to a good stance, then jam to a large ledge and belay. Traverse the ledge left around a corner to anchors. Rappel 90 feet — knot your rope ends!) to descend.
80 ft. Tom Kwasny, Brad Truax, 2004.

⓭ Cruxifixion 5.12d ★★★
The long and aesthetic vertical orange face right of *Dirty Old Men*. Begin with a difficult direct-start boulder problem, then mellow out on 5.12b to the chains.
90 ft. 9 bolts. Jared Hancock, 2006.

⓮ Blue Collar 5.12b ★★★★
This route climbs the face left of the *First Fall* dihedral. Make a big move (or a few thin moves) to the first bolt, then crimp and crank your way to a powerful, technical crux between the fourth and fifth bolts.
55 ft. 6 bolts. Jared Hancock, Tim Powers, 2004.

⓯ First Fall 5.8 ★★★★
A must-do for the 5.8 trad leader. Start in a blocky, left-facing dihedral. Climb up, then step left to a hand crack. Continue up through a bulge to the anchors.
60 ft. Karla Carandang, Jared Hancock, 2004.

⓰ Conquistador of the Crumbly 5.10+ ★
AKA *S-Crack*. Mixed gear and bolts, and not the best rock. Improvise a start to reach the high first bolt. Surmount the bolted bulge, then crack-climb to a bolt-protected traverse. Follow the curving finger/hand/fist crack to a set of anchors inside a high hueco.
75 ft. 2 bolts. Jared Hancock, Karla Carandang, 2005.

THE SANCTUARY

123

INNER SANCTUM

13 routes

Inner Sanctum is the section of cliffline right of the Sanctuary; its routes are mostly slabby to vertical. Two popular 5.10s, *Naughty Neighbors* and *Bad Company*, mark the beginning of the wall, while the excellent crimpfest *Psyberpunk* marks the end.

Approach: From the Sanctuary, hike right from *First Fall* a few hundred feet until you reach a dip in the trail where the trail switches back. Head back uphill from the dip and look for the first bolted line, which is *Tabernacle*.

If headed to Inner Sanctum from the parking area, follow the road to the right, located near the entrance to the parking area, and find a short trail on the left that leads to another road. This road winds downhill to reach the valley floor near a stream. Skip the first left on the road as it doglegs back left and immediately crosses the stream and instead continue along the road until you reach a field on the left. Walk through the field to a stream crossing and continue past the first trail on the left, which leads to the Sanctuary and Indy Wall. Eventually you will reach another trail on the left, which winds uphill to meet the cliff on the far right side of the Sanctuary. Walk right and down through a gully, then head back up and look for the first bolted line: *Tabernacle*.

Conditions: Most lines get wet during even light rain, though *Naughty Neighbors* and *Bad Company* stay drier than the rest.

❶ Tabernacle 5.12a ★★★
This is the first line encountered at Inner Sanctum and begins on a ledge. Climb through cryptic moves on the gently overhanging wall on the right side of a corridor. Exciting runout to the third bolt.
80 ft. 8 bolts. Justin Riddell, 2007.

❷ Baer Necessity 5.11b
Right of *Tabernacle* and left of a crack is this bolted line. Climb a steep layback seam to an overhanging face. It's currently really, really dirty.
60 ft. 9 bolts. Simeon Heimowitz, 2012.

❸ Naughty Neighbors 5.10d ★★★
Walk right from *Tabernacle* beneath an overhang and look for two bolted lines that begin on a ledge. This is the left line. Begin from the ledge and climb incut crimps, sidepulls, pockets, and plates up the slightly overhanging face.
55 ft. 5 bolts. Jared Hancock, Karla Carandang, 2004.

❹ Bad Company 5.10a ★★★★
This is the bolted route about 10 feet right of *Naughty Neighbors*. Fun vertical climbing on flakes, sidepulls, and jugs.
50 ft. 5 bolts. Tim Powers, Mike Susko, 2004.

❺ The Universe Next Door 5.8
Just right of *Bad Company* is a discontinuous crack system that jogs right and then back left after a short, blank face section.
55 ft. Greg Martin, Brian Boyd, 2004.

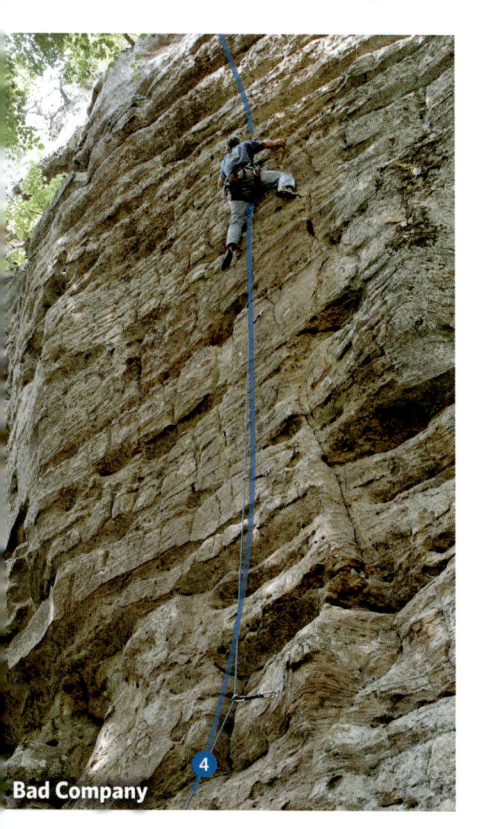

INNER SANCTUM

Bad Company

Netizen Hacktivist

Karmic Retribution 5.10d ★★★★
The next sport route right of *Bad Company*. Begin with positive crimps on a moderate slab, up to a prominent rib. Reach left up the steepening face to good pockets and an interesting finish below the large ledge.
75 ft. 5 bolts. *Jared Hancock, Karla Carandang, 2004.*

Crack 'n Up 5.7 ★★
Just right of *Karmic Retribution* is this easy crack. Walk up the initial wide section to a short offwidth layback followed by a few chimney moves, surmounting the occasional obstacle along the way.
50 ft. *Karla Carandang, Jared Hancock, 2004.*

Quaquaversal Crack 5.8+ ★★
Locate an obvious cave 40 feet up the wall. Begin on the easy, right-angling flake right of *Crack 'n Up* and climb up and right to a single bolt before entering the giant hueco. Stem, jam, and face-climb up and out of the cave. Exposed stemming will take you to the anchors.
75 ft. 1 bolt. *Jared Hancock, Karla Carandang, 2005.*

Netizen Hacktivist 5.9+ ★★★
Balance up the steepening slab right of the previous line until you reach an orange water groove. Ascend the sculpted shelves, edges, pinches, and pockets. Watch out for furry, flying, four-legged friends along the way.
70 ft. 7 bolts. *Jared Hancock, Karla Carandang, 2005.*

Cosmic Trigger 5.12b ★★★★
An obvious black arête with a golden, bolted face to the right. Moderate climbing on jugs and pinches leads to a good bouldery crux. Mantel past the final bolt to anchors on the roof.
70 ft. 7 bolts. *Greg Martin, Brian Boyd, 2004.*

Cybersex 5.7 ★
Just left of *Psyberpunk* is a large flake protected with large gear. Easy climbing leads to a ledge in the middle of the wall. A short crack leads to a large ledge. Put in a directional and belay off *Psyberpunk's* anchors.
65 ft. *Greg Martin, Brian Boyd, 2004.*

Psyberpunk 5.11c ★★★★
Move 60 feet right of *Cybersex*, past a large boulder/flake leaning against the main wall, then up to a small ledge. Mostly jugs to two crimpy face sections to exit jugs.
65 ft. 7 bolts. *Greg Martin, Brian Boyd, 2004.*

Consenting Adult 5.11b ★★★★
Great technical face climbing that features a very distinct crux mid-ride.
65 ft. 6 bolts. *Dustin Stephen, Scott Curran, 2016.*

THE STADIUM

MUIR VALLEY

25 routes

The Stadium is primarily for trad climbers — most of the lines require at least one piece of gear. Start on the left side and do *Tradisfaction*, *Kentucky Waterfall*, *Dreamtheiver*, and *In a Pinch* and you will be one respected hard traddy; each route is stout and high quality. For non-masochists, two of Muir's better sport 5.12s, *The Pessimist* and *Cheetah*, sit side by side on the far right edge.

Approach: If headed to the Stadium from the parking area, follow the road to the right, located near the entrance to the parking area, and find a short trail on the left that leads to another road. This road winds downhill to reach the valley floor near a stream. Skip the first left on the road as it doglegs back left and immediately crosses the stream. Instead, continue along the road until you reach a field on the left. Walk through the field, cross the stream, and continue past the first trail on the left, which leads to the Sanctuary and Indy Wall. Eventually you will reach another trail on the left, which leads to Inner Sanctum. Continue past this trail and within a couple of minutes the trail will head left and uphill to meet the cliff just beneath the splitter crack *No Bones About It*. *Tradisfaction*, *Kentucky Waterfall*, etc. are about 300 feet left, past a rocky area.

Conditions: *Tradisfaction* and *Kentucky Waterfall* are good candidates for rainy days. The other climbs can be hit or miss.

❷ **Tradisfaction** 5.10b ★★★★
Begin in a large left-facing chimney. Continue up to a ledge to enjoy this satisfying dihedral. Stem, jam, and layback to a pumpy finish. Classic.
80 ft. *Jared Hancock, 2004.*

❸ **Dreamtheiver** 5.12a ★★★★
The striking roof crack above *Tradisfaction*. Climb *Tradisfaction* to the anchors, then traverse right and set a belay in a cave. Crank out the roof and continue to the top of the wall.
35 ft. *Bart Bledsoe, 2006.*

❹ **In a Pinch** 5.11b ★★★
This climb is the next dihedral about 60 feet right of *Tradisfaction*. It starts as a thin, left-facing dihedral, which leads to a large roof protected by a bolt. Rap anchors are over the lip to avoid having to climb the chossy rock to the top.
80 ft. *Ken Thompson, Jeff Smith, 2004.*

❺ **Indecision** 5.8 ★★★★
This highly recommended route begins left of where the approach trail meets the cliff. Begin with easy face climbing left of the arête, then step right to gain the crack. Enjoy the ride and soak in the view of the valley from the top. Lower from rap anchors.
95 ft. *Ed Griffiths, Jeff Smith, Ken Thompson, 2004.*

❶ **Kentucky Waterfall** 5.11a ★★★
A variation finish to *Tradisfaction*. Start on *Tradisfaction* and traverse left, following the arching flake.
80 ft. *Loren Wood, 2004.*

Adam Brusven on *Tradisfaction*, 5.10b (opposite). Photo: Mike Wilkinson.

MUIR VALLEY

In a Pinch

No Bones About It

6 Psycho Billy Cadillac 5.10+ ★
If you just climbed *Indecision*, then leave it at that and go home with a smile. Otherwise, climb this line 15 feet to the right. Jug up steep rock past two bolts and a tricky roof move. Step right, then continue to the top with some bolt-protected face and crack climbing.
95 ft. 6 bolts J.J., Jared Hancock, 2006.

7 Walk the Line 5.9 ★★★
Begin five feet right of *Psycho Billy*. Climb overhanging rock past two bolts to a roof. Climb the left side of the roof to a soothing splitter crack. Follow the splitter to a slab topout protected by a bolt.
100 ft. 3 bolts Jared Hancock, J.J., 2006.

8 Flying J 5.12b ★★
Begin on jugs near an obvious overhanging arête left of a b beech tree. A steep start will take you to the high first bolt. big or find the pinch undercling, then continue slightly up a left on the lower-angled face, with protection in horizontals. Finish on an overhanging, bolt-protected face. Beware of th tree, which could possibly break your fall.
80 ft. 5 bolts. Nick Walker, Jared Hancock, 2006.

9 Ring of Fire 5.12a ★★★★
The line of glue-ins 10 feet left of *No Bones*. Cruxy steep climbing down low gives way to stimulating face climbing o quality orange pockets and a spicy anchor run.
80 ft. 9 bolts. Dustin Stephens, Steve Sandman, 2014.

10 No Bones About It 5.10b ★★★
A steep thin-hands start leads to a widening, right-arching crack. Traverse slightly up and right at the top of the arch and climb through soft rock to a short hand crack. Finish by traversing left to ledge with slings on tree. The first-ascent party found a lot of bones on the way up, hence the route name. It's possible to climb over to the anchors on *Scrumbulglazer* to avoid choss pushing for the last 30 feet.
90 ft. Ken Thompson, Jeff Smith, Ed Griffiths, 2004.

11 Scrumbulglazer 5.10d ★★★
This route is the left of two sport routes between *No Bones Abc It* and *ED*. Steep start with jugs and pockets. Good clipping hole with a thin, balancey crux, then sidepulls to the top.
60 ft. 6 bolts. Gregg Purnell, 2005.

12 Melancholy Mechanics 5.10d ★★★
The technical face right of *Scrumbulglazer* is fun, but slight dirty. It may have cleaned up over time.
60 ft. 6 bolts.
Gregg Purnell, Mark Ryan, J.J., Jared Hancock, 2005.

13 ED 5.7 ★★★
A left-facing dihedral with large holds. Step right after approximately 50 feet to anchors above a ledge.
50 ft. Ed Griffiths, Ken Thompson, 2004.

14 Augenblick 5.10c ★★★
This line, previously a mossy and crunchy toprope named *Stadium Slab*, is the bolted route just right of *ED*.
80 ft. 8 bolts. J.J., Jared Hancock, Karla Carandang, 2006.

15 Tug-o-War 5.11b ★★★★
Thin, techy, sustained slab on the face right of *Augenblick*.
80 ft. 9 bolts. Karla Carandang, Jared Hancock, J.J., 2006.

Treetop Terror 5.10d ★★★★

...s route begins 20 feet right of an arête. Climb a fingery
...e to reach a hand crack, which leads to a featured slab
...tected by bolts.
...olts. *Jared Hancock, Rob Copeland, Barry Brolley, J.J.,*
...rk Ryan, 2006.

Arêterection 5.11c ★★★★

...s is the obvious and aesthetic arête. Bouldery up to the
...d bolt. Although the climbing is better in the beginning left
...he arête, it's a bit more mellow on the right side.
...ft. 9 bolts. *Jared Hancock, JJ, Gregg Purnell, 2005.*

Environmental Imperialism 5.8 ★

...e dihedral above *Arêterection*. Much easier than it appears.
...ft. *Jared Hancock, 2005.*

Ascentuality 5.11a ★★★★

...ow the cliffline right past the previous line for about 100
...t to this route. Climb a technical face past three bolts to
...ch a steep, striking, orange dihedral. Clean and classic.
...ft. 3 bolts. *Jared Hancock, Karla Carandang, 2004.*

Endangered Species 5.11b ★★★★

...uldery face leads to an amazing sandtone tufa. Belay up
...h on a ledge system that is best accessed from the right.
...wo-bolt extension bumps the grade to 12- and is worth
...mbing if dry.
...ft. 6 bolts. *Dustin Stephens, Symon Ardila, 2015.*

Gnome Wrecker 5.10d ★★★

...eresting slab and face climbing left of *The Pessimist*. An
...kward anchor placement, but an otherwise enjoyable climb.
...ft. 7 bolts. *Dustin Stephens 2014*

The Pessimist 5.12c ★★★★

...s impressive line starts 80 feet right of *Ascentuality*.
...mb a short flake system to reach an obvious bucket. Bust
...ough an unlikely sequence to reach increasingly better
...lds. Move right and climb the striking and sustained orange
...eak to a horizontal break.
...ft. 6 bolts. *Matt Hoffman, Bob Peterson, Peter Morone, 2006.*

Cheetah 5.12a ★★★★

...e next bolted line on the orange-and-black-streaked wall.
...mb through powerful cruxes separated by good rests.
...ft. 5 bolts. *Bob Peterson, Matt Hoffman, Paul Coover, 2006.*

El Patron 5.13a ★★★

...stunning, overhanging orange streak.
...ft. 11 bolts. *Gregg Purnell, Mike Duncan, 2005.*

THE STADIUM

Augenblick

The Pessimist

㉕ Water Music 5.12c ★★★★

Long, varied, overhanging face with a unique obtuse dihedral
halfway up.
95 ft. 10 bolts. *Symon Ardila, Dustin Stephens, 2014.*

STRONGHOLD WALL

2 routes

A couple hundred yards past Ivory Tower wall, this 35-meter wall only has five routes currently. Three are difficult projects. The other two are exceptional 5.13a's that wouldn't be out of place at the Motherlode. At press time this crag was mostly a work in progress; check redriverclimbing.com for updated route info.

Approach: Hike as you would for the Sanct and the Stadium. Just after the bridge, when trail heads steeply uphill and left to the Stadiu go right on a smaller trail to cross the creek a head up the staircase. First you will come Ivory Tower, but walk further and you'll find t inspiring wall.

❶ Geronimo 5.13a ★★★★

120 feet? Yep. This traversing line on the far right side of t wall goes a long way. To reduce rope drag, back clean the first couple of draws. 70-meter rope mandatory!
120 ft. 13 bolts. Symon Ardila, Dustin Stephens, 2016.

❷ Rock the Casbah 5.13a ★★★★★

Start 20 feet left of *Geronimo* on a boulder. This "line of lea resistance" turned out to be pretty resistant. Static climbe should leave their prefered style on the ground.
105 ft. 12 bolts. Symon Ardila, Dustin Stephen, 2016.

There are three projects left of *Rock the Casbah.*

Stronghold Wall

IVORY TOWER

20 min 20 min 37.7301 -83.6318

Continuing left along the Tectonic Wall cliff line leads across a gully to the Ivory Tower. It currently contains a few decent lines and open projects but is still under development. *Astrodog* is a fantastic voyage that makes a visit worthwhile.

Approach: Follow the main approach to Tectonic Wall and continue on a new trail for 200 yards, down a staircase and back up the other side of a steep gully.

Song of Solomon 5.13b ★★★
...e farthest left line. A vertical start leads to a hard crux ...owed by superb moves on an overhanging, right-leaning ...te. Hard for the grade.
...ft. 7 bolts. *Adam Taylor, 2013. Equipped by Dustin Stephens.*

The Stallion 5.12b ★★★
...ping holds lead to an overhanging wave of rock with a ...ulder-problem crux at the last bolt. The two-bolt extension ...ove the first anchor is an open project.
...ft. 8 bolts. *Dustin Stephens, 2011.*

The Agile Process 5.11d ★★★
...rounded, mossy arête leads to moves out a big roof. This is ...decent warm-up, but stays wet after many days of rain.
...ft. 7 bolts. *Dustin Stephens, 2011.*

❹ Ivory Tower 4 Open Project
Left of *Astrodog* are two open projects. This left line opens with a bouldery start.
100 ft. Equipped by Dustin Stephens.

❺ Ivory Tower 5 Open Project
This open project is the right of the two lines left of *Astrodog*.
100 ft. Equipped by Dustin Stephens.

❻ Astrodog 5.12c ★★★★
This great line that goes to the top of the wall gets rave reviews. The tree that grows close to the wall has been trimmed and is no longer an issue for the climber. A 60-meter rope will barely get you down — tie a knot in the end.
100 ft. 12 bolts. Jimmy Farrell, Dustin Stephens, 2011.

❼ Ivory Tower 7 Open Project
Right and downhill of *Astrodog* is this project that starts with a low roof. Expect hard moves at the second and third bolt — and bring a brush.
85 ft. 9 bolts. Equipped by Dustin Stephens.

The Stallion

Astrodog

KIPP TRUMMEL
(the guy with the drill)

Kipp and Karen. Photo: Trummel collecti[on]

It's rare that we know who the first ascensionist of a route is if we haven't seen some superhuman rock star's thwarted attempts at it in the latest video. Even more rare is knowing who took time away from their climbing to jug up and down the ropes to drill and bolt the routes we play on. But if you bolt enough quality lines, people will eventually catch on to who you are and may even thank you for what you are doing. Kipp Trummel has done just that. Kipp has bolted over 250 lines including classics such as *Amarillo Sunset*, *Samurai*, *Iniquity*, and *Zendebad*.

Kipp, with his wife, Karen, moved to Lexington, KY, from Illinois in 2005 and immediately jumped into the bolting scene with his first route in the Red, *Supress the Rage*. Immediately afterward, he was greeted by the late and colorful local legend Terry Kindred, who asked him, **"What's up with the crappy anchor placement?"** Not long after that incident, Kipp had one of his red-tagged projects snagged by a local (which turned out to be a misunderstanding). It wasn't a great introduction to developing in the Red, but Kipp's thick skin helped him to shrug it off and keep drilling away.

Kipp's biggest task came in the winter of 2007 when Rick Weber, the owner of Muir Valley, offered to provide all the hardware if Kipp would put some routes up at what came to be known as Midnight Surf.

Not many people would jump at the "opportunity" to bolt a north-facing, severely overhanging wall using mostly glue-in bolts in the dead of winter. After **80 hours in a matter of a few weeks**, and a near-miss with a descending rope that had turned into an ice-covered deathtrap, Kipp had bolted some of the most unique and classic new routes in the Red. But you look at the first ascensionists these particular routes you'll noti[ce] Kipp is only on one of them. Wh[y?] Because **Kipp is known to giv[e] his buddies a shot at h[is] routes** even if he is close to sendi[ng] them. It is apparent that his joy com[es] from envisioning and bolting the lin[e] and in the words of Kipp, "leaving t[he] sending to those who actually train."

Most people say that route develope[rs] only bolt for themselves, and oth[er] climbers just reap the benefits [of] their selfish endeavors. Kipp is t[he] exception. **He bolts routes as [a] creative outlet** with no regard [to] whether the line is within his ability [or] not. So if you are ever out climbing a[nd] hear the sound of a hammerdrill a[nd] the clank of a five-piece Rawl bei[ng] pounded into sandstone, stroll on ov[er,] drop a six pack of Avalanche Ale at t[he] base of the static line, and yell than[ks] to the guy with the drill. ■

TECTONIC AND JOHNNY'S WALLS

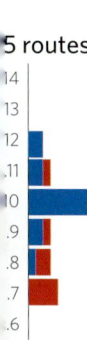

5 routes

These walls are great for climbers breaking into 5.10 and looking to experience the infamous RRG forearm pump. They have excellent 5.10s, including the extremely popular *Gettin' Lucky in Kentucky* and *Plate Tectonics*. Recent development at the left end of the Tectonic Wall has doubled the route count and diversified this small wall with some enjoyable 5.12s.

TECTONIC WALL

❶ LIDAR 5.8
Follow the cliffline 200 feet left of Tectonic Wall. Scramble to a belay ledge below a vertical crack that gives way to horizontal features near the top. Protect the crux and pull into the first horizontal, then stem and chimney to the anchors.
70 ft. 6 bolts. *Brett Stark, Rob Copeland, 2008.*

Approach: Follow the approach to the Sanctuary, but instead of taking the trail on the left after crossing the stream, take the trail on the right, which winds up the hill to the middle of Tectonic Wall and Johnny's Wall. If you walk right a few feet when the trail meets the cliff, you'll see a nice-looking wall with several bolted lines. This is Johnny's Wall, and the first route you come to is *59-Inch Drill Bitch*. The Tectonic Wall lies to the left; the first bolted route you encounter walking left from where the trail meets the cliff is *Tall Cool One*.

Conditions: The walls' slightly overhanging nature provides for decent rainy-day climbing.

❷ Excellent, Slithers 5.9+ ★★
Grunt, slither, and squeeze your way up the overhanging slot, with just enough footholds to keep it from being truly unpleasant. Several large cams up to BD #5 & #6 recommended. Can also be set up on toprope by climbing up and left from the *Serpentine* anchor.
40 ft. *Dustin Stephens, Rick Weber, 2013.*

❸ Serpentine 5.10b ★★★
Slither up the arête to an enjoyable finish. Thought-provoking and unique.
45 ft. 6 bolts. *Dustin Stephens, Rick Weber, 2013.*

LIDAR

Serpentine

Cottonmouth

Getting Lucky in Kentucky

4 Cottonmouth 5.12b ★★★
Wander up the gently overhanging face to some large moves on small, not-so-positive dishes. Dont expect any big holds until it's all over.
45 ft. 6 bolts. Justin Miniard, 2016. Equipped by Dustin Stephens.

5 Ball and Chain 5.12b ★★★
Finesse your way up the face to a burly boulder problem complete with a big dyno and an exciting run to the chains.
45 ft. 6 bolts. Chaz Ott, Dustin Stephens, 2013.

6 Dime a Dozen 5.11a ★★★
The rightmost sport route on this section of wall is balancey, with a section in the middle that will feel harder than 5.11a for short people.
45 ft. 8 bolts. Dustin Stephens, Rick Weber, 2013.

7 Frozen Bananas 5.10b ★★
Located in a cave to the right of *Dime a Dozen*. Negotiate a start to reach a flake and climb it to the roof. Then jam and stem out the roof to anchors around the corner.
40 ft.
Bryce Noonan, Bryan Battles, Cameron Link, Luke Rhoades, 2014.

8 Tectonic 5 Open Project
This project climbs to the shared anchor with *Frozen Bananas*.
40 ft.

9 Gettin' Lucky in Kentucky 5.10b ★★★★
The leftmost bolted route on this section wall. Enjoyable, pumpy, technical climbing on jugs, pockets, sidepulls, and underclings to a steep finish. Classic.
60 ft. 6 bolts. Jared Hancock, Karla Carandang, Tom & Ines Truesdale, 2004.

10 Plate Tectonics 5.10a ★★★★
The route right of *Gettin' Lucky*. A tricky start to enjoyable, pumpy climbing on huge plates. Classic.
65 ft. 6 bolts.
Jared Hancock, Karla Carandang, Rick & Liz Weber, 2004.

11 Fifth-Bolt Faith 5.10c ★★★
Fifteen feet right of *Plate Tectonics*. This route follows an interesting variety of holds: pinches, slopers, plates, underclings — you name it. Fun moves.
55 ft. 6 bolts. Jared Hancock, Mark Ryan, Karla Carandang, 200

12 Continental Drift 5.7 ★★
A mixed route between *Fifth-Bolt Faith* and *Tall Cool One*.
80 ft. 3 bolts. Harini Aiyer, 2008.

13 Tall Cool One 5.9 ★★★
Located 10 feet right of *Fifth-Bolt Faith*, on the left-facing wall. Move right from the first bolt on the face toward the crack to gain a ledge. Pull the small overhang to climb plate to the chains.
60 ft. 6 bolts. Tim Powers, Jeff Neal, Mike Susko, 2004.

Jessy Baker on *Plate Tectonics*, 5.10a (page 134). Photo: John Wesely.

14 Paraplegic Power 5.7 ★★

When walking to Tectonic Wall from where the approach tr meets with the cliff, this is the first route you will encounte It climbs the crack just right of *Tall Cool One*. Work left and pull the roof, protecting with a slung block and horizontals. Continue up a wide crack, then move left to the anchors on *Tall Cool One*.

60 ft. *Can Beck, Caleb Heimlich, 2007.*

JOHNNY'S WALL

15 59-Inch Drill Bitch 5.10a ★★★

The leftmost route on Johnny's Wall and the first bolted rou encountered when walking right from where the approach trail meets the cliff between Tectonic and Johnny's. Climb vertical plates, edges, and pockets. Jug up and right to the interesting finish.

45 ft. 5 bolts. *Karla Carandang, Jared Hancock, 2004.*

16 Bethel 5.10a ★★★

Follow incut plates to a big move and juggy finish.

50 ft. 5 bolts. *Tim Powers, Jeff Neal, Mike Susko, 2004.*

17 Spinner 5.10a ★★★

Similar to *Bethel*, with a more difficult finish. Pull over the bulge on subtle holds to the anchors.

50 ft. 5 bolts. *Tim Powers, Mike Susko, 2004.*

18 Mancala 5.10b ★★★

Start on the boulder right of *Spinner*. Pick a path up the jug plates to an interesting bulge and a fierce finish.

45 ft. 4 bolts. *Jared Hancock, Rob Copeland, J.J., Karla Carandang, 2006.*

19 Burning Bush 5.11a ★★★

Fifteen feet right of *Mancala* is another overhanging jug ha You may want to place a piece of gear in the crack betwee the first and second bolt. Climb jugs to a well-defined crim and-crank crux just before the anchors.

50 ft. 4 bolts. *J.J., Rob Copeland, Jared Hancock, 2006.*

20 Climbing With Crowbars 5.7 ★

Move 50 feet right from *Burning Bush* to locate this chimne with a nice blocky dihedral and crack system. Bolted ancho

50 ft. *Mark Ryan, Jenny Ryan, J.J., 2006.*

21 Thanks Holly 5.8 ★★

Right of *Climbing with Crowbars* is this slabby arête. Follow big holds to anchors above a final ledge.

45 ft. 5 bolts. *Mike Trabel, Mike Susko, 2006.*

Bethel

Burning Bush

Thanks Holly

2 Two Chicken Butts 5.9 ★★
Twelve feet right of the arête is a slabby wall loaded with more huge holds.
45 ft. 5 bolts. *Mike Trabel, Mike Susko, 2006.*

3 Mental Affair 5.8 ★
Begin eight feet right of a tree. Climb to a ledge and pull into a crack. Climb the crack to a face, then run it to the anchors.
45 ft. *JJ, Mike Susko, Holly Trabel, 2006.*

4 Brain Stem 5.7 ★
Shoot up a short, striking dihedral, then wander out a roof to locate a bolt on the slabby face above. Bolted anchors.
50 ft. 1 bolt. *J.J., Jane Maurer, Mark Ryan, Jenny Wagner, 2006.*

5 Grey Matter 5.10b ★
Toprope. Just right of *Brain Stem* is a thin, slabby arête. This toprope line climbs the face right of the arête. Make a few long reaches and enjoy some technical climbing to gain the juggy slab above.
40 ft. *Jared Hancock, J.J., Rob Copeland, 2006.*

JOHNNY'S WALL

137

LAND BEFORE TIME WALL

37.723
-83.631

7 routes Close to the car, with friendly grades and high stars, this popular crag offers some fun climbing — mostly short — on edges and pockets galore.

.14
.13
.12
.11
.10
.9
.8
.7
≤.6

Approach: Approach this and the rest of the Muir Valley crags via the "Main Trail South," the right fork of the trail leaving the parking lot. Head toward the valley floor, but before the floor and while on the staircase, turn right and follow the signs. Three minutes of easy trail, through a really cool arch, leads you to the wall.

❶ Basilisk 5.5 ★
The leftmost route on the wall is very short. Find the snake hold as you climb the featured face to a fun finish.
20 ft. 2 bolts. Isaac Heacock, 2010.

❷ Coprolite 5.8 ★
Cruise past small pockets and a hand jam on this subpar route, if you just have to climb it.
30 ft. 3 bolts. Isaac Heacock, 2010.

❸ Neanderfall 5.9 ★★
Smear up a slab to reach a bulge. Pull over it on plates to some slopers, then walk up to the ledge. Almost always wet.
60 ft. 5 bolts. Isaac Heacock, Tony English, 2010.

❹ Watering Hole 5.10a ★★★
Start on a ledge with a large hole in it. Climb past pockets, side pulls, and a challenging roof move. Stop at the first anchor if you plan to toprope this route. The original, higher anchor is set back on a ledge. If continuing to this anchor, it's recommended to top belay and rap off, or risk a stuck rope and/or rope drag over sharp edges.
50 ft. 5 bolts. Isaac Heacock, 2010.

❺ Ryanosaurus 5.9 ★★★
Start on the large block. Mantel onto a sloping ledge, then get your feet up to pull over the roof. Climb jugs to the top.
55 ft. 5 bolts. Ryan Jones, 2010. Equipped by Isaac Heacock.

❻ Prehistoric Extermination 5.8+ ★★★★
Climb through plated jugs to a balancey, tricky finish with a crimp and a sidepull.
55 ft. 6 bolts. Tony English, 2010. Equipped by Isaac Heacock.

❼ Sabertooth 5.10c ★★★
The grade of this route reflects a direct start below the first bolt. Traversing in eases the difficulty. Small pockets and crimps lead to good plates above. Mantel the top to the anchors. Toproping this route is not recommended due to significant rope rub on the ledge up top.
50 ft. 6 bolts. Isaac Heacock, 2010.

Prehistoric Extermination

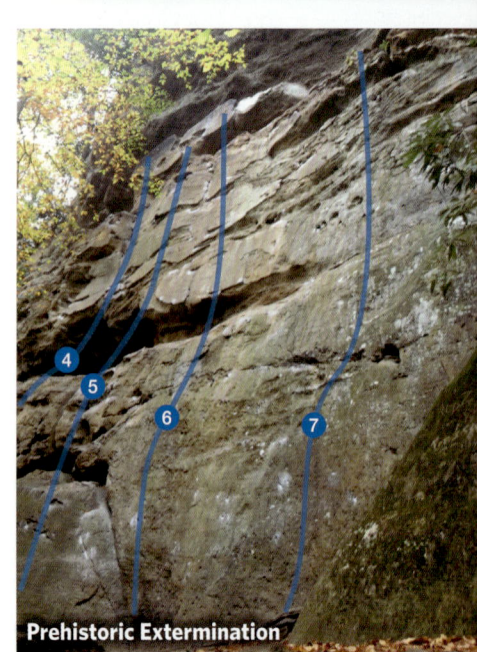

FRONT PORCH

The Front Porch has a nice overhanging face with a comfortable belay area, and shade most of the day.

Approach: Hike the "Main Trail South" to the valley floor then veer right past the bridge (not crossing it). Follow signs over a small bridge and follow the switchback trail leading to the beginner area of the wall on its left side.

❽ Dagon Open Project
Like its neighbor to the left but the bottom boulder problem is harder.
60 ft. 8 bolts. Equipped by Kipp Trummel, 2011.

❾ Dustopian Left Open Project
This route, and the following two, are grouped together about 75 feet right of the previous routes. Walk past a narrow section of ledge protected by a wire hand rail to gain the nice belay area.
80 ft. 8 bolts. Equipped by Dustin Stephens.

❿ Dustopian 5.12d ★★★
Start with a hard boulder problem to gain a ledge. After the ledge, good crimps and mail slots lead to a few long moves that guard the anchors
80 ft. 8 bolts. Blake Bowling, 2016. Equipped by Dustin Stephens.

⓫ Watching the World Burn 5.12b ★★★
Climb a sequential boulder problem and through some choss to gain a rest ledge. Do another boulder problem off the ledge, then head to the chains via sustained crimping.
80 ft. 8 bolts. Ralph Woolard, Blake Bowling, 2016. Equipped by Dustin Stephens.

Grandma's Rocker 5.4 ★★
is the leftmost route on the short wall located where the approach trail meets the cliff.
ft. 2 bolts. Kipp Trummel, 2011.

Porch Potato 5.4 ★★
middle route on this section of wall.
ft. 2 bolts. Kipp Trummel, 2011.

Dripity Dew Da 5.4 ★★
rightmost route on the short wall where the approach trail meets the cliff. Another very short slab climb.
ft. 2 bolts. Kipp Trummel, 2011.

---

st left of the first three routes listed is a rebar ladder at is used to access a ledge system. The remainder the routes begin from this ledge.

Mint Julip 5.11a ★★
ake a huge move to some OK holds, then fight choss and ab to a set of anchors.
ft. 7 bolts. Scott Brown, 2011. Equipped by Kipp Trummel.

Perros Grande 5.12b ★★
ares a start with *Silent Killer*, but instead of bustin' out ht at the suspect jug, take a left up through decent holds a slab finish.
ft. 7 bolts. Kipp Trummel, 2011.

Silent Killer 5.12c ★★★
me start as *Perros Grande*. Climb up on bad holds to a RY suspect jug that may not survive multiple ascents. Bust ht, taking care not to break too many holds.
ft. 8 bolts. Kipp Trummel, 2011.

Dead but Dreaming 5.13b ★★★
art on powerful sidepulls and slopers to get to the second lt, where better holds begin to appear. Get it back on the st ledge, then take on the headwall.
ft. 8 bolts. Kipp Trummel, 2011.

Dustopian

WASHBOARD WALL

MUIR VALLEY

9 routes

37.72
-83.62

20 min / 20 min

This overhanging wall has great adventure sport climbing, as well as shorter pumpers in the 5.11 range. To fully enjoy Washboard Wall, bring double ropes and trad gear. If not, run up *Barenjager* and *Brushfire Fairytales* and be done with it.

Approach: Take the "Main Trail South" to th[e] valley floor, cross the creek, and take the first tr[ail] on the left. Follow this trail north a few minute[s] until you see the sign for Washboard Wall on th[e] left. Follow the trail a couple of minutes to me[et] up with the main wall.

Conditions: Most lines stay dry in a downpo[ur] and see great sun in the early hours.

1 Sierra's Travels 5.9- ★
Leftmost route to the left of the big cave with a picnic table. Start directly under the first bolt, left-hand slopey crimp to a sidepull, then stand up and follow the obvious line to the anchors.
45 ft. 2 bolts. J.J. (free-solo), 2004.

2 Heard It on NPR 5.10c ★★★
This adventure climb begins with a high first bolt left of *Spider Crux*. Climb through 65 feet of 5.9 on sometimes questionable holds to reach a ledge. Continue through the overhanging pocketed face for 35 feet to reach the anchors. This route is kind of like NPR because you have to wait a long time for something good. Use a 60-meter rope.
100 ft. 11 bolts. Barry Brolley, J.J., 2004.

3 Spider Crux 5.10b ★★
Start under a small roof to gain this attractive, right-leaning hand-and-finger crack. Make a long move, then continue u[p] easier ground to anchors on the ledge. Belay, rappel off her[e] or continue up *Heard It on NPR*.
50 ft. J.J., Barry Brolley, 2004.

4 Cordillera Rojo 5.11a ★
A not-so-great adventure climb with lots of bad rock on the second pitch. Start immediately right of *Spider Crux*. Follow four bolts to the ledge system, then launch up the unrelenti[ng] and imposing headwall above. A 70-meter rope is not long enough to lower off, so use the intermediate anchor or figur[e] out another way down.
115 ft. 12 bolts. Barry Brolley, Keith Raker, 2006.

Photo: Andrew Bu[…]

WASHBOARD WALL

Barenjager 5.10d ★★★
his route ascends the overhanging face 10–15 feet right of
pider Crux. Follow a line of four bolts up pockets, flakes, and
dges to anchors.
0 ft. 4 bolts. *Jared Hancock, Rob Copeland, 2004.*

Brushfire Fairytales 5.11a ★★★
art 10–15 feet right of the previous route. Similar to
arenjager but slightly harder, with bigger, pumpier moves
d a sequential crux.
0 ft. 4 bolts. *Rob Copeland, Jared Hancock, 2004.*

Tradmill 5.7 ★★★
imb the obvious left-leaning ramp. Step around this
ostacle, then cruise up the left-leaning ramp over a small
ulge. Clip the chain anchors on the left, or continue into the
ormous cave. Build an anchor in the cave and belay, or
averse left along the ledge to the *Spider Crux* anchors.
0 ft. *Dave Hoyne, Jared Hancock, Karla Carandang,*
ob Copeland, 2004.

8 Sticks and Stones 5.11+ ★★★
Begin at the base of *Tradmill*. Climb up to the roof and hand-
traverse 10–15 feet right to gain the hand crack. Place some
gear, then crank through the thinning and steepening crack to
a good horizontal. Clip the bolt and make the move to the jug.
Crimp your way to the anchors.
35 ft. 1 bolt. *Jared Hancock, Rob Copeland, 2004.*

9 Bad Dentures 5.9 ★
Toprope. First recorded route in Muir Valley. Walk 100 feet
right of *Sticks and Stones*. Follow a ledge system up to an
arête that is often wet. Climb the left side of the slabby arête
to a large ledge with a tree.
70 ft. *Rick Weber, 2003.*

PRACTICE WALL

MUIR VALLEY

24 routes

The name says it all — it's a great place to learn. An abundance of very short, easy, and well-protected routes awaits those with shiny new quickdraws and ropes. Bring your cams as well, to learn placements on a couple of 20-foot cracks with bolted anchors.

Approach: Take the "Main Trail South" to the valley floor, cross the creek, and take the first trail on the left. Follow the trail north a few minutes until you see the sign for Practice Wall on the left, just after the sign for Washboard Wall. You will arrive beneath the short wall containing *Low Exposure*.

Conditions: The routes here are short, and most are less than vertical. A heavy rain could soak them, but the nature of the rock above should keep the climbs tolerable in a light rain.

Dragon's Mouth

❶ Creeping Elegance 5.11a ★★★
When the approach trail meets the wall just beneath *Slabalito*, continue walking left and slightly uphill, passing beneath a low roof for about 150 feet until you reach more short bolted lines and the obvious chimney that is *Dragon's Mouth*. This is the next bolted line, about 30 feet left of the *Dragon* routes. Slightly pumpy for how short it is.
45 ft. 5 bolts. Jim Taylor, 2008.

❷ Dragon's Tail 5.3 ★★
The low-angle, right-leaning wide crack that begins 15–20 feet left of the *Dragon's Mouth* chimney. This route merges with the last two bolts of *Dragon's Mouth*. Continue to the top of the cliff through a short 3rd-Class gully and rap from tree, or opt for the 5.6 finish to the *Dragon's Mouth* anchors.
60 ft. 2 bolts. Jared Hancock, Sierra Jones, J.J., 2005.

❸ Dragon's Mouth 5.6 ★★
The obvious short, bolted, dirty chimney right of *Dragon's Tail*.
55 ft. 6 bolts. Rick Weber, 2004.

❹ Crescent Moon 5.10a ★★
The next sport route, 15 feet right of the *Dragon's Mouth* chimney. Ascends the featured face on good edges and pockets with a few reachy moves. The difficulty may vary depending on which way you go at the second bolt.
35 ft. 3 bolts. J.J., Mark Ryan, Skip Wolfe, Jared Hancock, 2005.

❺ Crescendo 5.8+ ★★
Right of *Crescent Moon* is another vertical face. Begin with a tough start and end with a short overhanging section.
40 ft. 3 bolts. Jared Hancock, J.J., Skip Wolfe, Mark Ryan, Amy Moore, 2005.

❻ A Happy Ending 5.9 ★★★
Fifty feet right of *Crescendo* is this short, slightly overhanging right-facing dihedral. Climb past a single bolt up to a ledge, then continue to the top past five bolts. The original line stopped at the ledge.
35 ft. 6 bolts. Isaak Heacock, 2009.

❼ The Handout 5.11d ★★★
A short but steep line beginning beneath the head-height roof just right of *A Happy Ending*.
30 ft. 4 bolts. Isaak Heacock, 2011.

Slabalito to Short and Sweet

Slabalito 5.7 ★
Near the point where the trail first meets the cliff, locate this short, bolted line that begins left of the two trees on the obvious short slab.
20 ft. 2 bolts. Maria Gabriela Castro, 2007.

Shawty 5.8 ★
Another short bolted line, 15 feet right of *Slabalito*.
20 ft. 2 bolts. Unknown, 2007.

Low Exposure 5.9 ★★
Crimpy face 25 feet right *Shawty*. This short climb has a brief thin section before topping out onto the ledge. Shares anchors with the dihedral *Short and Sweet*.
25 ft. 3 bolts. Jared Hancock, Sierra Jones, Mark Ryan, 2005.

Short and Sweet 5.7 ★★
The short, left-facing dihedral just right of *Low Exposure*.
20 ft. Mark and Kate Calder, 2004.

Slither and Squeeze 5.2 ★
A few feet right of *Short and Sweet* is this short, unremarkable squeeze chimney.
20 ft. Jared Hancock (free-solo), 2004.

Kate's First Trad Lead 5.1 ★
The slabby crack in a right-facing dihedral with large face holds right of *Short and Sweet*.
20 ft. Kate and Mark Calder, 2004.

Acrophobiacs Anonymous 5.4 ★★
This may be the easiest sport line in the Red. The short slabby face right of *Kate's First Trad Lead* that trends up and left to shared anchors.
25 ft. 3 bolts. Jared Hancock, Karla Carandang, Jane Maurer, Mark Ryan, 2005.

Yu Stin Ki Pu 5.5 ★★
Approximately 20–30 feet right of the previous route is another short novice climb.
20 ft. 3 bolts. Jared Hancock, Skip Wolfe, Mark Ryan, 2005.

MUIR VALLEY

Beta Spewer

Sheet Rock

16 Sweet and Sour 5.5 ★★

This thin, slabby, left-facing dihedral offers sweet climbing, but is sour because it ends way too early. Bolt anchor.
20 ft. Jared Hancock, Skip Wolfe, Mark Ryan, 2005.

17 Ai Bang Mai Fa Kin Ni 5.7 ★★

It can happen if your foot slips. Another short route right of *Sweet and Sour*.
20 ft. 2 bolts. Jared Hancock, Karla Carandang, Jenny Wagner, Mark Ryan, 2005.

18 Mercenary of the Mandarin Chicken 5.9+ ★★

Short, right-leaning arête just right of the previous line.
25 ft. 2 bolts. Karla Carandang, Jared Hancock, Skip Wolfe, 2005.

19 Beta Spewer 5.10b ★★★

Around the corner to the right is this short, overhanging face with fun, flowing moves.
20 ft. 2 bolts. Jared Hancock, Karla Carandang, Skip Wolfe, Mark Ryan, 2005.

20 Smear Tactics 5.11b ★★★

Begins on the ledge above *Beta Spewer*. The name of the route gives you an indication of what you can expect, but only up to the first bolt, after which it eases up.
50 ft. 6 bolts. Jim Taylor, 2009.

21 BDSM 5.10b ★★★

This short, bouldery, overhanging crack is 30 feet right of *Beta Spewer*. Jam, crimp, and power your way to the ledge. Bolted anchor.
25 ft. J.J., Barry Brolley, Jared Hancock, 2005.

22 Night Foxx 5.11d ★★★★

Start 20 feet right of *BDSM*, beneath a ramp. Power through the overhang to gain the ramp, then make a committing third clip. Tackle the crux between the third and fourth bolts, then enjoy easier climbing to tough moves guarding the chains.
60 ft. 6 bolts. Isaak Heacock, Josh Thurston, 2009.

23 Sheet Rock 5.11d ★★★

The next route right of *Night Foxx* has a chain draw on the first bolt and starts on a right-facing flake. Stick-clipping is recommended.
60 ft. 7 bolts. Mark Jedele, Isaac Heacock, 2010.

24 Beastly Traverse 5.11a ★★★

This line follows the left-leaning ramp, beginning as an offwidth right of *Sheet Rock*, and resembles a 5.10 version of *Tradmill* at Washboard. The route is 5.10 trad to the first set of anchors. From there you can continue up bolt-protected, overhanging ledges for a 5.11a finish to another set of anchors.
90 ft. 6 bolts. Loren Wood, J.J., 2005.

GUIDE WALL

37.7278 -83.6275
20 min / 20 min

Similar to the Practice Wall, this short wall hosts a few great routes in the 5.7-5.8 range. A stick clip is recommended. Most of the routes start on a belay ledge, guarded by a rebar ladder, and may not be good for small children.

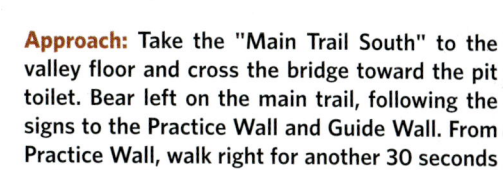

Approach: Take the "Main Trail South" to the valley floor and cross the bridge toward the pit toilet. Bear left on the main trail, following the signs to the Practice Wall and Guide Wall. From Practice Wall, walk right for another 30 seconds to Guide Wall.

❶ Parks and Rec. 5.8 ★★
The leftmost route on this wall is short enough to see what you'll get. A tough start leads to good crimping and the finish jug. A bolt protects the belay.
25 ft. 2 bolts. Isaac Heacock, Ryan Jones, 2010.

❷ Irish Mud 5.8- ★★
Another super-short climb that offers a quick run up small but positive holds, with fun movement. A bolt protects the belay.
25 ft. 2 bolts. Isaac Heacock, Ryan Jones, 2010.

❸ Fear of Commitment 5.7 ★★
Balance up to a hidden jug, then work your feet high to make a reach for some ledges. Get a high step to clip the anchor. A bolt protects the belay.
25 ft. 2 bolts. Isaac Heacock, Ryan Jones, 2010.

❹ The Archeologist 5.7 ★★
Climb the short dihedral to the top of the bulge. Grab jugs, then make a big move at the finish. A bolt protects the belay.
30 ft. 3 bolts. Isaac Heacock, Ryan Jones, 2010.

❺ Built for Life 5.8 ★★★
This is a decent climb with lots of cool moves for the grade: hand jams, crimps, mantels, and jugs.
45 ft. 7 bolts. Isaac Heacock, Ryan Jones, 2010.

❻ Mona Lisa Crack 5.8 ★★
Climb a short crack section to a sloping ledge, then over a bulge and up giant shelves to the anchor.
40 ft. 6 bolts. Isaac Heacock, Ryan Jones, 2010.

RECESS ROCK

MUIR VALLEY

20 min | 20 min | 37.72 / -83.62

4 routes
.14
.13
.12
.11
.10
.9
.8
.7
≤.6

This boulder was kept hidden by the trees and shrubbery for years, but recently cleaned up to host four easy slabs and one short vertical climb.

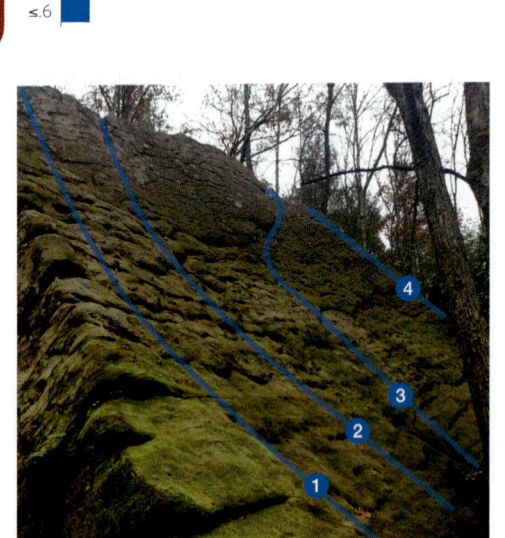

Approach: Follow the directions as you wou going to Washboard Wall (page 140). 200 fe or so after you pass the pit toilet, look for a trail your right, a sign, and a large boulder just insi the tree line.

❶ Child's Play 5.3 ★★★
The leftmost slab climb on this boulder. Start on the lumber deck, staying as far left as possible. Good for people who don't want to use their hands while climbing.
25 ft. 3 bolts. Eric Jones, 2016.

❷ T's Knobs 5.4 ★★★
The next route to the right of the *Child's Play* arête. A bit more challenging, especially toward the top where you must actually use your hands and be more precise with foo placements.
25 ft. 3 bolts. Whitney Maynard, Eric Jones, 2016.

❸ School of Rock 5.4 ★★★
Similar to the route to its left, but just a bit more footwork is needed to wander up the bolt line. Climb to the obvious left-facir crack system. Possibly the best route on the rock.
25 ft. 4 bolts. Erik Kloeker, Eric Jones, 2016.

❹ Who Pooped the Playground? 5.5 ★★
A slightly harder start in the flake system on the right side of this boulder leads to the right arête, where the climbing eases up and is quite fun.
25 ft. 3 bolts. Jenn Gifford, Eric Jones, 2016.

Recess Rock

BRUISE BROTHERS WALL

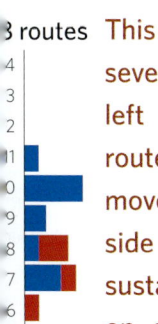

37.7242
-83.6269
20 min / 20 min

This popular wall has several great 5.10s. The left side contains shorter routes with more technical moves, while the far right side contains several long, sustained forearm pumpers on great stone. *Workin' for the Weekend* and *Return of Manimal* are two favorites that climb a gorgeous wall, with big moves between blocky roofs and features. The shorter but fierce *Jungle Trundler* is on you at the start but quickly eases up to a relaxing ride.

Approach: Take the "Main Trail South" to the valley floor, cross the creek, and continue straight past the first trail on the left. (This trail leads to Practice and Washboard walls.) You'll soon reach a fork in the trail. Follow the left fork uphill a few minutes and you'll eventually see the sector where *Jungle Trundler* is, to your left through the trees. An obvious short trail leads up to the wall. Staying on the mail trail about 100 more feet will bring you to *Workin' for the Weekend* and *Manimal*.

Conditions: This wall receives excellent sun, and most of its routes stay dry in the rain. Expect crowds.

Dirt in Eye 5.7 ★
The first four routes are located about 40 feet uphill and left of the logging road, on the small buttress left of the main Bruise Brothers Wall. Climb the hand crack in the short cathedral to a ledge under the first overhang. Once on the ledge, step right behind a boulder and up to rap hangers on the left side of the heuco.
? ft. Mike Susko, Mike Trabel, 2005.

Pine Needle Shuffle 5.6
Right of *Dirt in Eye* is a broken and wandering crack system with some ledges. Climb the crack to a ledge and traverse left to another crack. Continue up, then traverse right to the anchors on *Redeye Brew*.
? ft. J.J., Jared Hancock, 2005.

Redriveroutdoors.com 5.10a ★★
First bolted line right of *Pine Needle Shuffle*. Follows a small flake-like feature to anchors below the ledge.
? ft. 4 bolts. J.J., Jared Hancock, 2005.

Redeye Brew 5.8 ★★
Just right of *Redriveroutdoors.com* is another so-so bolted line. Climb up to a ledge, then follow pockets and edges to top out on another ledge.
? ft. 5 bolts. Jared Hancock, J.J., 2005.

❺ **Flutterby Blue** 5.9 ★★★
This is the first route on the left side of the main Bruise Brothers Wall. Continue hiking down the road from the previous lines to wooden stairs marking the start of the main wall. This line follows an arête with a tough start.
40 ft. 5 bolts. Mike Susko, Stacia Susko, J.J., 2004.

❻ **Tomthievery** 5.8 ★★
AKA *The Sultan Returns*. The blocky, right-facing dihedral about 15 feet right of *Flutterby Blue*. No anchors; traverse off left.
50 ft. Tom Kwasny, Dennis Rice, 2004.

❼ **Stay Off the Radio, Jeff!** 5.9+ ★★
Begin 15 feet right of *Tomthievery*. Start and finish on the slab and negotiate the daunting roof in the middle.
50 ft. 6 bolts. Chad Maurer, Mark Ryan, Jeff Colombo, 2011.

❽ **The Bee's Business** 5.7 ★★★
Next route right of *Stay Off the Radio*. Climb up easy ground to a slight bulge and find the hidden hold to reach the anchors.
50 ft. 6 bolts. Jenny Ryan, Mark Ryan, 2010.

❾ **Sweet Jane** 5.8- ★★
Next right-facing dihedral right of *Tomthievery*.
50 ft. 1 bolt. J.J., Jane Maurer, 2004.

147

MUIR VALLEY

Hey There, Fancy Pants

CH4

⑩ Trundling Kentucky 5.7 ★★
Fifteen feet right of *Sweet Jane* is a decent line with a little bit of everything. Clip the anchors high and to the left on the ledge.
50 ft. 5 bolts. Skip Wolfe, Jeff Colombo, Mark Ryan, 2011.

⑪ Hey There, Fancy Pants 5.10c ★★★
This is the second sport route right of the right-facing dihedral *Sweet Jane*. Follow an obvious, fingery flake up the vertical face, making a couple of long moves along the way.
55 ft. 5 bolts. J.J., Jared Hancock, 2004.

⑫ Jungle Trundler 5.11a ★★★
A bouldery start soon eases to moderate climbing and a short layback/finger-crack feature. Top out onto the large ledge and enjoy the view. May feel easier for tall climbers.
60 ft. 6 bolts. Jared Hancock, J.J., 2004.

⑬ Little Viper 5.10b ★★★
Climb a right-facing flake to very small roof. Clip the fourth bolt, crank a boulder problem, then follow pockets and edges.
50 ft. 6 bolts. Tim Powers, Mike Susko, 2004.

⑭ CH4 5.7 ★★
This is the first bolted route right of a wild-iris patch and intermittent waterfall. Short, fun climbing under a large roof.
30 ft. 3 bolts. J.J. (free solo), 2004.

⑮ Rising 5.11a ★★★
Steep roof above *CH4*. Doable from the ground in one pitch (AKA *Methane Rising*, six bolts). Follow bolts to chain anchor.
30 ft. 3 bolts. Barry Broley, J.J., 2004.

⑯ A-Beano 5.7 ★★
Next bolt line right of *CH4*. Hard first move, heady last move.
30 ft. 3 bolts. Mike Susko, J.J., 2004.

⑰ Immodium AD 5.7 ★★
Climb the crack right of *A-Beano*, sharing its anchors.
30 ft. J.J., 2004.

⑱ Don't Take Yer Guns to Town 5.10c ★★★
Climb a short dihedral to an easy slab and big roof. Hand-traverse right and make a long move to pull the roof. A one-move wonder.
50 ft. 5 bolts. Jared Hancock, Rob Copeland, 2004.

⑲ The Offering 5.7 ★★★
Begin near the right edge of the ledge. Follow easy crack system and ledges up and right to an exciting finish.
45 ft. 5 bolts. Dennis Rice, Mike Susko, Tim Powers, 2004.

⑳ The P. Heist Rockway to Heaven 5.6 ★★
The crack system that begins at the base of *The Offering*. up and right to the chain anchor on *Get on the Good Foot*.
60 ft. Mike Susko, Stacia Susko, 2004.

㉑ Put the Best Foot Forward 5.8 ★★★
This is a variation finish to *Get on the Good Foot*. Climb the route until it's possible to step up and left to the bolted face. Follow two bolts up the juggy slab to anchors just below the ledge.
55 ft. 2 bolts. J.J., Rick Weber, 2004.

BRUISE BROTHERS

Workin' for the Weekend

Get on the Good Foot 5.8 ★★★
low a right-angling crack and flake system 10–15 feet
nt of *The Offering* and *P. Heist* up and right to chain
chors under the large roof.
ft. *J.J., Tracy Crabtree, 2004.*

Send Me on My Way 5.9- ★★★★
ick and plunder the pleasantly plump and plentiful plates
t of the leaning crack. Then juice the jugs as they send you
your way to the anchors. Much fun. Highly recommended
the novice leader.
ft. 9 bolts. *Jared Hancock, Karla Carandang, Jenny Wagner,
rk Ryan, 2005.*

Ohio Climbing 5.8 ★★
ull squeeze job, but given the number of people who have
mbed this on TR, why not bolt it? A fun, juggy route with
od rests.
ft. 5 bolts. *Zac Kroeger, Mark Ryan, JJ Jones,
b Kroeger, 2013.*

Workin' for the Weekend 5.10c ★★★
art on an easy slab. Make a couple of long, pumpy moves
a small flake feature. Crimp or undercling through another
ort crux and pull over a large flake to the anchors.
ft. 8 bolts. *Jared Hancock, Karla Carandang, 2004.*

㉖ Return of Manimal 5.10d ★★★★
Moderate slab with big reaches to a giant roof at the top.
85 ft. 10 bolts. *Tim Powers, Mike Susko, 2004.*

㉗ Critters on the Cliff 5.10d ★★★★
Begin 15 feet right of *Return of Manimal*. Balance up the
moderate slab to steepening terrain. Reach through the
overhanging finger-crack section and stroll past a few more
bolts to the anchors.
75 ft. 9 bolts. *Jared Hancock, Tim Powers, Tony Panozzo,
Karla Carandang, 2004.*

㉘ Rat Stew 5.10a ★★★★
The rightmost route on Bruise Brothers. Balance up the
knobby face to a small ledge. Continue cranking up a slightly
overhanging face on good holds, through two solid black
sections, to an anchor under the final roof. Good moves.
Easier than it looks.
75 ft. 9 bolts. *Jared Hancock, Joel Bruhn, Tim Powers, 2004.*

SUNNYSIDE

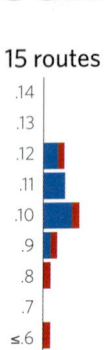

MUIR VALLEY

15 routes

If the crowds at Bruise Brothers Wall have got you down, head over to Sunnyside. Here you'll find more great routes in the 5.10-to-5.11 range, and even a 5.12. Begin on the highly recommended *Fear or Common Sense*, then head over to the tiered roofs of *Machete* and *Weed Eater*. If you've got mad edging skills, jump on the highly technical *Suppress the Rage*.

Approach: Take the Main Trail South to the valley floor, cross the creek, and continue straight pa the first trail on the left (which leads to Practi and Washboard walls). You'll soon reach a fork the trail. Follow the right fork toward Sunnysi (The left fork leads uphill to Bruise Brother Follow the trail downhill, then uphill until y meet the cliff just beneath *Fear or Common Sen* The rest of the routes are to the right.

Conditions: Don't let the name fool you Sunnyside actually isn't sunny all day. The w mainly faces west, so if you're an early riser y can avoid the sun on hot days. The steeper rout on the far right wall will stay dry in a downpou

Dog Wars

Mini Me

❷ **Fear or Common Sense** 5.11b ★★★★
Begin on the right side of the ledge 15–20 feet right of the previous route and follow the flake feature up the arête.
70 ft. 7 bolts. J.J., Barry Broley, 2004.

❶ **Dog Wars** 5.12 ★★★★
This is the overhanging finger-and-hand crack that splits the middle of the main wall where the approach trail meets the cliff. It is about 20 feet left of the bolted line *Fear or Common Sense*.
90 ft. 3 bolts. Ken Thompson, 2005.

❸ **Continental** 5.12a ★★★★
Boulder-problem start to a pocketed section resembling the Dark Continent. Long, sustained, pumpy moves up spaced-out slopers.
80 ft. 8 bolts. Jared Hancock, JJ on TR. Equipped by Brad Com

Virgin Bolter to Kokopeli's Dream

Mini Me 5.9+ ★★★

short, gently overhanging finger-to-hand crack. Boulder
e start, then follow the crack until it ends. Continue past
ickenheads to anchors.
0 ft. J.J., David Fromke, 2004.

Enganche 5.10b ★★

his route is 50 feet left of the entrance to a cave that forms
 hidden arch. Wide layback crack with two roofs. The upper
of is fun and exposed. May need some cleaning.
0 ft. Danny Rice, Chris Dent, 2004.

Virgin Bolter Tag Team 5.10b ★★

alk 50 feet right from the large cave near *Enganche* to a
ocketed wall with some bolted lines. This is the leftmost of
e bolted lines. Climb through the crux roof at the start, then
uise up moderate terrain to a steep finish.
5 ft. 6 bolts. Jared Hancock, Mike Hatchett, Mark Ryan,
ip Wolfe, 2005.

Machete 5.10b ★★★★

he middle bolted line, up a pocketed face to a small alcove.
ake out and fight the pump up and over a few roofs.
5 ft. 7 bolts. J.J., Jared Hancock, 2004.

Weed Eater 5.11b ★★★★

e sport route just left of the *Velveteen* chimney. Climb slabby
ockets to steep ledges to a steep finish on crimpy pockets.
5 ft. 8 bolts. David Fromke, J.J., 2004.

Enganche

9 Velveteen 5.5 ★★★

This is the obvious chimney between the left side of the
pinnacle and the main wall. Climb up through the cave and
spiral around to a ledge near the top at the right side of the
pinnacle. Fun.
40 ft. J.J. (free-solo), 2005.

Suppress the Rage

⓯ **Dingo the Gringo** 5.10c ★★★
The rightmost bolted line on the ledge. Solve the beginning sequence to reach easier slab climbing to the anchors.
45 ft. 5 bolts. Jared Hancock, Karla Carandang, Mark Ryan, Jenny Wagner, 2005.

BOWLING ALLEY

20 min 20 min   37.72 -83.62

Wanna get away from the crowds Muir? Start hiking. This short wall on has four routes, and is the southernmo wall in Muir Valley. Access it by a 3/ mile hike along Smokey Fork Creek.

Approach: Hike in as for Bruise Brothers, but lo for a Bowling Alley sign just before the trail lea uphill. Follow the lower trail along the creek to set of stairs. A couple hundred yards later, t cliff will be on your left. See map on page 138.

❶ **Steel Reserve** 5.10b ★★
It's only about 45 feet high, but you'll see loads of brittle ro along the way. But if you've walked all the way out here, you'll get on it, and with only four routes to choose from, yo may like it. If this cleans up, it may turn out to be an OK rou
45 ft. 5 bolts. J.J., Jane Maurer, 2005.

❷ **King Pin** 5.10a ★★
The second route from the left is a bit better than the first.
40 ft. 4 bolts. J.J., Jane Maurer, 2005.

❸ **Imminent Demise** 5.10b ★★★
If you started on the left side of the crag and made it to this point, you'll notice the routes are getting better. Too bad the are only four. Climb finger buckets to a nice ledge and rest. Continue on the pockets above through a slightly overhangi face and small roof.
45 ft. 4 bolts. Jared Hancock, Rob Copeland, 2005.

❹ **Espresso** 5.12a ★★★
Boulder problem to the first bolt, then good holds to the chains. If you boulder hard but have no endurance, this route's for you. Stick clip the first bolt.
40 ft. 4 bolts. Jared Hancock, Rob Copeland, 2005.

⓾ **Kokopelli's Dream** 5.9 ★★★
This sport route climbs the pinnacle, just right of the chimney. It begins as a technical slab and angles up and left to the arête. Balance on up with some underclings, then finish by laybacking on the arête. Harder variations can be toproped from the anchors.
40 ft. 4 bolts. Jared Hancock, Karla Carandang, J.J., 2005.

⓫ **Velvet Revolution** 5.11d ★★★★
A super-steep extension to *Kokopelli's Dream* that continues out the rock house. Fun and exposed, with a few powerful moves.
100 ft. 9 bolts. J.J., Jared Hancock, Tim Powers, 2005.

⓬ **Baccaus Goes Climbing** 5.8 ★★
Climb the wide, arching crack formed between the right side of the pinnacle and the main wall.
45 ft. Chris Moratz, Cindy Simpson, J.J., 2005.

⓭ **Suppress the Rage** 5.12a ★★★★
Walk right from the pinnacle to a small ledge with three bolted lines. This is the leftmost line and climbs the left-angling blunt arête. It's possible to bail right with a big move onto the face for a slightly easier but height-dependent crux.
50 ft. 6 bolts. Kipp Trummel, Eric Heuermann, 2005.

⓮ **Some Humans Ain't Human** 5.10c ★★★★
This technical line is the middle of the three bolted routes on the ledge. Begin with fun moves, then balance up solid sandstone on nice edges to the chains.
50 ft. 5 bolts. Rob Copeland, Jared Hancock, James Case, 2005.

METOLIUS
SUPER CHALK

Pat Goodman on Half Moon Tilt V8 - Cotton Top, WV Photo: Pat Goodman

PENDERGRASS-MURRAY RECREATIONAL PRESERVE

RRGCC

The Pendergrass-Murray Recreational Preserve (PMRP) is a 750-acre region owned and maintained by the Red River Gorge Climbers' Coalition (RRGCC). The PMRP contains over 500 sport and traditional rock climbs from 5.6 to 5.14, with more climbs being developed each year. This was the largest direct land acquisition ever made by climbers and permanently secures access to a significant amount of the climbing in the Red.

The RRGCC is a 501(c)(3) nonprofit organization dedicated to ensuring quality climbing opportunities for the recreating public by promoting responsible climbing. The historic PMRP purchase represents the RRGCC's dedication to ensuring quality climbing opportunities on public and private land. The purchase and maintenance of the PMRP is made possible solely through private donations and volunteer efforts. All donations made in support of the RRGCC and the PMRP are tax deductible; volunteer contributions in the form of trail work or pro-bono professional services are also welcome. You can make a donation and become an RRGCC member by visiting **rrgcc.org** where you will also find information about events and other activities.

History and Vision: On March 28, 1908, Dani Boone Pendergrass secured his first 530-acre parcel of land on Bald Rock Fork, which run through the heart of the Pendergrass-Murray Recreational Preserve. Pendergrass bought three more tracts, including the 325-acre Coal Bar Hollow, eventually totaling more than 100 acres. The land stayed in the Pendergrass family for three generations, being passed finally the granddaughter of D.B. Pendergrass, Matt Murray, and her husband, Lafayette. During the late 1990s, inspired by the discovery of the nearby Motherlode, climbers started exploring and developing the superb climbing potential of the many cliffs on this land. On January 20, 200 the RRGCC officially purchased the surface right to what is now the PMRP from the Murrays and secured climbing access for the future.

The vision of the PMRP is to create an outdoor recreational haven in Eastern Kentucky that encourages a love for the outdoors, facilitate human-powered recreation, and build appreciation and a sense of stewardship for this unique and beautiful land. As a public trust organization dedicated to responsible ensuring open, public access to rock climbing and other outdoor recreational opportunities while encouraging conservation, the RRGCC developing a variety of recreational opportunities including hiking and mountain biking, with a emphasis on the "recreational experience" in the unique natural and geological environment.

our membership dollars at work. Photo: Andrew Burr.

RULES OF THE PMRP

Climbing is a dangerous activity and should always be taken seriously. The RRGCC assumes no liability for your safety and personal property while visiting the PMRP. You climb and recreate on the PMRP at your own risk.

Before climbing at the PMRP you must submit a waiver via rrgcc.org. If you are interested in establishing new sport routes or traditional routes with fixed anchors at the preserve or plan to guide or bring an organized group, please e-mail rrgcc@rrgcc.org and the RRGCC will reply with contact information so that you can coordinate your activities with the PMRP property manager. Other rules and guidelines are as follows:

• Please climb responsibly and follow "Leave No Trace" practices.

• All dogs must be leashed, or under the direct control of their owners if not leashed.

• Stay off all tagged projects and do not touch or use any project ropes, draws, or other gear.

• Stay on established trails and do not mark or damage trees or other vegetation. RRGCC approval is required prior to the establishment of any new crags or trails.

• No hunting, trapping, digging for archaeological artifacts, or operation of motorized vehicles off established roads.

• No open fires due to oil-extraction activity in the area and the enormous threat a forest fire in a region of numerous oil wells would pose.

• Overnight camping (no long-term camping) is permitted as long as it's not in a climbing area, along a trail, or near oil equipment. Please remove all refuse and bury human waste.

PMRP OVERVIEW

Access: All crags at the PMRP are accessed from KY 11 south of Torrent via either Fixer Road or Bald Rock Fork Road, both maintained by Lee County. American Natural Gas, Inc., the owner of oil and gas rights on the property at the time of writing, uses many other roads on the Preserve to access its oil wells. Most of these are not shown on the maps, so it is important to look for and follow directional signs. It is absolutely imperative to park your vehicle in the designated parking areas only, and follow all posted rules and guidelines. Park off any gravel road and away from pipes, oil wells, or other oil-production equipment, and always yield the right-of-way to any oil worker or truck. Stay clear of all oil-production equipment — oil wells, injection sites, and storage tanks. They are dangerous and pose a serious risk to visitors. Blocking access to oil equipment may also endanger climbing access throughout the region.

The cliffs in the PMRP are approached from several main parking areas: Coal Bank Hollow, Sore Heel Hollow, and several spots along Bald Rock Fork Road including the new Flat Hollow lot. Note that the Bald Rock Fork and Sore Heel parking areas involve some rough driving. Although doable with skillful driving in a passenger vehicle **in good conditions**, 4WD is recommended.

PMRP: COAL BANK HOLLOW

Map labels:
- Dark Side
- Bright Side
- Solar Collector
- Gold Coast
- Crossroads
- Far Side
- FIXER ROAD
- CAVE FORK ROAD
- to 11
- rougher, slower way to 11
- 1/4 MILE
- COAL BANK HOLLOW
- (MANY ROADS NOT SHOWN)

Coal Bank Hollow: From Miguel's Pizza, drive 9 miles south on KY 11 and turn right on Fixer Road. Drive about 0.2 miles and take the first left to stay on Fixer Road. After a couple of miles on this road you will descend a steep, winding hill. At the bottom of the hill, the road turns to gravel. Drive 1.1 miles on the gravel road until you see a road on your right directly across from a black oil tank the size of a car. Turn right onto this road and head up a steep hill, then down another hill. Continue along the slightly rough road for about .5 miles, staying left (do not turn right onto a road that heads down a steep hill where oil-company equipment is located) until you reach an obvious parking area with an RRGCC kiosk.

PMRP

CLIFF	KIDS	RAIN	SUN	DRIVE	HIKE	ROUTES	GRADE RANGE	CLASSIC ROUTES
CROSSROADS page 78	✓		◐	20 min	15 min	34		
GOLD COAST page 85	✓	☂	☀	20 min	15 min	46		Golden Boy 13b; Black Gold 13c; God's Own Stone 14a; 24 Karats 14c
SOLAR COLLECTOR page 92	✓	☂	☀	20 min	15 min	18		Buddha Hole 11d; Supafly 12a
BRIGHT SIDE page 95		☂	☀	20 min	20 min	22		Crown of Thorns 11c; Dog Bites Fist Fights 12d
THE DARK SIDE page 100		☂	◐	20 min	20 min	31		The Force 13a; Elephant Man 13b; Darth Moll 13b; Swingline 13d
FAR SIDE page 106	✓		◐	20 min	10 min	12		
VELO CRAG page 193			☀	18 min	5 min	17		Lightning Rod Arête 10c
THE SHIPYARD page 196			●	18 min	10 min	18		Cabin Boy Fever 11b; Sail 12b
THE GETAWAY page 201			◐	18 min	10 min	10		Afros, Macks, and Zodiacs 12c
THROWBACK CRAG page 204			◐	18 min	5 min	11		Do the Hemlock Rock 10+; Don't Call it a Comeback 11d
CURBSIDE page 149	✓	☂	◐	25 min	5 min	16		
THE GALLERY page 152	✓	☂	☀	25 min	10 min	39		27 Years of Climbing 8; All That Glitters 12c
VOLUNTEER WALL page 160	✓	☂	◐	25 min	10 min	25		
LEFT FIELD page 163	✓		☀	25 min	10 min	12		
THE PLAYGROUND page 164		☂	☀	25 min	10 min	12		
SHADY GROVE page 166	✓	☂	◐	25 min	15 min	16		
MEGACAVE page 144		☂	◐	25 min	15 min	4		
BRONAUGH WALL page 168	✓	☂	☀	25 min	15 min	17		Two Women Alone 11b; Belly of the Beast 12c

COAL BANK HOLLOW

FLAT HOLLOW

SORE HEEL HOLLOW

158

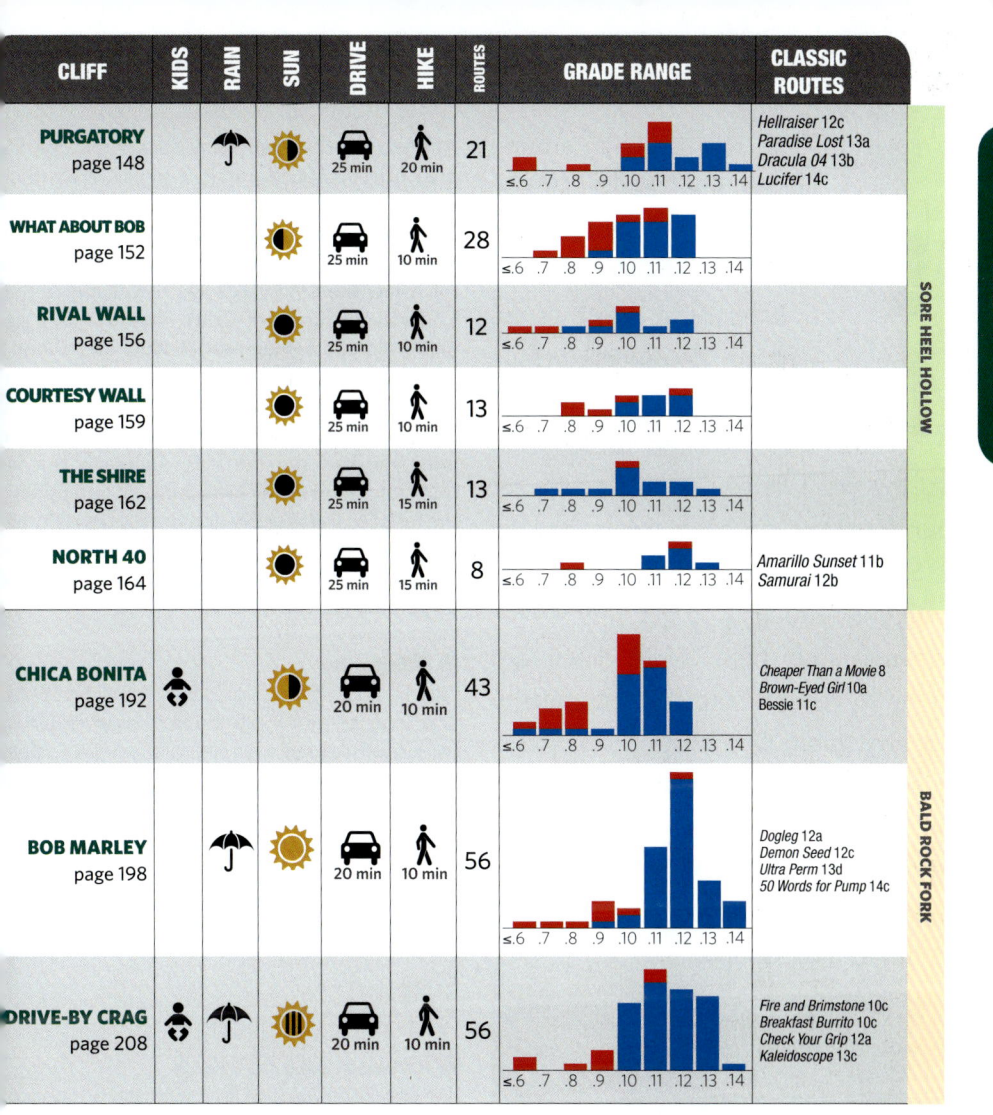

CLIFF	KIDS	RAIN	SUN	DRIVE	HIKE	ROUTES	GRADE RANGE	CLASSIC ROUTES
PURGATORY page 148		☂	◐	25 min	20 min	21		Hellraiser 12c / Paradise Lost 13a / Dracula 04 13b / Lucifer 14c
WHAT ABOUT BOB page 152			●	25 min	10 min	28		
RIVAL WALL page 156			●	25 min	10 min	12		
COURTESY WALL page 159			☀	25 min	10 min	13		
THE SHIRE page 162			☀	25 min	15 min	13		
NORTH 40 page 164			☀	25 min	15 min	8		Amarillo Sunset 11b / Samurai 12b
CHICA BONITA page 192	👶		◐	20 min	10 min	43		Cheaper Than a Movie 8 / Brown-Eyed Girl 10a / Bessie 11c
BOB MARLEY page 198		☂	☀	20 min	10 min	56		Dogleg 12a / Demon Seed 12c / Ultra Perm 13d / 50 Words for Pump 14c
DRIVE-BY CRAG page 208	👶	☂	◐	20 min	10 min	56		Fire and Brimstone 10c / Breakfast Burrito 10c / Check Your Grip 12a / Kaleidoscope 13c

SORE HEEL HOLLOW

BALD ROCK FORK

PMRP

CROSSROADS

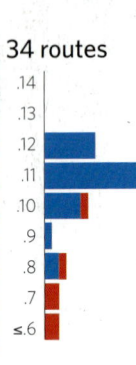

37.67
-83.73

20 min 15 min

34 routes

This crag has been around since the early 1990s, rediscovered a decade later, and now developed into a full-service sport venue hosting 35 routes (versus the original four on the left side, rumored to be Brian McCray FAs). If you're looking to get your forearms pumped, keep walking to Solar Collector or the Dark Side, but if you're looking to get your calves pumped, stop here. Most lines are slabby to vertical, and the rock quality is pretty good. One section resembles an ocean wave, where the crux of the lines is pulling over the crest. They're definitely worth checking out. For the beginning climber, *Boilerplate* is one of the better 5.8s around.

Approach: Drive to the Coal Bank Hollow parking area (directions on previous page). From there, walk a few feet past the kiosk to the signed trailhead on the right. Follow the trail down and across a small bridge, then along an old dirt road for a few hundred yards (as if walking to Solar Collector or the Dark Side). Take the first right on an old oil/logging road. Follow this about ? yards, then continue left on the road at the fork. Take this to an old oil rig. Behind this, the road forks again. Take the left fork and follow it around until you can see the cliff. To reach the first routes, look for a trail branching off and uphill to the left. For *October Sky* and the routes right of it, remain on the road a bit longer, passing another old oil pump, then cross a small footbridge to end up just beneath *October Sky*.

❶ **N4** 5.10c ★★★
After taking the wooden steps up to the left toward *Cannibal Love Generator*, the trail splits just past a large tree. This and the next two routes are on an outcrop to the left. It's not often that lines this short can be so much fun, but this one pulls it off. Forty feet of fun with a nice solid crux at the third clip.
40 ft. 3 bolts. Jeff Neal, Theresa Neal, 2011.

❷ **Love Potion #9** 5.9 ★★
Just right of *N4*. Fun face climbing for the first half, then sloping slots with tricky feet for the second half. Longer than it looks.
65 ft. 7 bolts. Theresa Neal, Jeff Neal, 2011.

❸ **The Country Boy** 5.11b ★★★
Just right of *Love Potion #9*. Begin with a reachy move right off the ground, then prepare for a strenuous reach-and-release crux between bolts two and three. After wondering how you pulled off the crux, enjoy a nice jug run to the chains. Don't worry, they're up there.
65 ft. 6 bolts. Jeff Neal, Theresa Neal, 2011.

❹ **Legalize It** 5.12a ★★★
The first line right of the previous three routes on the vertical wall that looks impossible but has just the right holds to be climbable.
55 ft. 4 bolts. Brian McCray?

❺ **Wake and Bake** 5.11d ★★★
Fifteen feet right of the previous line is another crimpfest, but with more holds than its neighbor. Begin on a ledge and step and reach up the slightly-less-than-vertical face. Shift slightly left just before the shuts.
55 ft. 4 bolts. Brian McCray?

Love Potion #9

Tati Mejia on *Yell Fire,* 5.10d (page 164). Photo: Elodie Saracco.

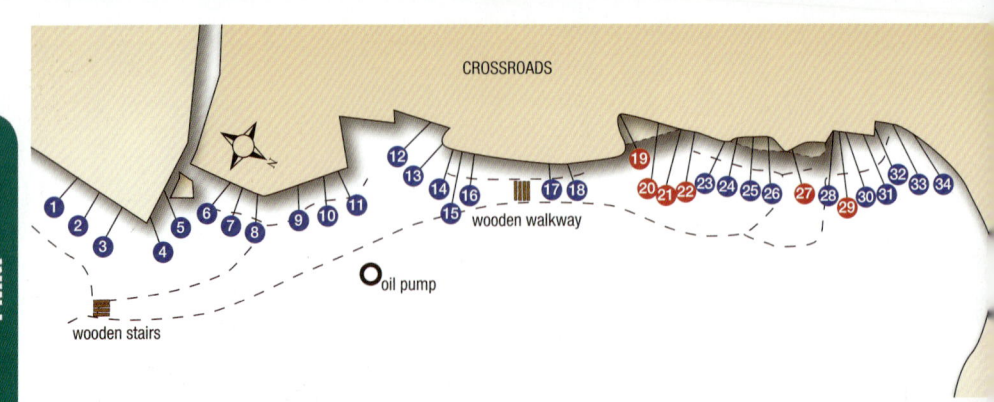

6 Hippie Speed Ball 5.11d ★★★★
Just right of the slab wall is an overhanging section of cliff with two nice-looking pocket lines. This is the leftmost line on the wall. Clip a high first bolt to begin. Pull through long moves on deep pockets to a crimp crux just before the shuts. Watch out for the tree from the last bolt to the anchors.
60 ft. 5 bolts. Brian McCray?

7 Cannabis Love Generator 5.11c ★★★
Just right of the previous line is another overhanging pocketed line. Climb deep pockets to an obvious crux. Continue on jugs to the anchors or gun for the anchors on the previous line for more value.
50 ft. 5 bolts. Brian McCray?

8 Praying Mantis 5.12a ★★★
Hugs the left-leaning arête 15 feet right of *Cannabis Love Generator*.
60 ft. 7 bolts. Kipp Trummel, 2010.

9 Evil Eye 5.11b ★★★★
Just left of *Happy Feet*. Crimpy and sequential face climbing leads to a slab with a jug rest. Clip a bolt and gaze into the eerie evil eye hold as you float out to a brick-shaped knob. Make a long scary move, clip another bolt, and breathe a sigh of relief as you soak up a squat rest. Finish on tiny crimps to the chains.
70 ft. 7 bolts. Rachel Stewart, Shadow Ayala, 2013.

Happy Feet 5.11c ★★★

...irty feet right of *Praying Mantis* is a less-than-vertical wall. ...is line begins left of a blunt arête and just right of *Evil Eye*. ...imb an easy start, then tiptoe up the face while improvising ...ur way through multiple blank sections.
5 ft. 7 bolts. Phil Wilkes, Josephine Neff, 2009.

Signed in Blood 5.12b ★★★★

...imb the blunt arête right of *Happy Feet* using squeeze, ...pes, and crimps.
5 ft. 6 bolts. Blake Bowling, 2012.
...quipped by Wes Allen and Kipp Trummel.

...he following routes are located about 120 feet right ...f Signed in Blood. Hike back down to the main trail, ...en walk right, past a second oil pump, to locate a ...mall wooden bridge branching left. Cross the bridge ...o meet the cliff at October Sky.

Amish Whoopie Cushion 5.11d ★★★

...eft of *October Sky* is a striking orange wall; this line is to ...e left of it. Jam or lieback up a short crack to gain a ledge ...efore the mangy slab. Tech your way up to the shallow ...eco, fire off a cool boulder problem on solid orange rock, ...d end with vicious crimps just before the chains. Have your ...ll partner hang the third draw.
...0 ft. 7 bolts. Will Sweeney, 2013.

Stomp U Out 5.12c ★★★★

...eft of *October Sky* is a striking orange wall. This is on the ...ft side and begins with a flake and a low roof. Traverse left ...ound the roof to gain the flake. Climb the enjoyable flake, ...en exit right into two bolts worth of tough bouldering on ...allow pockets and small edges
5 ft. 8 bolts. Ricky Parks, Kipp Trummel, 2012.

⑭ Hood Luck 5.12a ★★★★

This is the middle of the three lines on the golden wall. Climb through a dirty start to reach a ledge where the good stuff begins. Step off the ledge into some techy, powerful pocket pulling with just the right amount of fun thrown in.
70 ft. 8 bolts. Andrew Wheatley, David Linz, 2012.
Equipped by Jeff Neal.

⑮ Fairweather Friend 5.10d ★★★★

Fifteen feet left of *October Sky* (*Hood Luck* is 25 ft left) is this long, varied climb. Pull the bulge, walk the ramp, and enjoy good movement on solid stone. Like the other routes on this section, the sun can be brutal in summer until 2 PM or so.
80 ft. 9 bolts. Jeff Neal, 2012.

⑯ October Sky 5.11c ★★★★

This line is almost directly in front of the wooden walkway where the trail meets the cliff. Get your slab on for a brief session, then pinch and crimp through a crux to reach enjoyable face climbing. Reach into the "bass mouth" for the finale.
70 ft. 8 bolts. Jeff Neal, 2009.

⑰ Foot Jive 5.11d ★★★★

Move right of the foot bridge to locate two bolted lines, which begin with jugs but turn to attractive stone after the first bolt. This is the first on the left. Solve the very difficult entrance moves to earn the ticket to sustained crimping and high-stepping up this beautiful streak of sandstone.
65 ft. 8 bolts. Matt Johns, Jeff Neal, 2009.

Severn Bore

Banjolero

⑳ Buckwheat's Climb for Stef 5.6 ★
The first crack right of *Turkey Crossing* would be better if it were longer.
40 ft. Mike Susko, 2010.

㉑ Stefanie Bauer Route 5.7
Next crack right of *Buckwheat's Climb*. Challenging gear in some spots.
40 ft. Mike Trabel, 2010.

㉒ The Right Bauer 5.8+ ★★★
Climb the short finger crack system just right of *Stefanie Bauer Route*. Finish at the shared anchors.
30 ft. Unknown, 2013.

㉓ A1A 5.10b ★★★
Walk right a bit until you see a section of the cliff containing several bolted lines that surmount a roof shaped like a wave. This is the first of these routes on the left and borders the left edge of the wave roof. Take on a difficult start that quickly eases to fun climbing on solid stone.
50 ft. 5 bolts. Don McGlone, 2009.

㉔ Yell Fire! 5.10d ★★★
The next route right of *A1A*. Climb a flake to a stance below the roof. Use thin seams to get high feet and gun for the lip. Continue on easier ground to reach the short, overhanging, pockety finale to the chains.
80 ft. 10 bolts. Tania Allen, 2009.

㉕ Severn Bore 5.11c ★★★★
Just right of *Yell Fire* is another slab-to-roof problem. Tiptoe up to a decent stance just before the roof, then use thin seams and edges to extend as far as possible to a good hold in the flake. Thug over the lip, then enjoy less stressful climbing to an enjoyable, airy finish. Use a long draw for the roof bolt to save your rope.
60 ft. 7 bolts. Kipp Trummel, Scott Brown, 2009.

㉖ Red Tag Rape 5.11c ★★
This is the route on the far right of the wave. Climb a flake system to reach the crest of the wave. Make use of a pocket and a crimp to pull the lip, then fight for a stance. Move up larger holds to another fun, pockety finish.
80 ft. 10 bolts. Ray Ellington, 2009. Equipped by Wes Allen.

㉗ Wrong Turn 5.7 ★★
Move right to locate this right-angling crack. Enjoy decent protection and a few slabby moves, then top it off with a nice set of anchors.
50 ft. Jeff Neal, 2009.

⑱ Whippoorwill 5.11b ★★
Move 15 feet right of *Foot Jive* for more slabby goodness. As with the previous line, you will be rewarded with holds you can feel between your fingers if you make it through the nerd gate.
65 ft. 7 bolts. Jeff Neal, Theresa Neal, Matt Johns, 2009.

⑲ Turkey Crossing 5.4 ★★
Head right along the cliff line to an incut area. This is the wide crack on the left side.
45 ft. Jeff Neal, Theresa Neal, 2009.

Jingus Kahn — **Boilerplate** — **Swallow the Hollow**

Banjolero 5.10c ★★
[A]round the corner from *Wrong Turn* is this heavily featured [fa]ce. Climb to a ledge to reach the high first bolt, then [co]ntinue up the face on pockets and pinches, staying left of a [cr]ack. Move left onto the face before the chains.
[4]5 ft. 7 bolts. *Jeff Neal, Theresa Neal, 2009.*

The Rusty Philosopher 5.10a ★★★
[Th]is dihedral is between *Banjolero* and *Deeznuts*. Don't clip [th]e bolts of the other routes to get the full value. Easy to TR [fr]om the *Banjolero* anchors.
[4]5 ft. *Phil Wilkes, Russ Jackson, 2009.*

Deeznuts 5.8 ★★
[Cl]imb to the same ledge as *Banjolero* to reach the first bolt, [th]en continue up the face, staying right of a crack. Stand on a [bu]lging feature to clip the chains.
[5]0 ft. 6 bolts. *Don McGlone, Joel Petrino, 2011.*

Jingus Khan 5.12a ★★★★
[Ju]st right of *Deeznuts* is this overhanging and technical [cr]impfest on solid stone. Begin with a few bolts of sticky [fri]ction jugs and horns to reach a rest at a hueco. Move out of [th]e hueco into sustained big moves between decent edges.
[5]0 ft. 8 bolts. *Dustin Stephens, 2012.*

Boilerplate 5.8 ★★★★
[Ex]cellent route for the grade. Move right from *Jingus Khan* and [w]alk up a steep section of the trail to find this enjoyable line on [a] northeast-facing section of the wall. Begin on a small ledge, [th]en pull on solid plates to a steeper run for the chains.
[5]0 ft. 6 bolts. *Jeff Neal, Matt Johns, 2009.*

㉝ June Bug 5.11d ★★★★
For those who thought Crossroads was all slab. Right of *Boilerplate* is this steep and well-featured face. Begin with some big-move cruxes down low, then continue up through steep jugs to the chains.
55 ft. 7 bolts. *Jeff Neal, 2012.*

㉞ Swallow the Hollow 5.12a ★★★★
Walk downhill from *June Bug* to locate this striking line, which climbs easier than it appears. Begin off the boulder on the left and climb up to a stance beneath the meat of the line. Take on the steep face, making use of Scream-face holds to reach the obvious duck-bill feature. Shake out, then make more big moves culminating in a desperate finale for the chains. No gigantic cheater slings on the anchors!
70 ft. 9 bolts. *Kipp Trummel, 2012.*

㉟ Crossroads Crack Project ★★★
A hard boulder problem leads to a spectacular overhanging dihedral in the back of the amphitheater.
100 ft. 3 bolts. *Equipped by Dustin Stephens.*

CROSSROADS

COAL BANK HOLLOW

165

Heather Trevarthen's try-hard face, *Golden Boy*, 5.13b (opposite). Photo: John Wesely.

GOLD COAST

37.6770
-83.7338
20 min 15 min

26 routes This is a great hardperson's crag — the Gold Coast's striking main wall features some of the Red's most aesthetic and difficult sport lines, including *God's Own Stone* 5.14a and *True Love* 5.13d. Farther right you'll find several excellent traditional routes.

Approach: Drive to the Coal Bank Hollow parking area (directions on page 157). From there, walk a few feet past the kiosk to the signed trailhead on the right. Follow the trail down and across a small bridge, then along an old dirt road for a few hundred yards, passing a road branching off right (the approach for Crossroads). Keep following the main trail until you encounter the signed Gold Coast trail to the right; take this and head shortly uphill to end just beneath the bolted line *On the Prowl* on the cliff's far-right side. You can also access the Gold Coast by walking right from the Solar Collector; this is the quickest approach for the main wall routes 1–13.

❶ Damascus 5.12b
This is the leftmost bolted route and starts with a roof. Climb loose rock to a shelf about 20 feet up to begin. Clip a fixed chain, then climb out the short overhang. Continue up the slightly overhanging face to the anchors just before a large, ropey ledge.
50 ft. 6 bolts. Gus Alexandropolus. Equipped by Jason McClennan.

❷ Black Plague 5.12a
This line shares the first three bolts with the previous line, then heads right up a brown streak. Poor rock quality.
50 ft. 6 bolts.

❸ Black Gold 5.13c ★★★★★
This great route follows a drainage line and requires dry conditions. Move 30 feet right of the previous lines to a taller section of the wall. Climb past shelves to a large ledge 15 feet up, then head left up the striking dark streak to anchors in a hueco just before the top.
70 ft. 8 bolts. Bill Ramsey, 2001.

❹ God's Own Stone 5.14a ★★★★★
Start as for *Black Gold* but angle right after the first two bolts. Power up the golden face to the anchors just before a large horizontal. The crux is short lived; the route may feel easy for the grade if you have steel fingers.
70 ft. 7 bolts. Ben Cassel, 2003. Equipped by Hugh Loeffler.

❺ Twenty-Four Karats 5.14c ★★★★★
Just right of *God's Own Stone* used to be two longstanding open projects. In November 2010, visiting climber Jonathan Siegrist combined the top half of the first project with the bottom half of the second project to create this exceptional line. A bolt was added to link the two, and the old bolts were removed. The climbing consists of deadpoints and delicate movement on shallow pockets and sloping edges. In 2012, the original right project was resurrected when a local decided to put the bolts back in.
65 ft. 6 bolts. Jonathan Siegrist, 2010.

❻ Gold Star Project Open Project
As mentioned above, this is the original right project that was combined with the left project to create *Twenty-Four Karats*. It's now again ready for someone very, very strong.
65 ft. 6 bolts.

❼ 100 Ounces of Gold 5.14a ★★★★
Thirty feet right of the *Gold Star Project* lies this shallow-pocketed, fat-finger-challenged, rarely done, but excellent line that travels straight up a gold streak between two black streaks.
70 ft. 9 bolts. Ben Cassel, 2003. Equipped by Rob McFall.

❽ Golden Boy 5.13b ★★★★★
This route tackles the next line of bolts about 15 feet right of *100 Ounces of Gold*. One of the best lines of its grade in the Red. Relentless sloping edges with not much for a shake. Lynn Hill flashed this line in 2008. Think of that while you're struggling on it. Check out Joe Hedge's video of Lynn's feat on Vimeo.
70 ft. 7 bolts. Bill Ramsey, 2004. Equipped by Chris Martin.

Gold Coast Main Wall

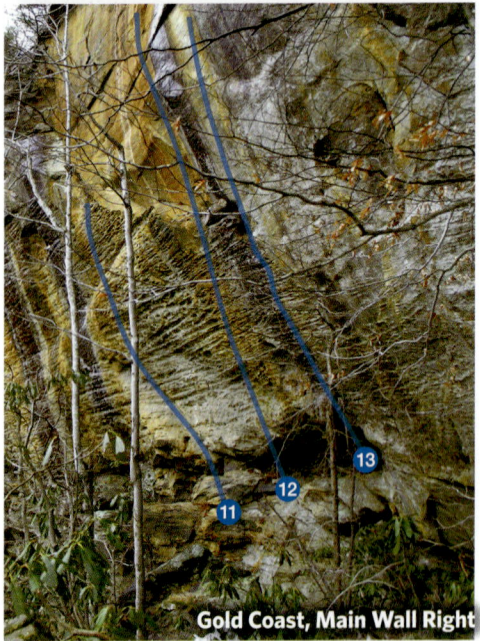

Gold Coast, Main Wall Right

⑨ True Love 5.13d ★★★★★

This crimping testpiece begins just right of *Golden Boy*. Climb the same start or slightly right to reach the face where the insanity begins. Power out about 15 desperate moves, which increase in difficulty as you approach the "I got it" jug. Continue down the home stretch to the chains, but don't get cocky till you clip 'em.

70 ft. 6 bolts. Dave Hume, 2001.

⑩ Sun's Out, Guns Out 5.12b ★★★

This route follows an obvious feature and begins on a high ledge right of *True Love*. Begin with a big cross move to a pocket, then bust up to a flake. Ride the flake to enter a sea of pockets and edges. Make the right decision on which holds to grab and you might have just enough left to beat the smackdown going for the anchors.

50 ft. 5 bolts. Dave Lins, Andrew Wheatley, 2010.

⑪ No Fluff 5.11d ★★★

Another shorty right of *Sun's Out, Guns Out* that packs a mean punch for its length and grade. So much fun you'll want to climb it twice.

45 ft. 5 bolts. Rob McFall, 2000.

⑫ Brilliant Orange 5.13a ★★★★

This is the next route just right of *No Fluff*. Originally ended higher on the wall, but the anchors have been lowered, making it an excellent and doable line. Climb long moves between bad crimps to reach the well-worth-the-trip last move.

70 ft. 8 bolts. Kenny Barker, 2005. Equipped by Rob McFall.

⑬ Mr. Roarke 5.12c ★★★

This is the last route on the gold-streaked, overhanging wall. Belay from the platform as with the previous two routes. Climb a sustained face until you reach the last bolt. Lower from here at 5.12c, or continue to the anchors to send an open project.

65 ft. 7 bolts. Equipped by Jeff Moll.

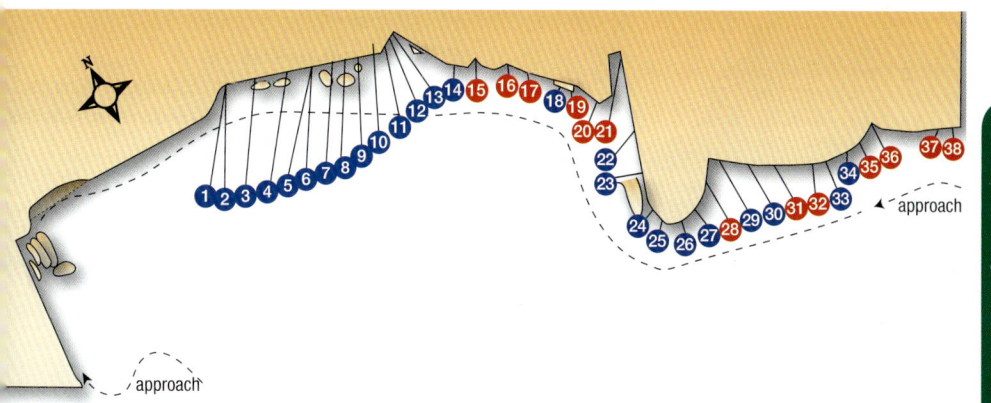

Gecko Circus 5.13b ★★★

Walk around a blunt corner 100 feet right from the previous ...es until the ground flattens. This is the first vertical bolted ...ute you see, and lies about six feet left of the detached ...nnacle climbed by *Erik's First*.
...0 ft. 7 bolts. *Tony Lamiche, 2007. Equipped by Josh Thurston.*

Erik's First 5.6 5.9- ★★

...st right of the previous line is a pair of nice-looking cracks ...scending a small pillar and sharing anchors. This route ...scends the left crack and gets a little wide toward the top.
...5 ft. *Blake Bowling, 2000.*

Erik's Second 5.6 5.9+ ★★

...his is the crack just right of *Erik's First* and shares the same ...nchors. Climb a slabby start to a thin crack, which widens ...ward the top.
...5 ft. *Blake Bowling, 2000.*

17 Smoothie Nut 5.10b ★★★★

This route ascends the striking, thin, left-facing dihedral 15 feet right of *Erik's Second*. Lower from bolted anchors.
60 ft. *Blake Bowling, Jason Tackett, 2000.*

18 Red Shift 5.11d ★★★★

Walk about 20 feet right from *Smoothie Nut* to locate this slab route, which begins atop a boulder. Climb the less-than-vertical face, which gets steeper toward the top, and end beneath a block. *Hand Drills and Handgrenades* (5.10d R) climbs the finger crack above the anchors, past two bolts on the face to a second set of anchors.
50 ft. 4 bolts. *Blake Bowling, 2000.*

19 Dark Matter 5.11a ★★★

Ascends the crack right of *Red Shift* to anchors on that route.
50 ft. *Blake Bowling, 2000.*

Smoothie Nut

Red Shift

169

COAL BANK HOLLOW

Zone of Silence

㉔ Amelia's Birthday 5.11b ★★
Begin on the ledge right of *Zone of Silence* and climb the pocketed face past four bolts to a 15-foot run to the anchor.
60 ft. 4 bolts. Hugh Loeffler, 2003.

㉕ Highway Turtle 5.11d ★★★
Step down around the corner from *Amelia's Birthday* to locate this line. Veer left up the overhanging face on holds that seem to all be facing the wrong way.
60 ft. 5 bolts. Nate Heide, 2003.

㉖ All Gold Everything 5.11d ★★★
Sequential, slopey, and steep, on solid orange rock.
50 ft. 6 bolts. Scott Curran, 2013.

㉗ Gold Nugget 5.12a ★★★
Around the corner from the previous few routes, on the same detached boulder, is this overhanging small wall of pockets, underclings, and tricky clips. Ledge topout if you want. Attentive belay required!
45 ft. 5 bolts. Dustin Stephens, Scott Curran, 2013.

㉘ From the Ashes 5.8+ ★
Walk right and around the corner from *Highway Turtle* to locate this crack-and-face system right of the large leaning block. Use caution placing pro on this line, since there is a possible death block waiting to detach. Rappel from a tree.
65 ft. Scott Hammon, Frank Waters, 2006.

㉙ Explanatory Gap 5.11c ★★★★
Excellent tricky face climbing up to a hard and committing crux at the roof.
50 ft. 5 bolts. Symon Ardila, Dustin Stephens, 2013.

㉚ Golden Shower 5.12a ★★★★
More tricky face climbing on perfect orange rock leads to a wild bouldery crux sequence out the roof. For the non-slabmasters, consider hanging the second draw with a stick clip. Not recommended when the shower is "turned on."
65 ft. 8 bolts. Chris Lamme, Dustin Stephens, 2013.

㉛ Futuristic Testpiece 5.4 ★★
Walk right from *Highway Turtle* until the trail heads down the hill and then back up to meet the cliff line again just beneath *Riptide Ride*. Walk left about 50 feet to locate this chimney system, which leads to the top of the buttress. Rappel from tree for the descent.
50 ft. Unknown.

⑳ Hot Pursuit 5.10b ★★★
This route starts in the dihedral to the right and uphill of the *Red Shift* area. Tight fingers and tips locks lead to a small squeeze chimney. Find some tricky gear, move into the upper dihedral, and top out on a nice belay ledge with bolted anchors.
60 ft. Scott Curran, 2013.

㉑ Not Named 5.9+
This line ascends the dirty dihedral 75 feet right of *Dark Matter*.
65 ft. Dan Beck, Joel Petrino, 2007.

㉒ David and Goliath 5.11c ★★
Spot a bolted line farthest up on the dirty slope right of *Not Named*. Climb through bouldery moves on pockets.
55 ft. 5 bolts. Adam Jones, Alex Southward, 2010.

㉓ Zone of Silence 5.12b ★★
Begins 15 feet right of *David and Goliath*. This line begs to follow what would be an excellent 5.12c, but climbers are staying right, on the path of least resistance, making it a not-so-great 5.12a/b.
55 ft. 5 bolts. Dave Hume, 2002.

170

Christophe Bichet weighs in on *Twenty-Four Karats*, 5.14c (page 167). Photo: Elodie Saracco.

Riptide Ride

32 Riptide Ride 5.10c ★★★★
This is the obvious thin dihedral that has a unique hueco about 20 feet up. It is located 50 feet right of *Futuristic Testpiece* where the trail meets with the cliff. Enjoy excellent climbing with challenging gear placements.
55 ft. Nate Heide, Matt Raymond, 2003.

33 Sunny the Boxer 5.9 ★★
Walk right from *Riptide Ride* until you come to a slab wall with a couple of bolted lines sharing the first two bolts. This line moves up and left after the second bolt to end in a slot.
85 ft. 8 bolts. Justin Elkins, Scott Hammon, Frank Waters, 2007.

34 Lucky Duck Soup 5.5 ★★
This short route shares the first two bolts with the previous line, but continues straight up to its own set of anchors.
45 ft. 4 bolts. Scott Hammon, Stephanie Carson, 2003.

35 The Perfect Pint 5.4 ★★
Climb a splitter crack in the slab to shared anchors.
45 ft. Tony Panozzo, Jared Hancock, Curtis Williams, 2003.

36 Chester Fried Chicken 5.4 ★★
Climb the arching dihedral eight feet right of the previous route to anchors.
45 ft. Scott Hammon, Stephanie Carson, 2002.

37 Fubar 5.10c ★★
A steep layback crack left of *Rebar* that eventually joins with it after the large hueco near the top.
60 ft. Dustin Stephens, 2009.

Rebar

38 Rebar 5.11a ★★★★
A bit right of *Chester Fried Chicken* and *Fubar* you'll see tw obvious cracks splitting the face. This route ascends the lef crack. Begin by climbing *Broken Chicken Wing*, then step le when the crack splits.
60 ft. Josh Thurston, Scott Lappin, 2002.

39 Broken Chicken Wing 5.9+ ★★★★
This route ascends the left-angling hand crack just right of *Rebar*. Climb hands and fingers to a nice rest, then tackle th last few feet for an exposed clipping stance. Chain anchors.
60 ft. Josh Thurston, Scott Lappin, 2002.

40 Green Tea 5.10a ★★
The curving crack just right of *Broken Chicken Wing*. Start b pulling a tricky boulder problem, then follow the path of leas resistance to the chains.
50 ft. Josh Thurston, Mike Thurston, 2005.

41 Norway on My Mind 5.9 ★★
Move right and just around the corner to this bolted line, which ascends a slabby face left of *Slow Jack*.
45 ft. 4 bolts. Don Byrd, Josh Thurston, 2006.

42 Slow Jack 5.7 ★★
Climb the clean dihedral just right of *Norway on My Mind*. Stop at the chains just beneath a roof.
45 ft. Josh Thurston, Mike Thurston, 2005.

Pyrite 5.11c ★★★★

...ght of the *Slow Jack* corner is this technical face climb. ...imb the dihedral to the first bolt. Mantel, crimp, and high-...ep to the chains.
... ft. 7 bolts. Dustin Stephens, Brad Dallefeld, 2012.

Should've Known Better 5.7

...alk right from *Slow Jack* to locate this line, which begins 30 ...et left of the bolted line *On the Prowl*. Climb a ramp with no ...otection to a tree just before the start of the crack. Continue ... the dihedral on soft rock until you reach a ledge where it ... possible to traverse 20 feet right to bolted anchors.
... ft. Scott Brown, Mason Allen, 2006.

On the Prowl 5.9 ★★★

...alk right to reach this bolted route, located just left of the ...vious arête where the alternate approach trail meets the ...ff. Begin from a small ledge 10 feet above the trail and ...ntinue up an enjoyable slab, using the arête when possible.
... ft. 5 bolts. Jared Hancock, Mark Ryan, Jenny Ryan, 2006.

Peer Review 5.10b

...ty feet right of the trailhead and *On the Prowl* are two ...ort, bolted lines. This is the first of the two and ascends a ...atured face. This route has become popular due to the fact ...at it may be a top contender for worst route in the Red.
... ft. 4 bolts. Mike Cole, JATD Crew, 2007.

7-11 5.7 ★★

...st right of *Peer Review* is another short, bolted line on an ...ête. Although a blank-looking face, it's possible to stem off ... the left.
... ft. 4 bolts. Scott Brown, JATD crew, 2007.

Slow Jack

On the Prowl

SOLAR COLLECTOR

37.67
-83.73

18 routes

The aptly named Solar Collector offers classic overhanging bucket hauls in the 5.11–5.12 range on a wall with several huecos large enough to crawl into and sit down.

Approach: Drive to the Coal Bank Hollow parking area (directions on page 157). From there, walk a few feet past the kiosk to the signed trailhead on the right. Follow the trail down and across a small bridge, then along an old dirt road for a few hundred yards, passing a road branching off right (the approach for Crossroads). Keep following the main trail, past the signed turnoff for the Gold Coast, until you reach a trail on the right, signed for the Solar Collector. Take this trail, which winds uphill to end just beneath the main Solar Collector wall near *Super Pinch*. If you continue on the main trail past the dogleg, it will take you to the Dark Side.

❸ Mona Lisa Overdrive 5.11b ★★★
This is the third bolted route from the left on the main wall. Start just right of the thin seam and boulder a tough start to better holds. Climb past the large hueco onto the face and continue to the anchors.
55 ft. 6 bolts. Rob McFall, 1999.

❹ Green Horn 5.11a ★★★
Move 10 feet right from *Mona Lisa Overdrive* to the next bolted line. Climb up to a large hueco, then negotiate a way out. Continue up the face to anchors.
55 ft. 5 bolts. Hugh Loeffler, 1999.

❺ Chickenboy 5.11b ★★★
This line is located a few feet right of *Green Horn*. Pull past tough start, then contine up the sustained face to anchors.
70 ft. 6 bolts. Neal Strickland, 2000.

❻ Psychochicken 5.11b ★★★
A good, natural trad challenge among the bolts. Play a dangerous game of connect-the-huecos, using the discontinuous seam system between *Psychopathy* and *Chickenboy* for pro. Continue to the old anchor above the *Chickenboy* hueco following the crack system on an old mixed route.
75 ft. Scott Curran, 2012.

❼ Psychopathy 5.12c ★
Ten feet right of *Chickenboy* is a line with a blank section about midway up. Climb the line just right of a brown streak. Try clipping the bolt at the crux, but you may have to skip it.
65 ft. 7 bolts. Jason McClennan, 2000.

❽ Ethics Police 5.11d ★★★★
Move a few feet right to the next line. Climb up to a large hueco, take a breather, then cross out of the hueco into the crux and a sustained, pumpy headwall to the anchors.
75 ft. 7 bolts. Rob McFall, 1999.

Solar Collector Left Side

❶ The Decline of Western Civilization 5.10a ★★★
This is the first bolted route on the left side of the wall as the trail reaches the cliff.
45 ft. 5 bolts. Dustin Stephens, Scott Curran, Jeremy Kiner, 2012.

❷ Super Pinch 5.10d ★★★
Second route from the left, which begins just left of a thin seam. Climb the slightly overhanging wall, with a long pull down low. Popular ... for being the hard warm-up that you wish you hadn't tried to warm up on.
50 ft. 5 bolts. Rob McFall, 1999.

nily Ventura in the moment on *Buddha Hole,* 5.11d (next page). Photo: Elodie Saracco.

Solar Collector Right Side

9 Buddha Hole 5.11d ★★★★
Climb up on slopers, then mantel into a hueco. Move out of the hueco and onto the face, make a couple of tough moves to another big hueco, then enjoy jugs to the anchors.
75 ft. 8 bolts. Neal Strickland, 2000.

10 Herd Mentality 5.12c ★★★★
Start up a harder-than-it-looks thin crack right of *Buddha Hole*. Climb past the big hueco and out left onto the face, continuing up through a long, sustained section of crimps to easier but still pumpy moves at the top.
70 ft. 8 bolts. Rob McFall, 1999.

11 Blue-Eyed HonkeyJesus 5.12b ★★★★
Stand on a short, flat boulder 10 feet right of the previous line and reach up to deep two-finger pockets. Climb into a huge hueco at 15 feet, then continue up the overhanging face.
70 ft. 8 bolts. Hugh Loeffler, 2000.

12 Supafly 5.12a ★★★★
This is the last bolted start before the dihedral on the main wall. Begin on a large boulder and make a big move to the hueco. Shift left and tackle the sustained face to the last bolt. Take a rest, then make some steep, tough moves to the anchors.
70 ft. 7 bolts. Chris Martin, 2000.

13 Space Junk 5.12c ★★★★
Begin by climbing *Supafly* to the sit-down rest, then launch up and right through big moves on solid edges to a rest just before the crux. Crank out difficult moves on bad holds, then cruise to the chains.
70 ft. 8 bolts. Jonathan Siegrist, 2012.

14 Yakuza 5.9 ★★★
This is the obvious, overhanging, left-facing dihedral at the right end of the main wall, just past the bolted lines.
90 ft. Barry Brolley, Clyde Stroman, 1997.

15 Brouwer Power 5.11d ★★★
Get your slab on. This is the first route on this section of wall past *Yakuza*. Burly low crux to cool balance moves.
70 ft. 7 bolts. Dustin Stephens, Shadow Ayala, 2013.

16 Buttsweat and Tears 5.10c ★★★
The next line of bolts, right of *Brouwer Power*, is another slab with nice slopers and even a few finger locks.
65 ft. 5 bolts. Scott Curran, Jimmy Klaserner, 2012.

17 Brambly Downslide 5.10a ★★★
Walk right from *Yakuza* to a slab with many water grooves before the black-and-tan Gold Coast starts. This route is the rightmost bolted route. Enjoy fun and technical slab climbing.
75 ft. 6 bolts. Bram Bell, Kevin Downs, JATD crew, 2007.

18 Spring Jammers and Widget Blocks 5.10d ★★★
This trad route is located about 10 feet right of *Brambly Downside*. A top anchor was placed with the intention of bolting it for the 2007 Jonny and Alex Trail Day. After a recon rappel, they decided it would go on gear. Start with a boulder problem, a few feet right of a wide, smooth swath of rock.
75 ft. Dan Beck, Matt Kiroff, JATD Crew, 2007.

BRIGHT SIDE

37.6786
-83.7357

22 routes

Although the Bright Side was ignored for years due to the quality of the surrounding areas, a few motivated developers jumped in head-first in 2011 to create a stellar climbing area with loads of excellent, clean lines. Since then it has exploded to 22 routes with room to grow. The wall contains two major sections: the beautiful arch wall and the steeper amphitheater wall. If you hike in just to climb *Crown of Thorns*, you can leave fully satisfied, as it's one of the best 5.11c's in the Red. Also don't miss *Dog Bites & Fist Fights*, a step up in the grade located on the mega-steep amphitheater wall.

Approach: This wall is situated between Solar Collector and the Dark Side. Approach as for the Dark Side, but just before crossing the wooden bridge, where the trail veers left, continue straight up a steep and winding trail that ends 25 feet right of the rightmost route, *Crazy Eyes*. You can also hike left from Solar Collector to reach the wall.

1 Smokin' on Kesha 5.11c ★★★★
The left of two lines that pass a ledge at 25 feet. Begin on a large, fat flake. Angle up and left on small crimps to reach reprieve on the ledge. Jug up to the blank section, which, unlike its neighbor to the right, lives up to its appearance.
70 ft. 8 bolts. Jimmy Hoctor, Scott Curran, 2012.

2 Chica Loca 5.11a ★★★
This is the right line through the ledge, and serves up a few bolts of crimp-and-pump to reach an intimidating finish that has more bark than bite. A bolt has recently been added to help keep the leader from hitting the ledge.
55 ft. 6 bolts. Nick Feiler, Andrew Wheatley, Mike Wheatley, 2012.

3 Sandy Malone 5.11a ★★★
Head up the short hill left from the amphitheater and *Pickpocket* to the rock patio where this reachy line begins.
40 ft. 4 bolts. Scott Curran, Kyle Waldrop, 2012.

Chica Loca

Sandy Malone

Eleanor Krause, *Golden Brown*, 5.12a (opposite). Photo: John Wesely

Amphitheater Wall

BRIGHT SIDE

COAL BANK HOLLOW

8 Skywalker 5.13b ★★★★
Begin with a difficult boulder problem (V6/7) to reach a long ride of 5.12+ climbing with decent rests to the top of the cliff.
95 ft. 12 bolts. Thomas Cunningham, 2011. Equipped by Dustin Stephens.

9 Fiat Lux 5.12d ★★★★
Fifteen feet left of *Dog Fights* is another long extravaganza guaranteed to sap the forearms.
85 ft. 8 bolts. Brendan Mitchell, 2013, Equipped by Mike Wheatley.

10 Dog Bites & Fist Fights 5.12d ★★★★★
While dogs were biting and fists were flying over at the Lode, a small group of developers enjoyed the peace of this newly found crag. Let's hope that sort of chaos is never seen here. Long and sustained — you may think you're at the Lode while climbing this gem.
85 ft. 10 bolts. Brad Dallefield, 2012.

11 LOMM Open Project ★★★
Right of *Dog Bites* awaits an open project for someone who's either not afraid to use a ladder or has some extremely inventive climbing technique to exit the gigantic hueco.
80 ft. 8 bolts.

12 Medicine Man 5.13a ★★★★
A wicked line left of *Crown of Thorns*, which doesn't provide any sit-down rest in the gigantic hueco.
75 ft. 8 bolts. Enzo Oddo, 2012 Equipped by Kipp Trummel.

13 Crown of Thorns 5.11c ★★★★★
Plenty of interesting features and just the right amount of pump delivers one of the best lines of its grade in the Red. Take the left bolt line leading up to a large hueco. Move out of the hueco roof, then angle left, making good use of a perfectly placed hand-sized hueco along the way.
70 ft. 8 bolts. Dustin Stephens, Max Pazirandeh, 2011.

14 Brownian Motion 5.12b ★★★★
This is the right of the two two lines that head into a large hueco at midheight, and moves out of the hueco into sustained crimping to the chains.
70 ft. 8 bolts. Dustin Stephens, Jimmy Farrell, 2011.

15 Golden Brown 5.12a ★★★★
This takes on the left of two prominent orange streaks. Slightly easier than its partner, and just as good.
60 ft. 9 bolts. Dustin Stephens, Lena Bakanova, 2011.

Pickpocket 5.10d ★★
alk left from the large amphitheater, being careful not to fall to the black hole that leads to the center of the earth. As ou walk beneath a low overhang and just before heading up short hill, look for this line that begins with a few gravelly ockets to reach a heavily featured wall.
0 ft. 5 bolts. Scott Curran, Jimmy Hoctor, 2012.

Bush League 5.12c ★★★★
his is the leftmost line (for now) in the large amphitheater, arked by an arête feature near the middle. Boulder the art, then jug-swim to the chains, passing decent rests that opefully restore the needed juice.
ft. 8 bolts. Scott Curran, Dustin Stephens, 2012.

Better Eat Yo' Wheatleys 5.13a ★★★★
nother bouldery and pumpy line right of *Bush League*.
0 ft. Adam Taylor, 2012. Equipped by Dustin Stephens.

Blowin' Loadz 5.12c ★★★★
g pockets separated by tough boulder problems. It's good, t save the loadz blowin' for later.
0 ft. 9 bolts. Frank Byron, 2012. Equipped by Dustin Stephens.

Hal Garner on the pockets of *Blowin' Loadz,* 5.12c (previous page). Photo: John Wesely.

Fresh Baked 5.12b ★★★★

Locate two streaks of orange rock on the multicolored face beneath the arch. This line climbs the right streak. Climb up to a ledge, then pull onto the pocketed gold streak, skirting the left edge of a hueco where the face flattens and more technical face climbing begins. The black streak can be wet in spring.
0 ft. 9 bolts. Symon Ardila, Dustin Stephens, 2011.

Deep Fried 5.11d ★★★

This is the rightmost bolted line beneath the large arch and left of the crack. Begin on a ledge and boulder up past a mini-arête to reach decent face climbing in the black streak.
5 ft. 8 bolts. Frank Byron, Dustin Stephens, 2011.

Epigyne Crack 5.8+ ★★★

Climb the wide crack starting on the a ledge about 15 feet up. The bolt anchor is tucked up high inside the arch.
0 ft. Dustin Stephens, Jimmy Farrell, 2011.

One-Zero-Six 5.11c ★★★

Scramble to the ledge to reach the start of this face climb, which crosses over a thin crack near the beginning. Move up the face on pockets and edges that diminish as you approach the chains. FA'ed in 106-degree temps, hence the name.
0 ft. 7 bolts. Andrew Wheatley, 2012.

Tongue-Punch 5.11d ★★★

The left of two mank-start routes, which promises to make up to you if you just stick with it for 25 feet. Boulder up the shallow groove on small crimps and big moves.
5 ft. 6 bolts. Andrew Wheatley, 2012.

Scalawagarus 5.11a ★★★

Fifty feet left of *Crazy Eyes*. This and the neighboring line begin with mank, but are well worth jumping on for the stellar post-mank climbing. Climb to a ledge 20 feet up, then continue past big moves including a jump to the tongue for the shorties. Big moves plus big holds make for a happy climber.
0 ft. 7 bolts. Nick Feiler, Mike Wheatley, 2012.

Crazy Eyes 5.9 ★★

As the approach trail meets the cliff, walk left about 25 feet to locate this line, which is marked by a roof midway up.
5 ft. 4 bolts. Scott Curran, Jeremy Kiner, 2012.

Arch Routes

Tongue-Punch

THE DARK SIDE

31 routes

The Dark Side has proven to be one of the Red's most popular cliffs for strong sport climbers. Only the Motherlode has more 5.13s. The lines are steep, sustained, and more pocketed than most at the Red. Many have distinct cruxes, often in the wall's unique "pocket band." Some of this band's pockets can feel sharp — especially if you're weak, tired, or flailing. *Shanghai* is a popular line, finishing with a series of long throws between perfect incuts on an otherwise blank face. *Tuskan Raider* is another classic, with a slopey boulder-problem start and a stout crux lunge. Less bouldery, but packing a mighty pump, *The Force* is probably the wall's most popular outing.

Approach: Drive to the Coal Bank Hollow parking area (directions on page 157). From there, walk a few feet past the kiosk to the signed trailhead on the right. Follow the trail down and across a small bridge, then along an old dirt road for a few hundred yards, passing a road branching off right (the approach for Crossroads). Keep following the main trail, past the signed turnoff for the Gold Coast and Solar Collector; continue straight on the trail, which crosses a creek and winds uphill to meet the lower buttress near the first two routes listed below. The approach trail is signed.

❶ **Catholics' Traverse** 5.8
As the approach trail meets the cliff it forks left. Follow this trail for several hundred feet, passing several bolted routes, and pass beneath a low overhang after a slight downhill. As you round the corner and look right you will see an impressive chunk of leaning rock hosting *The Departure* and *Dagobah*. This route is the chimney to the left. The FA party said he would never do it again, so let that be a hint.
90 ft. *Jimmy Klaserner, Quincy Stang, 2011.*

❷ **The Departure** 5.12c ★★★★
The left line on the leaning pillar right of *Catholics' Traverse*. Tough, sloping boulder problems with difficult clips will have you struggling more than you ever have on a 5.12c. Bring a stick clip for when you get shut down. Best attempted in frigid temps for maximum friction.
80 ft. 9 bolts. *Frank Byron, 2011.*

❸ **Dagobah** 5.12a ★★★
Just right of *The Departure*. Begin with four bolts of steep underclings and sloping pinches that lead to a ledge so big you'll think you climbed back to the ground. From the ledge choose your path, which includes either five bolts of crusty jugs or five bolts of forced but more enjoyable steep climbing.
80 ft. 8 bolts. *Scott Curran, Dustin Stephens, 2012.*

❹ **It's a Trap!** 5.10c ★★★★
About 200 feet right from *Dagobah* and 150 feet left of where the approach trail forks left is a blocky section of wall that splits from slab to steep at midheight. This worthy trad line begins on the left side of the wall and takes on the steep crack system. Begin with the dihedral, then launch into steep climbing with decent protection and a single bolt. There may be anchors before the steep climbing begins, which makes for a decent 5.8.
80 ft. 1 bolt. *Dustin Stephens, Scott Curran, 2012.*

The Departure ❷ ❸

Wookie Love Nest

Evil Emperor

Redneck Jedi

DARK SIDE

COAL BANK HOLLOW

Wookie Love Nest 5.12c ★★★★

Who says you can't have your slab and steep rock too? Take the demanding slab between *It's a Trap* and *Stormtrooper*, passing a tough move to pull the ocean wave at the third bolt. Put more time in on the slab, then shift gears to enjoy the more familiar kicked-out steepness to the chains.
90 ft. 9 bolts. Scott Curran, Dustin Stephens, 2012.

Stormtrooper 5.10b ★★★

Just right of *Wookie Love Nest* on the right side of the blocky wall is this thin crack system. Climb it and take the small gear along for the ride. Bolt anchor.
90 ft. Dustin Stephens, Scott Curran, 2012.

Evil Emperor 5.13a ★★★★★

Twenty-five feet left of *Redneck Jedi* is a very slightly overhanging golden face marked by a hueco 25 feet up. Excellent technical face climbing. To quote the equipper, Dustin Stephens: "Probably the best thing I've ever put bolts in."
90 ft. 8 bolts. Brad Dallefeld, Dustin Stephens, 2012.

Redneck Jedi 5.11a ★★★

Head left about 100 feet when the approach trail first reaches the rock to locate this dihedral with two bolts. Climb the dihedral and slab to chains.
90 ft. 2 bolts. Blake Bowling, 1999.

9 Young Jedi 5.11b ★★

The technical slab 15 feet right of *Redneck Jedi*. The most difficult moves are reaching the first bolt. The quality decreases reaching the second bolt, but the climbing is fun the rest of the way.
60 ft. 5 bolts. Blake Bowling, 1999.

183

Dark Side Ramp Routes

10 Grippy Green 5.12a ★★★★
As you reach the wall on the approach trail, head right. This slabby climb is the first route reached. Boulder up a blind, left-leaning flake for a few bolts, then continue up the slab to a hueco. Pull around the hueco, then climb more slab to reach a slightly overhanging headwall.
70 ft. 8 bolts. Neal Strickland, 2002.

11 Count Dookku 5.11c ★★★
Just right of *Grippy Green* is this sustained slab with a reachy crux.
85 ft. 10 bolts. Dustin Stephens, Will Sweeney, 2014.

12 Small Fry 5.9 ★★★
This lies on a short buttress a bit right of *Grippy Green* and before the Dark Side main wall.
40 ft. 4 bolts. Rob McFall, 1999.

13 Padawan 5.10a ★★
Another short warm-up. Climb the plated face 20 feet right of *Small Fry*.
40 ft. 4 bolts. Nick Walker, Jared Hancock, Karla Hancock, 2006.

14 Techulicous 5.12a ★★★
Walk right from *Small Fry* to reach the main overhanging wall of the Dark Side. On the left side of the wall you'll see a ramp leading up and left to a number of lines on a high section. Walk left beneath this ramp to locate tree stairs leading up to the start of this route.
50 ft. 4 bolts. Hugh Loeffler, 2002.

15 Mama Benson 5.12a ★★★
Start at the highest point and leftmost edge of the ramp mentioned in the previous route description. Climb up the ramp, clipping and unclipping bolts along the way to protect a fall, until you reach the start. Now climb the steep wall with big moves at the top.
50 ft. 6 bolts. Rob McFall, 2000.

16 Shanghai 5.12d ★★★★
This classic route begins high on the ramp, second route from the top. A pumpy start leads to the archetypal "cruel joke" finish.
50 ft. 6 bolts. Chris Martin, 2000.

17 Big Burley 5.13b ★★★
This route lies just right of *Shanghai* and is the third route from the left on the ramp. Power through pumpy moves to a bouldery finish.
60 ft. 6 bolts. Dave Hume, 2002.

18 American Dream 5.12b ★★★★
This is the lowest route on the ramp, and climbs a faint groove feature. Most people pre-clip the second bolt. Pull a tough move at the second bolt, then continue through wicked cross moves and sustained, pumpy climbing to the anchors.
65 ft. 5 bolts. Chris Martin, 2000.

19 The Death Star 5.14b ★★★★
This is the first route right of the ramp on the main wall. Begin with V11 climbing on thin pockets to reach a single-move V8. Wander through 13b climbing, then either fire left and up to a jug or move straight up to finish on *Darth Moll*. Both endings keep the grade the same.
70 ft. 9 bolts. Adam Taylor, 2012. Equipped by Brad Weaver.

20 The Return of Darth Moll 5.13b ★★★★★
One of the best and stiffest 5.13b's in the Red. Begin just right of the previous route. Climb straight up, then angle left and up through difficult cruxes.
65 ft. 8 bolts. Bill Ramsey, 2001.

21 Jedi Mind Trick 5.13b ★★★
Same start as the previous route but move right. Rarely done due to a tweaky shutdown move. Crank up to a dyno off a small pocket, then continue up easier ground to the anchors.
75 ft. 7 bolts. Dave Hume, 2002. Equipped by Neal Strickland.

22 The Force 5.13a ★★★★★
Classic. This route begins a few feet right of *Jedi Mind Trick* and climbs past a cool-looking stone embedded in the wall at about 25 feet. A jumpy start and some long pocket pulls gain the stone. Continue up the pumpy, bulging wall; may the Force be with you for the redpoint crux at the top.
75 ft. 7 bolts. Chris Martin, 2000.

23 Mind Meld 5.12d ★★★
This route begins just right of *The Force*. More bouldery but less sustained than that route. Boulder through sharp bowling-ball-grip pockets, make a difficult third clip, and continue on progressively easier terrain. Stout for the grade.
75 ft. 7 bolts. Hugh Loeffler, 2000.

Dark Side Main Wall

DARK SIDE

COAL BANK HOLLOW

THE DARK SIDE
17. Big Burley 5.13b
18. American Dream 5.12b
19. The Death Star 5.14b
20. The Return of Darth Moll 5.13b
21. Jedi Mind Trick 5.13b
22. The Force 5.13a
23. Mind Meld 5.12d
24. Elephant Man 5.13b
25. Tuskan Raider 5.12d
26. Straight Outta Campton 5.13b
27. Swingline 5.13d
28. Non Starter 5.13b
29. Phantom Menace 5.12d

185

Nathan Hoette, *Big Burley*, 5.13b (page 184). Photo: John Wesely.

Elephant Man 5.13b ★★★★★

...ep a few feet right from *Mind Meld* to locate this beast. ...art on slopey holds, then crank sustained, hard boulder ...oblems for the first five bolts.
5 ft. 9 bolts. Rob McFall, 2000.

Tuskan Raider 5.12d ★★★★

...art on the same slopey holds as *Elephant Man* but traverse ...eeply right. Climb the bulging wall and make a difficult ...ove to gain a huge hueco. Take a rest, then move left and ... to an easier finish.
5 ft. 9 bolts. Rob McFall, 2000.

Straight Outta Campton 5.13b ★★★★

...ack when it was graded sandbagged 5.13a, Dave Graham is ...mored to have fallen on this line, making it his first fall on a ...13a in several years. That should tell you something about ...is beast. Start right of *Tuskan Raider* and climb into and out ... the right side of the big, round hueco. If you've nothing left ... do at this cliff, then check out the Euro-style linkup starting ... *Tuskan Raider,* then moving right out of the large hueco to ...ish on this route. Dubbed *Straight Outta Locash* 5.13a.
5 ft. 6 bolts. Bill Ramsey, 2002. Equipped by Chris Martin, ...son Forrester, 2009.

Swingline 5.13d ★★★★★

...is line has become one of the most sought-after 5.13d's at ...e Red River Gorge. Same start as *Straight Outta Campton,* ...t swings right. Begin with 5.13a climbing to a very difficult ...ulder problem. Continue up the sustained face to the ...chors. Warning! This route has been known to give false ...pe and suck away the seasons of many climbers. Approach ...th caution.
5 ft. 7 bolts. Tony Berlier, 2003. ...uipped by Rob McFall, Chris Martin.

Non Starter 5.13b ★★★

...d up to the first bolt to begin, then step up to the steep ...all and power to the anchors. Rumor has it that Alex Megos ...sighted this from the ground, suggesting that the boulder ...oblem start is V8 and giving it a grade of 5.13c.
... ft. 7 bolts. Bill Ramsey, 2003. Equipped by Hugh Loeffler.

Phantom Menace 5.12d ★★★

...imb the cheater stone tower right of *Non-Starter* to reach ...e starting holds. Pull on and battle your way up the large, ...opey rail feature.
... ft. 8 bolts. Scott Curran, 2015.

Barn Dance

㉚ Barn Dance 5.10d ★★★★

Walk shamefully past the testosterone-filled cave 200 feet right to locate this interesting line. Begin with slab climbing out left instead of the nice line of pockets to the right. Continue up a vertical section with reachy moves that extend into the slab, where the bizarre iron formations await.
60 ft. Andrew and Mike Wheatley, 2012.

㉛ Praestantissimum 5.12a ★★★

Farthest right route at the Dark Side. A short boulder problem leads to good holds. Relax and sack up for the slabby top. End in a half-sunken hueco.
85 ft. 8 bolts. Scott Curran, 2012.

DARK SIDE

COAL BANK HOLLOW

187

FAR SIDE

37.67
-83.73
20 min / 10 min

12 routes

.14
.13
.12
.11
.10
.9
.8
.7
≤.6

This small crag only has a handful of routes, but they include some absolutely amazing lines: *Papa Love Jugs* hucks moves between three sinker huecos, while *Second Nature* powers through an extremely difficult boulder problem to reach a protruding lightning-bolt feature that runs the length of the wall.

Approach: Drive to the Coal Bank Hollow parking area (directions in the PMRP chapter intro, page 157). From there, when facing the RRGCC kiosk, the Far Side is directly uphill to your left. Avoid bushwhacking up the hill by walking back in the direction you drove in and heading up the dirt road to your right. Follow the dirt road as it winds up the hill to the cliff, and then walk right until you reach an obvious notch formed by two closely spaced walls. The first route listed ascends the striking arête on the left wall.

Second Nature

❶ Dirty Sanchez 5.12c ★★★
This route ascends the striking and seemingly featureless arête on the wall forming the left side of the notch. Pull over a small overhang to reach to the bald arête, then climb the arête until the bolts force you left onto the face, where a few troublesome bulges lead to the anchors.
50 ft. 4 bolts. Laban Swaford, 2005.

❷ Subject to Change 5.10d ★★★
Walk about 100 feet right from *Dirty Sanchez* — but do not hike down to the road — to a wall on the right side of the notch, facing the parking lot. This route ascends the short face via small crimps and fingery underclings.
40 ft. 4 bolts. Jack Hume, 2004.

❸ Far Side TR 5.12 ★★★
Five feet right of *Subject to Change* is a set of anchors that may eventually blossom into a line of bolts, if the equipper ever gets off his butt and bolts it. Until then, it's a fun toprope.
50 ft. Blake Bowling, 2000.

❹ Nameless 5.10d ★★★
Step 20 feet right to the next line, which begins behind a large tree. Climb past a crimpy start, then continue up the face on slopey ribs and the occasional good pinch.
40 ft. 5 bolts. Jack Hume, 2004.

❺ Digitalgia 5.11c ★★
Right of *Nameless* is another crimpy line. Beware the biting pocket.
50 ft. 5 bolts. Arthur Cammers, 2007.

❻ Papa Love Jugs 5.11d ★★★★
Pure fun. Walk back down to the road and follow it 100 feet to the right. Look for a north-facing, overhanging wall with lightning-bolt feature. This route is on the left and links three huecos. Scramble up to an overhang to start.
45 ft. 5 bolts. Nick Reuff, 2003.

❼ Second Nature 5.13a ★★★
This rarely traveled yet excellent line ascends the lightning bolt feature just right of *Papa Love Jugs*. Make a big move to a good right-hand jug, then power through the obvious crux. Continue up the feature with zigzagging sidepulls to an exciting finish. Stout for the grade. People now dyno through the crux. The route is much harder if you do it statically, as was originally climbed.
50 ft. 6 bolts. David Hume, 2003.

Al Dilluvio lives the *American Dream*, 5.12b, the Dark Side (page 184). Photo: Elodie Saracco.

Quantum Narcissist 5.13b ★★
st right of *Second Nature* is another difficult and technical
e angling right as it follows the margin of a slanting arête.
ry tough opening moves.
ft. 6 bolts. David Hume, 2003.

NAMBLA RAMBLA 5.11
irty feet right of *Quantum* and *Second Nature* is a vertical
ll containing four vertical lines. Not much is known about
ese lines, and only ATM is being climbed currently. None
them appear to be closed, and the grades and quality are
timates.
ft. 6 bolts. Unknown. Probably equipped by Joe Haynes.

⑩ Nose Ring 5.11
Next route right of *NAMBLA RAMBLA*.
50 ft. 6 bolts. Unknown. Probably equipped by Joe Haynes.

⑪ French Fighter 5.11
Just right of *Nose Ring*.
50 ft. 6 bolts. Unknown. Probably equipped by Joe Haynes.

⑫ ATM 5.11d ★★★
This is the fourth line right of *Quantum Narcissist* on the vertical face. Begin with a big move to a good edge, then continue up the crimpy face, interspersed with a few more big moves on small edges, to the chains.
50 ft. 6 bolts. Johnny Vagabulla, 2007.

PMRP: FLAT HOLLOW

Flat Hollow consists of four crags on the south side of Bald Rock Fork Road, across from Sore Heel Hollow. Some of the routes, at the Getaway in particular, were established back in the 1990s, but a limited trail system and lack of documentation have kept them off the radar. A dedicated parking lot, completed in 2013, along with further development of the cliffs, has now made this area a better destination, with a diversity of routes for every climber. Check out the Velo Crag for some excellent moderates with no line-ups, especially the five-star *Lightning Rod Arête* (5.10c). The Getaway crag is a classic Red River wall that offe[rs] some 5.10 warm-ups along with a pump[y] wall of 5.12s. Head to the Throwback Cra[g] for a handful of long, technical routes, [or] visit the Shipyard for all-day shade a[nd] the must-do route *Sail* (5.12b).

Approach: From the Motherlode parking lot (s[ee] cautions about the approach road, page 20[6),]continue on about 1/4 of a mile, looking for a lar[ge] culvert on the left leading to the new RRGCC F[lat] Hollow Parking Lot. You can park here for bo[th] the Flat Hollow crags and Sore Heel. For So[re] Heel, walk back toward the Motherlode abo[ut] 100 yards and follow the trail that starts wi[th] the walking bridge crossing the creek on yo[ur] left. The Flat Hollow crags are accessed direct[ly] from the Flat Hollow parking lot. Find approa[ch] descriptions in the intro for each specific crag.

Stacy Hodges lights up Lanterne Rouge, 5.9+, Velo Crag (page 194). Photo: Mike Wilkinson.

Jimmy Hoctor on *Lightning Rod Arête,* 5.10c (opposite). Photo: Mike Wilkinson.

VELO CRAG

37.6449 -83.7183
18 min / 5 min

Velo offers a good sample of sport and trad moderates. Don't dismiss the easy sport lines just because you crank 5.12 in the gym with your bros — these are quite high-quality routes with fun moves. And once you show your girlfriend how awesome and brave you are on the fledgling classic *Lightning Rod Arête* (5.10c), you can take whips off the tricky *Cat Amongst the Pigeons* (5.12a) trying to figure out how to rock climb the top.

Approach: Park in the Flat Hollow Parking lot, as you would for the Multi-Purpose Use Trail, Throwback Crag, and the Getaway Crag. Now walk back toward the main road, but instead of crossing the creek, turn right and up the hill on the oil road. Take this road to the end, about 150 yards, and look for a faint trail on the left, leading to the wall near *On Beyond Velodrome*, which has a large hueco about halfway up. To get to the *Lighting Rod Arête* area, take the faint trail left past *Ultegra*. It will hug the pinnacle and as the trail takes a sharp turn right, stop and look up at the striking arête that is *Lightning Rod*.

Old People Are Awesome 5.8 ★★★
the north side of the pinnacle, this chimney and offwidth parates the main cliff from the pinnacle where *Lightning d Arête* is located. Rap from chains.
ft. *Dan Beck, Rae Hartley, Drew Stewart, 2013.*

Lightning Rod Arête 5.10c ★★★★★
striking arête with a great top out and view of the PMRP. cess it by dropping down the lower trail just past *Ultegra*. ke the trail about 100 feet, up and through a wide crack the cliff line, and onto the other side of the pinnacle. Stick p the first bolt. At presstime, an excellent new route went in feet to the right: *Thunder Face*, 5.12c, by Rachel Goldman d Blake Bowling, 2016
ft. 8 bolts. *Dan Beck, Drew Stewart, 2013.*

Krypton 5.7 ★
d this route on the east side of the middle pinnacle. mb the dirty offwidth just left of the cave until you are ced to traverse right and mantel. Bushwhack to the . Rap from a tree or walk toward the point (westward) jump the gap onto the last pinnacle and lower from the chors of *Old People*.
ft. *Dan Beck, Rae Hartley, 2013.*

Spoke Junkies 5.5 ★
mb the crack above the cave, and right of *Krypton*.
ft. *Curtis and Audrey Gale-Dyer, 2015.*

❺ Ultegra 5.10a ★★★
The furthest left route on this section of wall. This route and the next few are located about 70 feet up the hill from where the trail meets the cliff. Climb large iron shelves until you have to actually start rock climbing. Clip the crux bolt, make a committing move near the vertical crack, and cruise to the anchors.
75 ft. 8 bolts. *Don McGlone, Greg Humberg, Matt Tackett, 2010.*

❻ Dura-Ace 5.8+ ★★★★
Super good for the grade. Trend up and left through nice iron edges.
75 ft. 8 bolts. *Don McGlone, Greg Humberg, Matt Tackett, 2010.*

8 Lanterne Rouge 5.9+ ★★★★
Same start as *Eddie Gets a Perm*, but only snap-links are required. A high first bolt protects the opening crack moves followed by a couple more of the same. Then step right onto the face for a pure sport experience to the anchors.
80 ft. 9 bolts. Don McGlone, Greg Humberg, Matt Tackett, 2010

9 A Cat Amongst the Pigeons 5.12a ★★★
This route is located about 30 feet left of where the trail meets the cliff line. A bouldery start leads to swimming on good holds. A big move guards the flake system, then there a great changing-corners section on micro-dihedrals. Really good, just needs some brushing.
75 ft. 8 bolts. Dan Beck, Matt Tackett, 2010.

10 On Beyond Velodrome 5.12c ★★★★
Just as the trail meets the cliff, this line is so striking you may leave your quickdraws and go buy trad gear just for it. Start in the back of the dihedral and climb the arête. As it steepens just know that a rest in the "velodrome" hueco is coming. Plug a #3 and tackle the bouldery top.
90 ft. Dan Beck, 2014.

11 Velo 11 Project
Just right of *Beyond Velodrome* are some top anchors. This and the following routes are right of where the trail meets the cliff line.

12 The Podium 5.10c ★★★★
A bit dirty and intimidating, but as badass as you are. Long, overhanging dihedrals and a roof crux just to round out the cliff.
95 ft. Don McGlone, Greg Humberg, 2010.

7 Eddie Merckx Gets a Perm 5.9 ★★★
Start in the dihedral as for *Lanterne Rouge*, but this time take some trad gear. Protect the crack with some wide pieces, then tackle the cool roof. Lower from anchors.
85 ft. Don McGlone, Greg Humberg, 2010.

On Beyond Velodrome

The Podium

Real Girls Don't Pumptrack

Velo 13 Project ★★★
There is an unbolted 5.11 route here with a jump start that leads to a vague flake. It may be bolted in the future.

A Spot of Bother 5.11 ★★★
It is said that the flake and face caused "a spot of bother" about whether it should be trad or bolted. If you don't like it spicy, you may feel the same.
100 ft. Matt Tackett, 2010.

My Quads Are Too Big 5.11b ★★★
A thin splitter that shares the anchors of *Real Girls*. Great jams and locks with a bit of face climbing thrown in. It's OK to clip the last couple of bolts of *Real Girls* as long as your partner doesn't see you.
80 ft. Dan Beck, Rae Hartley, 2014.

Real Girls Don't Pumptrack 5.10c ★★★★
Good exposure and movement on this hidden gem. The more it cleans up, the better it gets. Climb the arête.
80 ft. 8 bolts. Erin Crocker, Matt Tackett, Keenan Connor, 2010.

The Century 5.10c ★★★★
About 100 feet right, and around the corner from *Real Girls*, *The Century* is well worth the short walk. A bit of choss at the beginning will get you loosened up, then climb overhanging edges to a long lock off. Now a dynamic crux rewards you with 60 more feet of great edges, sidepulls, and gastons.
85 ft. 10 bolts. Merrick Schaefer, 2010.

18 Double Century 5.11d ★★★
Right of *Century*, this one doubles up the difficulty. A low crux leads to better holds above.
80 ft. 8 bolts. Shannon Stuart-Smith, Adam Nolte, 2016.

19 Summer Solstice 5.12b ★★★
Solid rock from beginning to end. Start on a small, arching flake, up through edges, then cut left to an obvious flake at mid-height. More crimps await you on the final approach to the anchors.
80 ft. 8 bolts. Shannon Stuart-Smith, Adam Nolte, 2016.

THE SHIPYARD

37.64
-83.72
18 min / 10 min

18 routes

.14
.13
.12
.11
.10
.9
.8
.7
≤.6

This grey-rock cliff offers the well-traveled climber something a bit different than straight-down pocket pulling. It can be a bit dirty, but well worth it if you know how to gaston, highstep, undercling, and stay in balance, all while carrying a pump. Expect nearly all-day shade, which makes it a great warm-weather area —and make sure to get on the must-do route *Sail*.

Approach: Park in the Flat Hollow parking lot, a you would for the Multi-Purpose Use Trail, Vel Crag, Throwback Crag, and the Getaway Cra; Walk west down the oil road about 20 yards to th bottom entrance of the Flat Hollow Multi-Purpos Trail (MPT). There are two entrances to the MP here; take the first trail you come to, just afte a large oil tank on the left. This trail follows th creek for about 300 yards, crossing it a couple (times. Continue past two "metal-pipe hurdles" fo an additional 75 yards, and start looking for an o oil road going up and right, just past a drainag Follow this road up for about 250 yards toward th cliff line on your left. As the road diminishes to trail, it will make a hairpin to the left, parallelin even closer to the cliff (see topo on opposit page). Routes listed right to left.

3 Avast Ye Project
Work in progress. This project has some crack moves and face climbing. Probably 5.11+.
Equipped by Blake Bowling, 2013.

4 Castoff 5.10d ★★★
Begin on *Boarding Pass* and split right.
65 ft. Blake Bowling, 2013.

5 Boarding Pass 5.11b ★★★★
Requisite for the area—if you don't like how this one climbs, stay ashore. Big moves off the ground quickly disappear befo a ledge rest. Climb dishes and edges as the pump grows. Tackle the crux, grab a shake, then climb a few more bolts to sweet anchor-clip stance.
70 ft. 8 bolts. Blake Bowling, 2013.

6 Climb Aboard 5.11d ★★★
Nerd gate at its finest. Very hard/tricky start, a cruxy middle, and a crux guarding the anchors. You're not done until you're fully on the ship. Start either back in the cave and climb out o jams, or stay further right and climb the thin slab.
65 ft. Blake Bowling, 2013.

Boarding Pass

1 Poop Deck Project
Work in progress at press time. Jump start to a very thin headwall. Probably 5.11.
Equipped by Blake Bowling, 2013.

2 Keelhaul Project
Work in progress at press time, up the scoop feature. Probably 5.11.
Equipped by Blake Bowling, 2013.

7 Davy Jones' Locker Direct 5.13 ★★★
A V8 start to *Davy Jones' Locker*. Start just left of *Climb Aboard* in a hueco. Head up and left on big but sandy holds, to a wicked three-move boulder problem where temperatur makes a difference. Merge with the other bolt line (crappy rock but cool moves) to a small roof and some of the cooles climbing on the wall. Too bad the bottom half isn't good.
70 ft. 7 bolts. Blake Bowling, 2013.

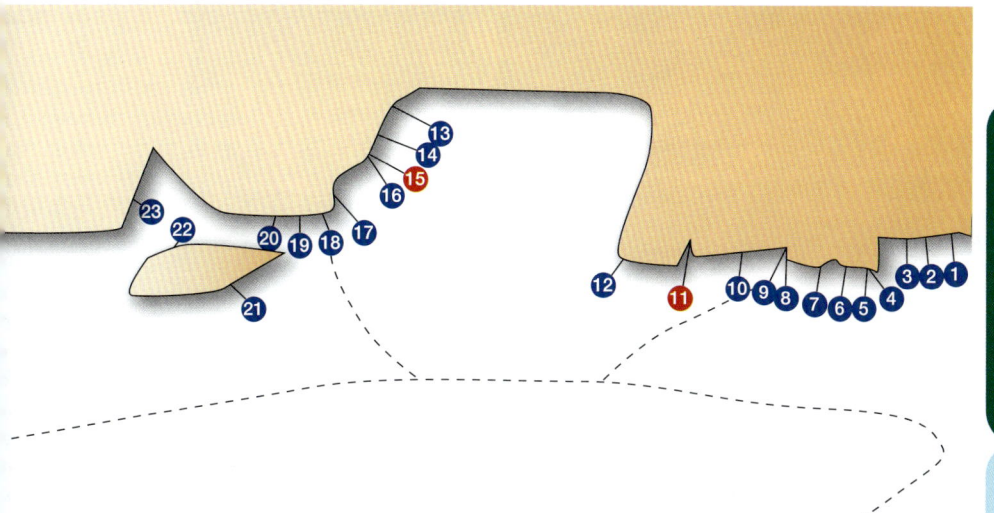

Davy Jones' Locker 5.12b ★★★ ☐
hares first section of *All Hands* then splits right. Climb dirty
opers and broken shelves to one of the finest sequences in
e Red, then tackle the crux.
0 ft. 8 bolts. *Blake Bowling, 2013.*

All Hands on Deck 5.11a ★★ ☐
ll hands, but no feet. Really fuzzy, so bring a brush until it
ets traffic. At some point, this route may continue through
e upper roof at a slightly harder grade.
0 ft. 4 bolts. *Blake Bowling, 2013.*

Bow to Stern 5.12a (Closed) ☐
his route is permanently closed due to a large section of bad
ck. Bolts will be removed in the future.
0 ft. *Blake Bowling, 2013.*

Uncharted Waters 5.11 ★★ ☐
imb the obvious crack system. No anchors. Dirty and loose.
0 ft. *Blake Bowling, 2013.*

Breakneck Speed 5.11c ★★★★ ☐
his blunt arête is the furthest left route on this section of
iff. It is 11b to the second-to-last bolt, then requires some
xtra try-hard. Pockets, edges, laybacking, big moves, small
olds—it has everything.
5 ft. 8 bolts. *Blake Bowling, 2013.*

Beechcomber 5.12- ★★★ ☐
art on steep pockets behind *Storming the Beech*. Move up
nd right to a thin section. "Stay off the beech!"—meaning,
o hand jams between the beech tree and the rock. That's
efinitely cheating.
0 ft. 8 bolts. *Blake Bowling, 2013.*

Davy Jones' Locker

FLAT HOLLOW

⑭ Storming the Beech 5.12b ★★★
Back-to-back boulder problems to a couple of cool sequences. Start on the pile of dirt, stick clip the first bolt, and attempt to figure out the opening sequence. Grab a few jugs and figure out the next crux. Shares the anchors with *Dead Man Chest Hair*.
50 ft. 5 bolts. Blake Bowling, 2013.

⑮ Dead Man Chest Hair 5.8 ★★★
The "Corpse" Don McGlone lives, and this is evidence of his appearance. The anchors are 3/4 of the way up the wall.
50 ft. Don Mcglone, Matt Tackett, 2011.

⑯ Jolly Roger 5.11c ★★★
AKA *Bess Booty*. Same start as *Batten*, then a few moves near *Dead Man Chest Hair*, then steep pockets to a big move. A bit contrived, but fun if you need something else to climb.
55 ft. 7 bolts. Blake Bowling, 2013.

⑰ Batten Down the Hatches 5.11c ★★★
Start left of *Batten* and *Dead Man Chest Hair*, on the blunt arête. Stick clip and climb on semi-choss to a very large move. Don't cheat left onto the other route for a rest. Climb the rest of the blunt arête on nice pockets and edges.
55 ft. 6 bolts. Blake Bowling, 2013.

⑱ Cabin Boy Fever 5.11b ★★★★
The warm-up of the wall. Good holds, good moves, and a runout to the chains.
55 ft. 5 bolts. Blake Bowling, 2013.

⑲ Sail 5.12b ★★★★★
Looks featured, right? Start in the middle of the wall and climb straight up. Jugs lead to more sidepull jugs to a shake. Clip and go through thin edges and small pockets. Simply awesome.
50 ft. 5 bolts. Blake Bowling, 2013.

⑳ Black Pearl 5.11d ★★★★
Start on *Sail* and traverse left, bypassing really fuzzy rock to long moves on good rock. A bit more crimpy than the others on this wall. The climbing is good, but short lived.
50 ft. 4 bolts. Blake Bowling, 2013.

㉑ Capstan 5.6 ★★★
Wander the "front" side of the bow, make one technical move, pass some sandy rock, and deal with lots of rope drag. Descend from the anchors of *Kiss the Manta Ray*.
45 ft. Blake Bowling, 2013.

㉒ Kiss the Manta Ray 5.8 ★★★
You can't miss this pinnacle, or ship's bow, where two routes are located: *Kiss the Manta Ray* and *Capstan*. Walk between the cliff and this pinnacle to a good stance. This sport route climbs up the side of the pinnacle that faces the main wall.
60 ft. 6 bolts. Rae Hartley, Dan Beck, 2014.

㉓ Pay the Devil 5.13b ★★★★
One of the most striking arêtes in the Red. Excellent boulder problems with great movement to a hero finish.
65 ft. 5 bolts. Ralph Woolard, Blake Bowling, 2016.

Hahn ready to *Sail*, 5.12b (opposite). Photo: Mike Wilkinson.

scarpa.com

You only get 26,320 days, more or less. How will you spend them?

SCARPA®
NO PLACE TOO FAR

THE GETAWAY

37.6452
-83.72225
18 min 10 min

0 routes Despite being bolted years ago, this crag has been unknown to many climbers and may no longer remain a sanctuary from the crowds. With only a handful of climbs, it could get crowded on a busy weekend, but with mostly .12s, you will likely be among fellow strongmen and -women.

Approach: Park in the Flat Hollow parking lot, as you would for the Multi-Purpose Use Trail, Velo Crag, and Throwback Crag. Walk west further up the oil road for about 200 yards as if you were going to the Throwback Crag, but before you get to that trail, you will see an oil rig on your left and a road leading up to it. Take two steps onto that road, and look for the other entrance to the Multi-Purpose Trail on your left. After about 400 yards, the trail go around the corner, very close to the cliff. Keep your eyes open for the very short trail leading to the base of the routes.

Brohymn

Brohemian Rhapsody

① Brohymn 5.10c ★★★★
This edging route fires nearly straight up the face. It looks more difficult than it really is; pockets and edges appear just as you need them.
70 ft. 9 bolts. Matt Tackett, Don McGlone, 2005.

② Brohemian Rhapsody 5.10c ★★★★
From the main cliff, head back down to the multi-purpose trail and follow it another 75 feet to the left. A faint set of steps lead back to the cliff line under this gorgeous feature. Climb the face, stem the crack, then mantel your way to the anchors.
70 ft. 9 bolts. Blake Bowling, Jeff Neal, 2005.

③ Bridge Suite 5.10c ★★
On the far left of this section of wall is a warm-up. It's dirty and breaky, but could possibly clean up to be a good climb.
50 ft. 7 bolts. Josephine Neff, 2013.

④ Notso Borneo 5.10a ★
Clip some of the bolts on the route to the right, until you can escape left. Climb the flake system on the left of the main wall. Rap from the anchors of the sport line, or from a tree.
50 ft. 3 bolts. Blake Bowling, 2005.

Blake Bowling, *Afros, Macks, and Zodiacs*, 5.12c (opposite). Photo: Mike Wilkinson.

AfroSquad 5.12b ★★★

art on the second-level ledge. This route is the last one on
's section of wall that goes to the top of the cliff. Start on
gs and climb plates and ledges to a stance. Breathe and
ad up through a couple of cruxes. Big moves await.
) ft. 8 bolts. *Porter Jarrard, Chris Martin, 1998.*

OG Pimp Juice 5.12a ★★★

st before a dirt gully leads you to the ledge and the routes
 the left side of this crag, this route starts on an arête
ature, then trends up and right. Gain the ledge and rest
fore tackling the sea of brilliant orange rock.
) ft. 8 bolts. *Porter Jarrard, Chris Martin, 1998.*

Pimpto-Bismol 5.12b ★★★

art on the left face of the block, climb to a mantel, then
gher on increasingly better rock. Pockets and iron edges
ad to a bulge. Climb directly over it, then up really cool
lds to the anchors.
 ft. 9 bolts. *Porter Jarrard, Chris Martin, 1998.*

Pimptastic 5.12b ★★★★

arting in the middle of the face just left of the "cave," climb
aight up to the ledge to an obvious rest. Boulder your way
 the next ledge where you can contemplate for a while.
lock good sequences on iron edges and pockets that lead
 a redpoint crux.
 ft. 9 bolts. *Porter Jarrard, Chris Martin, 1998.*

Afros, Macks, and Zodiacs 5.12c ★★★★

 the far right of the cliff, start in the steepest part of the
ve. Obed-like climbing with long moves on good holds.
ng out at the ledge and heckle your friends before you
ntinue up the best stone on the wall.
 ft. 9 bolts. *Porter Jarrard, Chris Martin, 1998.*

Gotta Get Away 5.11a ★★★★

is two-pitch route may make you try as hard as you
uld on the harder sport routes to the left. Start back in the
edral, climbing out the steepness. Belay anchors on the
dge make for a nice vantage point for your bros flailing on
 12's. Continue up the flaring crack, finding some actual
lds along the way. Rap from anchors. If you want to skip
 first pitch, the ledge is accessible from the right, but it's
it sketchy.
 ft. *Blake Bowling, Jeff Neal, 2005.*

Pimptastic

Photo: Mike Wilkinson.

203

THROWBACK CRAG

11 routes

With one of the easiest approaches in the PMRP, the Throwback is a great crag to get in some final pitches before darkness falls. With a handful of stellar, long, technical routes, it's not too far to walk back to your car with your tail dragging.

Approach: Park in the Flat Hollow parking lot, as you would for the Multi-Purpose Use Trail. Walk west further up the oil road for about 200 yards. Just as you crest the top of the hill you will see a small turnaround on the left. Just left of the turnaround, look for the start of the trail that leads to the middle of the wall at the route Yo, Ono (#10). Routes listed left to right.

Hand and Fingers

To Julie, With Love

① Search and Seizure 5.11d ★★★
This and the next two routes start at the far left of the crag, up on a small ledge. This one follows the arête, beginning in the crack created by a detached block. Move toward the arête, then balance back and forth on each side until you reach the anchors.
60 ft. 6 bolts. Adam Nolte, Shannon Stuart-Smith, 2016.

② Marmight 5.12a ★★★
Crimps and pockets on the beautiful face left of the obvious crack. The name is a wordplay on Marmite, the British spread made from yeast extract and known for its "acquired" taste. As the marketing slogan goes, you'll either love it or hate it.
80 ft. 8 bolts.
Shannon Stuart-Smith, Byron Hemple, Adam Nolte, 2016.

③ Hand and Fingers 5.11 ★★★★
The obvious finger crack seen from the road. Chill up to a decent stance, pull a cool move over/around a small roof, then head into the void of not-perfect fingers. There is adequate gear where you need it, but don't expect to be making every move on toprope as you lead it.
80 ft. Unknown.

204

To Julie, With Love 5.12c ★★★

In loving tribute to my late wife. Brief, crimpy start leads to easy jug climbing before encountering the first of two shallow arches. Move up right and into the first shallow flake exiting out left on to the face and then straight up with a few well-placed finger pockets and positive iron-oxide edges leading to the second shallow arch. Climb up and towards the lower right end of the second arch then out left onto the face on edges before heading straight up on heinous crimps. Climbing eases as you head up toward a well-featured short arête beside a giant hueco to finish."

~ Shannon Stuart-Smith

90 ft. 10 bolts. *Shannon Stuart-Smith, Byron Hempel, 2015.*

10-Pound Tumor 5.11c ★★★★

About 50 feet left of the hemlock tree, you'll see two long routes up the main wall. Expect crimps, edges, and a few pockets.

ft. 9 bolts. *Jeff Neal, Lee Smith, 2015.*

There's a Bad Moon on the Rise 5.12a ★★★★

Starting just left of the hemlock, this route tries to climb the blunt arête. Boulder up through the first couple of bolts to get in a full resting ledge. Figure out your beta to get to the next set of holds, then start the adventure, wandering a bit right and left as you move up on small-but-good edges. A couple of mantels along the way get you to the chains near the top of the cliff.

ft. 10 bolts. *Blake Bowling, 2016.*

Do the Hemlock Rock 5.10+ ★★★★

Climb the beautiful dihedral behind the hemlock tree to the bolt anchor. Although the first ascent is unknown, the quality is not. If you are into climbing trad, don't pass up this one. It is a bit green due to the shade, but good stances and bomber jams are plentiful.

ft. *Unknown.*

Don't Call It a Comeback 5.11d ★★★★★

This awesome route is located just right of the ominous dihedral and hemlock. Edges, underclings, pockets, mantels, and slabs ... this thing has it all.

90 ft. 10 bolts. *Dan Beck, Matt Tackett, Rae Hartley, 2012.*

Birth of a Legend 5.11d ★★★★

From the top of the trail, traveling left, this is the first route you come to. Similar to its counterpart, *Don't Call It a Comeback*, but shorter and a bit more friable.

5 ft. 8 bolts. 8 bolts *Dan Beck, Matt Tackett, 2012.*

Yoko Ono 5.12b ★★★★

Look up as the trail meets the cliff. Boulder problem low, then good climbing above. If you're short, you may hate this thing.

ft. 11 bolts. *John Wesely, Greg Humburg, 2014.*

Don't Call It a Comeback

Yoko Ono

⓫ **Live Music Is Better** 5.9 ★★

The warm-up of the wall. Just right of where the trail meets the cliff, walk around the corner and up a small hill to this arête route. Stick clip recommended, as the opening moves are cruxy. What's left is balance climbing on good edges.

70 ft. 6 bolts. *Don McGlone, Matt Tackett, Greg Humburg, 2010.*

THROWBACK CRAG

FLAT HOLLOW

205

PMRP: SORE HEEL HOLLOW

Approach: From Miguel's, drive 12.4 miles south on KY 11 toward Beattyville. Turn right on KY 498. Drive 1.2 miles to a sharp right curve. Just beyond this curve, take a sharp right on Bald Rock Road, a gravel road, and follow it slowly as it curves left toward a house, staying left at the first intersection. After 0.3 miles the road descends a steep hill. The hill can be drivable in a passenger car if the road has recently been graded, but it usually ruts out within a few days. 4WD is recommended. During busy seasons and inclement weather, this hill can become treacherous. Scope out the hill before proceeding down. If you have doubts, climb elsewhere — do not park atop the hill, as this area is used to access oil company equipment (and you are liable to be towed). Throughout the gorge, DO NOT park in front of oil wells or oil equipment.

Once down the hill, pass the Motherlode parking area and continue 0.3 miles to the first gravel road on the right. There is a "Sore He Parking" sign at this turnoff. Here, you ha two choices:

To drive to the Sore Heel parking area (roug and slow — 4WD recommended), turn right a follow the road up the hill past a row of lar, bright-blue storage tanks, make a sharp rig (0.2 miles after the turnoff), and follow the ro another half mile, eventually descending a sho hill to the Sore Heel Hollow parking area at t bottom of the hill on the right.

Alternatively, to avoid the rugged Sore H road, continue just past the Sore Heel turnoff a park in the new Flat Hollow parking lot, on t left. Walk back up Bald Rock Fork Road towa Motherlode about 500 feet, looking for a footbrid on your left, and take the shortcut trail to the So Heel parking lot. Regardless of your vehicle, t option is better and will get you to the crag faste

What are you planning on doing today ?

PETZL Access the inaccessible

ClimbTech

Sustainable solutions and Innovations in climbing hardware.

ClimbTech Removable Bolt
ClimbTech removable bolts are great for bolting and minimizing impact. New features include cable stiffener, ergonomic trigger, and one-piece cleaning bushing. ClimbTech RBs are safe, efficient and easy to use.

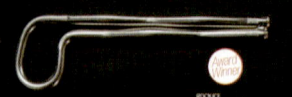

Wave Bolt Glue-In
The Wave Bolt is a glue-in rock climbing anchor, offering tremendous strength and increased resistance to corrosion. It combines the strength of glue-ins with the convenience of pitons. In vertical placements the Wave Bolt will not slide out of the hole – like other glue-in bolts do – prior to the glue hardening.

B.I.G.
ROCK ICE BEST IN GEAR 2014

ClimbTech Legacy Bolt
The new Legacy Bolt sleeve anchor now makes it possible to be installed and removed, allowing the same bolt hole to be used for rebolting. See new Legacy Bolt product videos at: climbtech.com/videos

more info at
climbtechgear.com

Follow us on Facebook /climbtech
Follow us on Vimeo /climbtech

CURBSIDE

5 routes

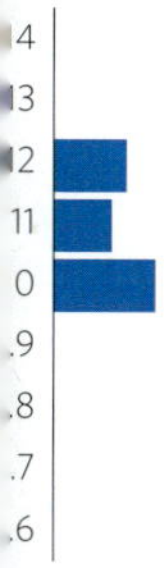

This wall's proximity to the road makes it a great place to warm up, or to bag a few new lines at day's end. Several route names are a play on those at Roadside; score bonus points by matching each route with its namesake! Most of the lines deliver a good pump, and some require a good bit of power.

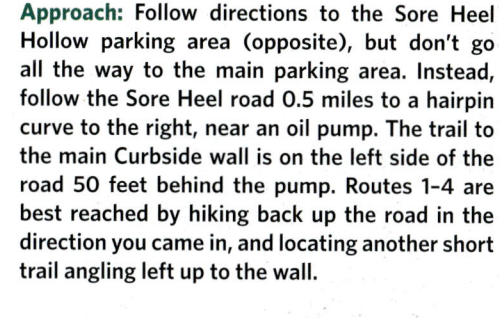

37.6514
-83.7190

Approach: Follow directions to the Sore Heel Hollow parking area (opposite), but don't go all the way to the main parking area. Instead, follow the Sore Heel road 0.5 miles to a hairpin curve to the right, near an oil pump. The trail to the main Curbside wall is on the left side of the road 50 feet behind the pump. Routes 1–4 are best reached by hiking back up the road in the direction you came in, and locating another short trail angling left up to the wall.

Conditions: Most routes stay dry in the rain. The wall faces east, so expect morning sun and afternoon shade.

❷ **Sudoku** 5.10a ★★
This line begins on the northeast-facing buttress directly at the head of the trail. Climb large holds to the anchors.
50 ft. 5 bolts. Kipp Trummel, Karen Clark, 2006.

❸ **Action Over Apathy** 5.10b ★★★
Begin five feet right of the previous line, on pockets. Move up to a short roof, don't wuss out left, and crank hard to a good ledge. Continue up, angling right, on pumpy underclings and sidepulls.
60 ft. 5 bolts. Kipp Trummel, 2006.

❹ **The Return of Frank Byron** 5.12c ★★★★
Move 20 feet right from the corner to a line of bolts beginning with a horizontal shelf. The holds are there, but they're tough to spot. Grab the shelf to start, then trend left on pockets and edges. Veer back right to the second bolt, clip it, then crank a few more moves to reach an incut slot. Shake, then follow easier ground to the anchors. Bouldering on a rope.
55 ft. 5 bolts. Ray Ellington, Kipp Trummel, 2007.

❺ **Curbside No Traction** 5.10c ★★★★
This is the leftmost line on the main Curbside wall. It's possible to head right from the previous lines, but easier to walk back down to the road, then follow the trail to the left near the next oil pump. From where the approach trail meets the wall, walk about 100 feet left and up to a ledge from which this and the next route can be accessed. This is the line on the left of the clean slab and begins left of a rounded flake-like feature. Burn rubber.
35 ft. 5 bolts. Kipp Trummel, 2006.

❻ **The Ankle Brute** 5.11a ★★★
This is the next slab line right of *Curbside No Traction*.
35 ft. 4 bolts. Kipp Trummel, 2006.

Waltz the Deal 5.10a ★★
locate this route, walk 40 feet left from the arête where alternate approach trail meets the wall. Scramble up a ort low-angle slab and pull over a bulge to reach the first lt. Continue up the face, staying just left of a wide crack.
ft. 8 bolts. Kipp Trummel, Karen Clark, 2006.

❼ The Second Labor of Hercules 5.10c ★★
The next two lines are located just left of the corner of the main Curbside wall. This is the line on the left and climbs the featured wall, using pinches and underclings.
50 ft. 7 bolts. Josh Thurston, Ron Bateman, 2006.

❽ Single Finger Salute 5.10c ★★
Begin with a tough start, then move up through pumpy moves to the chains. Better rock quality than the previous line.
55 ft. 5 bolts. Ron Bateman, Josh Thurston, 2006.

❾ Ghost in the Machine 5.10c ★★★
This is the leftmost line on the main east face of Curbside. Climb up through sloping holds to a large ledge. Pull off the ledge into a short section of steeper rock to reach the chains.
60 ft. 7 bolts. Ron Bateman, Rosanna Bateman, 2006.

❿ Subtle Thievery 5.11c ★★
Step right about 15 feet to the next line. Climb the sequential lower face to a good rest and contemplate the final boulder problem below the chains.
65 ft. 6 bolts. Josh Thurston, Ron Bateman, 2006.

⓫ Conscription 5.11c ★★★
An excellent pumper. Climb sustained pockets and edges, passing a tough move or two along the way. Beach onto a sandy ledge, finagle a rest, reach high to find the best holds you can, then highstep and heel-hook over the roof to a relieving finish.
65 ft. 6 bolts. Ron Bateman, Josh Thurston, Kipp Trummel, 2006.

⓬ Avalanche Run 5.11d ★★★
This line is marked by an obvious large roof with a fixed draw. Pull on positive holds to reach the intimidating roof. Locate key holds, release the feet, and hope the barndoor doesn't pull you off. Hang on to reach the chains.
65 ft. 6 bolts. Kipp Trummel, 2006.

⓭ Wildfire 5.12a ★★★★
This and the next few lines are steeper and less featured. Begin about 10 feet right of the previous line, on a boulder. Step out into a right-angling traverse. Bust straight up through the fingery face, make the last clip, then blast.
50 ft. 5 bolts. Paul Vidal, Kipp Trummel, 2006.

⓮ Outbreak 5.12b ★★
This is the next route right of *Wildfire* on the overhanging orange wall. Begin with a steep move to reach a sloping ledge. Trend right up the face, using bullet pockets and fing slots, to a reach-around move near the top.
55 ft. 5 bolts. Kevin Todd, Kipp Trummel, 2006.

CURBSIDE

SORE HEEL HOLLOW

Wildfire | 13 | 14 | 15

Thunder 5.12c ★★
...st route on the main overhanging Curbside wall. Begin 10 ...et right of *Outbreak*, on sandy holds. Blast through small ...ges on a blank section to reach a band of pockets. Gain ...lief on the pockets, then bear down for another blank run ...the anchors.
...) ft. 6 bolts. *Brian Arnold, 2008.*

Massive Attack 5.12a ★★★★
...long, slightly overhanging face climb to the right of the ...ain wall and directly right of a crack in a dihedral. Technical ...mbing leads to a no-hands ledge at midheight. Continue ...rough sustained, pumpy climbing to tough moves before ...e anchors.
...ft. 8 bolts. *Shadow Ayala, 2012.*

Photo: Mike Wilkinson.

211

THE GALLERY

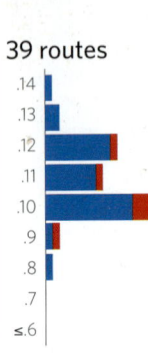

37.653
-83.717
25 min 10 min

39 routes

.14
.13
.12
.11
.10
.9
.8
.7
≤.6

This excellent wall is easily accessible and hosts a unique blend of striking lines. As you approach, you'll see one of the Red's most aesthetic cracks, All That Glitters, a must-do for elite trad climbers. If your technical face skills are up to par, try the amazing slab Random Precision.

Approach: Start at the Sore Heel Hollow parking area (directions on page 206). From there instead of hiking the trail that leads to the main Sore Heel Hollow areas (Playground, Shady Grove, Purgatory, etc.), walk back up the road to the top of the final hill. Atop the hill, take a sharp right and follow a road until it begins to head downhill 100 feet past some oil equipment on the right. Just as the road heads downhill, look for an old, overgrown road on the left. Follow this road which quickly narrows to a well-defined trail leading to the wall. The first route you encounter will be the obvious right-slanting crack *All That Glitters* (#26). Routes listed from left to right.

Conditions: Morning sun and afternoon shade.

Dain Bramage

❶ **Crimpy and the Brain** 5.9 ★★

At the very end of the cilff, just near where the last trail meets the rock, start on jugs that angle right up to a "spicy crimp and sloper section." Very, very sandy.

50 ft. 6 bolts. Steve Simpson, Angel Simpson, 2014.

❷ **All Draws & No Brains** 5.10d ★★

Just right of *Crimpy and the Brain,* and on the main front section of rock, start on the crispy holds to a "tongue" undercling, then power through a couple more small friable holds to gain access over the roof. Ledges and good holds appear as you get closer to the top.

50 ft. 6 bolts. Steve Simpson, Angel Simpson, 2014.

❸ **No Brain, No Pain** 5.10b ★★★

The rightmost climb on this section of rock. Powerful moves ease into pockets leading up the steep face.

40 ft. 5 bolts. Alan Prechtel, Steve Simpson, 2014.

❹ **Dain Bramage** 5.10d ★★★

Good, moderate, adventure climbing and the tallest of the routes in this section. Climb good edges to a ledge, pull an upper crux to another stance, then trend toward the arête and anchors.

80 ft. 8 bolts. Alan Prechtel, Steve Simpson, 2014.

❺ **Short by a Foot** 5.10c ★★★★

Good crimps and finger buckets to a mandatory mantel. Short and powerful for the grade.

40 ft. 5 bolts. Erik Kloeker, Will Sweeney, 2016.

❻ **Starry Night** 5.12a ★★★★

A crazy-steep line with permadraws just past the choss arch right of *Dain Bramage.* If you like steep, and you like jugs, then you will like this climb. Big moves on big holds lead you to more big holds and big moves.

65 ft. 6 bolts. Dustin Stephens, Will Sweeney, 2016.

❼ **Bottle Infrontome** 5.10d ★

Start 15 feet left of *Frontal Lobotomy* and stick clip as high as you like. Locate decent holds to work up the steep face, through a juggy roof, then up a wide crack peppered with jugs. The rock is very friable and sandy, but may clean up. Take a brush.

60 ft. 10 bolts. Alan Prechtel, Aaron Fraebel, Brian Bass, 2016.

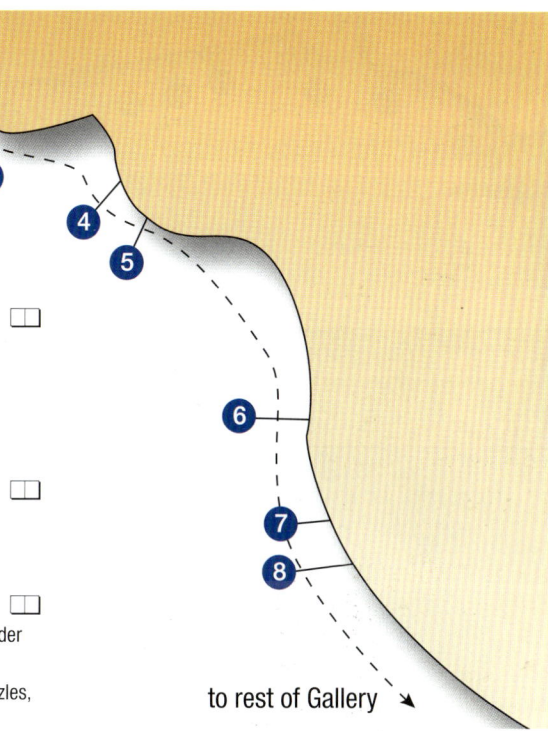

THE GALLERY

SORE HEEL HOLLOW

Frontal Lobotomy 5.10c ★★
 the far right side of the "cave," this route starts out
eep then gets into face/ledge climbing. A long draw is
commended on the fourth bolt.
5 ft. 8 bolts. *Alan Prechtel, Steve Simpson, 2016.*

Thin Skin 5.10b ★★★
imb the short dihedral just left of *Blank Canvas*.
5 ft. *Danny Rice, 2007.*

Blank Canvas 5.12c ★★★★
llow an arête and mini-dihedral through multiple boulder
oblems separated by good rests. If you haven't been
acticing squeezing blank corners and figuring out puzzles,
is may feel hard for 5.12c.
0 ft. 7 bolts. *Jason Forrester, 2005.*

Banksy 5.12c ★★★★
out 100 feet right of *Blank Canvas* is this striking, crimpy
dition marked by a black-stained half-moon rail. Begin by
mbing to a ledge to clip the first bolt. Excellent solid crimps
d powerful moves.
5 ft. 7 bolts. *Shadow Ayala, 2012.*

Crude Awakening 5.10b ★★★
st right of *Banksy* is this enjoyable face climb with an
-soaked start.
0 ft. 8 bolts. *Kipp Trummel, Brent Dupree, 2008.*

Clair Obscur 5.11b ★★★
ty feet right of *Crude Awakening* to this line, which serves
 a variety of movement up a wide black streak.
5 ft. 9 bolts. *Elodie Saracco, Shadow Ayala, 2012.*

DaVinci's Left Ear 5.10b ★★★
st right and around the corner from *Clair Obscur* is another
lted line. Climb the face on fragile holds, making use of
conspicuous underclings along the way.
0 ft. 7 bolts. *Blake Bowling, 2001.*

Smack Dab 5.11b ★★
mb the vertical face 10 feet right of the previous line. The
 is often wet.
0 ft. 6 bolts. *Blake Bowling, 2001.*

to rest of Gallery

Starry Night

213

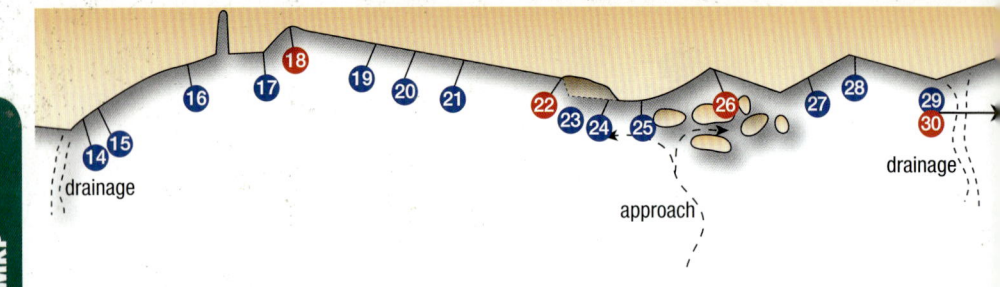

16 Different Strokes 5.11c ★★★
Move 30 feet right from *Smack Dab* to this line, which begins left of a wide chimney. Climb the pumpy face, making use of sidepulls and pinches the whole way. If you find a horizontal hold, you must be on a different route.
50 ft. 6 bolts. Terry Kindred, 2001.

17 Random Precision 5.11b ★★★★
This amazing, technical line begins 15 feet right of a wide chimney. Begin with a tough and balancey start and continu up the face, making use of precise foot placements and the random good hold. An extra bolt has been added after the fifth bolt, eliminating the original runout.
60 ft. 7 bolts. Terry Kindred, Blake Bowling, Bob Matheny, 2001

18 Stucconu 5.11+ ★★★
The obvious dihedral 50 feet right of *Random Precision*. Go gear leads to a very long, powerful move.
60 ft. Blake Bowling, 2001.

19 Zen and the Art of Masturbation 5.12d ★★★★
This is the first of two lines on the striking, gold, slightly overhanging face right of *Stucconu*. Begin with an easy star then quickly transition to heinous crimping interspersed wit mellow pocket climbing, to reach the upper headwall. Try to get a shake, then tackle the overhang to reach a jug. Trend left to hide in a large hueco for a bit, then creep out to take the finishing jugs to the chains.
70 ft. 7 bolts. Eric Stevenson, 2007.

20 American Graffiti 5.12d ★★
Between *Zen* and *The Shocker* lies this great face climb wi multiple cruxes and varied climbing.
85 ft. 8 bolts. Shadow Ayala, Rachel Stewart, 2012.

21 The Shocker 5.14b ★★★★
Begin left of the large hueco in the middle of the wall. Apparently this line has some stopper moves on it, but thes didn't seem to thwart the freakish strength of James Litz.
70 ft. 7 bolts. James Litz, 2008.

22 Darkside of the Flume 5.9 ★★
Climb the chimney and hand crack 50 feet right of the previous line. Lower from bolted anchors. Large cams and maybe some 2x4s may be helpful for pro.
70 ft. Blake Bowling, 2001.

23 Weak Sauce Closed Project
Just left of *Gold Rush*.

Ashley Schenck, *Gold Rush*, 5.11d (page 216). Photo: John Wesely.

Hal Garner loves *All That Glitters*, 5.12c (this page). Photo: John Wesely.

Gold Rush

24 Gold Rush 5.11d ★★★★
Right and around the corner from the *Darkside* wide crack is an overhanging and well-featured face. The dirty start gains a low roof. Pull over the roof on good jugs to the plated face. Pull on plates and good edges to a less-featured and more-overhanging section near the top. Get a good shake and crank through big moves on smaller edges to a surprise ending.
70 ft. 8 bolts. Terry Kindred, 2003.

25 Mosaic 5.12c ★★★★
Begin on a low ledge 20 feet right of *Gold Rush*. Follow a thin seam, then angle right and continue up the face near the left margin of a black-and-orange-streaked wall.
60 ft. 6 bolts. Blake Bowling, 2003.

26 All That Glitters 5.12c ★★★★★
The approach trail comes up just below this striking, right-angling crack, which has a bolt near the beginning. Crank through the lower crux move, then enjoy aesthetic crack climbing to the anchors.
70 ft. 1 bolt. Blake Bowling, 2006.

27 Calm Like a Bomb 5.13a ★★★
Walk right from *All That Glitters* to the next bolted line, which takes on a thin seam up an overhanging section of the wall. Begin on steep and slightly fragile rock to reach the seam. Sidepull and crimp through powerful moves to a decent rest. Get a shake and pull the difficult ending to reach the anchors shared with *Break the Scene*. If you suffer from a strange disease that some locals catch, then you won't use the incredibly obvious no-hands rest near the top.
70 ft. 7 bolts. Ben Cassel, 2006.

Calm Like a Bomb

The Tribute

⓫ Break the Scene 5.12a ★★★★
The bolted dihedral just right of *Calm Like a Bomb*. Pull a difficult start to the crack, followed by pumpy stemming to a sloping ledge near the top. Creep left into the overhang, trying not to lose your feet, and gun for the anchors. Don't cheat the last move by hanging 10-foot draws on the anchors!
75 ft. 8 bolts. *Terry Kindred, 2004.*

⓬ The Tribute 5.13 ★★
The next bolted line right of the *Break the Scene* dihedral. Climb mungy rock to an impossible move. Work magic, then continue up to the anchors on eroding jugs. The beginning boulder problem kept this route an open project for several years until Litz easily did it and called the line 5.12d/13a.
75 ft. 5 bolts. *James Litz, 2009.*

⓭ All That Quivers 5.10b ★★
Hike right from *The Tribute* to the bottom of a gully and locate an offwidth crack beginning halfway up the face. Start in the mud and climb the face to reach the crack. Take on the offwidth to a large ledge 15 feet from the top. Rappel from the ledge.
100 ft. *Danny Rice, Paul Coover, 2006.*

⓮ Happy Trails 5.10d ★★★
Move up from the gully until you reach an iron cable extending from the top of a cliff to the ground. Step over the cable and walk about 50 feet farther to locate the next bolted line, left of a rounded corner. Climb past a low overhang on fragile rock to start. Pump up the face past many eyebrow-like holds and feets that disappear when you get above them.
75 ft. 9 bolts. *Terry Kindred, 2005.*

Happy Trails

㉜ The King Lives On ... 5.10b ★★★
Just right of *Happy Trails*. Climb through edges to start, then enjoy rounded, sloping holds for most of the way to the anchors.
70 ft. 9 bolts. *Gary Drexler, Jared Hancock, 2004.*

THE GALLERY

SORE HEEL HOLLOW

27 Years of Climbing

A Brief History of Climb

㉝ Johnny B. Good 5.11a ★★★
Move right from the previous line to locate this route, which begins with a bulge leading to a low-angle section. Tread lightly on low-angle rock past thin sidepulls to a severely overhanging section near the top. Crank out the roof on big jugs to a pocketed section before the anchors.
85 ft. 9 bolts. Gary Drexler, Tim Powers, 2004.

㉞ 27 Years of Climbing 5.8 ★★★★★
Possibly the best 5.8 sport line in the Red! This is the next bolted line right of *Johnny B. Good*. Climb through a low-angle face to an interesting feature just before an overhang. Desperado past the feature, then crank through large pockets in the overhang to reach the anchors.
65 ft. 7 bolts. Alex Yeakley.

㉟ Gallery 35 Closed Project
The bolted line right of *27 Years of Climbing*, just past the wide crack. Several hangers are currently missing.
65 ft.

㊱ Murano 5.10b ★★★
Step just right from the previous line. Climb over a low roof to reach a series of plates. Continue up to an enjoyable slab.
75 ft. 9 bolts. Unknown.

㊲ Guernica 5.12b ★★★★
Right of *Murano* and left of *Brief History*. Lower from the first set of anchors for a three-star 5.11a, or take a breather and head out on an adventure through a hard boulder problem, then big moves and a mantel to the high anchors.
65-80 ft. 8-9 bolts. Dustin Stephens, 2013.

㊳ A Brief History of Climb 5.10b ★★★★
Walk right from *Guernica* to the next bolted line. Scramble up slightly suspect rock to reach the first bolt. Boulder past the next two bolts, then enjoy fun, steep climbing on good holds.
75 ft. 9 bolts. Blake Bowling, 2006.

㊴ A Briefer History of Climb 5.10b ★★★
Climb a direct start or the first several bolts of *A Brief History of Climb* to a ledge with bolted anchors. Clip a high bolt, then run with the difficult crack to a higher set of chains.
75 ft. 1 bolts. Blake Bowling, 2007.

㊵ Knot Sure 5.12b ★★
Head up the flake and face left of *Preacher's Daughter* to a ramp where easy and enjoyable climbing gives way to a desperately thin technical crux up top.
65 ft. 9 bolts. Sarah Gross, 2014.

㊶ The Preacher's Daughter 5.11a ★★★
Enjoy some jug-and-hueco-swinging fun on semi-decent vertical rock.
70 ft. 8 bolts. Jared Dean, Shadow Ayala, 2012.

Taylor Duncan, *Mosaic*, 5.12c (page 216). Photo: Elodie Saracco.

VOLUNTEER WALL

25 routes

Just before his death, John Bronaugh placed red tags at the base of this wall where he planned to drill new routes. In 2005, volunteers got together and continued where John left off. This took the route tally from 9 to 21. This wall is one of the few in the Red with a good selection of excellent 5.10 sport routes.

Approach: From the Sore Heel Hollow parking area (directions on page 206), walk uphill on a cleared dirt road a few hundred feet to the marked trailhead on the right. Take this trail then take the first trail on the left, which is marked with a wooden sign. Follow the trail a few minutes until you reach the first bolted line, *Generosity*. There is also another way to reach the wall: Instead of taking the first marked trailhead on the right, continue along the dirt road a few hundred more feet to the next trail on the right, also marked with a wooden sign. When the trail meets the wall, follow it left until you reach the *Swap Meet* (route #17).

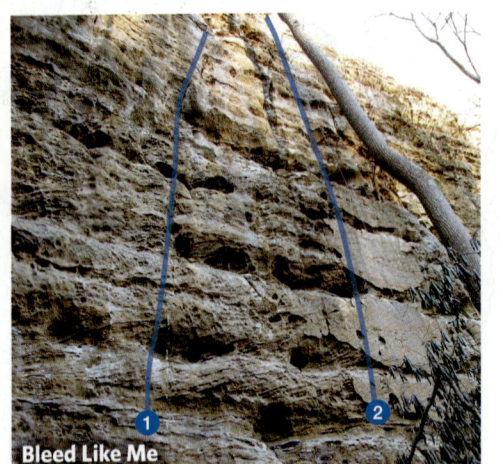

① Bleed Like Me 5.12b ★★★
This line is the leftmost on the wall before a large amphitheater. Climb past a dirty start to reach tough crimping through the first few bolts. Ease up for a bit, then bear down again at the last bolt. There's a good run to the anchors. This, *Same Way*, and *Hurt* were bolted and dedicated to John Bronaugh and his son Alex.
65 ft. 9 bolts. Blake Bowling, 2006.

② Same Way 5.11b ★★★
Next bolted line 20 feet right of *Bleed Like Me*. Pull past a sequence of large plates to a ledge. From the ledge, step up into pumpy pockets that lead through a series of subtle bulges.
65 ft. 8 bolts. Matt Tackett, Blake Bowling, 2006.

③ Pinkies Extended 5.10c ★★★
Plates and jugs lead to an upper crux.
65 ft. 7 bolts. Dustin Stephens, Aaron Saxton, 2013.

④ Smell the Glove 5.8 ★★★
Climb past two bolts that lead to the lieback crack. Descend from the *Pinkies* anchor.
65 ft. 2 bolts. Dustin Stephens, Aaron Saxton, 2013.

⑤ Hurt 5.10c ★★★
Begin on a boulder 50 feet right of the previous line. Climb around a large plate, which leads to pockets and edges on a more featured section of the wall.
65 ft. 8 bolts. Blake Bowling, Matt Tackett, 2006.

VOLUNTEER WALL

SORE HEEL HOLLOW

Darwin Loves You — 7

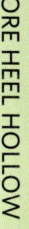

Donor — 9

A Chip Off the Old Sturnum 5.8 ★★
The right-facing dihedral around the corner from *Hurt*. Climb a ledge underneath a roof. Traverse underneath the roof a face holds, and continue up the crack to chain anchors. Inspect the anchor situation before lowering; there has been stress fracture surrounding them for a few years!
0 ft. Jason Haas, Sarah Maclean, 2005.

Darwin Loves You 5.9+ ★★★
This is the next bolted line 100 feet right of the dihedral. Begin with a reachy start, then continue up a short but fun face to a timebomb clipping jug.
0 ft. 4 bolts. Wes Allen, 2004.

Johnny on Roofies 5.11a ★★★
Move right from *Darwin Loves You* to the next bolted line. Pull small opening roof to easy moves leading to a tricky bulge. Continue on incut shelves to the top.
5 ft. 6 bolts. Unknown, 2004.

Donor 5.11b ★★★★
Pull a small opening roof in the center of the wall, just right of the previous route's start. Consistent climbing on crimps and slates, through a bulge midway, to sidepulls and open grips.
5 ft. 6 bolts. Unknown, 2004.

Let's Boogie 5.11b ★★★
Between *Donor* and *Wal-Martificaion of Trad*, this route climbs plates and sloping edges. Watch the run to the anchors.
0 ft. 5 bolts. Joel Anderson, Scott Curran, 2013.

⑪ The Wal-Martification of Trad 5.8 ★★
Move right from the previous line, past a large crack in a corner, to this route, which begins as a finger crack and shares anchors with *Family Tradition*.
50 ft. Steve Kaufmann, Jill Messer, 2004.

⑫ Family Tradition 5.10b ★★
Move a few feet right from the previous crack to the next bolted line on the wall. It starts as a bolted crack, then leads to rounded bulges.
50 ft. 7 bolts. Alex Yeakley, 2004.

⑬ Tong Shing 5.10d ★★★
Right of *Family Tradition* is this fun, bolted line on a featured face with grooves near the top.
55 ft. 6 bolts. Andy Pense, Sam Watson, JJ, Jared Hancock, 2005.

⑭ Anger Management 5.8+ ★★
The offwidth dihedral right of *Tong Shing*. Rap from a tree or walk off to the right.
65 ft. Jason Haas, Sarah Maclean, 2005.

Nice To Know You

⑮ Nice to Know You 5.10b ★★★★
This is the next bolted line right of *Anger Management*. Tiptoe to the first bolt, pull through the bulge, and launch into the slab moves and crimps. High-quality technical moves, interspersed with "thank you" pockets, keep the route interesting.
40 ft. 6 bolts. John Bronaugh, Ryan Adams, 2004.

⑯ Helping Hands 5.10d ★★★
Another fun line located right of *Nice to Know You*.
40 ft. 5 bolts. John Bronaugh, Ryan Adams, 2004.

⑰ Swap Meet 5.6 ★★
This short sport route is just right of *Helping Hands* on a corner. Climb past a dirty start, then continue up the face, passing a perfectly spherical hold along the way.
35 ft. 4 bolts. Ryan Adams, Tina Bronaugh, 2004.

⑱ Farley's Folley 5.10a ★★
Walk right from *Swap Meet* to the next bolted line, 10 feet left of *The Haas Memorial Route*. Boulder out the roof to start, then move up to and out another roof on large holds.
40 ft. 5 bolts. Curt Farley, 2007.

⑲ The Haas Memorial Route 5.10a ★★★★
Walk right from *Swap Meet* to locate this excellent offwidth dihedral. Start back in the cave and traverse out the roof crack to gain the wide dihedral. Leavittate up the offwidth to a ledge, then chimney to the top.
90 ft. Jason Haas, Sarah Maclean, Mark Johnson, 2005.

⑳ Stephanie's Cabaret 5.11c ★★
Walk right from *The Haas Memorial Route* to the next bolted line just before a cave. Climb through a dirty start, then crank through long moves and a couple of finger locks to the first set of anchors. The route continues to a second set of anchors at 5.12a.
50 ft. 6 bolts. Joe Leismer, 2005.

㉑ Labor Day Weekend 5.12a ★★★
Start under a low roof. Pull out from under the roof and up to the face angling left. Catch a quick breather before tackling a bouldery crux on crimps with a tricky reach-through as you move back and forth across the bolt line. A body-sized hueco midway up on the left offers a good rest before ending on s pockets, crimps, and pinches.
70 ft. 8 bolts. Shannon Stuart-Smith, Adam Nolte, 2015.

㉒ Four Shower Tokens, a Guinness, and My Girl 5.8- ★★
What more could a guy need? Start back in the cave just rig of *Stephanie's Cabaret*. Work up the face to gain the thin roc crack. Pull through a low crux, then enjoy large holds and ledges up the face. When you've had enough of the dihedra bail to the right-leaning crack on the main face. Follow it to the anchors of *First Time*.
50 ft. Mark Johnson, Jason Haas, 2005.

㉓ Normalised Bramapithecus 5.10d ★★★★
Ascends the slightly overhanging face just right of the previous trad line. Reach high for the start holds, then surmount a roof to gain the face.
65 ft. 8 bolts. Unknown.
Equipped by Norma Froelich and Bram Bell.

㉔ First Time 5.8+ ★★★
Walk 25 feet right from the previous line to this enjoyable rou that ascends black rock just left of a corner. Begin on a bould and climb through surprisingly good holds to the anchors.
50 ft. 5 bolts. Bill Strachan, 2004.

㉕ Generosity 5.10d ★★★
Just around the corner from *First Time*. Grab sandy holds to start and climb to a bulge. Crank over the lip and gain a stance. Continue up the slightly overhanging face, enjoying the improving quality of the rock with each move.
55 ft. 6 bolts. Paul Vidal, 2005.

LEFT FIELD

37.6529
-83.7156
25 min 10 min

This small wall is just left of and around the corner from the Playground. It's indicated by a sign just off the main Sore Heel Hollow trail.

Approach: From the Sore Heel Hollow parking area (directions on page 206), walk uphill on a cleared dirt road a few hundred feet to the marked trailhead on the right. Follow the trail a few minutes, then take a trail on your left signed Left Field, reaching the wall near *Lowered Expectations* (#3). Routes described left to right.

Flee From Fixer 5.5 ★
is trad climb is the leftmost route on this section of wall. mb the plates and flake to reach the anchors of *Return Zoe*. Suspect rock: use your own judgment regarding cement of gear, and tell your belayer to wear a helmet.
ft. *Geoff Graham, Kevin Downs, 2004.*

Return to Zoe 5.6 ★★
enty-five feet left of *Lowered Expectations* is this open edral trad climb. At 45 feet long, you hardly feel good about ing up your shoes for this one, but if you're in the area, why t, right?
ft. *Grady and Dean Marker, 2005.*

Lowered Expectations 5.5 ★★
the approach trail meets the wall, walk left of the blunk ète a few feet to locate this line on a less-than-vertical ce. Climb through large holds, angling right to the anchors. ossy and dirty, but everyone does it.
ft. 5 bolts. *John Bronaugh, 2004.*

Apoplectic Chick From Missouri 5.10b ★★★
gin right and around the corner from the previous line d climb through an overhanging section to a blank face. gotiate the blank section, then continue on larger holds to e anchors.
ft. 4 bolts. *John Bronaugh, 2004.*

Autograph 5.11a ★★★
gin a few feet right of the previous line. Climb to a large d comfy sidepull, then make a big move to a jug. Pump ough the overhanging remainder past a couple of bulges.
ft. 6 bolts. *John Bronaugh, 2004.*

Come to Me, Marie 5.8
alk right about 20 feet to a wide dihedral leading to a ueeze chimney. Stem the dihedral until you are forced to ve into the chimney. Descend from chains.
ft. *Mark Johnson, Jason Haas, Chris Nowak, 2005.*

❼ **If Trango Could Whistle** 5.8 ★
Locate a wide crack splitting the face 20 feet right of *Come to Me, Marie*. Ascend the crack using mainly face holds and the occasional chicken-wing. Walk off left, following the old pipelines down the slab.
100 ft. *Matt Tackett, Jason Haas, 2005.*

❽ **Hopscotch** 5.11a ★
Twenty feet right of the previous line is a slabby-to-vertical wall with numerous bulges. This is the leftmost bolted line on the wall. Begin by climbing to a ledge 15 feet up, passing one bolt. Climb the slab to a perplexing bulge near the top.
60 ft. 8 bolts. *John Bronaugh, 2004.*

❾ **No Love for Charlie** 5.11a ★★
Start as for the previous line, but move right five feet once you reach the ledge. Fight the pump past sustained edge climbing to the anchors.
60 ft. 7 bolts. *John Bronaugh, 2004.*

❿ **Jet Lag** 5.9 ★★
Walk right from the previous lines, under a large overhang, to a set of three routes that begin on the right side of the overhang. This is the leftmost route encountered and begins by climbing a fat flake leading to a small bulge. Pull the bulge and continue on big ledges to the anchors.
60 ft. 6 bolts. *Unknown.*

⓫ **Thru Space and Time** 5.10a ★★★
Step right from the previous line a few feet uphill to locate the next bolted line, which begins beneath a small roof feature 10 feet up. Balance up to the feature, then tech your way up the remaining enjoyable face to the anchors.
65 ft. 8 bolts. *Unknown.*

⓬ **Jack Move** 5.11b ★★
Move right from the previous line about 15 feet uphill to the next bolted line beginning with two slopey holds. Grab the slopers, find a foot, and move up left to a jug. Tiptoe up the face to a tough, long move midway. Finesse a bulge, then run to the anchors on larger holds.
65 ft. 8 bolts. *Unknown.*

223

THE PLAYGROUND

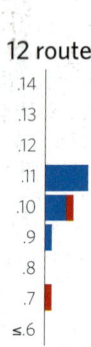

37.65
-83.71
25 min / 10 min

12 routes

This small wall has several great short lines on nice orange and black rock, bolted primarily by John Bronaugh before his passing, in 2004. It was one of the last crags he developed. The Playground is a fun area with good sport moderates.

Approach: From the Sore Heel Hollow parking area (directions on page 206), walk uphill a cleared dirt road a few hundred feet to the marked trailhead on the right. Follow the trail a few minutes and take a trail on your left signed "The Playground." The first route you reach is *Red Rover*.

Conditions: Routes #1–7 are slightly overhanging so stay fairly dry in the rain. Avoid routes #8– if it's raining, as they are slabs. These routes get great sun.

1 **Red Rover** 5.11b ★★
The leftmost route encountered where the trail meets the wall. Pumpy sidepulls lead to anchors.
65 ft. 6 bolts. John Bronaugh, 2004.

2 **Steal the Bacon** 5.11a ★★
Right of *Red Rover* is another bolted line. Climb up through some bulges to the anchors.
65 ft. 6 bolts. John Bronaugh, 2004.

3 **Chickenhawk** 5.10d ★★
A tough lead. Right of *Steal the Bacon* is an intermittent crack. Follow the crack, making liberal use of face holds along the way.
45 ft. John Bronaugh, 2004.

4 **Jungle Gym** 5.10b ★★★
Move a few feet right from *Steal the Bacon* to locate this bolted line. Fun ending with a funky lip move.
50 ft. 4 bolts. John Bronaugh, 2004.

Photo: Andrew Bu

Monkey Bars 5.10a ★★★★

is route begins just right of *Jungle Gym*. Climb up through e pockets and jugs to big moves on steep rock.

ft. 5 bolts. *John Bronaugh, 2004.*

Capture the Flag 5.11b ★★★★

is fun, powerful route begins just right of *Monkey Bars*. mb through great moves on small edges and pockets.

ft. 5 bolts. *John Bronaugh, 2004.*

Crack the Whip 5.11d ★★★

is powerful crimpfest begins right of *Capture the Flag*.

ft. 5 bolts. *Jason Haas, 2004.*

Octopus Tag 5.7 ★★★

the right side of the main wall is a clean chimney. Climb chimney to anchors. Despite appearances, no large gear needed to protect the line.

ft. *Ryan Adams, 2004.*

Balance Beam 5.11a ★★★★

st right of *Octopus Tag* is a slabby section of the wall. is is the leftmost bolted line on the wall. Climb the chnical slab to anchors.

ft. 7 bolts. *John Bronaugh, 2004.*

⑩ Teeter Totter 5.11c ★★★

This is the second route from the left on the slab wall. Sustained and desperate edging leads to the anchors.

65 ft. 8 bolts. *John Bronaugh, 2004.*

⑪ Slide 5.9 ★★★

This is the second-to-last route from the left on the slab wall. Start downhill a bit from *Teeter Totter*. Climb reachy moves through knobs and edges to the anchors.

65 ft. 8 bolts. *Bob Matheny, 2004.*

⑫ Tire Swing 5.10a ★★★

This is the farthest right route on the slab wall, just right of *Slide*, and has a bouldery, somewhat chossy start. Climb the slab to the anchors.

70 ft. 8 bolts. *Ryan Adams, 2004.*

SHADY GROVE

16 routes

Shady Grove is located a short ways beyond and around the corner from the Playground. It offers long, steep, pocketed climbs of varying difficulties. *Citizens Arête* and *Girls Gone Wild ... WOO!* are quite popular.

Approach: From the Sore Heel Hollow parking area (directions on page 206), walk uphill a cleared dirt road a few hundred feet to the marked trailhead on the right. Follow the trail few minutes, past The Playground, and then ta the trail on your left signed for "Shady Grove."

Conditions: Shady Grove was named for obvio reasons. It offers good relief from the h Kentucky sun during the summer. Although t routes have been around several years, a fe might still have some questionable rock, so clim with caution.

Citizen's Arête

❶ Citizen's Arête 5.11b ★★★★
This route begins just right of the obvious arête on the left side of the wall. Climb the face until you run out of holds, then make a big move left to the arête. Make another big move, then ride the arête to the anchors.
60 ft. 6 bolts. Shannon Stuart-Smith, 2004.

❷ Girls Gone Wild ... WOO! 5.10d ★★★★
The groove just right of *Citizen's Arête*. Grab a shelf and pull up and through a bulge. Continue up the face, staying just right of a flake.
60 ft. 6 bolts. Terry Kindred, 2004.

❸ Crucify Me 5.11c ★★★
Ten feet right from *Girls Gone Wild*, look for a high first bolt Climb up the steep face, making use of jugs and hidden pockets along the way. Tackle the crux toward the top and finish off on jugs to the anchors.
70 ft. 6 bolts. Terry Kindred, 2004.

❹ Who Knows? 5.11d ★★
Twenty feet right of *Crucify Me*. Climb steep rock for two bo to gain a large ledge. Continue up past a fat flake to anothe ledge, then up steeper rock to the anchors.
70 ft. 8 bolts. Blake Bowling, 2004.

❺ Which Is Which? 5.11c ★★
Step 10 feet right of *Who Knows?*. Crank a steep start to a har ledge. Continue up a more-vertical face to the overhanging headwall. Conquer the headwall and clip the chains.
70 ft. 8 bolts. Chris Martin, 2004.

❻ Who Is Who? 5.11d ★★★
Start five feet right of *Which Is Which?* on the same steep section of the wall. Crank through four bolts of pocket pulli to gain a vertical section. Climb past this, then deal with steepening rock to the anchors.
70 ft. 9 bolts. Blake Bowling, 2004.

Coming-Out Party 5.11d ★★★

[Th]is unique line is located 25 feet right of *Who Is Who?*, [jus]t past an overhanging crack in a dihedral. Boulder out [ext]remely steep rock to gain a large ledge. Climb the [ov]erhanging face past a few pods along the way.
[ ]ft. 9 bolts. *Shannon Stuart-Smith, 2004.*

Far From God 5.12b ★★★★

[Sh]ares the first bolt of *Coming-Out Party*. Power out the start [of] *Coming-Out Party* to gain a ledge, then veer right and [cli]mb the sustained, overhanging face to anchors.
[ ]ft. 8 bolts. *Chris Martin, 2004.*

False Idol 5.12b ★★★★

[Wa]lk 30 feet right from *Far From God* to locate this route. [Bo]ulder out a steep, pocketed start to gain a ledge. Continue [up] the sustained, overhanging face to the anchors.
[ ]ft. 10 bolts. *Blake Bowling, 2004.*

Irreverent C 5.12b ★★

[Ju]st right of the previous route is a hueco 25 feet up. This [ro]ute begins just left of the hueco and meets up with a water [gr]oove toward the top.
[ ]ft. 8 bolts. *Shannon Stuart-Smith, 2004.*

Imagine There's No Heaven 5.12b ★★★

[Th]is route takes on the next line of bolts right of *Irreverent* [an]d flows through fun movement sandwiched by tough [se]ctions. Should soon clean up into its predicted three stars, [so] give it some love and carry a brush.
[ ]ft. 8 bolts. *Shannon Stuart-Smith, Lee Smith, 2010.*

Taste the Raibow 5.13a ★★★

[Wa]lk right from *Imagine There's No Heaven* to this extremely [ov]erhanging, adventurous line. If *Pile Driver* leaves a bad [ta]ste in your mouth, just taste the rainbow and you'll feel [mu]ch better.
[ ]0 ft. 14 bolts.
[Be]ntley Bracket, 2009. Equipped by Mark Stevenson.

Pile Driver 5.12d ★

[Pu]t your beer goggles on for this one! Climb through several [b]oxied jugs and botched bolt placements to the chains.
[ ]ft. 11 bolts.
[Gr]eg Kerzhner, 2008. Equipped by Mark Stevenson.

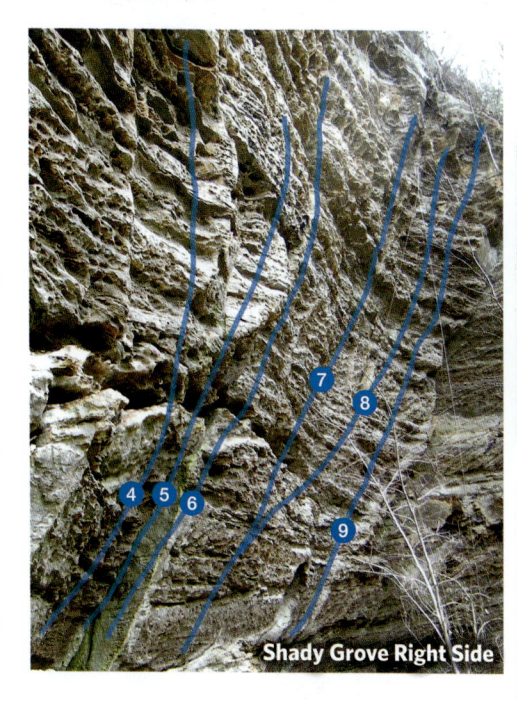

Shady Grove Right Side

⑭ **Listerine Girl** 5.9

Walk right from *Pile Driver* and head uphill about 30 feet to locate this line. Climb to a dish, then move out onto a tongue feature before tackling the roof. Finish on a well-featured slab to the chains.
75 ft. 9 bolts. *Jason Burton, Ron Snider, Ben Cassel, 2006.*

⑮ **Shaved Squirrel** 5.10d ★★★

Up the steep hill from *Listerine Girl* is a flat spot with two routes. This is the left route. Begin with a thin start, then move up into a good stance on the left side of a large hueco. Leave the comfort zone by tiptoeing left onto the face where the holds disappear and the climbing gets tough. Make a few thin moves, then enjoy larger holds to the chains.
60 ft. 7 bolts. *Ron Snider, Brian Clark, Jason Burton, 2006.*

⑯ **Street Fight** 5.10a ★★★

Shares the beginning moves of *Shaved Squirrel* but heads right from the hueco out into the business. Pull a few delicate moves, then run to the chains on Disneyland jugs.
65 ft. 6 bolts. *Ron Snider, Jason Burton, James Street, 2006.*

MEGACAVE

4 routes

.14
.13
.12
.11
.10
.9
.8
.7
≤.6

Located between Shady Grove and Bronaugh Wall, this newer crag mostly hosts very steep, hard open projects.

Approach: Use the approach as you would for Bronaugh Wall, but just as you cross the drainage past Shady Grove, start looking for a faint trail on the left that leads to the left side of the wall. You can reach the far right side of the wall by walking further toward Bronaugh wall, crossing the footbridge and taking another faint trail on the left.

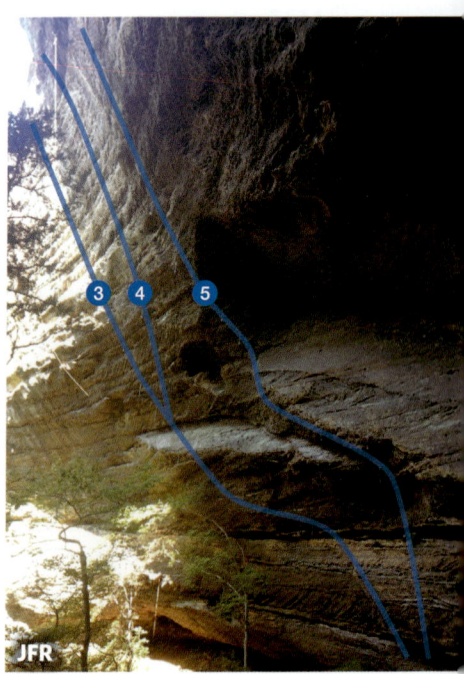

Open Project

JFR

❶ Megacave 1 Open Project
Located at the left end of the cave, a bit right of a massive hueco at mid-height. Needs a few more bolts.
Equipped by Daniel Woods, Jimmy Webb, Tyler Wilcutt, 2012.

❷ Megacave 2 Open Project
This one begins left of a tree growing up against the wall. Needs a few more bolts.
Equipped by Daniel Woods, Jimmy Webb, Tyler Wilcutt, 2012.

❸ Megacave 3 Closed Project
This route and *JFR* share a start a bit right of the tree growing against the wall. Follow the left branch of bolts when the two lines diverge near a huge hueco midway up the wall.

❹ JFR 5.13b ★★★
This route and the project to the left share a start a bit right of the tree growing against the wall. Follow the right branch of bolts when the two lines diverge near a huge hueco at mid-height.
115 ft. 16 bolts. John Flunker, 2013.

❺ Megacave 5 Open Project
This project starts right of *JFR*, then climbs a strip of overhang between two slabbier sections. It breaks onto the headwall just right of the big hueco.
100 ft. 13 bolts.

MEGACAVE

SORE HEEL HOLLOW

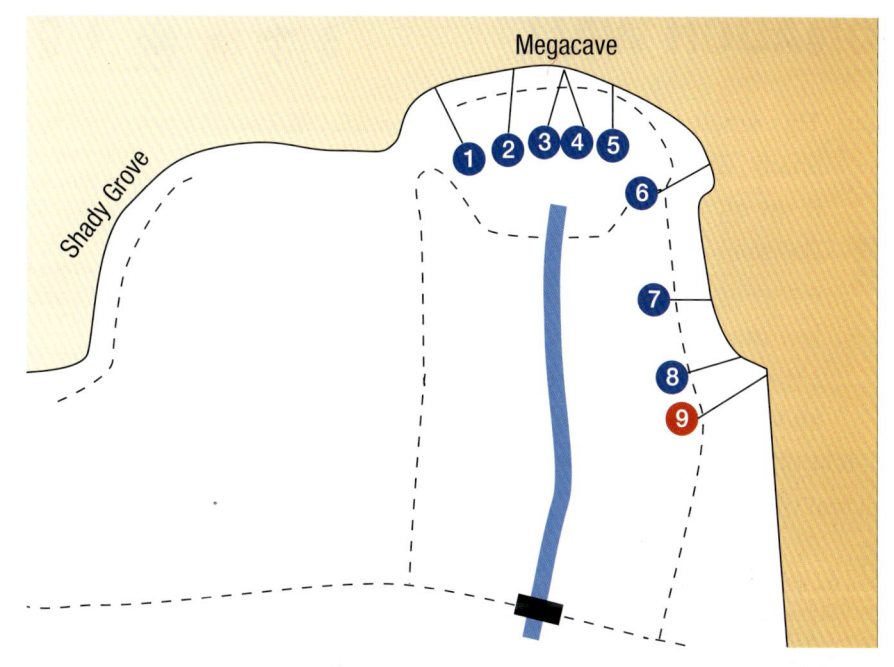

Iam Dunk

Burnout

Slam Dunk 5.12d ★★★
st to the right of the main cave is this fingery, powerful line.
arts off a boulder with thin moves.
ft. 9 bolts. Steve Sandman, Dustin Stephens, 2012.

Megacave 7 Open Project
e route on the consistently angled wall near the right end
the crag needs a few more bolts.
uipped by Daniel Woods, Jimmy Webb, Tyler Wilcutt, 2012.

🔵8 **Burnout** 5.11b
The pumpy orange face on the right side of the crag gets morning shade.
70 ft. 8 bolts. Dustin Stephens.

🔴9 **Shotgun Funeral** 5.11a
The obvious dihedral right of *Burnout*. Climb it until you can clip the last bolt of *Burnout* and finish at that route's anchors.
70 ft. 1 bolt. Dustin Stephens, Scott Curran.

229

BRONAUGH WALL

37.65
-83.70
25 min / 15 min

17 routes

This small wall lies between Shady Grove and Purgatory. Right off the trail, *Jingus* and *Collision Damage* are good warm-ups. There are even a few must-dos here, including *Little Teapot*, *Belly of the Beast*, and *Like a Turtle*. Each climbs completely differently, yet all lie within several feet of each other.

Approach: Drive to the Sore Heel Hollow parking (directions on page 206). Approach as fo Shady Grove, but continue along the main tra a few minutes until you see the wooden sig marking the trail to Bronaugh Wall on the le The trail heads slightly uphill and wraps arou the cliff, ending just beneath *Little Teapot*.

Conditions: This wall faces east, maki for a good summer-afternoon retreat. Th overhanging section is quite steep, and rout #3–6 stay dry in the rain.

❶ My Mind Escapes Me 5.10a ★★★★
Just as the trail meets the rock, and before you turn right, look straight up for this very aesthetic water groove. Get your slab skills ready and remember it's only 10a.
55 ft. 7 bolts. *Ashley Hudson, John Flunker, 2014.*

❷ Fever Pitch 5.10d ★★★
Just right of *My Mind Escapes Me*.
45 ft. 5 bolts. *Dustin Stephens, John Flunker, 2015.*

❸ Spyder's Hangout 5.10a ★★
This short route starts from a ledge just left of *Little Teapot*. Stick-clipping the first bolt is recommended.
35 ft. 3 bolts. *David Scott, Stephanie Meadows, Justin Bartlett, Elodie Saracco, 2010.*

❹ Little Teapot 5.12a ★★★★
This fun little line takes on the short, black face that begins on a high, sloping ledge. Reach through a series of crimp ledges to a bouldery crux just before the anchors.
45 ft. 3 bolts. *Blake Bowling, 2005.*

❺ Muffin Top 5.10d ★★★
Start just left of *Jingus* on a ramp of sorts leading to big jugs and a tricky move or two. This is a great warm-up or a good route for those breaking into harder 5.10s.
65 ft. 7 bolts. *Dustin Stephens, John Flunker, 2013.*

❻ Jingus 5.11b ★★★★
Move right from the previous line about 15 feet to the first line on the overhanging section of the wall. Pull through the steep beginning, then continue up on coarse pinches and ledges to the anchors.
55 ft. 7 bolts. *Alex Yeakley, 2004.*

❼ Collision Damage 5.11d ★★★
Pump through pinches and pockets to reach the more verti and slightly licheny finish.
50 ft. 6 bolts. *John Bronaugh, 2004.*

❽ Crumblies 5.12a
About five feet right of the previous line is this adventure. Sho for a high pinch to start, then move up to a 50-pound flake waiting to blow. Tread lightly around the flake, then continue the right-angling face on holds that magically disappear whe you're done or even while you are using them.
55 ft. 7 bolts. *John Bronaugh, 2004.*

❾ Belly of the Beast 5.12c ★★★★
This is the rightmost bolted line on this section of wall. Beg under a roof and yard out on jugs to gain the overhanging face. Climb through long moves on good holds to a well-defined crux. Keep it together for the rest of the route, because it ain't over.
60 ft. 9 bolts. *Shannon Stuart-Smith, 2005.*

❿ Spread Eagle 5.11a ★★★
The intimidating corner tucked in to the right of *Belly* offers up some of the craziest moves and most bizarre positions in the Red. Burl out the crux start in the left chimney/crack, then shimmy up the offwidth and out the hanging chimney system, clipping the *Dirty Girl* anchor if you are light on big cams. Save a finger-sized piece or two for the exit. The righ start would probably bump this down into the 5.10 range, b expect some loose rock. Bring several large cams in the BD 5-6 range, and a decent amount of everything else. Belay o lower from the ledge anchor for the slab sport route right o *Dirty Girl*.
90 ft. *Blake Bowling, Terry Kindred, 2003.*

Little Teapot (4)

Like a Turtle (13, 14, 15)

BRONAUGH WALL

SORE HEEL HOLLOW

Dirty Girl 5.10a
rectly behind *Belly of the Beast*, you'll find this dirty seam that fades after about 40 feet of climbing. Two bolts protect e upper part.
ft. 2 bolts. John "Fred" Aragon, 2007.

Nanotechnology 5.11b ★★★★
DSSR (Yet Another Dustin Stevens Slab Route). If you're o slab climbs, get on this route. Balance and tech your way the insecure crux.
ft. 7 bolts. Dustin Stephens, John Flunker, 2013.

Two Women Alone 5.11a ★★★★
ntinue walking right from *Belly of the Beast*, past the slabs. is is the first route with some actual holds on it. Climb ough thin holds and plates on a vertical wall.
ft. 7 bolts Julia Fain, 2005.

Like a Turtle 5.11b ★★★★
ve down the hill 15 feet right from *Two Women Alone*. ulder through the start on thin incuts to reach a series of ge plates. Ponder the moves on the thin face from the last , then shoot for the iron-oxide turtle-head feature. Navigate ough long reaches to a welcome jug at the anchors.
ft. 7 bolts. Julia Fain, 2005.

15 Take the Scary Out of Life 5.10d ★★★
This originally mixed line has recently been updated with more bolts, so extra gear is no longer needed. Start off a large, flat boulder and climb through plates and incuts to reach an intermittent crack.
55 ft. 7 bolts. Shannon Stuart-Smith, 2005.

16 Bring Up the Bodies 5.11c ★★★★
Climb the left side of the giant hueco, then gently up and right through the gamut of holds to a definitive crux. Plot twists keep you guessing. Named after the award-winning British novel.
90 ft. 10 bolts. Shannon Stuart-Smith, Enoch Harding, Julia Fain, Eva Bach, 2012.

17 Upworthy 5.10c ★★★
Pull-up start on the obvious two-handed jug. Wander your way through pockets and edges.
70 ft. 8 bolts. Shannon Stuart-Smith, Byron Hempel, 2014.

18 The Odyssey Closed Project
This climbs out the massive cave that looks like the Motherlode without the slab start.
Equipped by Adam Taylor.

PURGATORY

25 min   20 min   37.65 / -83.70

21 routes

Purgatory has excellent, difficult sport lines, including one of the Red's toughest, *Lucifer*. Canadian Mike Doyle spent several weeks over winter 2006 working this open project, a severely overhanging power-endurance climb. On the last day of his trip, he sent. During the same period, Kenny Barker sent the extension to his already difficult *Paradise Lost*, which he named *Paradise Regained*. It was a good winter for Purgatory. 5.13b seems to be the popular grade here, but don't expect them all to come easy, as each one packs a powerful series of cruxes.

Approach: Purgatory is the last cliff on the ma Sore Heel Hollow trail. From the main Sore He parking area (directions on page 206), walk a dirt road past the kiosk. Take a small trail the right, which leads up to the main trail. Tu left on the main trail, then hike about 10 minute passing Left Field, the Playground, Shady Grov and Bronaugh Wall. Continue past Bronaug Wall a few more minutes on the main trail a look for the next trail on the left, which lea slightly uphill to Purgatory.

❶ Stirrin' the Grits 5.11c ★★★
From where the trail meets the cliff, walk left of the arch to locate two bolted lines on a slab. This is the farthest route left and may feel right on the grade for six-foot-tall granite climbers. Otherwise, try harder than you normally would on a 5.11c slab. And if you're a Red River local, don't even try.
65 ft. 7 bolts. Matt Johns, Kipp Trummel, 2011.

❷ Skunk Love 5.11b ★★★★
Another tough slab line right of *Stirrin' the Grits*. This one is actually doable for non-slab-masters. Girls, put your boyfriend on this at the end of the day after he sends *Paradise Lost* and laugh at him while he struggles, then hike it with your smooth technique. The crux is low and requires some brow-furrowing.
65 ft. 8 bolts. Kipp Trummel, 2006.

❸ Mist of Funk 5.10b ★★★
This is the obvious, nice-looking dihedral right of the slab wall. Boulder up to a ledge, then layback up and around the first roof to a no-hands rest in a large hueco. Continue to a higher ledge and belay. Tackle the surprisingly short second roof and top out.
90 ft. Jason Haas, Matt Tackett, 2005.

❹ Looking Through the Devil's Window 5.6 ★★
This wide, left-leaning ramp up a green face begins 30 feet right of *Mist of Funk*. Layback up the clean crack to bolted anchors near the entrance of a cave.
40 ft. Jason Haas, Matt Tackett, 2005.

❺ Butterfly Gangbang 5.8+ ★★
Thirty feet right of *Devil's Window* is this left-leaning flake, which starts as a hand crack and has a tree 50 feet up on a ledge. Climb the widening hand crack, past the tree, to the top of the cliff. Rap from a tree to descend.
80 ft. Matt Tackett, Jason Haas, 2005.

❻ Believer 5.11b ★★★★
This is the first bolted route encountered after walking through the arch. Look to your left 10 feet after you walk through the arch, for a face with a few bolted lines. Climb finger pockets to a sit-down rest, then take on the overhanging headwall above.
60 ft. 6 bolts. Tony Reynaldo, 2005.

❼ Special Boy 5.11c ★★★★
Move right from *Believer* to the next bolted line. Begin with thin start, which leads to better holds and fun climbing with a nice hueco rest midway. Keep it together for the long run the anchors.
75 ft. 7 bolts. Kenny Barker, 2004.

❽ Fallen Angel 5.11c ★★★
Locate a beautiful crack splitting the face right of the previous lines. Crank through sporty moves to reach an expanding, right-facing dihedral near the top, which offers bit of relief. Rap anchors. Bouldery.
70 ft. Kenny Barker, 2004.

Kai Lightner vs *Lucifer*, 5.14c (page 234). Photo: Elodie Saracco.

Fallen Angel

Paradise Lost

⑨ Gluttony 5.12a ★★★★
Step right from *Fallen Angel* to locate this bolted line. Climb up a slab and crack, then move out onto the face at the third bolt. Crank through a shoulder-busting move to gain better holds. Continue up the overhanging face on perfect pockets to reach the vertical run to the anchors.
75 ft. 7 bolts. Kenny Barker, 2005.

⑩ Fat Man's Misery 5.4 ★★
Climb the start of *Gluttony* to a ledge and build a belay (bring a #5 Camalot). Crawl through the cave on the belay ledge for 30 feet to reach the anchors of *Looking through the Devil's Window* on the opposite side of Purgatory and rappel.
40 ft. Jason Haas, Matt Tackett, 2005.

⑪ The Proverbial Donkey 5.11a ★
Start in an alcove 20 feet left of *Dracula*, behind a large boulder. Work up the face to gain a fist crack in a roof. Be careful not to fall as you'll have a good chance of hitting the boulder beneath. The second is also in danger of swinging into the boulder, as it isn't possible to protect the low section. Work up the crack system, over several ledges, to reach a comfy belay ledge directly under a 15-foot roof. Bail out here for a higher-quality climb at 5.10b R, or continue out the roof on shaky jams and bad feet to chain anchors just past the lip of the roof.
100 ft. Jason Haas, Jordan Wood, 2005.

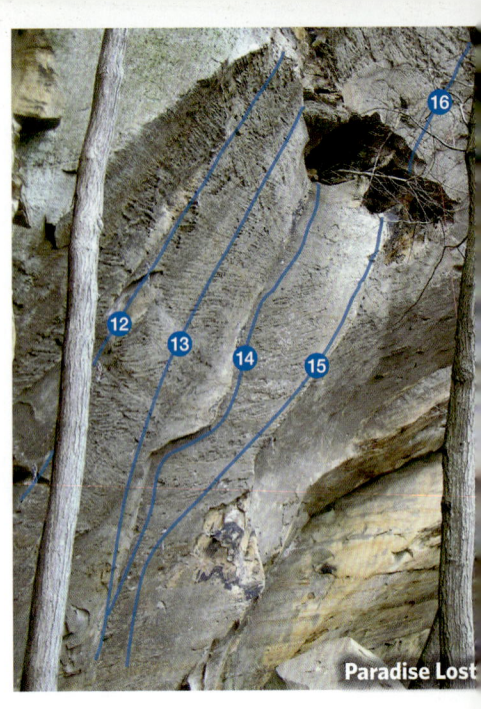

⑫ Dracula '04 5.13b ★★★★★
Move right from the previous lines to the big-boy wall and gush over the first line you come to, which starts as a sharp corner. Boulder desperate moves up the corner to reach a "rest." Continue up, then bust left to a gaston followed by a difficult clip. Crank out a few more tough moves to reach a much-needed relief jug. Throw through a big move to reach the final decent hold, then kiss it goodbye as you move left into the crux awaiting at the chains. The last bolt was recently added. Crazy, huh? Yeah, it was scary before ...
60 ft. 7 bolts. Kenny Barker, 2005.

⑬ Lucifer 5.14c ★★★★★
Sorry, Mike, this is no longer the most difficult line at the Re Begin just right of *Dracula '04*. Climb relatively easy moves to the third bolt, then bust left through a V7 boulder problem to reach a quick shake at the fourth bolt. Recharge, then boulder through a more difficult section, reach a moderate rest at the fifth bolt, and endure the redpoint run to the brea At the break, ponder on what a badass mofo you are, then finish it up.
100 ft. 9 bolts. Mike Doyle, 2006.

⑭ The Castle Has Fallen 5.13b ★★★★
Climb the first three bolts of *Lucifer*, then head straight up the thin seam with a wicked-hard boulder problem at the to Skip the lines and climb this one.
60 ft. 6 bolts. Ben Cassel, 2005.

Leor Gold, *Believer*, 5.11b (page 232). Photo: John Wesely.

15 Paradise Lost 5.13a ★★★★★
Formerly 5.13b, but the first ascensionist downgraded it to 5.13a since everyone was choosing to stand on the obvious ledge that he avoided. Regardless, this line is the must-do route at Purgatory. Begin by climbing the flake marking *The Castle Has Fallen,* then traverse right to reach a sit-down rest on the notorious ledge — or avoid it for nostalgia's sake (and the original grade). Recruit your fast-twitch muscles to work through powerful movements up the striking, overhanging arête. Save a few grunts for the final crux after the last clip.
65 ft. 6 bolts. Kenny Barker, 2004.

16 Paradise Regained 5.13b ★★★★
From the anchors of *Paradise Lost,* continue up the sustained headwall. 70-meter rope necessary. Stiff for the grade!
105 ft. 11 bolts. Kenny Barker, 2006.

17 Hellraiser 5.12c ★★★★★
Walk right from *Paradise Lost* past a large amphitheater. This is the next sport line and follows a distinct line of pockets through grey rock. Climb through fragile holds a few feet to reach a good hold. Reach hard through the crux, then flow to the anchors on large holds.
65 ft. 7 bolts. Kenny Barker, 2005. Equipped by Lee Smith.

18 The Gimp 5.10a ★★★
Walk right from *Hellraiser* to the next bolted line. Pull on plates to reach a slab. Start up the vertical section, then make a tricky move to the next clip. Continue on larger holds to the anchors.
60 ft. 6 bolts. Tony Reynaldo, Drew Cronin, 2005.

"The BAT" on *Paradise Lost*, 5.13a (opposite). Photo: John Wesely.

Back in the Days of Bold 5.11c ★★★
 ep right around the corner from *The Gimp* to locate this
 roken finger crack. Work your way up the low finger crack
 n the left, then boulder up and right to regain the crack.
 ollow the flaring crack until it ends, then friction on an easy
 ut sparsely protected slab to the chains.
 5 ft. *Jason Haas, Matt Tackett, 2005.*

Jumbo Shrimp 5.10a ★
 ight of *The Gimp* is this slightly dirty route that moves up
 rough some technical, vertical face and surmounts a small
 ulge before continuing on big holds to chain anchors.
 0 ft. 5 bolts. *Tony Reynaldo, 2008.*

21 The Seventh Circle of Dante 5.10a ★
Walk 60 feet right of the previous crack to find this route at
the end of the ledge. Start in a large hueco and climb the face
to a wide crack. Work up the crack until it flares, then fades.
Protect out of a pocket and continue up the slab to reach a
rappel tree.
65 ft. *Jason Haas, Sarah Maclean, 2005.*

237

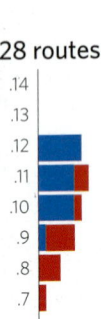

WHAT ABOUT BOB WALL

25 min | 10 min | 37.650 -83.714

28 routes

.14
.13
.12
.11
.10
.9
.8
.7
≤.6

What About Bob Wall is the easily accessible stretch of cliffline above the main Sore Heel Hollow parking area. It offers a unique blend of lines, from man-eating roof cracks to calf-blowing slabs. Most of the bolted lines range from slabby to slightly overhanging, so don't expect the Red's typical steep, pumpy pocket climbing.

Approach: From the main Sore Heel Hollow parking (directions on page 206), walk south (opposite the main road leading to the Gallery) toward the edge of the lot, near a stream, to locate a trail leading off to the right (west) into the woods. The trail that immediately crosses a wooden footbridge heading east onto a wide dirt road leads to Rival and Courtesy walls; the What About Bob Wall trail is opposite that trail. Follow the trail about five minutes, crossing a small stream, until the trail heads uphill and forks near a large boulder directly in front of the cliff. Reach routes #1-16 by taking the right fork. For routes #17-31 (described right to left), go left.

Conditions: This wall faces mainly northwest to west, so expect shade and afternoon sun.

For the first 16 routes, take the right fork near a large boulder in the approach trail. Routes listed left to right.

❸ Running in Place Open Project ★★★
Right of the previous line is a crack system leading to a vertical face. Begin by climbing the crack, clip a bolt, then plug gear up to a bulge where the crack ends and the face climbing begins.
40 ft. 3 bolts. Equipped by Kipp Trummel in 2008.

❹ Hirsute Open Project ★★★
This is the next bolted route right of *Running in Place*. Begin on large holds and make a few long moves to reach a three bolt blank section. Have fun figuring it out.
60 ft. 8 bolts. Equipped by Kipp Trummel in 2008.

❺ Gluteus 5.9 ★★
The leftmost crack of a trio. Climb an offwidth pod to a wide hand crack and improvise your descent.
45 ft. Jason Haas, Matt Tackett, 2006.

❻ Maximus 5.9 ★
The middle crack. Climb a hand crack in a right-facing dihedral over a few ledges to a fixed piece. Lower from fixed anchors.
40 ft. Jason Haas, Matt Tackett, 2006.

❼ Hole 5.8 ★
This is the rightmost crack. Begin in a wide, left-facing dihedral that quickly pinches down. Ascend the arching crack to the shared anchors of *Maximus*.
40 ft. Matt Tackett, Jason Haas, 2006.

❶ Pongosapien 5.11d ★★★
As the approach trail meets the main wall near a large boulder, it forks left and right. If you take the right fork and head up to the cliff about 30 more feet you will arrive beneath a cluster of three cracks (*Maximus*, etc). Left of these cracks is a ramp leading to a ledge. *Pongosapien* is the leftmost bolted line off this ledge. Climb to a low ledge, grab a flake, and dig through your bag of tricks to reach a pair of small crimps on the face. Crimp hard for a few bolts, then relax on easier fun climbing, passing through a body-sized hueco just before the chains.
50 ft. 6 bolts. Kipp Trummel, 2008.

❷ Gild the Lily 5.12b ★★★
Right of *Pongosapien* is another crimpfest on black rock.
50 ft. 5 bolts. Kipp Trummel.

Kentucky Flu

Optical Rectitus 5.11a ★★★★
This is the bolted line just right of the previous cracks. Climb the blunt arête, making use of what few holds it has to offer.
0 ft. 6 bolts. Matt Tackett, Aaron Tackett, Amy Tackett, Steph Meadows, Morgain Sprague, 2006.

Weathertop Stings 5.10b ★★
From the previous lines, walk right to a scramble with a fixed rope. Grab a high iron-oxide ledge, then scoot out left. Head up on friable holds to chains just above a large hueco.
5 ft. 5 bolts. Matt Tackett, Jared Hancock, Jeremy Egleston, Don McGlone, 2006.

Tumble Dry Low 5.12b ★★★
Next line right of *Weathertop Stings*, and begins on the same ledge. Scramble up to the ledge to start. Crimp up the vertical face past some tough moves.
5 ft. 5 bolts. Kipp Trummel, Matt Tackett, 2008.

Tobacco Crack Ho 5.8 ★
This line ascends the face 20 feet right of *Weathertop Stings*, making use of natural protection. Climb pockets to a fragile ledge, then step right to get a placement. Move left at the top to belay and rap from bolted anchors.
5 ft. Don McGlone, Jeremy Egleston, 2006.

Stem Cell 5.10a ★★
This is the next bolted line 25 feet right of *Tobacco Crack Ho*. Stem between the boulder and face or traverse in from the left to start. Continue up the arête while occasionally breaking out left onto the featureless black rock to clip.
5 ft. 4 bolts. Don McGlone, Jeremy Egleston, 2006.

Cultural Wasteland 5.9 ★★
Walk right from *Stem Cell* to locate this short but fun crack.
5 ft. Jason Haas, Jeremy Egleston, Jared Hancock, Don McGlone, Matt Tackett, 2006.

⓮ Threat Level Blue 5.9 ★
Move right from *Cultural Wasteland* to the next short, bolted line. Pull over a low overhang at the start to reach a high jug. Leave the comfort of the jug behind for the funk movement that lies ahead. Make a committing move to clip the chains, then move left for better-quality routes.
35 ft. 3 bolts. Jared Hancock, Don McGlone, Jeremy Egleston, Matt Tackett, 2006.

⓯ Stuck Buckeye 5.8 ★★
Hike right from the previous lines about 200 yards to locate two enormous roof cracks about 40 feet apart. This line tackles the left roof crack. Climb hands to a squeeze chimney in an overhanging dihedral. If you don't get stuck, rap from a tree to descend. Otherwise, wait for the buzzards.
75 ft. Ken Thompson, 2006.

⓰ Farewell Drive with a Spit in the Eye 5.11a ★★★
This is the right roof crack. Work up the initial hand jams and maneuver yourself into the chimney. Carefully traverse the roof until you can turn the lip. Rap from a tree to descend.
50 ft. Jason Haas, Matt Tackett, 2006.

The following routes are reached by taking the left fork near a large boulder in the approach trail. Routes listed right to left.

⓱ What About Bob 17 Project ★★★★
As the approach trail meets the main wall near a large boulder, the trail forks left and right. If you take the left fork, this is the first bolted slab line just past a large boulder. Currently an open project in the 5.12+/5.13- range.
80 ft. 9 bolts. Equipped by Kipp Trummel.

⓲ Kentucky Flu 5.10c ★★★★
Begin 15 feet left of the previous line. Edge up to a large hueco, then shift left onto the face to begin this enjoyable ride. Tiptoe up the left edge of a water groove on little black knobs and the occasional incut crimp. Pull onto a large ledge near the top and scramble up and left for the chains. Make sure to turn around and soak in the view.
80 ft. 9 bolts. Matt Tackett, Don McGlone, 2005.

239

SORE HEEL HOLLOW

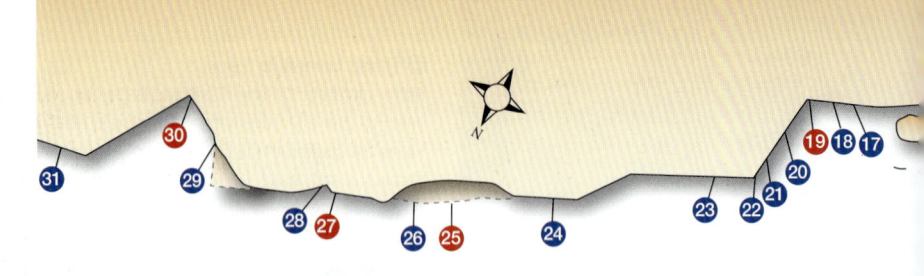

⑲ Adventures of the Leper Nurse 5.9 ★★★
Twenty-five feet left of *Kentucky Flu* is an obvious clean dihedral. Fight to the top and lower from anchors.
50 ft. Matt Tackett, Jeremy Egleston, 2005.

⑳ Code Red 5.12d ★★★★
This line takes on the vertical face 10 feet left of the dihedral. Bust through the blank start and keep it together for the next few bolts. Bring lots of shoe rubber.
80 ft. 9 bolts Kevin Todd, 2005.

㉑ Duputyren's Release 5.12b ★★★★
Ten feet left of *Code Red* is another spectacular face climb.
80 ft. 9 bolts. Justin Riddel, Colleen Reed, 2009. Equipped by Kipp Trummel.

㉒ GSW 5.12a ★★★★
The slabby arête 10 feet left of *Duputyren's Release*.
80 ft. 9 bolts. Brad Weaver, Eric Heuermann, 2006.

㉓ Drip Wire 5.11a ★★★
Tough for the grade (cough, cough ... sandbagged). Move 20 feet left from the arête to the next bolted line, which has a high first bolt. Climb through a slightly dirty start to reach a roof. Hyper-extend or heel-hook and lock-off to surmount the roof. Claw up to the chains on small-to-nonexistent edges.
80 ft. 7 bolts. Kipp Trummel, 2005.

㉔ Dr. Synchro 5.12a ★★★
Move left from *Drip Wire* to locate this bolted slab line with long, difficult movements.
95 ft. 13 bolts. Matt Tackett, Eric Cox, 2004.

㉕ Brass Gunkie 5.10 ★★★
Stemming and liebacking up a steep corner just right of *No Sleep Till Campton*. Use the first four bolts of that route, then traverse right to get some small/medium protection. Climb an orange face and up the corner. Move right and up a hand crack to a bolt, and finally the anchor. A 60-meter rope may NOT reach the ground.
100 ft. 5 bolts. Kirk Aengenheyster, Dustin Stephens, 2013.

㉖ No Sleep Till Campton 5.10c ★★★★
Walk left 70 feet from *Dr. Synchro* until you reach a dip in the trail. This sport route starts when the trail starts back uphill, and just above a low overhang. Traverse in from the left and make a long move to reach a jug. Continue up the vertical face, passing through a couple of long reach moves to decent-sized holds. Midway up, enjoy the change in scenery when the rock becomes orange and pockety for a few moves. Reach far left to a crack, which will lead you to a well-deserved monster jug beneath a roof. Heave over the roof and enjoy the grand finale of fun moves to the chains.
80 ft. 11 bolts. Don Mcglone, Matt Tackett, 2005.

㉗ Alternative Medicines 5.7 ★★★
Twenty-five feet left of *No Sleep Till Campton* is this long and enjoyable crack system. Shares anchors with *No Sleep Till Campton*.
75 ft. Matt Tackett, Jeremy Egleston, 2005.

㉘ The Speed of Enzo 5.10c ★★
Named after a not-so-speedy beagle found near PMRP, this route starts 10 feet left of *Alternative Medicines* on solid edges.
60 ft. 6 bolts. Shannon Stuart-Smith, Enoch Harding, Eva Bach, Julia Fain, 2013.

WHAT ABOUT BOB

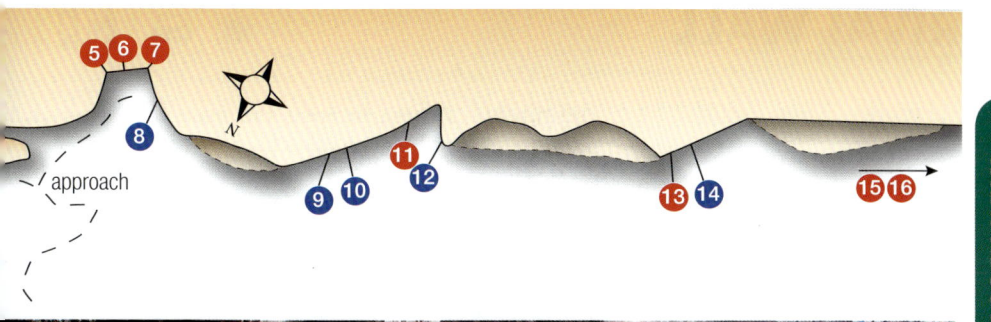

SORE HEEL HOLLOW

Brothel Doc 5.11a ★★★
alk left about 100 feet until you reach an overhanging, atured arête where the trail heads sharply uphill. This line gins 15 feet left of the arête. Stick-clip the first bolt and gin with a bouldery start, then enjoy the tricky moves that low. The first set of anchors is for the trad route *Kindred irits*; this sport line goes to the top.
ft. 10 bolts. Matt Tackett, Amy Tackett, Jason Haas, 2006.

Kindred Spirits 5.11a ★★
side the cave 20 feet left of *Brothel Doc* is a wide crack at gradually pinches down as you near the lip. Work out the edral and roof to a no-hands rest in a pod. Emerge from e pod to a hand crack that leads to bolted anchors.
ft. Jason Haas, Matt Tackett, Terry Kindred, 2006.

31 Bowling Pain 5.11c ★★★
Move 50 feet left of *Brothel Doc* to the next bolted line. Climb a slab past a small roof at the third bolt. Continue up and over a right-angling arête to take on a heavily featured, overhanging headwall. Accidentally poached by Blake Bowling after Matt told him to "check it out."
80 ft. 10 bolts. Blake Bowling, 2006. Equipped by Matt Tackett.

241

RIVAL WALL

☀ 🚗 25 min 🚶 10 min 📱 37.65 -83.71

12 routes This cliff is definitely worth a visit. *Lobster Claw* is an excellent forearm blaster, while just left of the main approach trail are the long and surprisingly moderate sport lines *Delayed Gratification* and *Hatfield*.

.14
.13
.12
.11
.10
.9
.8
.7
≤.6

Approach: From the main Sore Heel Hollow parking lot (directions on page 206), cross the footbridge on the left to reach a wide dirt road. Follow the road uphill and take the first trail on the right. The cliff is about 50 feet uphill from the main trail. The approach trail meets the cliff at *McCoy*. Routes are described left to right.

Conditions: This wall, like the others on this side of Sore Heel Hollow, faces north to northwest so expect shade or afternoon sun. The corridor containing *Lobster Claw* and the project to its left is a great shady spot in summer. Most of the sport lines stay dry in a light rain.

Hatfield

❶ Hatfield 5.10d ★★★★
When you reach the cliff from the approach trail there will be three bolted lines to your left. This is the farthest left. A long and sustained pumper that doesn't offer as many tasty iron-oxide relief jugs as the line to the right.
80 ft. 9 bolts. *Jared Hancock, Matt Tackett, 2006.*

❷ Delayed Gratification 5.10c ★★★★
Just right of *Hatfield*. Begin by climbing a right-leaning flake to reach up to a decent edge, then skate up to a large horizontal. Continue up the face, staying just left of a blunt arête, making long moves between solid iron-oxide horizontals.
80 ft. 9 bolts. *Bram Bell, Bill Strachan, JATD crew, 2006.*

❸ McCoy 5.10c ★★★
This is the first bolted route at the head of the trail and the third from the left. Begin with an off-balance and reachy start to reach some blocks that require a bit of trickery to move past. Continue on less brain-demanding moves to the anchors.
70 ft. 9 bolts. *Jeff Neal, Matt Johns, 2012.*

❹ Tourette Syndrome 5.11a ★★★
This route is approximately 60 feet right of *McCoy* on a slightly overhanging pocketed face. Start just right of a big tree and head to the first ledge. Gain the upper headwall and continue up enjoyable holds to the anchors.
75 ft. 9 bolts. *Sarah Gross, Tim Kuhn, 2014.*

❺ Epic Indicator 5.9+ ★★
Walk right 100 feet from where the approach trail meets the cliff then take the left trail, which leads to a ledge. Walk out onto the ledge to the left of the following two sport lines to locate a short overhanging hand crack that starts about five feet off the deck. Work up the crux hand crack and onto good holds on the face above. Continue to work up the crack with questionable gear to the top of the wall. Rap from a tree to descend.
70 ft. *Matt Tackett, Jason Haas, 2006.*

❻ Rorschach Inkblot Test 5.8+ ★★
This is the left line of two sport routes that start from a ledge. Surmount the low overhang, making use of whichever holds you can find. Continue on larger holds to the anchors.
50 ft. 5 bolts. *Yasmeen Fowler, Don McGlone, JATD crew, 2006.*

RIVAL WALL

SORE HEEL HOLLOW

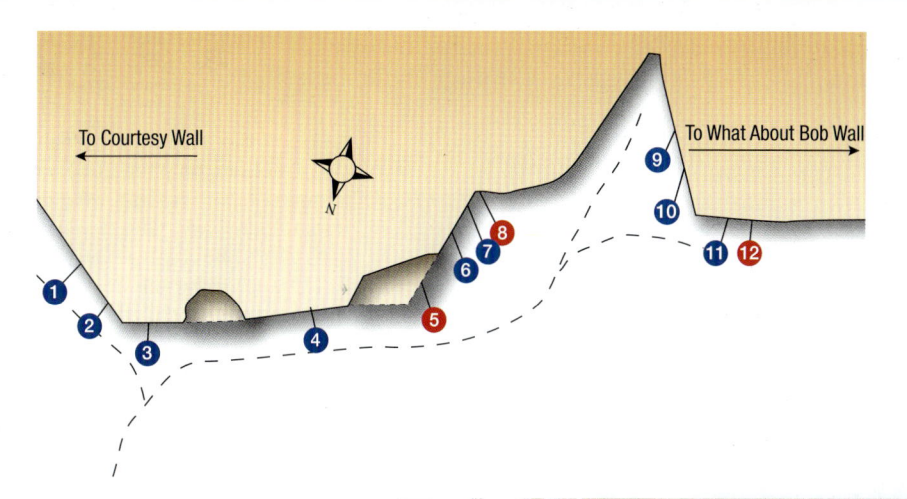

Monobrow 5.10a ★★★
ve a few feet right from *Rorschach Inkblot Test* to the next
ted line, just left of an arête. Climb the face, making use of
 arête when you're at a loss for holds.
ft. 5 bolts. *Brad Combs, Don McGlone, JATD crew, 2006.*

The Cheerleader Catch 5.6 ★★
s is the wide, left-facing dihedral just right of *Monobrow*.
mney up the dihedral, fiddling in a small cam or nut at
ut one-third height, then running it to the top. Top out or
er from the anchors on *Monobrow*.
ft. *Jason Haas, Matt Tackett, 2006.*

Cork Eye 5.12a ★★★
een feet right from *The Cheerleader Catch* is a corridor.
 the right side of the corridor is a pocketed and slightly
rhanging face, which hosts this and the following two
rt lines.
ft. 7 bolts. *Kipp Trummel, 2007.*

Lobster Claw 5.12a ★★★★
ve a few feet right from *Cork Eye* to the next bolted line.
gin just right of a low hueco. Climb large pockets to reach
 first bolt, then precisely stab your way through tiny
kets to a breather near the top. Don't get too confident,
ause you still have to make it to the chains.
ft. 7 bolts. *Kipp Trummel, 2006.*

Days of Thunder 5.9
ve right and just around the corner from *Lobster Claw* to
 next bolted line. Climb a dirty start to gain better rock
ve. Take on a slopey crux near the top, then run it on jugs
he anchors.
ft. 5 bolts. *Mark Ryan, Jenny Ryan, Jared Hancock, Karla
cock, 2006.*

Epic Indicator

Monobrow

⑫ **May as Well** 5.7
This line follows the crack system just right of *Days of Thunder*. Climb the initial wide crack that starts on top of a small roof, then traverse left to another crack. Work up the cracks and pods to a ledge with several small trees. Continue up to a higher ledge and larger trees to rappel, or bail from the anchors on *Days of Thunder*.
80 ft. Matt Tackett, Jason Haas, 2006.

243

Kevin Thompson, *Aural Pleasure*, 5.11a (opposite). Photo: Mike Wilkinson.

COURTESY WALL

37.6517
-83.7113
25 min   10 min

Located between the Shire and Rival Wall, Courtesy Wall contains some difficult and technical bolted lines and a few nice trad routes. The sport lines are not severely overhanging, but still deliver a wicked pump. If you want to [te]st out the style, jump on *Tweaked Unit*.

Approach: From the main Sore Heel Hollow parking lot (directions on page 206), cross the footbridge on the left to reach a wide dirt road. Follow the road past the first trail to the right (leading to Rival Wall) and look for the next trail on the right. Follow this trail a short way to reach the main wall near *Welcomed Guest*. This wall may also be reached by hiking 200 feet left from Rival Wall, past a breakdown in the cliff.

Conditions: This wall, as others on this side of Sore Heel Hollow, faces north to northwest, so expect mostly shade with some afternoon sun.

Go Home Yankee 5.12a ★★
[Fro]m the approach trail, walk right to reach a nice-looking [wa]ll sporting three lines. This is the rightmost line and [tak]es on the face left of the arête. Your experience could be [co]ntrived or technical, depending upon your patience.
[?0] ft. 7 bolts. *Matt Tackett, 2007.*

Wearing Out My Welcome 5.12a ★★★★
[Th]e middle of the three lines on the attractive face, which [be]gins with a short, shallow arête. Continue up and right to [rea]ch an overhanging dihedral leading to the anchors.
[?0] ft. 8 bolts. *Jason Haas, Matt Tackett, 2006.*

Welcomed Guest 5.11d ★★★★
[Be]gin on the arête 15 feet left of the previous line. Climb the [ne]ar-blank arête to a small, pocketed roof. Work over the [roo]f, then move up and right to the anchors.
[?0] ft. 10 bolts. *Jason Haas, Matt Tackett, 2006.*

Kiss It All Better 5.8 ★★
[Fro]m the approach trail, walk left to locate this obvious, wide, [rig]ht-facing dihedral. Climb through easy but slightly dirty [ter]rain and enjoy a great view at the top. Rap from slings on [a t]ree.
[?0] ft. *Dan Beck, Catherine Harrison, 2006.*

STD 5.10a ★★★
[Mo]ve left 20 feet around the corner from *Kiss It All Better* to a [sec]tion of the wall hosting three sport lines. This is the right [on]e. Climb large iron-oxide jugs to a blank section. Make a [bi]g reach, then continue on with the reach-and-step routine.
[?0] ft. 7 bolts. *Sandy Davies, Tina Bronaugh, Dana Weller, 2006.*

Welcomed Guest

❻ **Tweaked Unit** 5.11b ★★★★
This is the bolted line 10 feet left of *STD*. Begin with a high left sidepull and pull up to a couple of jugs. From the jugs, pull a tough move to get past a blank section. Enjoy the last few large holds as you approach the sequential pumpfest that lies ahead. Clip the chains from a big, comfy hueco.
70 ft. 9 bolts. *Wes Allen, Stephanie Meadows, JATD crew, 2006.*

❼ **Aural Pleasure** 5.11a ★★★
Shuffle 10 feet left of *Tweaked Unit* to the next sport line. Climb jugs up a left-leaning arête. At the third bolt, move sharply left into the business half of the route. Flexibility will help the shorties get through the well-defined crux.
70 ft. 7 bolts. *Wes Allen, JATD crew, 2006.*

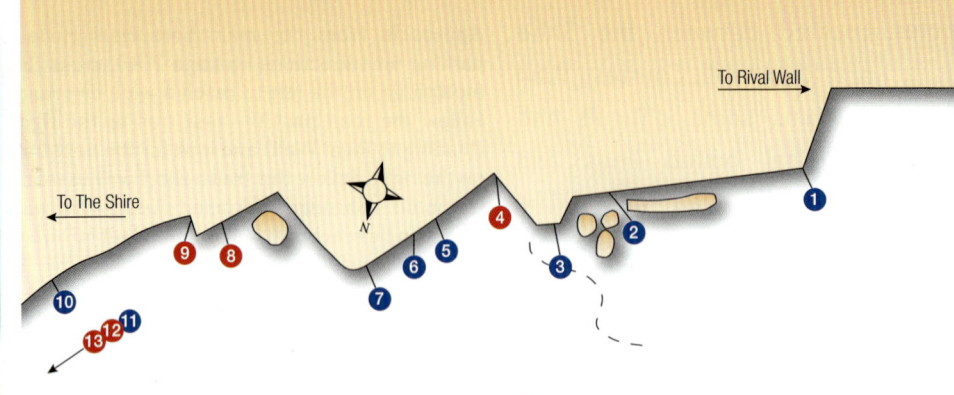

8 The Climbing Corpse Cometh 5.10d ★★

Walk 70 feet left of *Aural Pleasure* to find this appealing finger-and-hand crack splitting the face next to a large black streak. Work your way up the initial grungy face to a large pod, then tackle the splitter crack. Lower from chains.
60 ft. Jason Hass, Matt Tackett, Don McGlone, 2006.

9 Jackie the Stripper 5.12b ★★★

This line takes on the left-facing dihedral just left of *The Climbing Corpse Cometh*. Work through mellow moves, then let the stemming madness begin. Formerly an aid climb called *Zombie Sloth*. Lower from chain anchors to descend.
70 ft. 2 bolts. Jordan Wood, 2008. Equipped by John "Fred" Aragon, Mike Cole, 2006.

10 Seam Project ★★★

Walk 50 feet left from the previous line to locate this gently overhanging bolted seam.
90 ft. 8 bolts. Equipped by Wes Allen.

11 Buenos Hermanos 5.10b ★

This bolted line is located left of *Seam Project*. Climb iron-oxide ledges to reach tricky slab climbing above.
50 ft. 5 bolts. Jeff Castro, Dan Spalding, 2012.

12 Trad Is His Son 5.9 ★★

Walk left from the previous line about 150 to 200 feet until you reach a small dip in the trail. This line starts with a broken face and moves left into a right-leaning crack. Lower from bolted anchors near a small tree.
65 ft. Matt Tackett, Jeremy Egleston, 2006.

13 And They Called It a Route 5.8

This discontinuous crack system begins about 20 feet left of *Trad Is His Son*. Begin on iron-oxide jugs to gain a thin crack which quickly fades. Traverse right to more cracks and fiddle in gear. Pull a layback move to reach a ledge with anchors. The first ascentionists do not provide a money-back guarantee.
50 ft. Matt Tackett, Jason Haas, 2006.

SHANNON STUART-SMITH
(RRGCC founder)

In 2004, the Red River Gorge Climbers' Coalition (RRGCC) made the largest-ever acquisition of private land for rock climbing. The Pendergrass Murray Recreational Preserve (PMRP) consists of 700 acres of pristine sandstone hosting some of the world's best sport climbing. It took a strong organization of climbers to make this happen — a group formed eight years earlier thanks to efforts led by Shannon Stuart-Smith.

Between growing up in an Air Force family and working as a horse exercise rider, jockey, and trainer, Shannon traveled extensively in her earlier years until taking a job at a horse track in Lexington, KY, in 1979. At age 25, she moved to Los Angeles to attend UCLA, and then returned to Lexington to earn a law degree from the University of Kentucky. Instead of heading to the office she went straight back to "rustlin' horses like mad" at the renowned Keeneland horse track.

At age 40, Shannon started climbing with her usual determination. After a leading class and a few trips to the New River Gorge, she discovered the sandstone paradise of the Red less than an hour away. Within a year of climbing at the Red, she learned of a major threat to access: a local anti-logging group had recently sued and won against the Daniel Boone National Forest for not following the National Environmental Policy Act (NEPA). Out of fear of being accused of a committing a similar NEPA violation, the Forest Service was drafting a climbing management plan that threatened to close most established crags on the national forest, including Military Wall and Left Flank.

Shannon and her climbing partner at the time, Kristin Snyder, immediately took action. They created red trifold pamphlets explaining the situation and placed them at the Slade rest area. For $5 you could join their two-person organization, the Red River Gorge Climbers' Coalition, its mission to "Protect, Promote, and Ensure Responsible Climbing." Soon several locals jumped on board, including the guidebook author, attorney, and strong local personality John Bronaugh. Shannon's spare bedroom became the RRGCC office; she became Executive Director, while Kristin served as Director of Operations. John Bronaugh offered his publication skills to serve as editor of the RRGCC newsletter, *The Crag Rag*. The familiar oval-biner-on-red-background decal began showing up all around the gorge.

Shannon's approach to preserving access was to try to resolve the conflict between the Forest Service and climbers. She contacted the local NEPA officer, Rita Wehner, offering to take her climbing in exchange for a day at the office.

This knowledge exchange would hopefully help the Forest Service to understand that climbers could work with them to bring the existing routes into NEPA compliance and prevent closure. The plan worked, and on February 7, 2000, the RRGCC and the Forest Service signed a memorandum of understanding — the routes would remain open! Shannon would go on to serve as Executive Director of the RRGCC through 2004 and then as Board Secretary until 2007, when she retired from the Board. The Forest Service experience taught two important lessons eventually leading to the successful purchase of the PMRP: the need for a more permanent, long-term solution to secure climbing — and the power of climbers being organized.

Shannon lives with her wife, Julie Fain, and their dogs in Lexington, KY. Both still climb regularly, but you may never see them since they love to seek out the newest routes at the newest crags. Shannon doesn't keep a public tick list on any websites, but if she did you would quickly realize that she climbs well and climbs a lot. ∎

Photo: Ludovic Bacquet

THE SHIRE

37.651
-83.710
25 min | 15 min

13 routes
.14
.13
.12
.11
.10
.9
.8
.7
≤.6

This small wall contains a handful of decent moderates and a couple of tough lines.

Approach: From the Sore Heel Hollow parking area (directions on page 206), follow the main dirt road that leads to Rival and Courtesy walls until it narrows to more of a trail. Eventually you'll reach a large fin-shaped boulder on the left, at which point the trail veers right and uphill to the main wall; do not take the left fork at the large boulder.

Conditions: The main wall, home to routes #1- can be quite cold. As with most walls in this area it faces north to northwest, so expect a bit of afternoon sun.

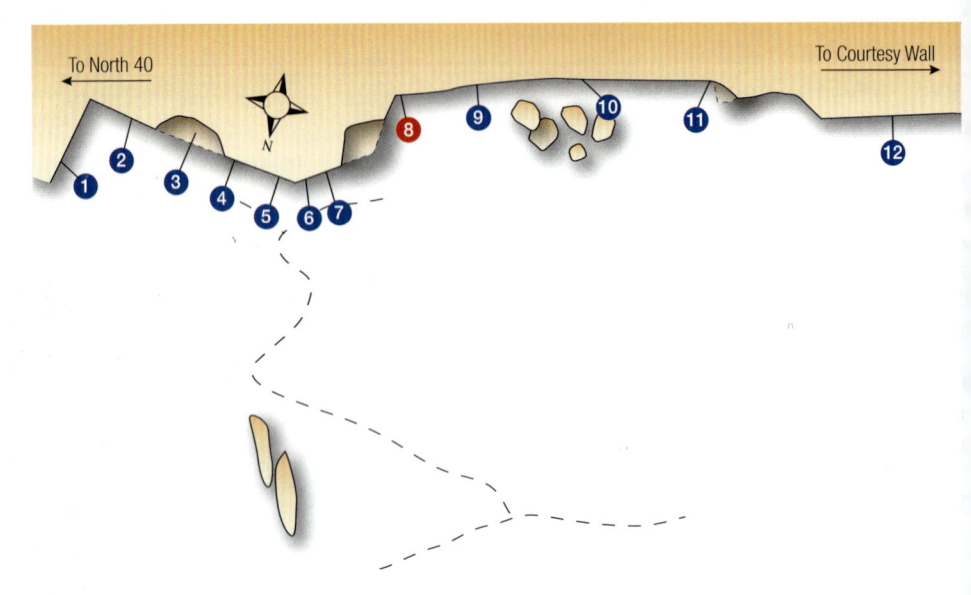

To North 40 ← — → To Courtesy Wall

❶ **My Name is Earl** 5.11d ★★★
As the approach trail nears the cliff you will see four bolted lines on a slightly overhanging, plated face. This line ascends the short arête on the adjacent wall, just left of a dihedral. It's short, but give it a chance.
30 ft. 3 bolts. Josh Thurston, 2007.

❷ **Pee-Wee** 5.7 ★★
This is leftmost route on the main face and begins just left of a large rock shelter. Fun final moves!
35 ft. 4 bolts. Ron Bateman, Josh Thurston, Betsey Adams, 2006.

❸ **Audie** 5.8 ★★★
This route follows the line of bolts beginning just above the rockhouse. Start in the rockhouse or left of it, and traverse to the first bolt. Continue on plates and pockets to anchors.
35 ft. 4 bolts. Ron Bateman, Jared Hancock, Matt Tackett, 2006.

❹ **Miranda Rayne** 5.9 ★★★★
Move right a few feet from *Audie* to step it up a grade and gain some more height to the anchors.
60 ft. 7 bolts. Ron Bateman, Eric Cox, 2006.

❺ **The G-Man** 5.10c ★★★
Once you've graduated from the previous three lines, move right to take on the toughest line on the wall. Begin just left of an arête and stick-clip the first bolt. Climb through pumpy moves on sloping pinches to the anchors.
40 ft. 6 bolts. Ron Bateman, 2006.

❻ **Significant Other** 5.10b ★★
Move right a few feet and around the corner from *The G-Man* to locate this and the next line. Climb a mossy start to gain a ledge, then continue up the fingery face to the anchors.
40 ft. 4 bolts. Josh Thurston, Bob Peterson, 2006.

248

● **Bulldozer** 5.10a ★★

tep right a few feet to the next bolted line. Climb the slabby
ice past thought-provoking moves.
0 ft. 4 bolts. *Ron Bateman, Betsey Adams, 2006.*

● **Buffalo Crickets** 5.10b ★★

wenty feet around the corner from *Bulldozer* is this left-
icing dihedral. Crank past a tough start, then continue up
ie crack. Near the top, the crack widens and becomes
xtremely dirty. Protect in horizontals on the arête to the left.
escend from a bolted anchor.
5 ft. *Josh Thurston, Betsey Adams, 2006.*

● **Iron Mike** Open Project ★★★★

wenty-five feet right of *Buffalo Crickets* is a striking line of
olated shallow pockets and crimpers. Start up the first four
olts of easy iron rails and get a quick rest. While recovering,
:ope the path of least resistance and try your luck with the
istained and heady crux.
0 ft. 8 bolts.

● **K.S.B.** 5.10d ★★★★

/alk right about 150 feet past *Bulldozer* to a large,
verhanging wall. This climb starts with some steep iron-
dge pulling and ends on a vertical face.
0 ft. 4 bolts. *Ron Bateman, Josh Thurston, Matt Tackett,
chard Strange, 2006.*

● **Earth-Bound Misfit** 5.12c ★★★★

ove about 50 feet right from the previous line to this
riking thin dihedral, which begins about 20 feet off the deck
nd ends on a perch. Contains some difficult clips and a little
t of spice. Named after the loss of the author's friend Terry
ndred.
0 ft. 4 bolts. *Blake Bowling, 2007.*

● **Team Wilander** 5.11d ★★★

venty-five feet right of the dihedral is this bolted line, which
egins in a cave. Crank through the initial cave, then emerge
the first bolt and enjoy gymnastic moves to the finish.
0 ft. 4 bolts. *Ron Bateman, 2007.*

● **Mis-Conception** 5.12b ★★★★

venty-five feet right from the previous route is this
eceptively difficult line. Climb through sloping holds to a
dpoint crux just before the anchors.
0 ft. 5 bolts. *Mike Uchman, Josh Thurston, Ron Bateman, 2007.*

NORTH 40

☀ 🚗 25 min 🚶 15 min 📱 37.65 -83.70

8 routes

.14
.13
.12
.11
.10
.9
.8
.7
≤.6

This crag has only a handful of routes, but many are superb. *Amarillo Sunset* (5.11b) and *Samurai* (5.12b) are two of the Red's best at their grades. Get ready for big reaches and hard pulls — a true classic can never be a gimme!

Aproach: Drive to the Sore Heel Hollow parking area (directions on page 206). Follow the approach to the Shire (page 248), then continue walking past the last line at the Shire for a few minutes until you see an obvious large amphitheater. *Amarillo Sunset* is on the right, just before the trail heads sharply downhill. Routes described right to left.

Conditions: North 40 faces primarily north to northwest, so expect shade, or at most a bit of afternoon sun.

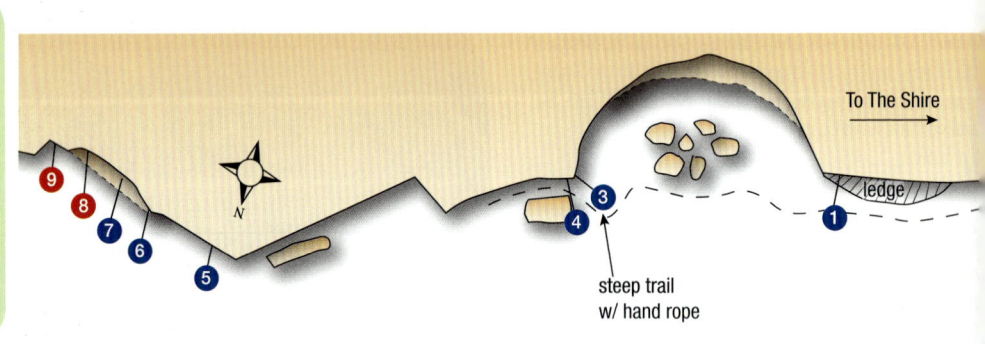

To The Shire →

steep trail w/ hand rope

❶ **Amarillo Sunset** 5.11b ★★★★★
One of the best for the grade in the Red — unless you're a shortie! Start from a ledge just right of a large ravine. Gorilla-swing through monster holds while savoring the excellent exposure.
50 ft. 7 bolts. Kipp Trummel, 2006.

❷ **Tequila Sunrise** 5.11b ★★★★
Just left of *Amarillo Sunset*, and sharing the last few bolts, is this other fun route. Unfortunately, it was chopped by an unknown climber. It may or may not have been re-equipped.
65 ft. 6 bolts. Shadow Ayala, Aaron Brouwer, 2013.

❸ **Swine Flew** 5.13b ★★★★
Hike down from *Amarillo Sunset*, through the ravine, and up to the other side with help of a hand rope. Begin this route by climbing the steep arête that hovers above the ravine to reach a blank, intimidating headwall above.
80 ft. 8 bolts. Bentley Bracket, Kipp Trummel, 2006.

❹ **Samurai** 5.12b ★★★★★
Step left a few feet from the arête, look up, and bow to the opponent. Take a stance, breathe, then slice through a series of difficult and unique moves along a striking feature. Claim victory at the chains.
55 ft. 6 bolts. Ray Ellington, Kipp Trummel, 2006.

❺ **Barbed Wire** 5.12b ★★★
Walk left from *Samurai* a few hundred feet to the next bolted line, which begins just right of a blunt arête. Step hard through a difficult start, then power-smear through the crux and jet for larger holds up high.
55 ft. 6 bolts. Kipp Trummel, 2006.

❻ **Yosemite Sam** 5.12a ★★★
Move left and downhill a bit from *Barbed Wire* to the next bolted line. Grab the best holds you can find, then power through the tough start. Pump out for the rest of the line and don't lose it up high.
55 ft. 7 bolts. Kipp Trummel, 2006.

❼ **Outlaw Justice** 5.11d ★★★
Move left a few feet from *Yosemite Sam* to the next bolted line. Make some tricky moves around a feature to gain fun climbing above.
55 ft. 8 bolts. Kipp Trummel, 2006.

❽ **Pistol Gripped** 5.12a ★★★
Technical face-climbing skills will be rewarded with a perfect hand crack above.
55 ft. 4 bolts. Kris Hampton, Justin Riddell, Kipp Trummel, 2006.

❾ **Summer Breeze** 5.8 ★★
Twenty-five feet left of *Pistol Gripped* is this obvious crack system. Follow the crack up and right until it fades to chains.
50 ft. Josh Thurston, Jordan Garvey, 2006.

Amarillo Sunset

Swine Flew

Samurai

Barbed Wire

NORTH 40

SORE HEEL HOLLOW

Dan Brayack shows *Where's the Beef?*, 5.12c, Bob Marley (page 270). Photo: Mike Wilkinson.

PMRP: BALD ROCK FORK

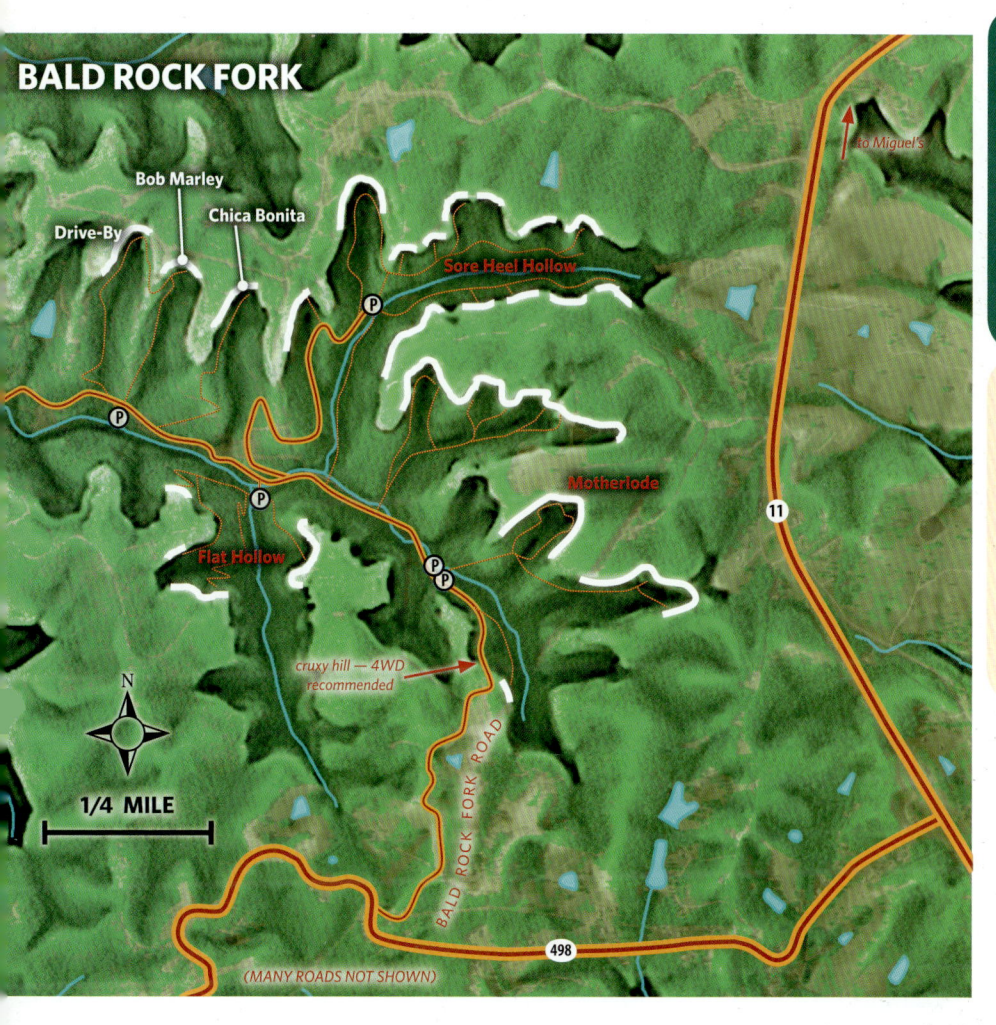

Bald Rock Fork Approach: From Miguel's, drive 2.4 miles south on KY 11 toward Beattyville. Turn right on KY 498. Drive 1.2 miles to a sharp right curve. Just beyond this curve, take a sharp right on Bald Rock Road, a gravel road, and follow it slowly as it curves left toward a house, staying left at the first intersection. After 0.3 miles the road descends a rough, steep hill. The hill can be drivable in a passenger car if the road has recently been graded, but usually ruts out within a few days. 4WD recommended. During busy seasons and inclement weather, this hill can become treacherous — scope it out before proceeding down. If you have doubts, climb elsewhere. Do not park atop the hill, as this area is used to access oil company equipment and you are liable to be towed. Throughout the gorge, DO NOT park in front of oil wells or oil equipment.

After the hill, continue past the Motherlode parking area, on the right, and remain on the road for a total of 1.4 miles (0.6 miles past the Motherlode parking) until you see a wooden sign indicating the RRGCC parking area on the left.

CHICA BONITA WALL

37.6514
-83.721
20 min 10 min

43 routes

Chica Bonita Wall is an area that you will either love or hate. The east-facing wall is best known for its trio of excellent slabs, *Brown-Eyed Girl*, *Baby Blue Eyes*, and *Bessie*, as well as the classic, arching crack *Cheaper Than a Movie*. Remember though, these are slabs, so don't get suckered by the loads of stars if you hate slab climbing.

Approach: Park at the Bald Rock Fork parking area (directions on previous page), as for Drive-By and Bob Marley crags, and walk back down the road toward the Motherlode a couple hundred feet until you reach two roads forking off uphill on the left. Take the road that veers right up the hill. There will be a sign near its intersection with the main road indicating the Chica Bonita Wall. Follow the dirt road uphill, passing a short road with an oil pump on the right. As the road curves around left, look for an obvious trail and sign. The trail makes a straight shot to *Darling Dirtbag* (route #4). The first few routes, including *Laying Pipe* and *Friend Zone*, are located on the backside of this section of cliff, and can be reached by taking the faint trail up and left around the cliffline.

Conditions: The cliff faces directly east, so expect sunshine from morning to early afternoon. Routes #5-12 are situated inside a large rockhouse, so are climbable in a heavy rain. The other lines are slabby for the most part, so won't stay as dry.

❶ **Laying Pipe Under the Bridge** 5.7 ★★★
Instead of taking the trail that drops down to the right from the oil pump, take a trail on the left. After roughly 300 feet you will come to this obvious line that has an old oil pipeline coming down from the top of the cliff near it. This line ascends the hand crack right of the pipe to the top of an arch.
70 ft. Dan Beck, Matt Tacket, 2008.

❷ **The Friend Zone** 5.6 ★
Located 30 feet right of *Laying Pipe*. Protect this intro to offwidth with a selection of big cams (#3-#6 Camalots). It sucks when you first realize you are in the friend zone, but once you're OK with it, it is a lot of fun! Rap from a pine tree.
50 ft. Curtis and Audrey Gale-Dyer, 2015.

❸ **Tight Lipped 2** 5.11c ★★★
Just right of *The Friend Zone* is a technical face climb. Start just left of the small flake, and angle up and right.
55 ft. 6 bolts. Troy Davidson, Sarah Gross, 2014.

❹ **Darling Dirtbag** 5.8 ★★
As you walk in to Chica Bonita, this is the arête, crack, and face system immediately before the rockhouse hosting *Quicky* through *The Dude Abides*. Climb the arête, then move into a hand crack. Stay in the hand crack to reach a slab leading to the top. Bring small cams for the top. Now and forever known as the single route in the RRG that Lee Smith doesn't like.
90 ft. Dan Beck, Nicole Bunda, 2008.

❺ **Quicky** 5.8 ★
This line ascends the first short dihedral on the left side of the rockhouse. There are no anchors — downclimbing is the only possible descent.
25 ft. Jason Haas (free solo), 2005.

❻ **Fresh Off the Bone** 5.11d ★★★
As you enter the first large rock house, this route will be just above you. Tackle the roof section and get ready for great holds and a "great ride."
65 ft. 9 bolts. Troy Davison, 2014.

❼ **Mary Pop-Parazzi** 5.5 ★
An easy, short-attention-span route.
25 ft. 3 bolts. Jenny Ryan, Mark Ryan, Keith Raker, Neil Arnold, 2009.

❽ **Pocahontas Path** 5.7
The next short line just right of *Mary Pop-Parazzi*. Bored yet?
25 ft. 3 bolts. Jenny Ryan, Mark Ryan, Keith Raker, 2009.

❾ **The Spice of Life** 5.10b ★★★
Locate a wide crack 30 feet right of *Quicky*. Climb the face next to the crack to a ledge. It is possible to get a piece of pro in a pocket on the face. From the ledge, traverse out the massive roof to another ledge with chain anchors. Entertaining, to say the least.
70 ft. Jason Haas, Matt Tackett, 2005.

CHICA BONITA

BALD ROCK FORK

Fresh Off the Bone

The Spice of Life

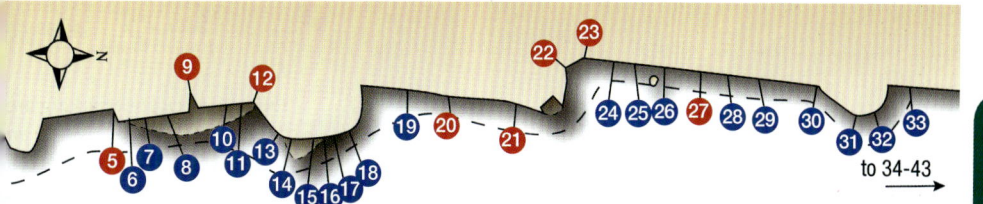

Brolo El Cunado 5.8 ★★
Just right of the start of *Spice of Life* is another moderate three-bolt route. Climb the nonexistent flake feature to a few jugs, then pockets and edges to the anchors.
30 ft. 3 bolts. *Nathan Ross, 2016.*

Raindancer 5.10a ★★
This short sport route takes the line of bolts just left of the next dihedral on the right side of the rockhouse. Negotiate a rough start to reach good pockets above.
30 ft. 3 bolts.
Fred Hancock, Matt Tackett, Mike Cole, Mark Ryan, 2006.

Rinse and Repeat 5.7 ★
Climb the short dihedral to a set of anchors.
30 ft. *Jesse New, Mike Cole, Jared Hancock, 2006.*

The Dude Abides 5.11a ★★★
Just right of *Rinse and Repeat* is another bolted line. Climb to an edge, then continue up a pocketed face to the chains.
50 ft. 7 bolts. *Don McGlone, John "Fred" Aragon, 2006.*

The Dude Abides

255

Ridin' the Short Buzz

Flying the Bird

Honduran Rum

⑯ Hot Drama Teacher 5.11a ★★★
Climb through a series of plates and horizontals to a short roo
Jam or claw through the roof, then continue to the chains.
90 ft. 9 bolts. Merrick Schaefer, Matt Tackett, 2005.

⑰ Ridin' the Short Buzz 5.9 ★★★
Climb the short, plated face just right of *Hot Drama Teacher*
Climb slow and the buzz will last longer than Salvia.
35 ft. 4 bolts.
Jared Hancock, Karla Hancock, Mark Ryan, Jenny Ryan, 2006.

⑱ When Rats Attack 5.10b ★★★
Climb the arête through a series of bulges and ledges.
55 ft. 5 bolts. Mark Ryan, Jenny Ryan, 2006.

⑲ Flying the Bird 5.10c ★★★
Right of the *When Rats Attack* arête is a large, dirty chimne
This bolted line climbs the slab 20 feet right of the chimney
Not for the "mantelly disabled."
50 ft. 5 bolts. Aika Yoshida, Barry Brolley, Mark Ryan, JJ, 2008.

⑭ Cold Hard Bitch 5.12b ★★★
Starting on the arête between *The Dude Abides* and *Helluva Caucasian*, this short route packs a punch.
40 ft. 5 bolts. Nathan Ross, 2016.

⑮ Helluva Caucasian 5.12a ★★★
Work your way to the roof, gather your beta, and make a big move over the lip. Don't feel bad if you take a whip, this route has seen its share of failed onsight attempts. Be prepared for the long run to the anchors.
90 ft. 10 bolts. Blake Bowling, 2009.

⑳ Honduran Rum 5.10c ★
Fifty feet right of the previous routes is a section of cliff separated by a large ledge midway up. This line ascends th thin crack system starting 15 feet up and behind a tree. En on the middle ledge at bolted anchors.
70 ft. Jason Haas, Cory Weber, 2005.

Be My Yoko Ono 5.8 ★★★

...e abundance of large face holds on this line makes for a ...at beginner's lead. Move 40 feet right to a crack system ...rrounded by large plates. Climb jugs to a higher hand ...ck. Rap from anchors to descend.
... ft. *Jason Haas, Matt Tackett, 2005.*

Let's Get Drunk and Think About It 5.10a ★

...e looks good now, but wait until you climb her. This next ...e is cursed with good looks but a whole lot of mud. Walk ...out 200 feet right from the previous line to a section of ...ll with two impressive-looking cracks. This line ascends ...e crack on the left. Climb the dihedral to a ledge with a tree ...d belay. Ascend the cleaner, right-arching flake to the top. ...p from a tree to descend.
... ft. *Jordan Wood, Jason Haas, 2005.*

Cheaper Than a Movie 5.8 ★★★★★

...is line, one of the best and longest in its class, is definitely ...rth a visit to Chica Bonita Wall. Climb the gorgeous, right-...gling crack until you can traverse right to the anchors on ...ssie for the descent. A 60-meter rope barely gets you to ...e ground, so tie a knot in the end.
...0 ft. *Matt Tackett, Jason Haas, 2005.*

Brown-Eyed Girl 5.10a ★★★★

...mediately right of *Cheaper Than a Movie* is a wide slab of ...ndstone containing a few incredible calf-burners. This is ...e first line on the wall and thins out near the top.
... ft. 6 bolts. *Nick Walker, Jared Hancock, Mark Ryan, 2006.*

㉕ Baby Blue Eyes 5.10c ★★★★

Climb the next bolted line just right of *Brown-Eyed Girl*. Begin on a small flake, then head straight up the clean section of rock, passing a large horizontal slot along the way.
75 ft. 7 bolts. *Amy Tackett, Matt Tackett, 2006.*

㉖ Bessie 5.11c ★★★

Walk 20 feet right from *Baby Blue Eyes* to the next bolted line on the slab. This is the best of the lines on this wall, but also the most difficult and beta intensive. Keep pressure on your toes for the runouts near the top!
100 ft. 10 bolts. *Matt Tackett, Amy Tackett, 2005.*

257

You Take Sally

Size Doesn't Matter

27 Sexy Sadie 5.10b ★★
This heady line is recognized by the short crack system that starts about 20 feet off the ground right of *Bessie*. Climb through a well-protected crux near the end of the initial crack, then continue up the slab, passing the occasional horizontal placement.
100 ft. Don McGlone, 2007.

28 You Take Sally 5.11d ★★★★
Locate the obvious hueco about 25 feet up and right of the previous lines, with routes going out the left and right side. This line climbs up and left of the hueco. Pure slab climbing and the hardest on the wall.
80 ft. 9 bolts. Matt Tackett, Don McGlone, 2007.

29 I'll Take Sue 5.11a ★★★★
An easier version of *You Take Sally*. Climb up to the hueco, then crux out of it. Get your friction on!
80 ft. 9 bolts. Don McGlone, Matt Tacket, 2006.

30 Size Doesn't Matter 5.11a ★★★★
Another tough-to-onsight, no-holds line right of *I'll Take Sue*. If those holds were just a bit bigger, then you would've gotten up a little quicker. Maybe size does matter.
80 ft. 8 bolts. Natasha Fischer, Reece Nelson, Ron Bateman, Matt Tackett, 2007.

31 That's What She Said 5.10c ★★★★
A great intro route for the slab-shy. Begin just right of *Size Doesn't Matter* on the ledge near where the trail cuts downhill. Climb through stop-and-go terrain with bolt placements just where you want them.
90 ft. 12 bolts. Matt Tackett, Don McGlone, 2007.

32 She Might Be a Liar 5.11b ★★★★
Want to end the day with some spice? Begin on the same ledge as the previous line and take on awkward movement requiring full commitment.
75 ft. 8 bolts. Dan Beck, Matt Tackett, 2007.

33 Motor Booty Pimp Affair 5.10b ★
This is the next route right of *She Might Be a Liar*, but must be approached by heading downhill on the trail and cutting around the outcropping that forms the ledge from which the previous lines begin. Inferior to the phenomenal lines on the main wall.
95 ft. 12 bolts. Dan Beck, Matt Tackett, Don McGlone, 2007.

34 Thunda Bunda 5.10d ★
Look for an offwidth beginning in a low roof right of the previous lines. Get your ass off the ground and continue up to a large hueco where it's possible to traverse left to another wide crack and set a belay. Thrash up to another hueco, move left, and take the face to the top. It's tricky but possible to climb over to the anchors on *Motor Booty Pimp Affair*, but 60-meter rope will get you down from the tree above the anchors if you don't want to commit to reaching them.
110 ft. Ben Strohmeier, Dan Beck, 2008.

35 Falkor 5.10d ★★★
Begin with the same tough start as *Thunda Bunda*, but head straight up instead of moving left. Continue up a sparsely protected face to the top. Rap from a tree above the anchors *Motor Booty Pimp Affair* if you've only got a 60-meter rope.
110 ft. Dan Beck, Matt Tackett, 2008.

Marriage Counseling

Old English

CHICA BONITA

BALD ROCK FORK

Marriage Counseling 5.11c ★★★
...low the trail to the right and head downhill around a
...ttress for about 100 feet to reach the next line. Locate
...ess-than-vertical crack beginning on a flat boulder just
...ht of a low overhang. Climb through easy moves to reach
...arge hueco about 30 feet up. Move left out of the hueco
...good holds to a stance beneath an overhanging, right-
...gling crack system in black rock. Pump up through the
...erhanging crack to bolted anchors at a large ledge.
...ft. Sam Elias, Beck Kloss, 2005.

Old English 5.10c ★★★★
...erhanging, jugs, no-hand stances — what's not to like?
...t on the large ledge and move left to the large flake.
...ft. 8 bolts. Scott Curran, 2013.

Colt 45 5.12b ★★★★
...arting on the same first bolt as *Old English*, head straight
... Several boulder problems will keep your attention just
...fore the devious pocket crux at the top.
...ft. Scott Curran, 2013.

King Cobra 5.12a ★★★
...xt in line is another steep 12. Mantel past the second
...t to take a break. Small pockets lead you to the final rail.
...antel again to clip the chains.
...ft. 8 bolts. Scott Curran, 2013.

40 Sister Catherine the Conqueror 5.12b ★
Look for a line of bolts near some small boulders with a large roof at midheight. If you aren't afraid of commitment to the choss, you may find some enjoyment in this route. The top gets pumpy if you can just hang in there mentally to reach it.
95 ft. 10 bolts. Dan Beck, 2008.

41 Sorostitute 5.7 ★
This dirty line is about 300 feet right of *Marriage Counseling*. Climb the dihedral in the back of an amphitheater to a sandy ledge, then rap from fixed gear to descend.
50 ft. Jason Haas, Cory Weber, 2005.

42 Chucklehead 5.11c ★★★
Continue walking about 200 yards past *Sorostitute*, skirting a large, detached block that overlooks an oil pump, then cross over some oil pipes, all while bushwacking rhodos, to reach a pair of nice-looking bolted lines. This is the left of the two and begins with sloping moves, then kicks out midway for the steeps the Red is known for. Worth the trek.
55 ft. 6 bolts. Kipp Trummel, Scott Brown, 2011.

43 Good Gravy 5.10b ★★★
Just right of *Chucklehead* is an another great line on solid stone. Holds so good you'll think you're in the gym.
55 ft. 6 bolts. Kipp Trummel, Russ Jackson, 2011.

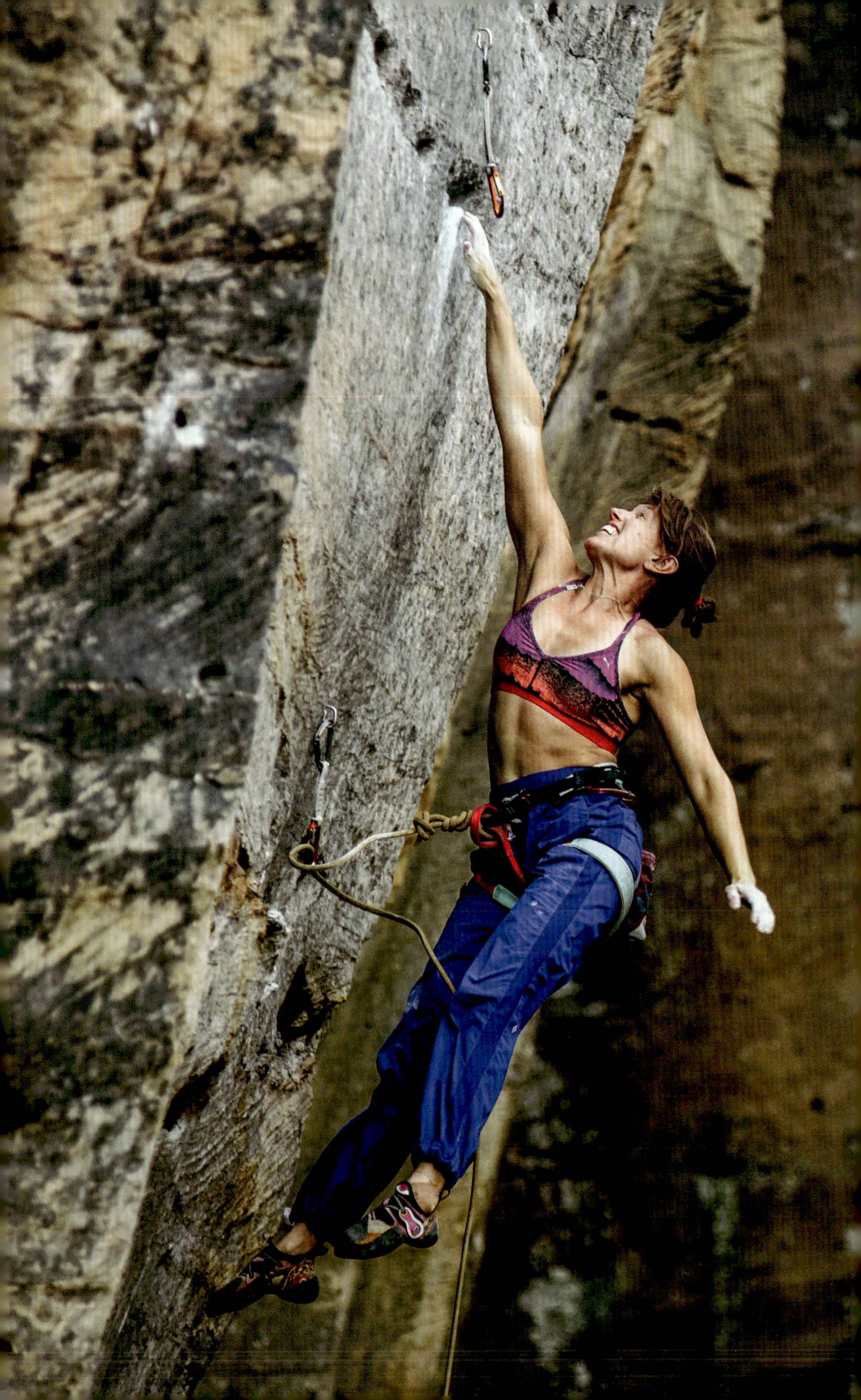

Jess Wickstrom about to send *Dogleg,* "5.12a," Bob Marley (page 265). Photo: Gabi Fox.

BOB MARLEY CRAG

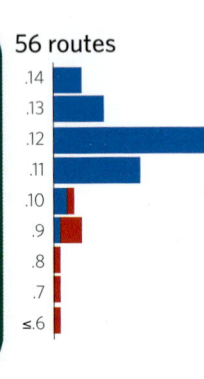

37.65
-83.72

20 min / 10 min

PMRP
BALD ROCK FORK

56 routes

Once a ghost crag full of unfinished routes, hanging ropes, impossible projects, and a handful of short, awkward roof climbs, this crag has now matured into one of the Red's best for difficult routes. The attention started with the 2007 Petzl Roc Trip, when the longstanding project *50 Words for Pump* was listed as the men's "Ultimate Route." Some of the world's best threw themselves at this beast, until Mickaël Fuselier of France got the first send, giving it a grade of 5.14c. During the trip, Sean McColl of Canada semt another open project, *MILF Money*, 5.13b, and Daniel DuLac bolted a tough new line, *El Encuentro*, 5.13b. In 2008, Joe Kinder established *Southern Smoke* 5.14c, leaving behind a possible direct start. In 2011, Adam Taylor climbed *Southern Smoke Direct*, which at 5.14d stood as the hardest route in the Red, despite being flashed by Adam Ondra the following year. In 2015 Alex Megos raised the bar even further by climbing *Southern Smoke Direct* and making the first ascent of *Your Heaven, My Hell*, 5.14d — in a single day.

The once "awkward" roof routes are now some of the most popular 5.11s and 5.12s around. *Dogleg* still stands as the Red's toughest 5.12a for the vertically challenged, if now overshadowed by a better line that branches left after the original novelty start (*Demon Seed*, 5.12c). As for easy lines, there's still not much. However, you probably have a good shot at convincing your partner to belay you on *Ultra Perm* now that a new trail puts Drive-By Crag just a five-minute walk away. Or head the other direction to check o some recently added "moderate" face climbs the right end of the crag in the 5.11 and 5.12 rang

Approach: From the Bald Rock Fork parking ar (see direction on page 253), walk back out the road. Cross the road and head straight up gravel road 0.2 miles to reach a trail that cuts le and uphill to the wall, near the routes *Dogleg* a *Demon Seed* (#14-15).

Conditions: This crag is a dry, sandy bead perfect if it's raining and you can climb 5.12 above. The sun shines directly on the wall, b the steep nature of most routes puts you in t shade, your belayer in the sun.

About 50 Words for Pump

This could have been named 50 words drama! A project for more than a decade, th high-quality pumpfest finally saw its FA duri the 2007 Petzl Roc Trip. The route had a tou and scary clip in the crux section, which is ho it was originally climbed, but shortly after the F Mike Doyle added two bolts slightly right of t original, which did away with the scary clip. Sor climbers thought this new sequence a let grade easier and also unnecessary, while othe argued it now followed the line of least resistan — and that a route's crux should not be clippir A similar incident and discussion happened w the route *50 Bucks* (AKA *Triple Sec*), 5.12d, at M Valley (what's up with the number 50?!).

Adam Taylor of Lexington, KY, added ev more controversy by smashing the new hange after his project draws were removed from a not replaced on the original bolts for a suppos photo shoot. The climbing blogs exploded a rap artist Odub even put out a song expressi his strong opinion. As Steve Petro once sa "Welcome to ole Kentuck."

❶ **Where's JJ?** 5.10a ★

From the main wall with *Toker*, walk left on the trail that connects Bob Marley with Drive-By. As you pass through th gap, you'll see two routes on the stand-alone block. This is the left one.
45 ft. 4 bolts. Mark Ryan, 2012.

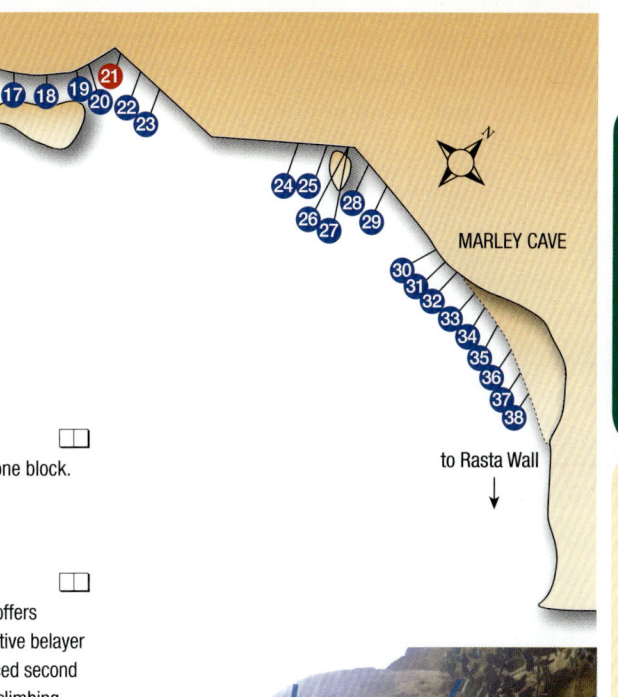

Waiting on JJ 5.9

...cated just right of *Where's JJ?* on the stand-alone block. ...is one is not quite as good as its partner.
...ft. 5 bolts. *Eric Davenport, Mark Ryan, 2009.*

Mentee 5.11c ★★

...the far left side of the the main wall, this route offers ...chnical moves up a mostly vertical face. An attentive belayer ...d nerves of steel are required due to the misplaced second ...d third bolts. Above that is some thin, deceptive climbing ...hind a tree. Your beta may include back-stepping on said ...e for the crux, or just trying hard on eroding crimps.
...ft. 7 bolts. *Sarah Gross, 2014.*

Mentor 5.11+ ★★

...*entor* is the big brother to *Mentee*. Same breaky face ...mbing, but thinner and more powerful. Start at the far left ...d of the ledge and stick-clip one of the first two misplaced ...lts. Don't fall in the beginning or you can shred your rope.
...ft. 7 bolts. *Sarah Gross, Troy Davison, 2014.*

Gettin' Ziggy With It 5.7 ★★★

...is is the leftmost crack climb at Bob Marley. Walk left of the ...rt of *Toker* to the end of the ledge and begin climbing just ...ht of *Mentor*. Finish at the *Mentor* anchor.
...ft. *Sarah Gross, 2014.*

DreadLocked 5.12b ★

...rt from the ledge, 25 feet left of *Toker*, and stick clip the ...st bolt. This route starts on steep pockets that lead to a ...ux, then a quick rest, but don't take the finish lightly.
...ft. 7 bolts. *Troy Davison, 2013.*

Crosley 5.11c ★★★★

...ere's now more than one warm-up at BMC! Begin on the ...me boulder as for *Toker*, but trend left at the start and ...mb through overhanging plates and pockets. Reserve some ...ce for the demanding lock-off move near the end. Not ...any crosleys here, but it still delivers a pump.
...ft. 8 bolts. *Andrew Wheatley, Mike Wheatley, Phil Wilkes, ...thur Cammers, 2010.*

8 Toker 5.11a ★★★★

The standard warm-up. Walk left from where the approach trail meets the cliff, past the arête of *Sugar Magnolia*, to this route, which begins above a large boulder. Stand on the boulder to reach the initial jug, then monkey over the roof to gain a stance. Climb large plates to an overhanging finish.
70 ft. 8 bolts. Jason McCleanen, 2005.

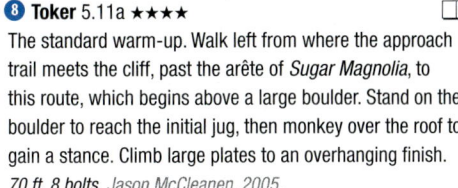

Toker

Mikael Mrotek expects *No Redemption,* 5.13b (opposite). Photo: Elodie Saracco.

9 Contact High 5.12c ★★

This new, squeezed-in route is just right of *Toker*, and climbs the arête. If you and your three buddies simultaneously climbed *Toker* through *Archangel*, you could high-five each other all the way. Start on the boulder and pull hard on soft stone to reach better holds and better rock.
70 ft. 10 bolts. *Sarah Gross, 2015.*

10 Moment of Truth 5.12c ★★★★

The striking steep corner. Wimp out at the anchors of *No Redemption* or continue with "soul-climbing" up the airy face to the bolted anchors. Bring up the second, or extend the anchor with some slings. Take a standard rack, long slings, and a new-style #6 Camalot.
90 ft. 2 bolts. *Andrew Gearing, Dustin Stephens, 2012.*

11 Archangel 5.12a ★★★

This line is the obvious line of bolts really close to the huge dihedral crack *Moment of Truth*. Although close to the crack, it is possible to stay on the face and climb pockets and crimps.
65 ft. 10 bolts. *Sarah Gross, 2014.*

12 No Redemption 5.13b ★★★★

In the wall right of *Moment of Truth* is this superb, technical line with long moves on quality rock.
70 ft. 9 bolts. *Kenny Barker, 2006.*

13 Sugar Magnolia 5.13d ★★★

The prominent orange arête just right of the classic *No Redemption*. Crank through small edges, then angle left to the arête and continue up the extremely thin face.
65 ft. 10 bolts. *Adrew Gearing, 2006.*

14 Demon Seed 5.12c ★★★★★

Twenty feet right of the arete is a tall, vertical orange face with two obvious lines that share a start. Climb the first five bolts and long moves of *Dogleg*, then branch left when *Dogleg* doglegs right. Climb through continuous long moves on small holds using the ramp for feet. You'll need a 70-meter to get down.
105 ft. 9 bolts. *Andrew Wheatley, 2009.*

15 Dogleg 5.12a ★★★★★

Start as for *Demon Seed*, with gigantic moves between horizontals, to reach the sequential face above. Angle right to the anchors. Note: you might find this much harder if you're under 5' 1".
90 ft. *Keith Moll, 2006.*

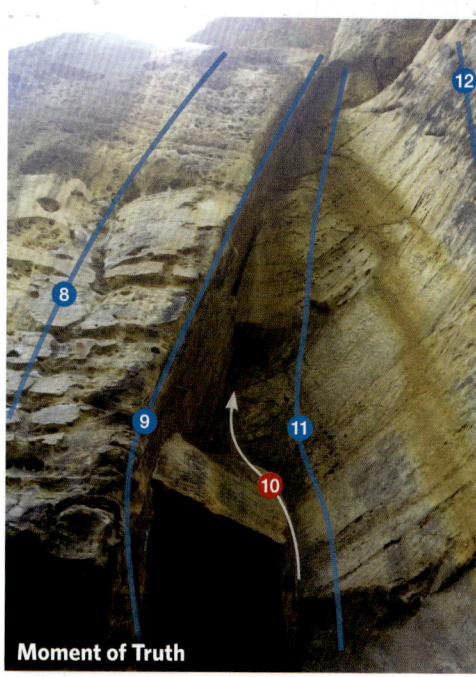

Moment of Truth

Dogleg

Stone Pipe

16 Stone Pipe 5.12c ★★★

The no-star route *Beeper* had a low self-esteem to begin with, and now it will be teased with potential ascents, only to find that climbers are just using it for its starting bolts. Begin on *Beeper*, then bail left onto the gorgeous golden face for a much better ride.

90 ft. 10 bolts. Jordan Stein, 2011. Equipped by Andrew Wheatle

17 Beeper 5.11d

About 20 feet right of *Dogleg* is an arête with a high dihedra Begin on the large boulders near its base. Grab the arête and follow it over soft rock and up into a thin crack. Continue up the crack to the anchors. Caution! Rock turns to crap up high

70 ft. 8 bolts. Keith Moll, 1996.

18 Slampiece BAM! 5.13a ★★★

Fingerlocking and liebacking on a sport line?
Just left of this line is an open project equipped by Troy Davidson in 2015: 50 feet, 7 bolts.

50 ft. 6 bolts. Brendan Leader, 2012.

19 MILF Money 5.13b ★★

Tough boulder problem to 5.9 choss. The line begins with tough pulls on very shallow pockets, then cuts directly right to meet up with climbing on sand for the remaining two-thirds of the route.

60 ft. 7 bolts. Sean McColl, 2007.

20 Granny Panties 5.12c ★★

The bolted line just left of *Tony's Happy Christmas Crack*. Boulder through several bolts of quality moves and finish on easier choss to the chains.

70 ft. 6 bolts. Kenny Barker, 2007.

21 Tony's Happy Christmas Crack 5.8 ★★★

The obvious hand crack in a dihedral. Climb the crack to a s of anchors 35 feet up. It's possible to continue past suspect rock and 5.11 climbing to the anchors on *Mas Choss*.

80 ft. Jack Hume, Tony Tramontin, Steve McFarland, Gene Hume David Hume, 1994.

22 Mas Choss 5.11c ★★★

About 15 feet right of *Tony's Happy Christmas Crack* is this slab route with striated holds. Climb some tough moves to a small roof. Move left at the roof and reach up to a large flak Continue up the face to the anchors.

80 ft. 7 bolts. Kellyn Gorder, 1996.

23 Route 22 5.12a ★★★

Move 15 feet right from *Mas Choss* to the next slab line. Climb the small edges and ledges up and right to a reasonable stance. Angle a little left to a small overhang, the power over thinning holds to the anchors.

80 ft. 7 bolts. Dave Hume, 1996.

Tony's Happy Christmas Crack

nna Liina Laitinen, *Ultra Perm*, 5.13d (page 269). Photo: Edwin Teran.

Kai Lightner fires *Southern Smoke*, 5.14c (opposite). Photo: Elodie Saracco.

Your Heaven, My Hell 5.14d ★★★★

...unch through a hard boulder problem into 5.14 climbing. ...rst sent by German phenom Alex Megos: After spending ...most the entirety of his U.S. trip at the New River ...orge, Megos took a one-day trip to the Red. On his 16th ...onsecutive climbing day, he sent this project in a single ...ession, right after ticking *Southern Smoke Direct*, thus ...imbing the region's two hardest routes, back-to-back. ...5 ft. 6 bolts. *Alex Megos, 2015. Equipped by Adam Taylor.*

Fifty Words for Pump 5.14c ★★★★★

...ee introduction to this crag for the controversy surrounding ...is route. Hike down and around the corner from the ...revious lines and you'll be standing directly beneath this ...uge, intimidating, steep beast identifiable by the crack ...ature in the first third of the route. Good luck. ...0 ft. 10 bolts. *Mickaël Fuselier, 2007. Equipped by Hugh Loeffler.*

Southern Smoke Direct 5.14d ★★★★★

...limbs straight up through a desperate boulder problem to ...eet up with *Southern Smoke* for solid 5.14-level endurance. ...dam Taylor suggested that the route could possibly be 5.15a ...ue to how hard he worked it compared to *The Golden Ticket* ...hich original consensus had at 5.14d (now 5.14c). However, ...e route was flashed by Adam Ondra in 2012, after which he ...uggested a grade of 5.14d. ...00 ft. 11 bolts. *Adam Taylor, 2012. Equipped by Joe Kinder.*

Southern Smoke 5.14c ★★★★★

...his ultimate stamina route begins as for *Ultra Perm*, but ...mmediately transitions left onto the face for 5.14a climbing ...o the relentlessly overhanging face to meet up with *Ultra ...erm* just where its hard climbing begins. ...0 ft. 10 bolts. *Joe Kinder, 2008.*

Ultra Perm 5.13d ★★★★★

...ne of the best routes east of the Mississippi. Climb the initial ...ce, then move left to the overhanging wall. Enjoy a few ...olts of confidence-building moves on big holds to prepare ...r the smackdown that awaits. Dive into a tough boulder ...roblem that doesn't seem to let up until you turn the lip. ...he size of your fingers may be the difference between you ...arking this "hard" or "soft" on your scorecard. ...0 ft. 9 bolts. *Dave Hume, 1997. Equipped by Chris Martin.*

Skinny Love 5.12d ★★★

...arts 30 feet right of *Ultra Perm*. Overhanging jug-swimming ...ads to a rest. Rest up, then take on a short section of poor ...imps and pinches leading to the anchors. ...0 ft. 10 bolts. *Andrew Wheatley, 2011.*

50 Words for Pump

Skinny Love

Horn to ... Beef

30 Horn 5.11d ★★★★

Walk 30 feet around the corner to the next set of steep lines in a large overhang. This is the leftmost route encountered and begins on a boulder. Grab pockets on the heavily featured face and move left. Continue up the face to anchors above the lip of a small roof.

50 ft. 5 bolts. Chris Martin, 1997.

31 Flush 5.11d ★★★

Start the same as the previous line but head straight up and over the lip.

50 ft. 4 bolts. Chris Martin, 1997.

32 Velvet 5.11d ★★★★

Just left of the *Tacit* crack is another steep line of pockets with anchors just past the lip.

50 ft. 5 bolts. Chris Martin, 1997.

33 Tacit 5.12a ★★★★

This route climbs a lot better than it looks. Begin near a crack above a boulder. Crank up the steep, pocketed face to a roof. Creep out the roof on large holds and pull past the lip to a good horizontal. Continue up past a bulge to the anchors.

50 ft. 6 bolts. Porter Jarrard, 1997.

34 Reticent 5.12d ★★★

Five feet right of *Tacit* is the start to another pocketed line leading to the large roof. Begin on a boulder and climb through slightly sharp holds to the roof. Power through a sequence of pockets in the roof to great holds just over the lip. Move up the face on small edges to the anchors.

50 ft. 6 bolts. Porter Jarrard, 1997.

35 Blood Bath 5.12c ★★★★

Some small boulders mark the beginning of this climb. Grab pockets and head up the steep wall to a horizontal just below the roof. Shake out and move through the roof to good holds just past the lip. Continue up over a bulge on the headwall to the anchors.

50 ft. 5 bolts. Chris Martin, 1997.

36 Where's the Beef? 5.12c ★★★★

Start 10 feet right of the previous route. Climb through steep pockets and crimps to a horizontal roof. Pull the roof, making use of sharp pockets, then crank over the lip to a ju Continue up the easier face to anchors.

50 ft. 5 bolts. Chris Martin, 1998.

Andrew Balog mans up to *Demon Seed*, 5.12c (page 265). Photo: Elodie Saracco

38 Eyeball Chaw 5.12a ★★★

Just when you think there's no more room for another route ... Begin right of *Bettavul Pipeline* and jug out and up to the headwall, where a difficult move awaits.
60 ft. 8 bolts. Brendan Leader, 2012.

Rasta Wall

Hike right about 150 feet from the main wall to reach Rasta Wall. You'll drop down into the lowest part of the valley and up the other side a bit until you see the following route.

39 El Encuentro 5.13b ★★

If only it weren't a water streak. A gorgeous, slightly overhanging bolted face. Often wet. Bolted and climbed during the 2007 Petzl Roc Trip.
90 ft. 11 bolts. Daniel Du Lac, 2007.

40 Ultrathon 5.11c ★★★

Opening boulder problem to decent climbing. With better rock it might be a gem. Start on the small ledge, and follow the numerous bolts all the way to the rim.
100 ft. 19 bolts. Troy Davidson, 2014.

41 The Rube Goldberg Experiment 5.9+ ★★★★

The first reasonable crack right of the main wall. Climb the crack and face to the lip of the wall.
90 ft. Hume brothers, 1998.

42 Levitation 5.11d ★★★

Just past *Rube Goldberg* are two routes that start side by side. This one climbs a crack through cool moves to a set of anchors midway up the wall. If you stop here, it's 11b. If you tackle the crux above, take full credit.
90 ft. 15 bolts. Sarah Gross, 2014.

43 Elevation 5.11a ★★★

Begin just right of the starting crack of *Levitation*.
90 ft. 16 bolts. Sarah Gross, 2014.

44 Marley 44 Open Project ★★★

Starting on a small ledge, same as *Rasta*. Work your way through a short, steep section of mediocre rock. Clip a bolt and figure out how to get through the very thin crux.
45 ft. 5 bolts. Equipped by Troy Davidson.

45 Rasta 5.10d ★★★

Start on a small ledge that also hosts the start of the open project. Climb the flake, a crack feature, across a bulge, the the crack again to the anchors.
60 ft. 7 bolts. Troy Davidson, 2014.

37 Bettavul Pipeline 5.12a ★★★

Begin near a pipeline that was drilled from the top of the crag and missed by a couple of feet at the bottom. Race up the steep wall on jugs.
55 ft. 5 bolts. Mark Johnson, Drew Cronan, 2006.

BON MARLEY CRAG / BALD ROCK FORK

ippy Wick

One Love

Marley 46 Closed Project ★★★
st right of the gaping chimney is this gritstone-looking
mb on black rock. With 15 bolts, it may be a good idea
have your partner hang the massive pack of quickdraws
eded to redpoint it.
ft. 15 bolts. Equipped by Sarah Gross.

Fungus Among Us 5.12c ★★★
is route skirts the left edge of a massive hueco. Technical
e climbing on slopey edges — fun if you're into that sort
thing.
ft. 7 bolts. Scott Curran, 2013.

Red-Eye Flight 5.13a ★★★
the middle of the wall, going through the left side of the
per roof, this enduro-thon has at least 12 bolts. Take a
uple more just in case.
ft. 12+ bolts. Troy Davidson, 2014.

Hippy Wick 5.12b ★★★
is route goes nearly straight out the roof in the center of
e wall.
ft. 10 bolts. Troy Davidson, 2014.

Marley 50 Closed Project ★★
s skirts the right side of the roof that is midway up the
ll.
ft. 11 bolts. Equipped by Troy Davidson.

51 Marley 51 Closed Project ★★★
Sharing the start and the first few bolts with its companion to
the right, this one trends up and left after the arête feature.
90 ft. 10 bolts. Equipped by Greg Martin, 2014.

52 Marley 52 Closed Project
Currently the furthest right route on the wall, sharing a start
with the previous route. Gain the ledge, climb the arête
feature above the roof, then bust out right.
80 ft. 9 bolts. Equipped by Greg Martin, 2014.

53 Green Machine 5.12a ★★★
A technical arête just right of a dihedral. Grope and balance
your way up the left face and parts of the arête to reach the
exciting crux up high.
45 ft. 4 bolts. Sarah Gross, 2014.

54 One Love 5.12c ★★★★
Climb the face just right of the *Green Machine* arête. Colder
weather will help the crux feel doable. Really cool.
45 ft. 5 bolts. Greg Martin, 2014.

55 Ivory Poacher 5.12a ★★★
Follow the trail about 75 feet right of the previous routes.
Just as it connects with the cliff again, *Ivory Poacher* and
Loan Shark appear. Start just left of the crack (*Loan Shark*),
through a series of edges and big moves to reach a feature,
then continue to the chains.
50 ft. 7 bolts. Troy Davidson, 2014.

Technical Difficulties

Cromper's Mom

Tickets to the Shitshow

⑤⑥ Loan Shark 5.9+ ★★★

Start off a boulder and short left-facing corner, then transition to the clean and attractive right-facing corner that ends at a bolt anchor below the big roof. Put up the day of Rocktoberfest 2012, when the RRGCC made their final payment to the Access Fund to formally own the PMRP.
55 ft. Zachary Lesch-Huie, Dustin Stephens, 2012.

⑤⑦ Uncle Ferdouz 5.10d ★★★

Very short but worth it. A roof start leads to a perfect finger crack with a few face holds and an anchor below the roof.
35 ft. Siamak Pazirandeh, Dustin Stephens, 2012.

⑤⑧ Peel It Back 5.12b ★★★

Starts with a hard boulder problem off the ground and finishes with one too. A bit more powerful, but less sustained than *Technical Difficulties*.
45 ft. 5 bolts. Siamak Pazirandeh, Dustin Stephens, 2012.

⑤⑨ Technical Difficulties 5.12b ★★★★

Technical, sustained, slightly overhanging face. If it's rained recently, expect to spend your first burn on this route locating the holds hidden in the black streak.
45 ft. 5 bolts. Dustin Stephens, Siamak Pazirandeh, 2012.

to Marley Cave

RASTA WALL

Cromper's Mom 5.5 ★★★

e route originally used to access the top of the cliff actually
rned out to be a damn good chimney, with a spectacular
inset view over the Bald Rock valley! Will be updated at
me point with a belay anchor and a couple bolts on the
protectable top half (5.4). In the meantime, this gaping
aw stays true to its name — don't climb this expecting
uch protection up in there.

ft. *Dustin Stephens, Zachary Lesch-Huie, 2012.*

Tickets to the Shitshow 5.9 ★★★

the far right of this crag you can find this fist and offwidth
ack. Expect it to be a bit dirty from the lack of traffic, but
 excellent arm-bar shuffle nonetheless. Take pro to a #5
malot.

ft. *Dustin Stephens, Siamak Pazirandeh, 2012.*

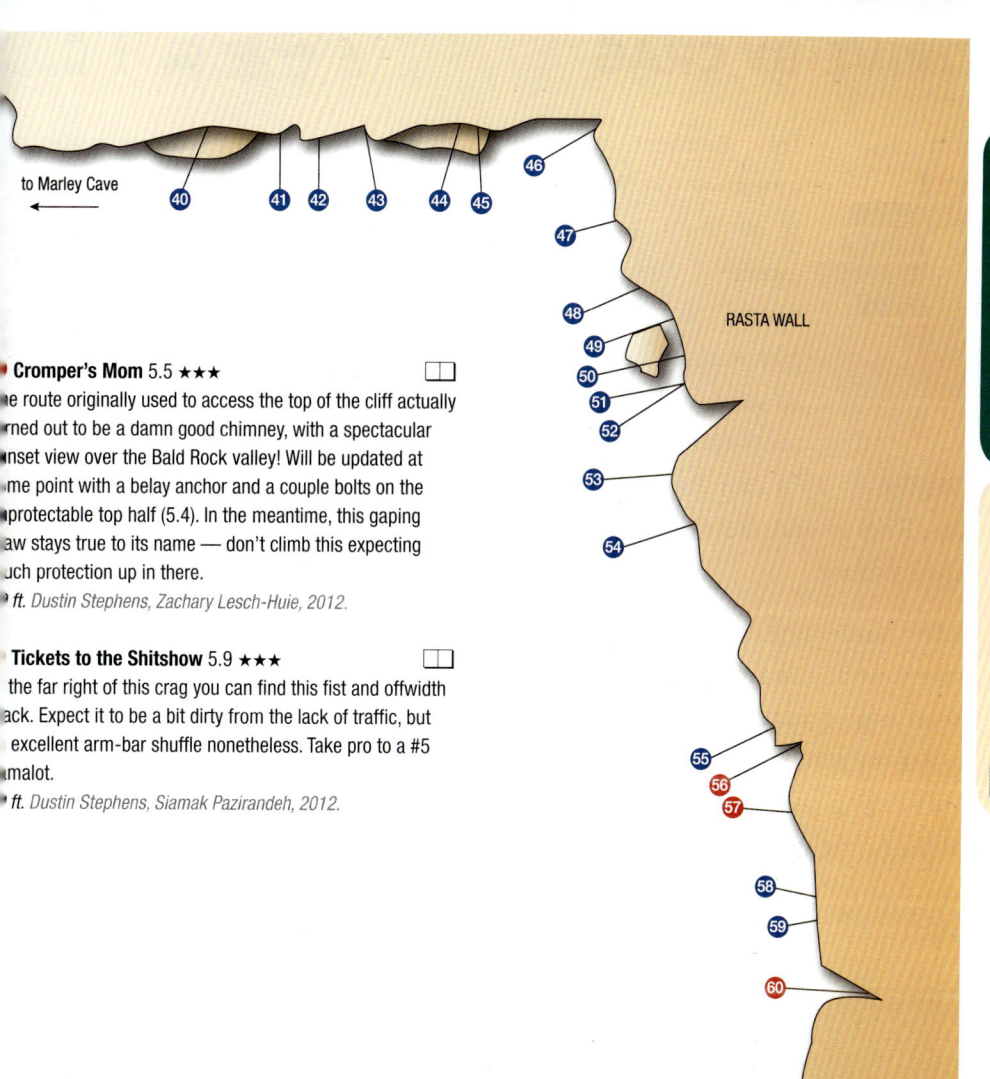

BOB MARLEY CRAG

BALD ROCK FORK

275

DRIVE-BY CRAG

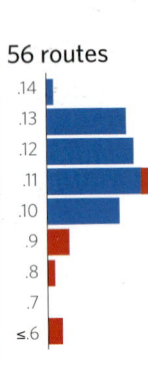

37.653 / -83.724

56 routes

This excellent crag has something to offer climbers at all levels, with several excellent 5.13s including one of the Red's top 5.13c pumpfests, *Kaleidoscope*. At an esier grade, jump on the spectacular 5.12a *Check Your Grip*. Warm up or cool down on two of the best 5.10s around, *Breakfast Burrito* and *Fire and Brimstone*.

The harder lines tend to be slopey and steep, while the rest tend to be slightly overhanging and crimpy. Expect to stand in line for almost every route at the main area during peak season, or seek solace at the far right end of the cliff.

Approach: From the Bald Rock Fork parking are (directions on page 253), walk out onto Ba Fork Road Road, turn left, and hike about 10 feet to the next dirt road on the right. Hike u this until it intersects with another road. Sta right and continue uphill about seven minute (do not turn left on the next road) until the roa curves around to the right. About 100 feet aft the curve, look for a small wooden ladder on th left that leads up a short, steep bank and enc directly beneath *Check Your Grip* and *Whipp Snapper*. It's also possible to approach from Bc Marley by walking left past *Toker* and followin the trail along the cliff and through a notc to the rightmost route in this sector, *Linka Disequilibrium*. Continuing left along the cli leads through the massive cave and hits the ma area near *Kaleidoscope*.

Conditions: The slightly overhanging wa provide good shelter from the rain. The wa receives morning-to-midafternoon sun, arrive late in summer. Expect large crowd including babies, dogs, beginner groups, ar arguing couples.

❶ Hotdog in a Hallway 5.9 ★★★
A steep, gaping chimney on the far left side of the crag, just l of *Guilty Pleasure*. Stem up, protecting with mostly medium-sized cams, to a wild step-across at the top. Belay from the t to keep your rope from getting stuck while lowering.
60 ft. Dustin Stephens, 2015.

❷ Guilty Pleasure 5.11d ★★★★
Located just around the corner from the main wall. A must- for the technical climber.
55 ft. 6 bolts. Dustin Stephens, 2014.

❸ Slick and the 9mm 5.10b ★★★
This is the leftmost route on the main wall, just right of whe the wall turns a corner. Climb over a bulge and up to ancho in the middle of the face. From the anchors, it is possible tc traverse right to a left-facing dihedral and continue to anotl set of anchors about 40 feet higher. The second pitch is tra and goes at 5.9.
60 ft. 7 bolts. Kellyn Gorder, 2000.

❹ Slut Men 5.11d ★★
Start under an arching overhang. Hang on for the ending.
70 ft. 8 bolts. Danita Whelan, 1996.

Guilty Pleasure

Bigna Buchli, *Easy Rider*, 5.13a (page 284). Photo: Javier Pérez López-Triviño.

Brea Holland breathing *Fire and Brimstone*, 5.10d (opposite). Photo: Elodie Saracco.

Hakuna Matata

Fire and Brimstone

Breakfast Burrito

DRIVE-BY CRAG

BALD ROCK FORK

Crimps and Bloods 5.12a ★★★

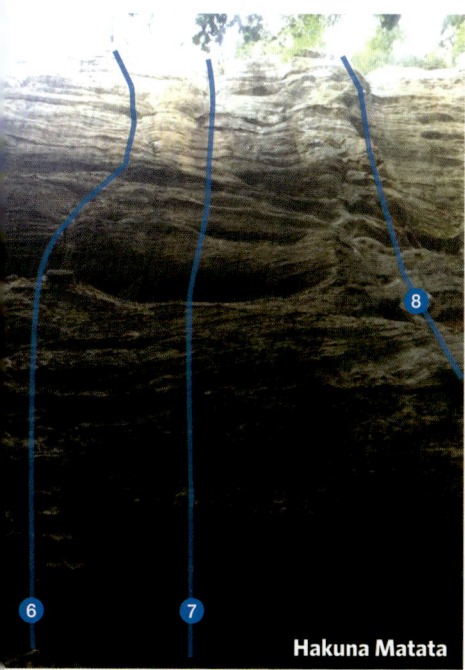

Located 10 feet left of the thin crack/seam of *Hakuna Matata*, this crimpfest is the longest route on the wall. There are just enough rests along the way to keep the grade palatable, but it delivers a nice punch at the end.
75 ft. 10 bolts. *Shadow Ayala, Rachel Stewart, 2013.*

Hakuna Matata 5.12a ★★★★

This sustained route follows a thin crack/seam system on the left side of a gently overhanging golden face. Boulder up to a small ledge, then climb crimps and fingertip locks to the anchors.
75 ft. 9 bolts. *Kellyn Gorder, 1996.*

Extra Backup 5.12a ★★★

A shorter climb on the golden face right of *Hakuna Matata*. Climb small crimps past well-spaced bolts to the anchors.
50 ft. 6 bolts. *Dave Hume, 1997.*

Fire and Brimstone 5.10d ★★★★★

This route begins in an obvious dihedral. Climb the funky dihedral to a stance. Pull through a series of good edges, then head right for the saddle sit-down on the arête. Continue up through easier moves to the anchors.
90 ft. 10 bolts. *Kellyn Gorder, 1997.*

Naked Lunch 5.12a ★★★★

A great plated jug line just left of *Breakfast Burrito*. Nope, it's not a squeeze job — you just never noticed this gorgeous line. Like keeping a straight face, this climb becomes more difficult the higher you get. A gimme for some. Watch out for gigantic talking insects.
ft. 8 bolts. *Shadow Ayala, Sam Speed, 2012.*

279

A Wave New World

Check Your Grip

⑩ Breakfast Burrito 5.10d ★★★★★
Classic. About 40 feet left of the approach trail is an attractive, plated face with an alcove about 60 feet up. Climb up to the alcove, take a deep breath, then brave the exposed arête and steep face to the anchors. Recently re-equipped.
80 ft. 8 bolts. Gene Hume, 1995.

⑪ A Wave New World 5.10c ★★
Left of *Make a Wish* is this very featured runnel. Climb through the boulder problem at the third bolt, then enjoy easier but still-interesting climbing.
50 ft. 8 bolts. Dave Quinn, 2014.

⑫ Make a Wish 5.10b ★★★
Walk left from the approach trail about 20 feet to find this line. Boulder up to good holds, move right around a flake/overhang, then surmount a ledge. Climb pockets and small edges, then jugs to the top of a point of rock.
75 ft. 8 bolts. John Bronaugh, Christina Bronaugh, 1999.

⑬ Death Wish 5.12a ★★★
The extension to *Make a Wish*. The rock is questionable at best, but it has been "cleaning up" now for some time.
90 ft. Shadow Ayala, Rachel Stewart, 2013.

⑭ Whipper Snapper 5.12b ★★★
At the end of the approach trail is an overhanging face with many bolted lines. This route is the first line encountered and begins just right of a crack. Climb up to a tough move near the third bolt, then save some steam for more hard moves higher.
80 ft. 9 bolts. Unknown.

⑮ Check Your Grip 5.12a ★★★★★
About 10 feet right of *Whipper Snapper*, mantel the start and climb up to a ledge beneath an overhanging face. Pull a bouldery sequence, then continue rapidly up the sustained face to anchors.
80 ft. 7 bolts. Neal Strickland, 1998.

⑯ Big Sinkin' Breakdown 5.11c ★★★
Crank out a difficult boulder problem to a shelf, then continue up the overhanging face to a nice sit-down rest above the last bolt. Check out the view, then gun to the anchors.
85 ft. 7 bolts. Hugh Loeffler, 1998.

⑰ Primus Noctum 5.12a ★★★★
This route is marked by an obvious slab section near the beginning. Climb up past the slab, pull a roof, then continue up the face to a long, exciting runout before the anchors.
75 ft. 8 bolts. Porter Jarrard, 1998.

⑱ Spirit Fingers 5.11c ★★★★
Scramble up to a large ledge just right of *Primus Noctum* to start. Climb edges and pockets up the enjoyable face.
70 ft. 7 bolts. Craig Smith, 1997.

⑲ Whip-Stocking 5.11a ★★★★
This is the next bolted line right of *Spirit Fingers*, around a blunt corner. There is a large alcove near the top and to the left of the line. Climb the plated face to anchors just above a roof.
80 ft. 8 bolts. Porter Jarrard, 1997.

DRIVE-BY CRAG

BALD ROCK FORK

Deeper is Better 5.10b ★★★★
...ust a few feet right of *Whip Stocking* and not quite to the ...rête of *Yadda Yadda*, this new route has many of the same ...ood moves as the rest of the wall, but at a lower grade. Use ... nice hand-jam down low to gain access to a ledge. Climb ... edges and plates to finish in a hueco.
...0 ft. 6 bolts. Savannah Norris, Joe Leismer, 2016.

Yadda Yadda Yadda 5.11b ★★★
...scend the arête with interesting and reachy moves.
...0 ft. 6 bolts. Kellyn Gorder, 1997.

Throne of Lies 5.12c
...e extension to *Yadda Yadda Yadda*. Angle up and right on ...mall crimps to a second anchor.
...5 ft. 11 bolts.
...raig Smith, Charmagne Duplantier-Cox, Ian Kirk, 2015.

Lord of the Ring 5.11b ★★★
...scends the thin finger crack in a dihedral right of *Yadda ...adda Yadda*. Climb to a ledge then move through steeper ...rrain to the chains on *Yadda*.
...0 ft. Cody Landry, 2013.

Head and Shoulders 5.11d ★★★★
...his burly route ascends the bolted flake system just right of ...e dihedral. Stop at the first set of anchors.
...0 ft. 8 bolts. Kellyn Gorder, 1997.

㉕ Knees and Toes 5.12b ★★★
An extension to *Head and Shoulders*. Continue up past two long bolt runs on tough, powerful terrain. Stacked on top of *Head and Shoulders*, these moves will feel hard!
90 ft. 11 bolts. Audrey Sniezek, 2007. Equipped by Mike Doyle.

㉖ Beer Belly 5.13a ★★★★
Begin on *Head and Shoulders*. Climb to the fifth bolt, clip it, then traverse right. Be prepared to get gymnastic at the crux, which meets you pretty quickly into the traverse. Keep gunning to the right and give it all you got for the final pop move before the chains.
90 ft. 12 bolts. Mike Doyle, 2007.

㉗ Super Charger 5.13d ★★★★
Climb the powerful, slanting face to reach a ledge beneath the main overhanging wall. Move up through increasingly difficult-to-hold slopers, pinches, and the occasional hand-sized hueco.
90 ft. 11 bolts. Tobias Wolf, 2009. Equipped by Joe Kinder.

㉘ Dirty, Smelly Hippie 5.13b ★★★★
Begin by climbing the right arête of the 30-foot block. From the ledge, continue up a flake, then leave its comfort to battle the steepness. Aim for the butt crack above where you will meet the crux. Pull the lip to gain a stance, look up, and ask yourself why the anchors are "up there" and not "right here."
90 ft. 10 bolts. Dave Hume, 1997.

281

29 Spank 5.13a ★★★★

This route ascends the overhanging face a few feet right of *Dirty, Smelly Hippie*. Begin by climbing left of the dihedral, then move right at the good stance to take on the severely overhanging face. Shake it out at the obvious jug near the top, then slap and pinch to the anchors. Most people skip the last bolt, but be careful if you do!
70 ft. 8 bolts. Dave Hume. Equipped by Chris Martin.

30 Absolute Zero 5.13b ★★★

Begin by climbing *Spank*, then trend right when you reach the first ledge. From the ledge, make a scary clip, then sma right to reach your friend for the next few bolts, Mr. Fat Flak Dig and squeeze while slapping for chalk spots. You won't b alone if you pull up a stick clip at this point.
80 ft. 8 bolts. Ethan Pringle, 2010.

Hal Garner channels *Angry Birds,* 5.13c (next page). Photo: John Wesely.

The Nothing 5.14a ★★★

his route starts up a faint crack system about 15 feet right
f the previous route. Hard boulder problem! A gimme 5.14
r those who spent the winter in Hueco.
0 ft. 10 bolts. *Dave Hume, 1999.*

32 The Galaxy Project Project

This line is currently being bolted. Follows the fat flake 30
feet right of *The Nothing.* If *The Nothing* wasn't already taken,
it would have been a great name for this non-line.
90 ft. *Equipped by Strange.*

283

Thug Life

㉝ The Business 5.11d
About 15 feet right of *The Galaxy Project*, climb pockets to the left side of a hueco, then continue through more pockets to the anchors. You have no business climbing this route surrounded by so much good rock.
65 ft. 8 bolts. Eric Lowe, 1998.

㉞ Pimp Juice 5.13a ★★★
Walk right of *The Business* to reach a cluster of long routes left of the obvious striking arête that is *Kaleidoscope*. This is the leftmost line and is marked by a large black flake feature. Mostly endurance climbing broken up by a reachy boulder problem.
95 ft. 9 bolts. Kevin Wilkinson, 2011.

㉟ Angry Birds 5.13c ★★★★
Work up a pump to meet the beast at bolt five. Bust through the first boulder problem to reach a ledge. Exit when ready, then rage through three more bolts of insanity, complete with a *Madness*-like sloping beach move. Milk a recovery jug for all it's got, then bust another boulder problem and dive for the toilet seat. One more long move gets you to the chains, where you can be glad everything fell into place just so.
100 ft. 12 bolts. Kevin Wilkinson, 2010.

㊱ Easy Rider 5.13a ★★★
Begin on the ledge right of *Angry Birds* and head up a ramp to gain consistent climbing with decent rests. Pace yourself, and save enough juice to enjoy the last 20 feet of excellent climbing, which make it all worthwhile. Apparently, climbers have discovered a lie-down no-hands rest before the final crux. 5.12d? Time will tell.
100 ft. 12 bolts. Mike Doyle, 2007.

㊲ Kaleidoscope 5.13c ★★★★★
The overhanging arête on the left side of a steep amphitheater. Begin by climbing through delicate and spicy moves to gain the steeper, right-angling arête. Battle through big moves and a couple of difficult clips while fighting the relentless Red River pump. Stop at the first, original anchor, or, at the same grade, continue to the rim past four more bolts.
80 ft. 12 bolts. Monique Forestier, 2006. Equipped by Team Such Extension added by Blake Bowling, 2016.

㊳ Thug Life 5.13d ★★★★
Fitting name. The striking line of features right of *Kaleidoscope* that climbs out the gigantic steep cave.
100 ft. 10 bolts. Kevin Wilkinson, 2011.

Basque hero Patxi Usobiaga styles *Kaleidoscope*, 5.13c (opposite). Photo: Javier Pérez López-Triviño.

Arachnophobia

Giblets

㊟ The Sharma Project Project
This line climbs out the insanely steep amphitheater 50 feet right of *Kaleidoscope*. Not finished. Question of the day: Where does he plan to start this thing?
Equipped by Chris Sharma.

㊵ Arachnophobia 5.12d ★★★
This route lies on the right side of the amphitheater, just off the trail leading to Bob Marley Crag. It involves a cruxical first half before reaching the Red's familiar steep jug hauling. Don't spray the "almost onsight" if you fall going for the chains, though, because it may happen way more than once — it's tough up there.
80 ft. 9 bolts. Jonathan Siegrist, 2011.

㊶ Harshin' My Mellow 5.10b ★★★
Near the leftmost part of this section of wall, this and its counterpart route, *The Hanging Tree*, are pretty good for the grades and offer an escape from the crowds at Drive-By.
60 ft. 6 bolts. Dustin Stephens, 2013.

㊷ The Hanging Tree 5.11b ★★★
Just right of *Harshin' My Mellow* is its harder brother. Start on the boulder and climb through a bulge crux. Traversey — cleaning on TR is recommended.
65 ft. 7 bolts. Dustin Stephens, 2013.

㊸ Captain Turtlehead 5.9 ★★
Clip the first bolt of *Pottsville*, then move up and left to the crack. Follow this to the top, trending right up high on the juggy slab to the *Pottsville* anchor. With lots of lichen but very solid rock, this route has been described as a "North Carolina training route." A #4 to #5 Camalot or two are helpful.
80 ft. 1 bolts. Dustin Stephens, Scott Hammon, 2013.

㊹ Pottsville Escarpment 5.10a ★★★★
The long, pretty slab just left of the *Mud on the Rug* dihedral. Start on *Mud on the Rug*, then immediately move left on a big iron jug to the high first bolt. Continue through awesome balancey moves and cool mantels.
80 ft. 8 bolts. Scott Hammon, Dustin Stephens, 2013.

㊺ Mud on the Rug 5.6 ★★
This route ascends the dihedral 25 feet left of *George of the Jungle*. Rappel from a tree to descend.
100 ft. Barry Little, Kerry Gorder, 1996.

㊻ Jungle Direct 5.10 ★★
Scramble up into the alcove beneath the A-shaped chimney to the right of *Mud on the Rug*. Stem up into the chimney and pull the roof. Proceed straight up the *George of the Jungle* crack until it takes a 90-degree turn to the right. Step up and slightly left onto the face and proceed directly upward through the line of three bolts to the anchors.
80 ft. 3 bolts. Bill Strachan, Will Winford, 2012.

DRIVE-BY CRAG RIGHT

to Bob Marley

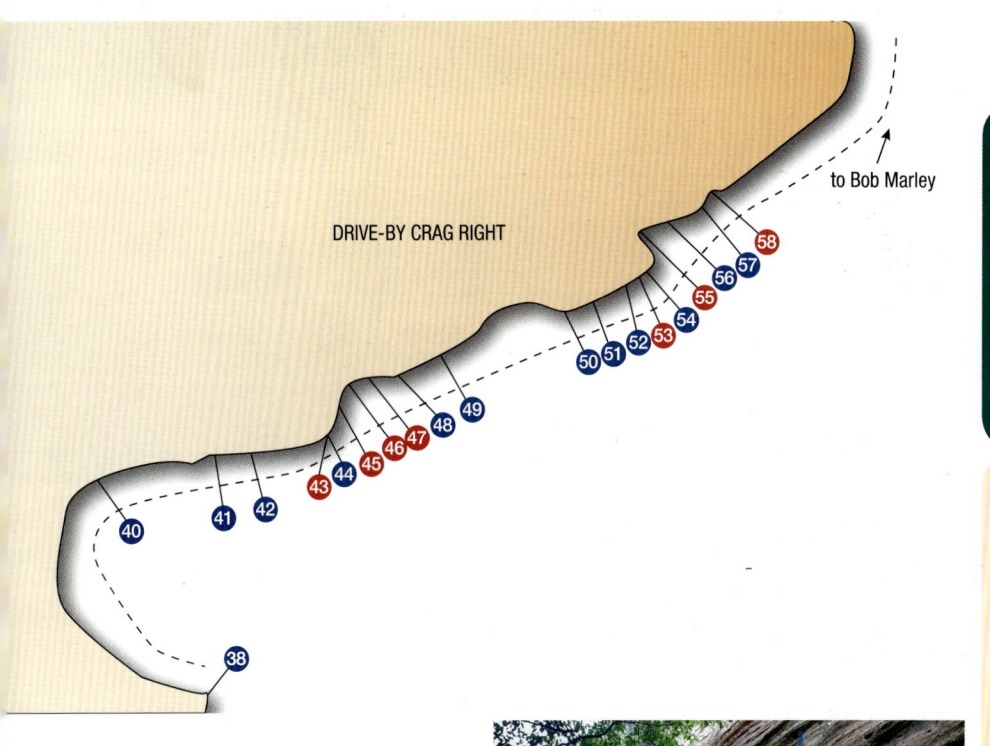

George of the Jungle 5.9 ★★
...wenty-five feet right of *Mud on the Rug* is a crack that starts ...out 20 feet off the ground. Climb the initial part of *Mud on ...e Rug,* then traverse right to a ledge. Follow the crack to ...e top past a difficult offwidth section.
...0 ft. *Jason Haas, 2004.*

Giblets 5.11c ★★★
...ontinuing right along the cliff toward Bob Marley Crag, look ...r a left offshoot trail leading shortly up to a slabby wall ...sting several bolted lines. This is the leftmost line. Jam a ...ort crack to reach a distorted hueco beneath the third bolt. ...ep up onto the face to begin climbing through several cruxes ...quiring lots of foot switching and bitching about no holds.
... ft. 7 bolts. *Kipp Trummel, 2011.*

Return to Sender 5.10c ★★
...teen feet right of *Giblets*. Use advanced stick-clipping skills ... nab the first bolt. Climb up to the roof and tread lightly on ...e gigantic mud blob to pull onto the face. Enjoy a long ride of ...gh-stepping and slot-sloping to a great view from the chains.
... ft. 8 bolts. *Kipp Trummel, 2011.*

Junior's Gesture 5.11a ★★★
...mb up to a ledge to clip the high first bolt, then continue ... a blunt arête to meet the crux after a couple of mud jugs. ...ovel onto the face, making use of sloping ledges that just ...n't feel as good as you want them to. Once you get your ... over the hump, it's fun climbing to the chains.
... ft. 8 bolts. *Jeff Neal, 2011.*

Murder at Frozen Head

51 Murder at Frozen Head 5.11b ★★★
Begin on a flat boulder. Climb the face to a no-hands rest on a ledge. Tiptoe off the ledge onto the face, then back onto the ledge several times until your belayer seems irritated, then commit to anything you can grab to make the leg-shaking clip. If you make it to the fourth bolt, it's in the bag.
65 ft. 6 bolts. *Jeff Neal, 2011.*

287

DAVE HUME
(the secret weapon)

Back in the early 1990s, the Red was still in its route-development infancy. Porter left the scene for a while, and drills began firing up on the oil fields and private land of the Southern Region.

A huge hollow was discovered that contained enough potential to call it The Motherlode, and a cast of characters including Chris Snyder, Jeff and Keith Moll, Brian McCray, Brian Toy, Hugh Loeffler, and Chris Martin unleashed their hammer drills to, in just a few short years, create the world-class crag they'd envisioned. However, **behind the testosterone-fueled twenty-somethings stood a mild-mannered teenager who served as a secret weapon: Dave Hume.**

Hume had begun climbing early in life. His family was introduced to climbing when Dave was seven, during a trip to the Tetons. Dave's dad, Jack, signed up for a class with big-wall veteran Chuck Pratt and brought Dave's brother, Gene, along. After further instruction closer to home with Martin Hackworth, Jack brought the family out on weekend trips to the Red. On Dave's first outing, Jack took the boys up to Fortress Wall and put up *American Wall*, a 5.4 R face climb that begins with difficult moves way right in a crack. Up next to follow was Gene. Gene struggled with the crack and wound up taking a nasty pendulum. Terrified at this introduction, Dave opted out that day. Instead, his first attempted climb was *Green Corner* at the Daniel Boone Hut crag, a climb that scared him to tears. Despite this inauspicious beginning, climbing became a regular activity for Dave and the Hume family. Further trips to the Gorge, Joshua Tree, and other areas out West had them hooked, and when Climbtime, Kentucky's first climbing gym, opened in Lexington, the Humes were among its earliest members.

By age 12, Dave was climbing 5.13 sport routes and placing regularly in regional climbing competitions. He went on to climb in national and international events with Chris Sharma and Katie Brown as one of the first in a new generation of young climbers competing against people twice their age. Dave also began establishing the Red's most difficult lines including the first 5.14, *Thanatopsis* at The Motherlode, which he did when only 16. Like many of his hardest lines, *Thanatopsis* went down with his father belaying. Soon after *Thanatopsis*, Dave achieved worldwide recognition by nabbing the quickest ascent to date of *Just Do It*, the coveted JB Tribout 5.14c testpiece at Smith Rock, Oregon.

Around this time, Dave caught the bug for exploring the Red's vast untapped potential. Some of his most memorable days were spent discovering crags like Bob Marley, Drive-By, and Coal Bank Hollow, where he and his fami established some of the first routes

If you've attempted one c Dave's RRG lines, it's mor than likely you had to pull u the stick clip. His bouldering skil are exceptional, and these naturally le to routes demanding significant fing strength. Prime examples include *Clean Well Lighted Face* 5.14a, *Nagypap* 5.13d, *True Love* 5.13d, and *The Nothin* 5.14a. These are far from your typic Red River endurance hauls.

These days, Dave doesn't get the Red much, but not because h stopped climbing. He earned his Ph in Atomic Physics from the Universi of Colorado Boulder and works at th University of Heidelberg in German performing research with lase cooled atoms aimed at fundament questions in quantum mechanics. Th research might lead to advancemen in sensor precision and more accura atomic clocks. So yes, **not onl is Dave Hume a freakishl strong climber, but he's als a very smart dude.** It's OK hate on Dave for being so damn goo at everything, but on the flip side he one of the most kind and humble guy you'll ever meet. ∎

The Dangling Particle

Linkage Disequilibrium

Amyloid Plaque 5.13a ★★★
...13 slab line? It probably doesn't need a description, ...cause nobody else will climb it. Look for the blank one ...h no holds.
... ft. 7 bolts. Brad Dallefield, Kipp Trummel, 2011.

Dementia 5.6 ★
...mb the angling crack that trends left to join *Amyloid Plaque* ...the chains. Use a crashpad or some creativity to protect ... beginning.
... ft. Kipp Trummel, Theresa Neal, 2011.

Sojourner Truth 5.10c ★★★
...ce up on large plates that end abruptly at a bulge, where ... real climbing begins. Move up past some nice moves to a ...e just before the chains. From the hole, peek out and stare ...the chains for awhile while wondering how to reach them ...hout falling.
... ft. 6 bolts. Kipp Trummel, 2011.

End of Days 5.8+ ★★
...e big crack in the dihedral right of the previous lines.
... ft. Jeff Neal, Theresa Neal, 2011.

The Dangling Particle 5.11a ★★★
...gin just right of the wide crack. If you got your ass kicked ...the slabs to the left, then jump on this climb — which has ...ual holds — to regain your confidence.
... ft. 6 bolts. Kipp Trummel, Brent Dupree, 2011.

57 Das Krue 5.12a ★★★
Just right of *The Dangling Particle*. Just because it's close to that route doesn't mean it has holds, too. Take a look at the holds in the beginning to determine if you want to attempt it, or head down the trail and over to jugs at Bob Marley.
50 ft. 6 bolts. Brad Dallefield, Kipp Trummel, 2011.

58 Linkage Disequilibrium 5.11b
Currently the rightmost line at Drive-By, this discontinuous crack system offers a full-value trad experience. Insecure jams in flared pods, with an "engaging" exit mantel move. Save a few small and medium cams for the top.
90 ft. Andrew Gearing, Dustin Stephens, 2013.

MOTHERLODE REGION

This cluster of four cliffs, including the most famous in the Red, is located just east of the Sore Heel Hollow and Bald Rock Fork areas of the PMRP. For most of its climbing history, the land was private and access was only through the permission of the current land owners. In January 2017, the RRGCC announced that, with help from Trango Climbing Gear and the Access Fund, it had bought the land, permanently securing climbing access to these world-class crags.

Approach: All the crags in this chapter are approached from the Motherlode parking area. To reach it, drive 12.4 miles south on KY 11 from Miguel's toward Beattyville. Turn right on 498. Drive 1.2 miles to a sharp right curve. Ju beyond this curve, take a sharp right on Ba Rock Road, a gravel road, and follow it slowly it curves left toward a house, staying left at t first intersection.

After 0.3 miles the road descends a steep h The hill can be drivable in a passenger car if t road has recently been graded, but usually r out within a few days. 4WD is recommende During busy seasons and inclement weath this hill can become treacherous. Scope o the hill before proceeding down. If you ha doubts, climb elsewhere — do not park atop t hill, as this area is used to access oil compa equipment and you are liable to be towed.

If you think you can make it back up the h park at the bottom in the well-worn parking ar on the right, or in a smaller gravel pulloff on t right a few yards farther on. Do not park ne to the oil derrick on the other side of the roa

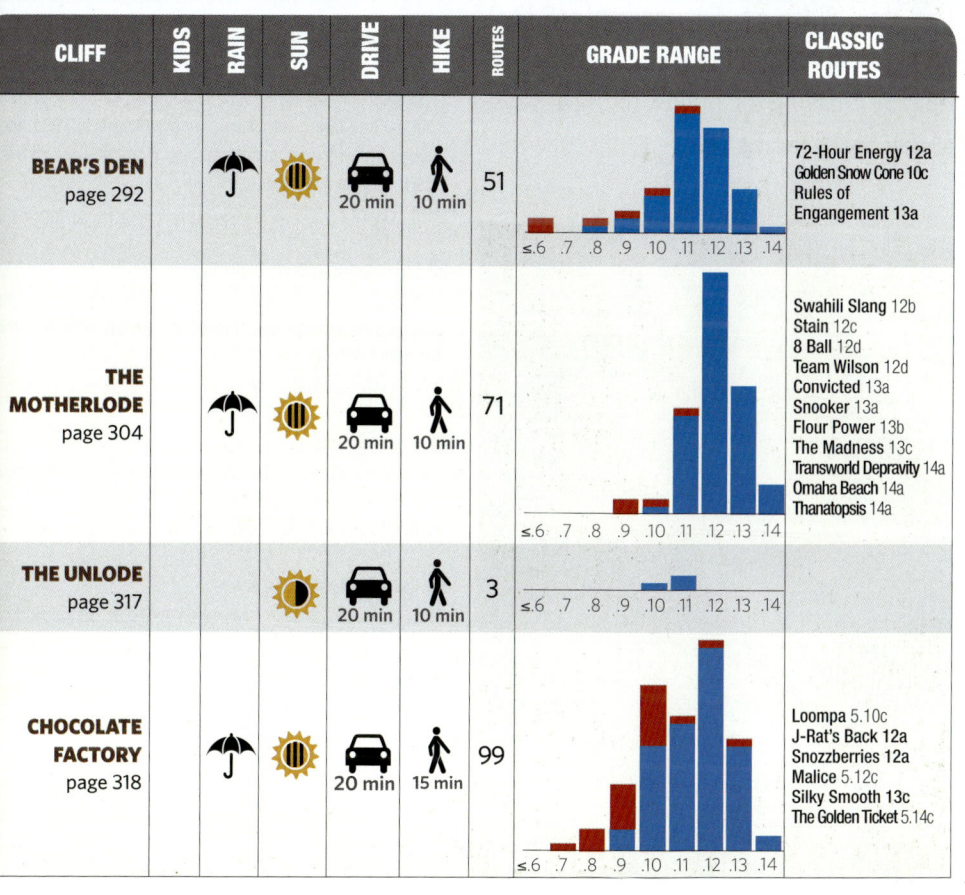

Here it comes again. Josh Pugel on *BOHICA*, 5.13b (page 310). Photo: John Wesely.

CLIFF	KIDS	RAIN	SUN	DRIVE	HIKE	ROUTES	GRADE RANGE	CLASSIC ROUTES
BEAR'S DEN page 292		☂	☀	20 min	10 min	51	≤.6 .7 .8 .9 .10 .11 .12 .13 .14	72-Hour Energy 12a Golden Snow Cone 10c Rules of Engangement 13a
THE MOTHERLODE page 304		☂	☀	20 min	10 min	71	≤.6 .7 .8 .9 .10 .11 .12 .13 .14	Swahili Slang 12b Stain 12c 8 Ball 12d Team Wilson 12d Convicted 13a Snooker 13a Flour Power 13b The Madness 13c Transworld Depravity 14a Omaha Beach 14a Thanatopsis 14a
THE UNLODE page 317			☀	20 min	10 min	3	≤.6 .7 .8 .9 .10 .11 .12 .13 .14	
CHOCOLATE FACTORY page 318		☂	☀	20 min	15 min	99	≤.6 .7 .8 .9 .10 .11 .12 .13 .14	Loompa 5.10c J-Rat's Back 12a Snozzberries 12a Malice 5.12c Silky Smooth 13c The Golden Ticket 5.14c

BEAR'S DEN

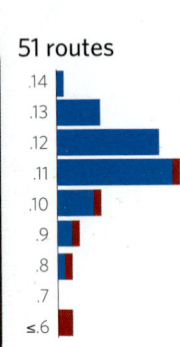

51 routes

Deeper into the holler, past the hustle and bustle of the Motherlode, is the sleepy crag of Bear's Den. Steady development began in 2010 and has so far yielded over 50 high-quality routes. The majority of the climbing is on a steep, south-facing wall similar in character to the Motherlode, if not quite as good. While this is not the crown jewel of Red River climbing, you'll still find great stone and pumpy classics like *Pinkalicious* (5.11b), *72-Hour Energy* (5.12a), and the five-star *Rules of Engagement* (5.13a), which rivals any Lode route. Escape the heat by crossing the hollow to the always-shady north-facing side.

Approach: Hike the Motherlode trail, taking the right path as if going to the Undertow Wall side. At the top of the steep mud hill there will be a faint trail that leads to your right. After a few minutes on this trail you will come to the first several trails angling uphill to the left. Use the first trail that cuts uphill to the wall to access routes #1-10, or continue on to the second trail for routes #11-28. The third trail leads to the steep amphitheater routes (#29-41) at the back of Bear's Den.

Routes #42-53 are located on the south side of the holler. Approach on the main trail as you would for routes on the north side. Just before you get to the third access trail, the main trail crosses a small drainage and goes up a hill. At the top of the hill, start to look for an obvious, but overgrown, logging road that cuts downhill to the right. Follow the logging road downhill, across the stream, and uphill to meet the cliff at the C Tree Wall and the route *Spicer* (#47).

❶ Tar Baby 5.9+ ★★★
Short, pumpy, and fun. Currently the leftmost route at the crag. After turning off the Motherlode trail, continue along until the trail trends left around a point. About 300 feet later a small trail will lead up and left directly to the base of this climb, and the next few.
40 ft. 6 bolts. FA Mike Wheatley, 2013.

❷ Low-Hanging Fruit 5.10d ★★★
Climb edges and pockets to a hard left after the last bolt and sneak up on the anchors. This route is slowly cleaning up and not easy for the grade.
60 ft. 5 bolts. Mike Wheatley, 2011.

❸ Psychopomp 5.11b ★★★
This one suffers from a few perma-sand holds, but offers some good moves. Some use a long draw on the last bolt.
60 ft. 6 bolts. Mike Wheatley, 2011.

❹ Clay City Exit 5.11a ★★★
The best of the routes on this section of cliff. Steep climbing on jugs just until you start getting pumped, then it backs off for a nice mellow 5.11.
65 ft. 6 bolts. Mike Wheatley, 2011.

❺ Deep in Dis Bear 5.9+ ★★★
The overhanging crack system right of the three sport lines. Face holds and jams lead to a water groove with just enough pro in horizontals.
95 ft. Kirk Aengenheyster, Dustin Stephens, 2013.

Psychopomp

Matt Hodges on *Psychopomp*, 5.11b (opposite). Photo: Mike Wilkinson.

MOTHERLODE REGION

Sam's Boy Toy

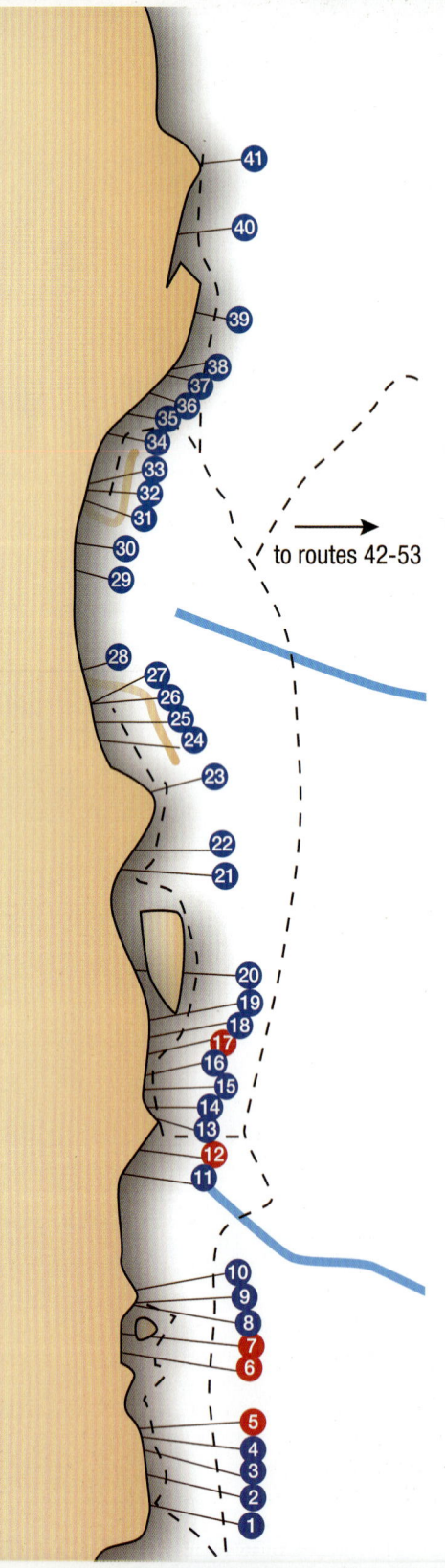

❻ Bear's Den Project 6 5.11a ★★
As the trail travels close to the cliff line and you're walking under a small roof, step out and look up for a bolt line on the upper slabs. But how do you get to it?
70 ft. 5 bolts.

❼ Bearly Legal 5.8+ ★★★
Between *Deep in Dis Bear* and *Don't Do it*, scramble up to a large ledge. Get to a stance with a crack to your left. Around the corner is this left-leaning crack system. Laybacks and jams lead to a bolt anchor.
60 ft. Scott Curran, Will Sweeney, 2013.

❽ Don't Do It 5.6 ★★
Take the first trail that leads to the sport lines and keep walking right along the cliff line until the trail turns right, down, and around a boulder section. It then goes straight back up the hill to the base of this climb. You should be standing on the far left of a rather large amphitheater. This line is the "first pitch" of the sport line *Devil Made Me Do it*. Climb the obvious hollow flake.
60 ft. Matt Seto, 2011.

❾ Devil Made Me Do It 5.11b ★★
After you grovel your way to the top of the trad line *Don't Do it*, crimp on up for a few bolts of good climbing.
70 ft. 5 bolts. Dave Linz, 2011.

294

Karsten Delap, *Pinkalicious*, 5.11b (below). Photo: Mike Wilkinson.

Sam's Boy Toy 5.11c ★★★

mediately left of the start of the cave, this route has small lds and some space in between them. Start on the slab, t a breather, then climb pockets up the overhanging finish. ft. 8 bolts. *Andrew Wheatley, Alex Southward, 2011.*

get directly to the following routes, continue 200 et past the first side trail, to a second trail that is cated just past a small drainage.

In Red We Trust 5.12b ★★

ar the middle of the cave, 75-feet left of *72-Hour Energy*, s small arête feature offers some powerful crimping and ol, bouldery moves. Shares anchors with *Wet Willy*. ft. 4 bolts. *Andrew Wheatley, 2011.*

Wet Willy 5.10a ★★★

e obvious crack at the far right of the cave/arch may look midating, but comes in at low 5.10 and offers a full trad erience. Climb the hand crack until you can slide in. Hand d head jam your way to the final chimney where you can ch down and clip the anchors of *In Red We Trust*. ft. *Will Sweeney, Tyler Schoeppner, 2013.*

Wet Willy

⓭ Pinkalicious 5.11b ★★★★

Great climbing on solid rock. Start on the arête that is formed by the far right side of the cave. Pull a couple of boulder problems off the ground until you can sneak around the corner onto the thin face.

60 ft. 7 bolts. Andrew Wheatley, Nick Feiler, 2013.

MOTHERLODE REGION

Zero Dark Fiddy

Golden Snow Cone

Off the Couch

⑭ Zero Dark Fiddy 5.13a ★★★★
Between *Pinkalicious* and *72-Hour Energy* is the hardperson's feature of this wall. It thwarted several strong climbers until Dru Mack and Scott Curran finally got at it. Climb the vert to a stance, then take on the hard, crimpy headwall.
75 ft. 8 bolts. Dru Mack, Scott Curran, 2013.

⑮ 72-Hour Energy 5.12a ★★★★
Perfect yellow slab climbing to a stance, then perfect overhung pockets and edges to a smack-down near the top. Possibly the best route on this section of wall.
70 ft. 8 bolts. Andrew Wheatley, 2011.

⑯ Golden Snow Cone 5.10c ★★★★
The warm-up on the wall. Climb the flake feature to the "golden snow cone," then up pockets.
55 ft. 6 bolts. Scott Curran, Jimmy Hoctor, 2013.

⑰ Wild Turkey Crossing 5.6 ★★★
If you hate climbers, climb this when the wall is full of people. Take the flake feature that crosses the wall across the sport line and finishes at the anchors of *Pinkalicious*.
60 ft. Clifton Gifford, Eric Jones, Isaac McShane, 2013.

⑱ Shadow Enhancement 5.11d ★★★
This one offers some sports action if you're on the shorter side. Just enough pockets and feet to get through the blank section, then a cruise to the anchors.
60 ft. 6 bolts. Andrew Wheatley, 2011.

⑲ Barren Gold 5.12a ★★★
Often wet, this is the real deal for some technical crimping solid stone. Start left of the large boulder and climb just left the blue-streaked section.
60 ft. 6 bolts. Andrew Wheatley, 2011.

⑳ Off the Couch 5.10d ★★★
The furthest right climb on this immediate section of wall starts behind the large boulder where your friends can star and point out beta. Start on good holds that quickly get smaller and force you to make some technical moves above.
60 ft. 5 bolts. Andrew Wheatley, Patrick Murphy, 2011.

Rachel Avallone, day three, *72-Hour Energy* 5.12a (opposite). Photo: Mike Wilkinson.

MOTHERLODE REGION

Eye of the Tigger

Brokeback Finger

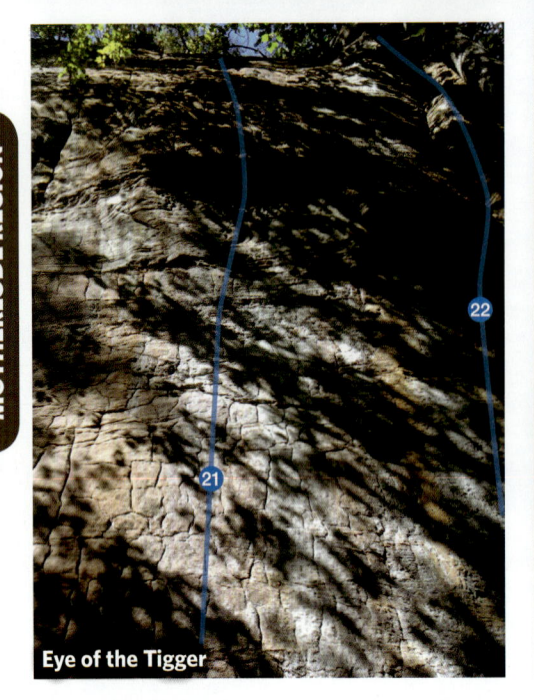

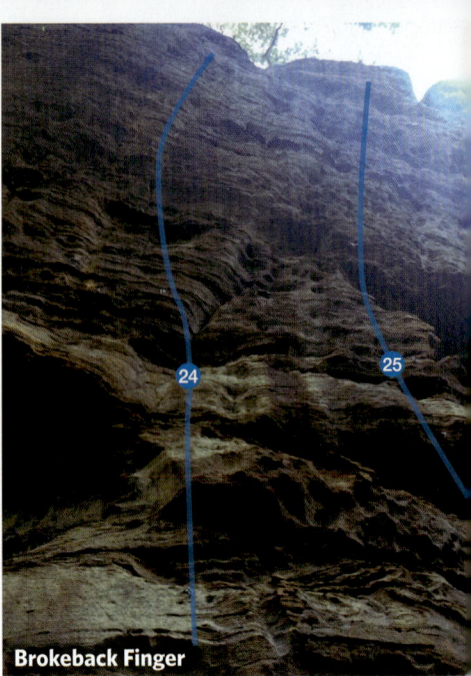

㉑ Eye of the Tigger 5.12b ★★★
As you pass *Off the Couch,* hiking right, the trail dives down and around a large boulder to rejoin the cliff line at this route, which is unlikely to have any chalk on it. If you can find the minimal holds and unlock the puzzling sequence, you have a chance.
45 ft. 6 bolts. Kipp Trummel, 2013.

㉒ Pooh and Piglet, Too 5.10d ★★★
Just right of *Tigger*, climb the wandering pockets behind a tree, over a roof, and up a small crack system.
50 ft. 7 bolts. Karen Clark, Kipp Trummel, 2013.

㉓ Gandee Candy 5.8 ★★★
About 75 feet right of the previous two routes, this starts on a partially detached pillar, then hops onto the main wall. Great route for the new leader, but pay attention to the ledge-fall potential.
65 ft. 6 bolts. Jimmy Hoctor, Scott Curran, 2013.

㉔ Brokeback Finger 5.12d ★★★
About 50 feet right of *Gandee Candy*, this and the next few lines start on a ledge that overlooks the large amphitheater of the "Steep Wall." Bouldery crux.
60 ft. 7 bolts. Jason Forrester, Andrew Wheatley, 2014.

㉕ Cindy Groms 5.12b ★★★
Just right of *Brokeback* is another steep pocketfest with a few ledge holds to help out.
65 ft. 6 bolts. Unknown, 2015.

㉖ Godbolt 5.12b ★★★
Sharing the same first bolt with *Inches and Fractions*, this one gets better the higher you climb. As with many of the routes here, save some juice for the top.
65 ft. 6 bolts. Preston Godbolt, 2015.

㉗ Inches and Fractions 5.12d ★★★
At the shared first bolt, trend right through fun moves, then a couple of bolts of hard crimping. Take the "surfboard" rest before the enduro run to the anchors.
65 ft. 6 bolts. Kyle Fisher, Andrew Wheatley, 2015.

㉘ Itchy and Scratchy 5.12d ★★★
An old route, the rightmost one starting from the ledge. Traverse on rather large holds, then trend up pockets and edges for a long endurance climb.
100 ft. 9 bolts. Bill Ramsey, 1995.

㉙ Bear's Den 29 Project
Starting in the bowels of the cave, left of the belay ledge for *Rules of Engagement* and its neighbors, are two projects. They both start in the wettest part of the overhang and climb directly out of the cave.

㉚ Bear's Den 30 Project
See above.

To get to the next several routes, walk a few hundred feet past the second left turn off the Bear's Den trail, over a drainage, to the third trail on the left. Go left at this three-forked intersection.

Inches and Fractions

All That Twitters

Squirrels Gone Wild

BEAR'S DEN

All That Twitters 5.13a ★★★
t the far left of this section of wall, deep in the amphitheater, his route starts on choss but leads to better rock and a rest efore some hard bouldering under the roof. The reward is .11+ climbing to the anchors.
00 ft. 11 bolts. *Jason Forrester, 2015.*

Rules of Engagement 5.13a ★★★★★
ight of *All That Twitters* and starting at the far left edge of the elay ledge, this one has it all: tough boulder problems, rests, nderclings, pinches, long runs up top ... If the Lode scene is o much, this out-of-the-way line will give you the deep pump u climb at the Red for, and put a smile on your face.
00 ft. 9 bolts. *Jason Forrester, 2010.*

Squirrels Gone Wild 5.13b ★★★★
tart under the large hueco located about 6 feet off the round. Hard boulder problems and jug pulling.
00 ft. 11 bolts. *Mike Anderson, 2015.*

G.I. Joe Closed Project ★★★
orty feet right of *Squirrels*, and still left of *Room With a ïew*, this steep powerhouse starts with difficult bouldering, en 5.12 crimpy climbing to the last bolt where you should repare to launch," according to the equipper. 5.13b?
00 ft. 12 bolts. *Equipper: Kipp Trummel.*

Room With a View Open Project ★★★
n the right side of the amphitheater, this one is easy to spot: ook for the flake system with the room-sized cave/hueco in e middle of the wall. Probably 5.13.
00 ft. 9 bolts. *Equipper: Kyle Fisher.*

㊱ **Routeburglar** 5.12a ★★★★
Start off the boulder and climb the small, angling dihedral/fin feature to a sit-down rest. Good, overhanging, RRG climbing lies above.
80 ft. 9 bolts. *Mike Anderson, 2010.*

299

Routeburglar

37 Bear Down 5.11d ★★★
AKA *Squatter*. Sharing the same start as the next line to the right, this is a nice warm-up as long as you're warmed up enough to "Bear Down" at the top.
80 ft. 7 bolts. *Mike Anderson, Janelle Anderson, Shaun Corpron, 2010.*

38 Mooch 5.11b ★★★
The last route on this section of wall, it also can be a good warm-up for the harder routes to the left. It shares the first bolt with the previous route.
80 ft. 8 bolts.
Mike Anderson, Janelle Anderson, Shaun Corpron, 2010.

39 C Quest R 5.10b ★★
A couple hundred feet right of the "Steep Wall" and *Mooch* lies this lone slab climb.
60 ft. 9 bolts. *Mike Wheatley, 2013.*

40 Levi Yoder 5.11c ★★★
75 feet right of *C Quest R*, and about 275 feet past the "Steep Wall," look for an 8-foot-high hueco. This slab climbs out of the right side. Attentive belayer required when clipping above the hueco.
60 ft. 6 bolts. *Kipp Trummel, Eric Heuermann, 2013.*

Loaded for Bear

41 Rumspringa 5.9 ★★
Currently the last route on this side of Bear's Den, this is fun but "not for the leader at their limit." The fastest way to get directly to this route is to not take any of the three trails on your left walking in, but just stay straight and walk directly under this route and get a nice view of the rear amphitheater.
50 ft. 5 bolts. *Jeff Neal, Kipp Trummel, 2013.*

Twelve Wall

This is the furthest left section of wall on the right side of the Bear's Den hollow. To get there, take the main trail as you would for all the previous routes, but just before you come to the third cutoff trail, you'll cross a drainage and come up a hill. Look for an obvious, but overgrown, logging road going down and to the right to the bottom of the drainage. Walk down the logging road, cross the stream, and bear up and left on the hillside, following the road. You will meet the cliff at a large tree stump with three bolted routes. This is Cut Tree Wall. The Twelve Wall is to your left (toward the back of Bear's Den), and Project Wall is to your right.

42 Loaded for Bear 5.12b ★★★★
The furthest left route on the Twelve Wall has a tough finish.
60 ft. 7 bolts. *Jason Forrester, 2010.*

43 Bear Belly 5.12b ★★★★
Start on the large flake/ramp to a hard slab crux. Save juice for the pockets up top.
60 ft. 7 bolts. *Jason Forrester, 2010.*

Twelve Wall

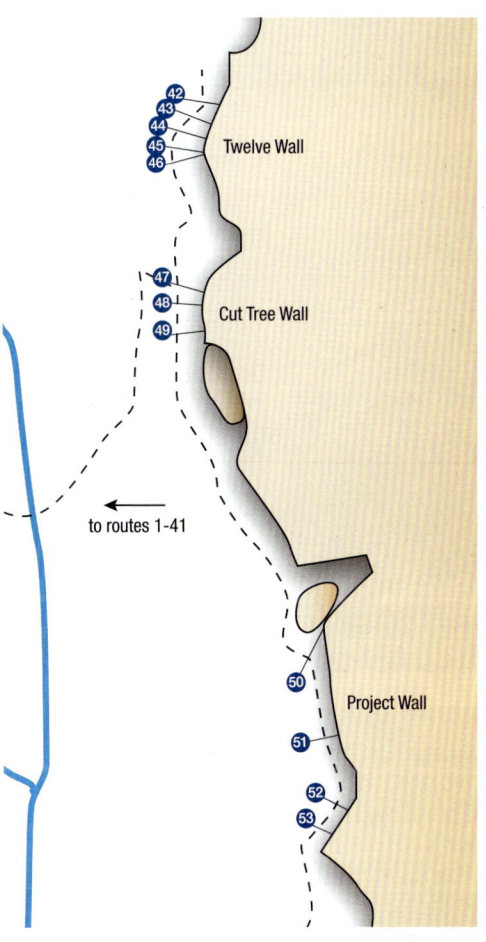

Ticks and Beer 5.12c ★★★★

...milar to its brothers to the left, this one also has thin, ...achy moves to some good, pumpy RRG climbing. Climb to ...e top of the flake, then set off.
...0 ft. 7 bolts. *Jason Forrester, 2010.*

Unbearable 5.12b ★★★★

... the far right of the Twelve Wall, and where the trail meets ...e cliff, this climb shares a start with *Two Rons*. Climb the ...unt arête for a bit, then bust out left through thin, reachy ...ocket moves.
...0 ft. 8 bolts. *Kyle Fisher, 2010.*

Two Rons Don't Make a Right 5.11b ★★★

...art as for *Unbearable*, then take on the blunt arête. "It's a ...eat warm-up," said the climber to his enemy.
...0 ft. 8 bolts. *Kyle Fisher, 2011.*

...ut Tree Wall

Spicer 5.11c ★★★★

...uper-good route. This is the leftmost route at Cut Tree Wall, ...d follows the obvious arête. You can't miss this one if you ...und the trail from the other side. For the most part, climb ...e left side of the arête ... no other spoilers.
...5 ft. 6 bolts. *Mike Wheatley, 2010.*

Bromance 5.11d ★★★

...e middle route on this wall follows the cool wave mini-
...ête feature. Hard for the grade.
...0 ft. 6 bolts. *Andrew Wheatley, 2012.*

BEAR'S DEN

Project Wall

50 Arête-Headed Stranger 5.11c ★★★
Another arête! Located on the left side of the Project Wall, 7 feet right of Cut Tree Wall. Start on huge, dirty holds that lea to a couple of great rests. Find your way to the steep part where the holds reappear after a short section of, well, not being very present.
80 ft. 10 bolts. Jason Forrester, 2010.

51 Bearly There 5.14a ★★★★
The beautiful blank face in the center of the Project Wall. It's all there, but bearly.
60 ft. 9 bolts. Adam Taylor, 2012.

52 Ursa Minor 5.11b ★★★
At the far right of Project Wall, just past a dirty dihedral, two pocketed routes await. Kinda like climbing at the Dark Side, but a bit easier. *Ursa Minor* is the left one, which climbs through good pockets, and is the better of the two.
45 ft. 4 bolts. Mike Wheatley, 2012.

53 Ursa Major 5.11a ★★★
Currently the furthest right route at Bear's Den. Start close t the swamp, through more pockets that make you think of th Dark Side. Less liked than its brother to the left.
50 ft. 5 bolts. Mike Wheatley, 2012.

49 Here Comes Palin 5.11c ★★★
The rightmost of the three routes on the Cut Tree Wall is a "Brad Combs 5.11c," but everyone else might find it to be a bit harder.
60 ft. 6 bolts. Brad Combs, 2012.

Sarah Brengosz knows *Two Rons Don't Make a Right*, 5.11b (page 301). Photo: Elodie Saracco.

THE MOTHERLODE

37.646
-83.709
20 min / 10 min

71 routes

.14
.13
.12
.11
.10
.9
.8
.7
.6≤

Map labels: GMC Wall, Warm-Up Wall, Madness Cave, Undertow Wall, Buckeye Buttress, left-side approach, right-side approach, N

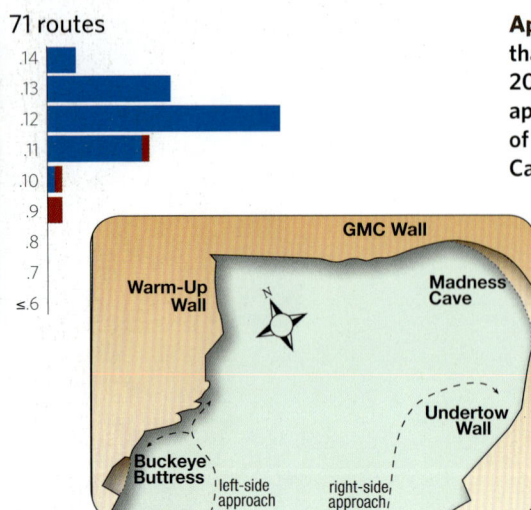

The Motherlode is the Red's hard (5.12-and-up) sport-climbing Mecca — and one of the best sport crags in the world. If you don't like taking big whips on steep rock, "the Lode" is not for you. The Lode is a place to get fit, see the best climbers, and gawk at freakish displays of strength. To truly appreciate this cliff, you need to climb solid 5.12.

The Motherlode is a huge amphitheater, broken up into several distinct sectors/walls: The western side offers technical face climbing on solid, slightly overhanging, streaked walls. The central curve forms the Madness Cave and has some of the Red's longest and steepest routes. The Undertow Wall forms the eastern side of the horseshoe; a good 150 feet long, 75 feet tall, and overhanging at a solid 25-degree angle, it hosts a slew of classic pumpfests.

Approach: Drive to the big muddy/dirty pullo that is the Motherlod parking area (see pag 206 for directions). Locate the obviou approach trail that leads uphill from the bac of the big muddy/dirty pulloff. For the Madnes Cave or Undertow Wall, stay right at the majo fork; this branch meets the cliff at th Undertow Wall's left side beneath Tea Wilson. If you're headed to the cliff's wester side, including Buckeye Buttress, Warm-U Wall, or GMC Wall, stay left at the majo fork and follow a trail that reaches the cli just right of Buckeye Buttress.

Conditions: The Lode is one of the Red's be wet-weather destinations. The overhangin walls offer great shelter from the rain. It possible to climb all day at the Lode an escape or follow the sun, depending on which sid of the amphitheater you climb on. The walls on th left side — Buckeye Buttress, Warm-Up Wall, an the GMC Wall — get morning-to-midday sun. Th Madness Cave starts getting sun the early afternoon. The Underto Wall is a good warm-weathe destination; it stays shady most of the da receiving only an hour or two of evening sun.

Access: The RRGCC, with help from Access Fu and Trango Climbing Gear, has permanent secured access to this iconic crag. Your he is still needed to pay off the loan! For mo information, or to donate, visit www.RRGCC.or

A number of vehicles in the parking area hav been broken into, so remove all valuables fro your car when climbing here. Beginning in 201 a community effort began to replace every bo at the Motherlode with stainless-steel glue-in To date the crag is nearly complete. Many thank to the several folks involved with the work and a those who made donations.

ckeye Buttress

One-Eyed Willy Up the Back 5.11c ★★
m the end of the approach trail for the western side of
e wall, walk left past a few bolted lines and scramble up
d around some boulders beneath a large overhang. Just
t of the overhang is a bolted line on the arête, which is
d *Sucker*. This route is just around the corner left of *Trad
cker*. Climb just left of the arête, pull over the roof, and
mb through small finger pockets at the top.
ft. 5 bolts. *Keith Moll, 1994.*

Trad Sucker 5.11b ★★★
is route ascends the line of bolts just right of the arête.
rt on a large boulder. Be careful clipping the first bolt.
ft. 4 bolts. *Keith Moll, 1994.*

The Chronic 5.12b ★★
e start of this route faces *Trad Sucker* and is on the right
the overhanging back wall. Climb a slab left of the arête
til you reach a crack, then make a big move left to the
erhanging headwall.
ft. 6 bolts. *Tim Cornette, 1994.*

Twisted 5.11b ★★★
rt as for *The Chronic* but follow the crack a little longer,
n make a big move left. Crank up through the overhanging
ll to a ledge.
ft. bolts. *Tim Cornette, 1994.*

⑤ The Reacharound 5.12c ★★★
Start the same as the previous two routes but move right around the arête, then continue up the seam and face to the anchors.
60 ft. 5 bolts. *Brian McCray, 1994.*

⑥ Stain 5.12c ★★★★★★
This route begins around the corner 15 feet right of *The Reacharound*. Blast through the first few bolts, then make an exciting move to a jug out right. Gain a shake, then head left on pockets and straight up through sequential moves on slopers and edges. Save some juice for the last move to the anchors.
50 ft. 6 bolts. *Chris Snyder, 1994.*

⑦ Buff the Wood 5.12b ★★★★
This route begins just right of *Stain* and is marked by a short finger crack about 15 feet up. Boulder up to the finger crack and make the clip. Take a rest, then move right on crimps and deadpoint to a crimp rail. Launch for a jug, then continue up the face to a pocket problem. Make some big moves, then clip the chains.
50 ft. 5 bolts. *Jeff Moll, 1994.*

⑧ Golden Touch 5.13b ★★★★
This beautiful line follows a golden streak just right of *Buff the Wood*. Power up to a delicate crux requiring the use of a credit-card-sized edge for most. Keep it together for the final moves before the anchors.
45 ft. 5 bolts. *David Hume, 1995.*

MOTHERLODE REGION

⑨ Fall of the Anticlimber Open Project
The grey streak right of *Golden Touch*. Estimated to be 5.14b.
50 ft. 4 bolts. Equipper: Adam Taylor.

⑩ Heart-Shaped Box 5.12c ★★★★
This line starts about 15 feet right of *Golden Touch*, on a ledge. Scramble up to the ledge to make the first clip. Crank through on decent edges and make the move to the heart-shaped box. Shake out and climb smaller crimps to the anchors.
50 ft. 5 bolts. Brian McCray, 1995.

⑪ Overdrive 5.9 ★
This route ascends the crack system just right of *Heart-Shaped Box* to the top. Walk off left or locate a rappel tree.
70 ft. Grant Stephens, 1994.

⑫ Leftomaniac 5.11b ★★★
Start on *Rug Muncher*, then move up into the hueco and up and over the roof. Clip the last bolt and take a hard left. If you head too far left, watch the fall/swing.
70 ft. 7 bolts. Dustin Stephens, 2013.

⑬ Rug Muncher 5.11d ★★★
Where the trail meets the cliffline, you should see the large hueco at about 30 feet on this semi-contrived, but fun route. Climb the techy face to the hueco, then bust out right. Not your typical RRG ladder.
55 ft. 8 bolts. Dustin Stephens, 2012.

⑭ Ball Scratcher 5.12a ★★★
This rounded arête is located where the approach trail meets the wall when walking over from *Heart-Shaped Box*. Balance up the creepy arête to the anchors.
40 ft. 5 bolts. Jeff Moll, 1994.

⑮ The Cream Machine 5.10 ★★★
A slab/water-groove about 35 feet right of *Ball Scratcher*. Techy start with an "appropriate" amount of bolts. Steep jug climbers will back off this thing and say it sucks. They probably just can't climb it.
60 ft. 6 bolts. Josh O'Brian, John Seymer, 2011.

⑯ All In 5.11d ★★★★
This golden route was passed over for years. About halfway between the previous and next routes lies this vertical gold streak. Look for a faint trail that leads up on a shoulder where this route begins, in a crack/flake. Perfect edges/knobs/cracks on wicked-hard rock. 11d? That's what the FA says.
60 ft. 7 bolts. Andrew and Mike Wheatley, 2013.

Warm-Up Wall

⑰ Three Wasted Bolts 5.11a ★★
Follow the trail right from *Ball Scratcher* about 100 feet. The route begins where the trail meets a rock patio. Climb jug plates to a large ledge, using natural protection. Continue u the bolted face to anchors.
50 ft. 3 bolts. Unknown, 1996.

⑱ Ben 5.11a ★★
Right of the previous line is a plated face with two routes. *Ben* is the left route, and despite big holds has been known to drop a hammer on the ego just before the chains.
60 ft. 6 bolts. Miguel's Pizza Crew, 2011.

⑲ Laura 5.11b ★★
A bit tougher and a little taller than *Ben*. These routes stand together as a memorial to Ben Strohmeier and Laura Fletch
70 ft. 7 bolts. Miguel's Pizza Crew, 2011.

⑳ Crescenta 5.9 ★★
The obvious wide crack a few feet right of the previous rou Walk off left or locate a rappel tree.
70 ft. Grant Stephens, 1994.

㉑ Breathe Right 5.11c ★★★
This is the first bolted line on the main Warm-Up Wall, just right of *Crescenta*. Climb large holds up and through a sequential section. Relax on large holds again to the ancho
60 ft. 7 bolts. Brian McCray, 1995.

㉒ Injured Reserve 5.11a ★★★
Just right of *Breathe Right* is another bolted line. Follow lar holds to a slopey crux. Negotiate this section, then continue to the anchors on more forgiving holds.
60 ft. 5 bolts. Chris Martin, 1994.

㉓ Trust in Jesus 5.11b ★★★
The last bolted route on the Warm-Up Wall. Angle up and ri through sharp plates and tough moves.
50 ft. 5 bolts. Keith Moll, 1994.

㉔ Purdy Mouth 5.12b ★★★
Walk right from *Trust in Jesus* to a route that begins just ri of a chimney in a corner. From a ledge and pull a difficult, sharp start.
70 ft. 5 bolts. Hugh Loeffler, 1997.

㉕ Mr. Sandy 5.14c
An old project 10 feet left of *Take That, Katie Brown*. Sent by visiting Czech phenom Adam Ondra, who described it as having a "nice boulder problem."
70 ft. Adam Ondra, 2012.

Buckeye Buttress

Warm-Up Wall

THE MOTHERLODE

left-side approach

GMC Wall

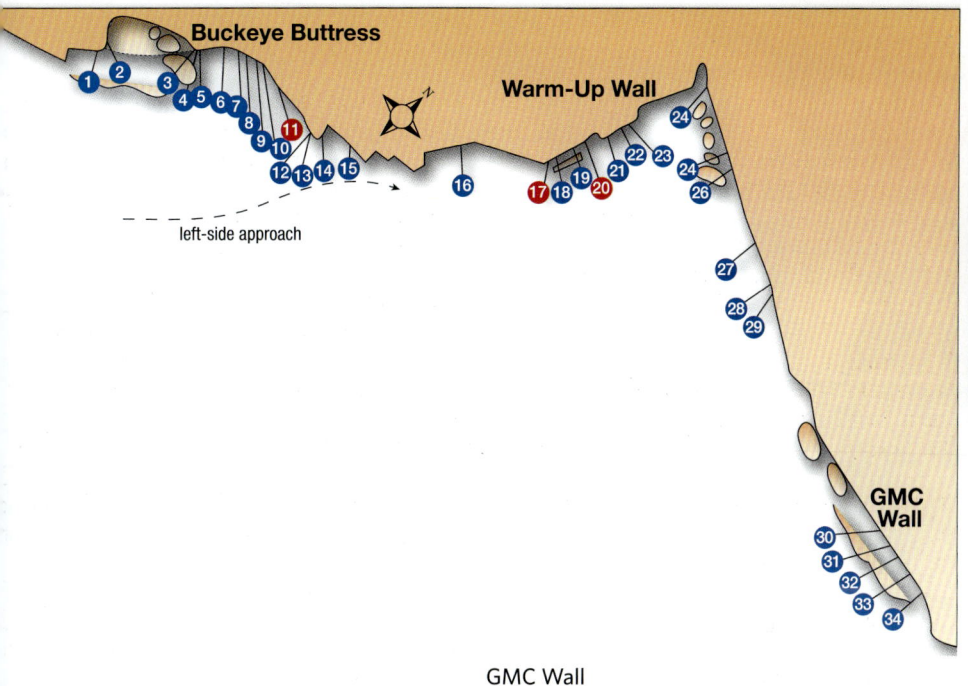

Take That, Katie Brown 5.13b ★★★★

s reachy route ascends a line of pockets just right of a
wn stain on the wall, 50 feet right of *Purdy Mouth* and
ar a small drainage. Named with Ms. Brown's consent as a
gue-in-cheek tribute to her kicking everyone's ass — as
"Thank God we finally found a route she can't onsight."
ft. 8 bolts. *Hugh Loeffler, 1997.*

Swahili Slang 5.12b ★★★★★

s picturesque line just begs to be climbed but is rarely
veled due to its less-than-vertical nature. Walk right from
e That, Katie Brown 50 feet to locate a line of bolts near
arching ramp with bright-orange stains. Follow the line
through very technical moves and over a small roof just
ore the anchors.
ft. 8 bolts. *Jeff Moll, 1995.*

So Low 5.12b ★★★

other rarely traveled line that features technical and
oyable edging, 20 feet right of *Swahili Slang*. Begin near a
ge hueco close to the ground. Climb the plated face right
he hueco to a slab finish.
ft. 9 bolts. *Brian McCray, 1995.*

Techno Destructo 5.12b ★★★

another vertical edging challenge that doesn't see much
fic. This route begins just right of a large tree a few feet
t of *So Low*, and climbs similarly.
ft. 10 bolts. *Brian McCray, 1995.*

GMC Wall

30 False Positive 5.12c ★★★★

The leftmost route on this section of wall starts on a flake
hidden by trees. Technical face climbing, a deadpoint, a wicked
hard mantel, and an insecure traverse to a hidden crimp.
70 ft. 7 bolts. *Dustin Stephens, 2013.*

31 Thanatopsis 5.14a ★★★★★

About 100 feet right of the previous routes, find a sandy
ledge. This route is at the left end of an obvious, steep, blank-
looking face. Stout for the given grade. The first ascentionist,
Dave Hume, spent two or three years trying this route. Shortly
after he succeeded, he did *Just Do It* (5.14c) at Smith Rock in
a mere four tries.
60 ft. 6 bolts. *Dave Hume, 1996.*

32 Cut Throat 5.13b ★★★★★

Tough for the grade. This route moves up through crimps on
steep rock a few feet right of *Thanatopsis*. Begin by grabbing
a shelf about six feet up, then fire up the face and crank
through a small overhang just before the anchors.
70 ft. 8 bolts. *Jeff Moll, 1995.*

33 8 Ball 5.12d ★★★★★

Begin below a right-facing dihedral. Grab a slopey hold about
six feet up, crank up to a ledge, then move left to a flake.
Climb the flake for a few moves, prepare your guns, then race
up the vague dihedral and left face before your arms melt.
7 bolts. *Chris Snyder, 1995.*

Patrick Bailey plays *Snooker*, 5.13a (opposite). Photo: John Wesely.

GMC Wall

Snooker 5.13a ★★★★★
...st left of the huge hueco. Begin with a bouldery start to ...ledge. Mantel the ledge, then climb slanting crimps to ...pocketed section. Make a desperate move left to a jug ...neath the roof. Get a shake and climb small crimps on the ...adwall to anchors.
... ft. 8 bolts. Dave Hume, 1995.

Hot for Teacher 5.12c ★★★
...is line starts by traversing right on the ledge where ...nooker begins. Climb up a blank face to reach the bottom ...ht side of the giant hueco. Traverse the edge of the hueco, ...en pull up right and over a roof to the headwall above. ...ntinue over bulges to the anchors.
... ft. 7 bolts. Chris Snyder, 1995.

White Man's Overbite 5.13c ★★★★
...st right of Hot for Teacher. Using a semi-permanent ...ck of cheater stones, reach up and grab a jug. Boulder ...a steep section and up to a mantel. Continue up the ...erhanging wall on crimps and sloping holds to a relief jug ...t before the finishing moves. Solid for the grade.
... ft. 9 bolts. Dave Hume, 1995.

White Man's Shuffle 5.13d ★★★★
...gin by climbing White Man's Overbite, then move right ...er the sixth bolt. Longer, more slopey, and substantially ...der than White Man's Overbite. Solid for the grade.
... ft. 11 bolts. Bill Ramsey, 2003.

38 Cosmic Sausage 5.13a ★
This is the rightmost line on the GMC Wall. Begin near the right edge of a large overhang and climb out the overhang on flakes. Turn the lip and bushwhack up the face to a large hueco near the top. Continue up the final and cleaner section of the face to the anchors.
100 ft. 11 bolts. Jeff Moll, 1995.

Madness Cave

39 Hell or High Water 5.12c ★★★
Walk right from Cosmic Sausage to the beginning of the obvious Madness Cave. This new addition to the Cave (although some may argue it's not *really* in the Cave) clocks in at 5.12, a first for this sector. Begin 15 feet left of Transworld, with a boulder problem start to reach a no-hands rest. Travel through great stone, past a short chossy traverse to reach the meat of the route, which consists of 80 feet of steep climbing on big holds — just what you'd expect for the Cave, only without the power-sapping cruxes found on the lines to the right.

The extension to the second set of anchors is called *Hell or High Chains* (5.13a). FA: Adam Taylor.
110 ft. 13 bolts. Shadow Ayala, Jesse Koerner, 2012.

THE MOTHERLODE

40 Transworld Depravity 5.14a ★★★★★
This is the leftmost line in the cave proper. Begin by climbing through roughly 60 feet of 5.12c moves to a rest. When recovered, power through a hard move to reach sustained tough climbing, which leads to another hard move. Finish by romping up a relaxing 5.13a section to the anchors. It is possible to lower from the route with one 70-meter rope.
110 ft. 14 bolts. *Bill Ramsey, 2001.*

41 BOHICA 5.13b ★★★★
"Bend Over ..." This is the second-from-the-left bolted rou[te] in the Madness Cave, just right of *Transworld Depravity*. Th[e] first third is high-quality, steepish .12a or so, to a good res[t.] Milk it, because the next section is extremely steep. Power endurancy, body tensiony, big moves. This one stays with y[ou] all the way to the anchors. It's a blast!
100 ft. 13 bolts. *Jeff Moll, 1995.*

Dru Mack actualizes *Transworld Depravity*, 5.14a (opposite). Photo: John Wesely.

Last of the Bohicans 5.13d ★★★★

...e extension to *BOHICA*. Crimp past a difficult boulder ...oblem above the first anchors, then fight the penultimate ...mp to anchors at the top of the headwall. Low in the grade. ...5 ft. 15 bolts. *Bill Ramsey, 1998.*

43 Flour Power 5.13b ★★★★★

A bit harder than *BOHICA*, this route begins by climbing through a roof 8 feet right of *BOHICA* to reach a steep face. Climb through the steep face to a more vertical section and a good rest on a small ledge before the overhanging headwall. Climb the steep headwall, heading toward a faint dihedral near the top. Rest as well as you can at the base of the dihedral, then punch right and up to the anchors.
100 ft. 15 bolts. Chris Martin, 1997.

Lee Smith, *Flour Power* 5.13b (page 311). Photo: John Wesely

Madness Cave (Starts)

Pushin' Up Daisies 5.13c ★★★★

This two-bolt extension to *Flour Power* takes the route to the top of the cliff! From the chains, make a hard move off a slopey ledge to reach easier climbing. Then make a committing deadpoint move off crimps to reach the jug at the top of the cliff.

20 ft. *Brad Weaver, 2008.*

Omaha Beach 5.14a ★★★★★

One of the best routes of its grade in the country. Begin a few feet right of *Flour Power*, climb up to the left side of a large alcove, then take on the steeply overhanging headwall. The lower two-thirds of this route was originally a project named *Ice Cream Man* until Bill Ramsey extended it and made the first ascent in 1999. Shortly after, this line was onsighted by then-local Katie Brown! Several holds have since broken, dropping the grade from 5.13d to 5.14a. The name comes from "the Beach," a slopey and somewhat sandy "rest" at two-thirds height. The crux is getting off the Beach — just like on *D-Day*.

120 ft. 13 bolts. *Bill Ramsey, 1999.*

The Madness 5.13c ★★★★★

Twenty-five feet right of *Omaha Beach*, move through a low roof to a no-hands rest in an alcove before the headwall. Face up the steep headwall and crank past a bulge near the top to reach the anchors.

120 ft. bolts. *Brian Toy, 1997.*

47 Forty Ounces of Justice 5.13a ★★★★

This route gives mortals a taste of the angle of the Madness Cave. Originally considered a crumbly, subpar route compared to its neighbors, but 20 years of traffic have cleaned it up and earned it another star. Step right from *The Madness* about 15 feet to the next line of bolts, near a small tree. Power out the steep wall on increasingly larger holds to reach a decent stance just before the less steep but slightly more difficult finish.

110 ft. 14 bolts. *Porter Jarrard, 1997.*

48 Buck Eye 5.13b ★★

Another long cave route right of *40 Ounces*. This one hasn't had much traffic so expect some breakage before it qualifies for the Cave. Do it some justice and jump on it with a brush.

Joe Kinder, 2011.

Undertow Wall

49 The Sauce 5.12b ★★★

Walk right from the Madness Cave to a shorter and less overhanging wall hosting an abundance of lines. *The Sauce* is the first route encountered on the wall and begins to the right of a large tree growing up into the wall. Climb the face to a good stance just before the wall takes a turn for the steep. Pump up the steep face and save some sauce for the roof before the anchors.

60 ft. 6 bolts. *Chris Martin, 1995.*

50 Leave It to Beavis 5.12d ★★★★

This is the bolted line 15 feet right of *The Sauce*. Climb through a large hueco, then continue up the steep face on big jugs to some challenging pulls on smaller holds at the top.

90 ft. 8 bolts. *Chris Martin, 1995.*

MOTHERLODE REGION

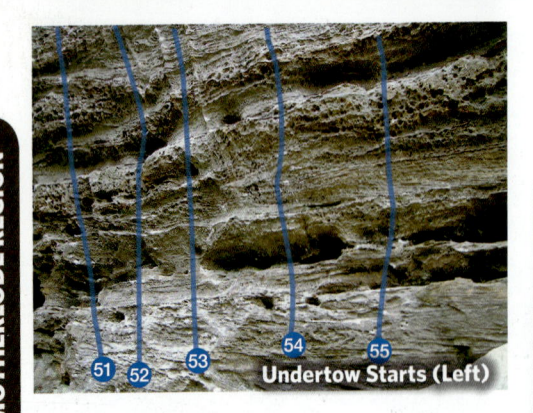

51 Tuna Town 5.12d ★★★★
This route begins near the right side of the large, low hueco that the previous line climbs through. Pump up the steep wall on incredibly big holds to a runout and exciting crux section at the top. Blow the finishing moves and you're going for a huge ride!
85 ft. 10 bolts. Jeff Moll, 1995.

52 The Flux Capacitor 5.12d ★★★
You'll either love it or hate it. Begin just right of *Tuna Town* on a flake. Climb up to a ledge, then take on a vertical rib system to a decent stance. Continue up past a bulge to reach the anchors.
95 ft. 10 bolts. Chris Martin, 1995.

53 Harvest 5.12d ★★★★
This route ascends the next line of bolts about 10 feet right of *The Flux Capacitor* and follows some distinctive rib-like features. It can be mossy and green after rain, so try to catch it in dry weather. Begin on a slopey ramp. Interesting moves up the groove and ribs lead to a rest on the right. One more hard move leads to an easier finish.
85 ft. 11 bolts. Jeff Moll, 1994.

54 Hoofmaker 5.13a ★★★★
Move 10 feet right from *Harvest* to the next line, which begins on a boulder. Climb up to a horizontal shelf, then crank out past a roof to some decent holds. Recover for an endurance haul on the sustained face to the anchors.
90 ft. 10 bolts. Porter Jarrard, 1997.

55 Team Wilson 5.12d ★★★★★
Begin left of a large stack of boulders. Climb up to a horizontal, then take on a blank face to reach another horizontal. Rest here, then race up the long, strength-sapping headwall to the anchors. Tough for the grade.
85 ft. 9 bolts. Chris Martin, 1995.

56 Resurrection 5.12c ★★★★
This route begins on top of a large boulder to the right of *Team Wilson*. Power through the start, then move left through horizontals and continue up through pockets to the anchors.
80 ft. 7 bolts. Chris Martin, 1995.

57 Subman 5.12d ★★★★
AKA *The High Hard One*. Locate the line of bolts 10 feet right of *Resurrection*. Grab a shelf, then head up and left on sloping holds to a jug rest. Continue up the face on crimps to a corner-like feature, up this, and over a final bulge. Clipping the chains is often interesting!
80 ft. 8 bolts. Jeff Moll, 1995.

58 Crime Time 5.12d ★★★
Five feet right of *Subman*. Climb up to a mouth-like feature that is often damp. Make some tough moves and continue up the pumpy face, staying left of a faint dihedral.
75 ft. 7 bolts. Brian McCray, 1995.

59 Skin Boat 5.13a ★★★★
This route starts a few feet right of *Crime Time*. Climb ledges for a few feet, then make a move to a half-moon-shaped jug that is often damp. Crank through edges and small pockets to the second bolt. Move up to two opposing jugs, then hang on for as long as you can, hopefully all the way to the anchors.
80 ft. 7 bolts. Jeff Moll, 1995.

Undertow starts (Right)

The Low Easy One

Convicted 5.13a ★★★★★
About 15 feet right of *Skin Boat* is a route that's less sustained but more cruxy than other climbs hereabouts. Boulder the initial section to a small flake, then continue up through pinches and sidepulls to powerful moves on sloping holds at the top.
70 ft. 7 bolts. *Jeff Moll, 1995.*

Ale-8-One 5.12b ★★★★
Begin just right of *Convicted* and to the left of a low, flat boulder. Climb a flake up to the first bolt, then traverse right and make a tough move to gain a jug. Get a shake and traverse back slightly left to begin the business. Make big moves up the overhanging face to a tough finish on edges and gastons.
65 ft. 7 bolts. *Brian McCray, 1995.*

Chainsaw Massacre 5.12a ★★★★
Classic enduro-climbing, and a good introduction to the Undertow Wall and the steeper routes at the Lode. Begin atop a low boulder. Climb up, then make a tough move left to a good shake. Paddle up on good edges in a groove between two blank walls, keeping enough energy in reserve to clip the anchors.
60 ft. 7 bolts. *Jeff Moll, 1994.*

The Verdict 5.12b ★★★
This often-wet route begins on the right side of the low, flat boulder that provides the start for *Chainsaw Massacre,* and takes a line of pockets just left of a large brown streak. If you find it dry, it's worth climbing.
70 ft. 8 bolts. *Jeff Moll, 1995.*

Sam Krieg Will Bolt Anything (SKWBA) 5.12a ★★★
This line begins just right of *The Verdict.* Formerly not as popular as the lines to the right, but has cleaned up and is getting more attention.
70 ft. 8 bolts. *Sam Krieg, 1997.*

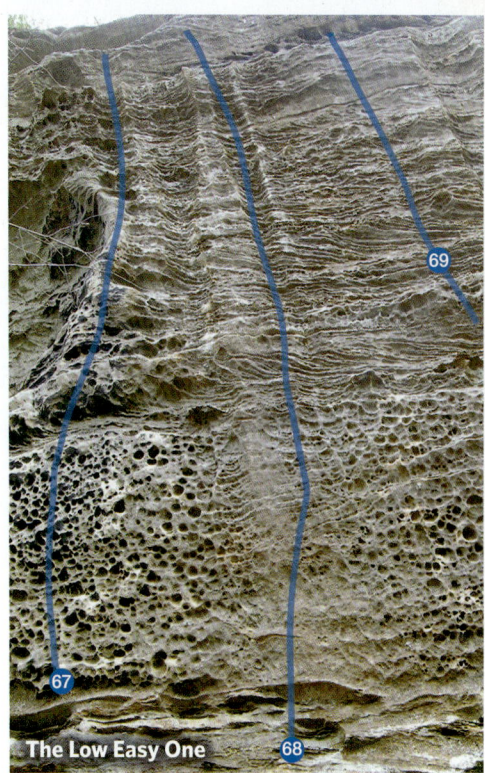

Kick Me in the Jimmie 5.12a ★★★★
This route begins slightly uphill and about 30 feet right of *SKWBA*. Start atop a small boulder, then move up and left to a big sloper move before the anchors.
60 ft. 7 bolts. *Jeff Moll, 1994.*

Burlier's Bane 5.12a ★★★
This route begins beneath a large hueco just right of *Kick Me*. Climb through pinches and sucker jugs to anchors.
60 ft. 6 bolts. *Roxanna Brock, 1995.*

Rocket Dog 5.12b ★★★★
This moves up through an obvious black stain. Grab a high ledge and step up to the slopers. Climb slopey pinches for about 10 feet, then make a move right to a jug. Continue up through the groove on pockets to the anchors.
50 ft. 5 bolts. *Chris Martin, 1995.*

The Low Easy One 5.12b ★★★
Walk down some boulders right of *Rocket Dog* to the start of this route. Climb pockets to a pointy brown shelf. Get a shake, then continue up on pockets to the anchors.
50 ft. 5 bolts. *Roxanna Brock, 1995.*

Dru Mack on *Omaha Beach*, 5.14a (page 313). Photo: John Wesely.

69 Stella 5.11d ★★★
Start about 10 feet right of *The Low Easy One* and left of an arête. Grab a low shelf and pull up into the business. Crank on gastons and pinches to the anchors.
50 ft. 6 bolts. Roxanna Brock, 1995.

70 Snapper 5.11a ★★★
This route begins about 30 feet to the right and around the arête from *Stella*, just left of a wide dihedral. Climb the near-vertical face on small holds.
50 ft. 7 bolts. Jeff Moll, 1995.

71 Stabbed in the Back 5.10a ★
Yes, this is a crack climb. Climb the wide dihedral just right of *Snapper* to the top. Rappel from a tree to descend.
80 ft. Jeff Moll, 1995.

72 Scrambled Porn 5.12a ★
Begin just right of the wide dihedral. Climb the blank face to a hand ledge about 15 feet up. Continue up the vertical face passing another horizontal break, to anchors.
60 ft. 6 bolts. Blake Bowling, Terry Kindred, 2003.

THE UNLODE

routes This little wall has a short approach and offers a couple of short, steep, alternative warm-ups for Motherlode visitors.

37.6465
-83.710
20 min 10 min

Approach: From the Motherlode parking (see page 206) hike back up the gravel road for a few minutes to an old, overgrown logging road heading down the slope on your left. Follow this road a few hundred feet until you see the cliff to your right.

Undesirable 5.11c ★★★
This bolted route begins just right of a large tree. Climb overhanging rock to the anchors. Short but pumpy.
45 ft. 5 bolts. Kellyn Gorder, 1996.

Unworthy 5.11a ★★
Just left of *Undesirable*, climb steep rock on larger holds to the anchors. Beware of swinging into the tree while cleaning.
45 ft. 4 bolts. Kellyn Gorder, 1996.

Unbridled 5.10c ★★★
Locate this route by walking left from *Unworthy* about 200 feet to a less-steep face.
45 ft. 6 bolts. Kellyn Gorder, 1996.

CHOCOLATE FACTORY

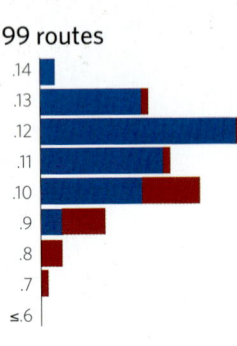

37.6497
-83.7139

99 routes

The Chocolate Factory is best known for two of the Red's most difficult routes: *Pure Imagination* and *The Golden Ticket*, both 5.14c. Aside from the insanely difficult, this wall still has plenty to offer, with good lines from 5.9 to 5.14+ and about 50 new routes since the last edition. There's even a lot for the traddies, including one of the Red's hardest gear routes, *Charlie* (5.13b). The climbing tends to involve more crimping and face climbing than jug hauling, so bring some finger strength.

Approach: Park as for the Motherlode (see page 206) and walk down the road (W) toward the Sore Heel Hollow parking area for about 200 feet, then walk across a small foot bridge on your right. The trail follows the creek for about 75 feet, then turns into an old logging road about 100 yards later. Just as you enter the tree line, the first cutoff trail shoots up and to the left. Follow this trail to the left end of the cliff for routes #1-34.

This zone can also be reached by staying on the logging road another 200 yards to the next fork in the trail. Going left here will lead directly to routes #12-16. The right branch will immediately cross a land bridge.

About 50 yards beyond the land bridge, the trail will fork yet again. Going left leads to the central sector with *Oompa* and *Pure Imagination* (routes #50-81).

Take the right branch to access routes at the right end of the cliff. About 150 yards down this trail, you get to choose left or right one more time. The left trail meets the cliff line near *Breakin' the Law* (routes #81-95.) The right trail leads to the hard, steep climbs around *Buttercup* (routes #96-108).

Conditions: There's plenty to do here on a lightly rainy day, as most of the routes are slightly overhanging. *Oompa* and *Loompa* will more than likely remain dry during the heaviest rains. Due to the extensive length and changing direction of the cliff, you're always bound to find sun or shade.

The best way to approach routes #1–34 or so is by following the first trail that breaks left off the main trail not far after leaving the road. The trail heads up and right to meet up with the cliff near For Your Health, *although you may see* Twinkie's Little Sister *first, due to its features, and chalk in the roof.*

❶ **For Your Health** 5.11a ★★★
This route is to the left when the trail meets the wall. Boulder up to a small roof, traverse right and head for the anchors.
90 ft. 10 bolts. Scott Curran, 2013.

❷ **Twinkie's Little Sister** 5.12c ★
When the trail meets the cliffline, this route should be quite visible. Steep enough to be named after the classic *Twinkie*, but lacking that route's rock quality.
80 ft. 7 bolts. Martin Schepers, 2012.

Twinkie's Little Sister

CHOCOLATE FACTORY LEFT | CHOCOLATE FACTORY CENTER | CHOCOLATE FACTORY RIGHT

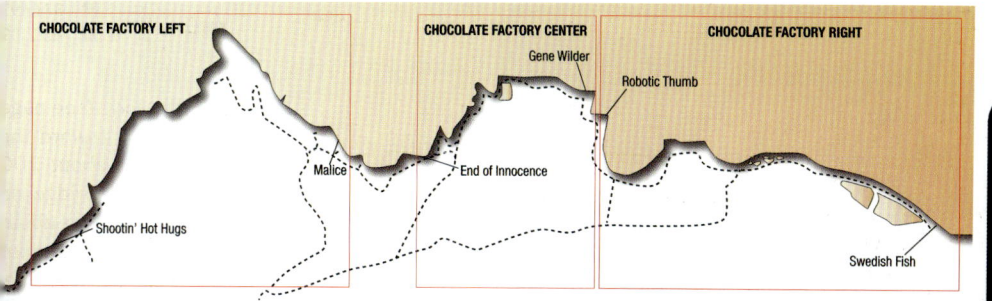

Gene Wilder
Robotic Thumb
Malice
End of Innocence
Shootin' Hot Hugs
Swedish Fish

The Juggernaut 5.10b ★★★★
his climb and *Shootin' Hot Hugs* begin on the ledge to the
ght of *Twinkie's Little Sister*.
5 ft. 7 bolts. Dustin Stephens, Lena Bakanova, 2014.

Shootin' Hot Hugs 5.12a ★★★
ook for bolts on a nice-looking golden wall beginning above
15-foot-high ledge.
0 ft. 7 bolts. Troy Davison, 2012.

Chocolate Factory 5 Closed Project
en feet right of *Shooting Hot Hugs*, this red-tagged project is
till under construction. It starts from the same ledge as the
revious two routes, and follows the left side of the large arch.

Climactic Crush 5.11b ★★★★
ght of *Shootin' Hot Hugs* is a similar route, but a bit easier.
0 ft. 9 bolts. Andrew Wheatley, 2012.

EGBG 5.10a ★★★★
ight of *Climactic Crush* is this nice 5.10. A low crux, then
ng wandering climbing on jugs.
0 ft. 12 bolts. Mike and Andrew Wheatley, 2012.

R. Kell Ethics 5.10c ★★★
ght of *EGBG* is this trad line that runs really, really close
 EGBG. Stay in trad mode while sharing some of the same
olds. Overcome a hard start out the roof with good pro,
ly to be rewarded with a stretch of poor rock quality. Don't
orry, it gets better. Belay the second from a tree. Lower to
e anchors of *EGBG*, then the ground.
20 ft. Meghan Curry, Art Cammers, 2012.

Icebreaker 5.12a ★★★★
art on the right side of the blunt arête where *Eternal Fire*
arts. Hand traverse left to climb on thin edges, sidepulls and
ockets. Technical and powerful, this route has it all.
5 ft. 9 bolts. Dustin Stephens, Margarita Martinez, 2012.

Eternal Fire 5.13c ★★★★
ty feet right of *Shootin' Hot Hugs* is a gorgeous orange wall
osting two sought-after, difficult lines. This is the one on the
ft. Pull a difficult crimp problem (or dyno past it as the FA
d) to reach stellar and difficult climbing on the face above.
 ft. 7 bolts. Andrew Gearing, 2011.

Shootin' Hot Hugs

Eternal Fire

Toxicodendron

The Dainty Butterfly

⓫ Cat's Demise 5.13b ★★★★★
Just right of *Eternal Fire* is another power sapper with easier opening moves but a tougher finish. Race past moderately steep pinches and slopers to a much-needed rest before the last bolt. Shove a leg in, get everything back, then pick your poison. If you've got your crimpers trained up, then reach straight up for a tiny right-hand seam and pull hard on it and bust for the ledge. If you've logged some time on the slopes, move left from the rest on insane pinches and slopers to reach the anchor ledge. Either way is a tough boulder problem. Bring a bail biner.
70 ft. 7 bolts. Dave Hume, 2009.

⓬ Toxicodendron 5.11b ★★★★
After you've been beaten up by *Cat's Demise*, get some confidence back by getting on this overlooked gem. Start on the flake and follow chalk and bolts to the steep finish.
70 ft. 7 bolts. Andrew Wheatley, 2012.

⓭ Chocolate Factory 13 Closed Project
Just right of *Toxicodendron*.

⓮ Unknown

⓯ Sarahinity 5.12b ★★
This route is in a cove before you get to *2-Fold*. Technical face climbing with decent clipping holds.
65 ft. 9 bolts. Troy Davison, 2014.

⓰ 2-Fold 5.12c ★★★
Walk right from *Cat's Demise* about 100 feet to locate a trio of challenging crimp lines on solid orange stone. Starting in a cave left on the left, climb on slopers and bad holds to a non-existent rest before heading for the anchors.
85 ft. 10 bolts. Troy Davison, 2014.

⓱ Bleak December 5.12b ★★★
This is the center line and begins with a left-arching crack. Follow the crack until it fades, then move up into some difficult cranking on small edges. The ending shares some personality with the *Butterfly* to the right.
55 ft. 6 bolts. Andy Mann, 2011.

⓲ The Dainty Butterfly 5.12c ★★★★
Begin with a couple of face moves to reach a crack. Climb the crack, then scoot right onto the face for a couple of moves to reach the final decent rest before the showdown. Shift left back onto the face for the second half of the route, which gets more difficult with each bolt run until the holds diminish in time for the finish.
55 ft. 6 bolts. Troy Davison, 2011.

⓳ Unfastidious Moth 5.9 ★★★
An offwidth and handcrack leading to a dirty flare.
60 ft. Blake Bowling & Steve Kauffman, 1997, Matt Tackett, 200 Joel Handley, Ryan Smith, 2013 ... who knows?

⓴ Kentucky Grape Vine 5.12b ★★★
Does Troy only bolt 12b? This powerful route packs a punch into just 45 feet.
45 ft. 5 bolts. Troy Davison, 2014.

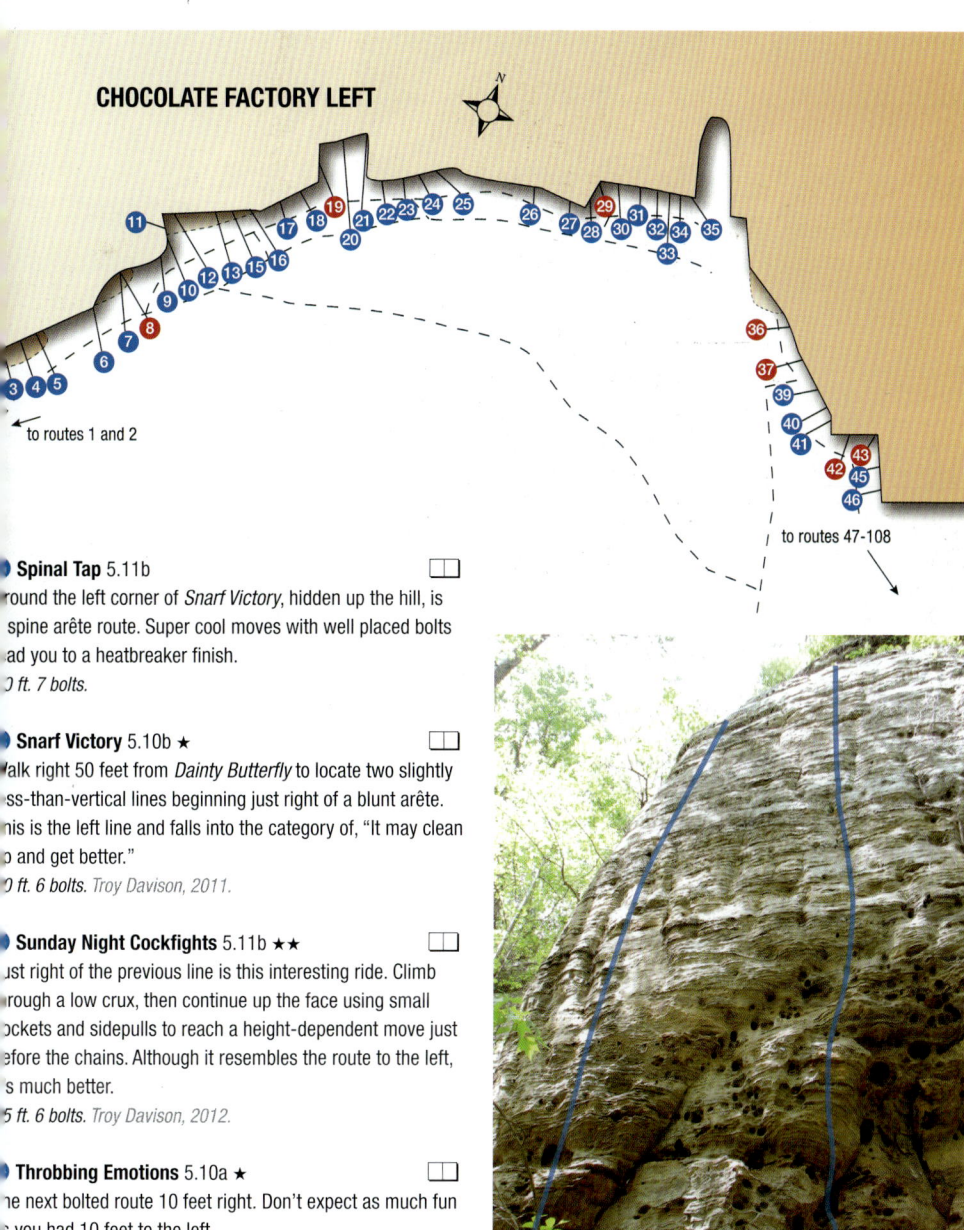

CHOCOLATE FACTORY LEFT

to routes 1 and 2

to routes 47-108

Spinal Tap 5.11b
round the left corner of *Snarf Victory*, hidden up the hill, is spine arête route. Super cool moves with well placed bolts ad you to a heatbreaker finish.
0 ft. 7 bolts.

Snarf Victory 5.10b ★
alk right 50 feet from *Dainty Butterfly* to locate two slightly ss-than-vertical lines beginning just right of a blunt arête. nis is the left line and falls into the category of, "It may clean o and get better."
0 ft. 6 bolts. *Troy Davison, 2011.*

Sunday Night Cockfights 5.11b ★★
ist right of the previous line is this interesting ride. Climb rough a low crux, then continue up the face using small ockets and sidepulls to reach a height-dependent move just efore the chains. Although it resembles the route to the left, s much better.
5 ft. 6 bolts. *Troy Davison, 2012.*

Throbbing Emotions 5.10a ★
ne next bolted route 10 feet right. Don't expect as much fun s you had 10 feet to the left.
5 ft. 6 bolts. *Alan Grau, 2012.*

Grandpa Joe 5.9 ★★★
ood rests, decent clipping stances — what else could you sk for in a 5.9?
0 ft. 7 bolts. *Josephine Neff, 2013.*

Bareback 5.13a ★
alk right from *Sunday Night Cockfights* about 75 feet to cate this blank face just right of a nice-looking seam exiting hueco. The seam looks good, huh? Apparently it's not as ood as it looks.
5 ft. 7 bolts. *Adam Taylor, 2013.*

Sunday Night Cockfights

321

㉗ Butane Junky 5.12a ★★★
Just left of the obvious *Wonkaholic* arête. This slab line will probably shut you down and make you cry. Enjoy.
75 ft. 10 bolts. Troy Davison, 2012.

㉘ Wonkaholic 5.10a ★★★
Just around the corner from *Butane Junky* is this interesting moderate. Climb through four bolts of large plates to reach a ledge where the holds get smaller and tougher to reach. If you know how to fist jam, the end may be a little easier.
55 ft. 7 bolts. Blake Bowling, Steve Kauffman, 1997.

㉙ Old School Chocolate 5.7 ★★
This ascends the dihedral just right of the previous line. Or, leave the gear in the car and climb the excellent bolted line just right, which follows the good part of the crack for 25 feet.
55 ft. Blake Bowling, Steve Kauffman, 1997.

㉚ Hip to the Jive 5.11b ★★★★
A fun and pumpy ride beginning with three bolts of easy crack climbing, then exiting right onto a steepening face filled with shallow pockets and sloping pinches.
60 ft. 7 bolts. Bentley Brackett, 2010.

㉛ Snozzberries 5.12a ★★★
Begin on a flake feature right of *Hip to the Jive*. Carefully climb the feature (which may be reinforced), then scoot right into a hueco. Hide out for a bit, then boulder out to reach the pumpy headwall.
80 ft. 8 bolts. Kevin Quinn, Dan Beck, 2012.

㉜ Naked 5.12a ★★★★
Thirty-five feet right of the two previous bolted lines is this steep, pocketed route.
55 ft. 6 bolts. Blake Bowling, Steve Kauffman 1997. Fully bolted by Greg Martin, 2000?

㉝ Fatman 5.12a ★★★★
Big holds at the start lead to a bouldery crux. Then it eases up to the chains.
60 ft. 5 bolts. Craig Lewis, 2013.

㉞ Grumpalump 5.11d ★★★
Just left of an arête is the type of route you traveled all the way to the Red for: sustained, pumpy climbing on good pockets with a nice finger-stab crux near the middle.
50 ft. 5 bolts. Blake Bowling, Steve Kauffman, 1998.

CHOCOLATE FACTORY

Unknown 12 5.12+ ★★

The rightmost bolt line on this wall follows the blunt arête on very small, crisp crimps.
50 ft. Unknown.

The Wondrous Boat Ride 5.10 ★

From *Grumpalump,* walk down to the trail and follow it beneath a large overhang. Scramble up and find the next crack system, which looks great but doesn't climb as well. Finish at the bolt anchor.
50 ft. Mike Conley, 2009.

The Mad Hatter's Tea Party 5.9 ★★★

Walk right from the *Boat Ride* to the next crack. Pull a tough start to reach a stance, then jam the crack up and over a roof to reach the anchors.
50 ft. Russ Jackson, Scott Hammon, Arnoldo Hutchinson, Frank Waters, Kipp Trummel, 2009.

Unknown

Wobbler 5.11d ★★★★

Begin with a few big moves, then race through sequential pockets and small crimps, with no good rest to be had. Pull a small roof to gain the chains, throwing a huge wobbler if you fall, because you have to do it all over again.
55 ft. 6 bolts. Ray Ellington, Kipp Trummel, 2009.

40 Stalker 5.11d ★★★

Just right of *Wobbler.* Start with the comfort of a pair of good holds, which quickly diminish to relentless crimping up the slightly overhanging face. Grab a good shake at set of slots, then crimp even harder through the obvious crux near the top. As with *Wobbler,* don't blow it going for the chains.
55 ft. 6 bolts. Ray Ellington, Kipp Trummel, 2009.

323

41 One Side Makes You Taller 5.11a ★★★
Begin 10 feet right of *Stalker*, in a short flake. Climb the short section of flake, then exit on large plates and knobs, trending left to a decent rest. Step off the rest and crimp a little harder on smaller edges to reach the chains.
65 ft. 6 bolts. Russ Jackson, 2009.

42 Ballnuts & Brassies or Busted Ankles 5.12a ★★★
This route follows a striking left-angling finger crack beginning midway up the wall. Climb moderate rock to reach an alcove where you will want to get the best protection you can. Pull out into the finger crack and attempt to balance the desire to send with the desire to protect yourself. If you survive the crack, traverse right, then continue up on face holds with decent protection.
70 ft. Dan Beck, 2012.

43 Through the Looking Glass 5.11d ★★★★
The overhanging acute dihedral right of the previous lines. Climb 35 feet of blocks to reach a ledge. Take a deep breath, then dive into relentless stemming and body smearing with difficult placements along the way.
75 ft. Russ Jackson, 2009.

44 Chocolate Factory 44 Project
The line of bolts on the wall left of *Malice*.

45 Malice 5.12c ★★★★★
Right of the acute dihedral is a concave, gold-and-black-streaked wall with two bolted lines that share a start. This is the left line and is a must-do. Climb up a short, easy slab to reach the overhang. Pop over to a large reinforced jug feature (which may possibly be crowbarred off in the future). Reach hard for slopers, then leave the safety of the jugs for some of the best moves and holds at the Red. While recovering after the overhang, switch gears and make a difficult move to gain the vertical wall, then relax to the chains.
60 ft. 8 bolts. Kipp Trummel, 2009.

46 Hookah 5.12a ★★★
Start the same as *Malice*, but move up and right instead of going to the jug feature at the start of the overhang. Pull a tough cross move, then bust up and right past a sloper crux. You're racing the pump clock on this one, so move quick. En with easier climbing near a crack.
60 ft. 8 bolts. Ray Ellington, Kipp Trummel, 2009.

47 Wonderland 5.10b ★★★★
This mixed line is about 50 feet right of *Hookah* and begins with a short crack. Pass a small section of face, then up to a nice-looking thin dihedral. Maneuver around a bulge at the top of the dihedral, then continue up the crack to the chains
80 ft. Russ Jackson, 2009

48 The Juice 5.12a ★★★
This route starts on a boulder 50 feet right of *Wonderland* a is marked by a thin seam near the beginning. Technical and difficult climbing.
55 ft. 6 bolts. Andrew Wheatley, David Lins, 2010.
Equipper: Kipp Trummel.

49 Peach Pit 5.9+ ★★
Squeeze past the boulder next to *The Juice* and look for a large hole in the wall with a chossy boulder inside (the "peach pit"). Climb the overhanging hand crack on the right side to a lichen-covered ledge. Continue straight up through the slab, finding sparse and contrived pro along the way. En at the same tree as *Down the Rabbit Hole*.
90 ft. Nathan Webster, Jesse Amundsen, 2013.

50 Down the Rabbit Hole 5.9 ★★
Walk right from *The Juice* up to a small clearing to locate th crack. Thrash your way up the obvious offwidth until you ca gain the face when the crack narrows. Get a last good piece then run out the dirty slab to the top.
85 ft. Russ Jackson, Scott Brown, 2009.

51 End of the Innocence 5.10b ★★★
This and the following three routes are right of *Down the Rabbit Hole*, at the head of the main trail where it meets the cliff. Walk back down to the trail, then head back toward the fork near the top of the main trail. Look for a large boulder o your left with a trail bordering its left side. Head uphill to me up with three bolted slab climbs. Walk 25 feet left from these lines to a crack at the left end of a roof 10 feet up. Scramble up to reach the crack. Place some small gear above your head, then crank through the initial layback moves to easier climbing above.
80 ft. Phil Wilkes, Art Cammers, 2009.

Michaela Kiersch sends *GoldenTicket*, 5.14c (page 330). Photo: Andy Wickstrom.

End of Innocence

Chocolate River

Sugar Rush 5.10a ★★★

...is is the leftmost of the three bolted slab climbs mentioned ...ove. Great climbing ends at an excellent view from the chains.
... ft. 6 bolts. *Jeff Neal, Russ Jackson, 2009.*

53 Augustus Gloop 5.9 ★★★

Right of *Sugar Rush*. Start on large ledges or traverse in from the right. Fun slabbing on solid stone.
60 ft. 6 bolts. *Jeff Neal, Russ Jackson, Rick Estes, 2009.*

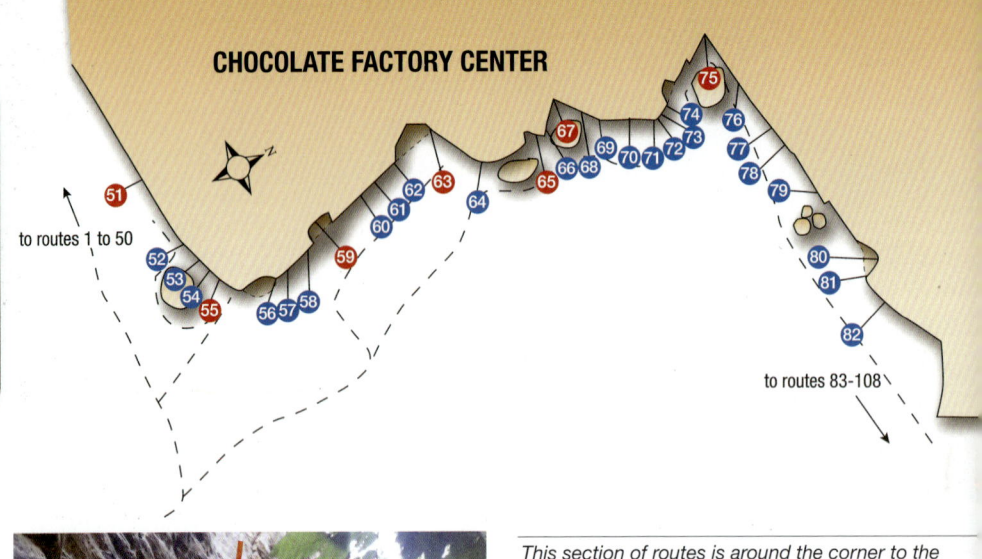

CHOCOLATE FACTORY CENTER

This section of routes is around the corner to the right of the slab lines by Sugar Rush. If you followed the main trail up to the cliff instead of taking the left branch up to Cat's Demise, then continue straight pa the obvious trail on the left near the top of the trail to the next trail on the left, which leads directly up to thi zone — a vertical wall containing several bolted lines.

56 Team Tough on Tour 5.11a ★★★
Climb the blunt arête left of *Keepin' It Real*.
70 ft. *Dave Quinn, 2014.*

57 Keepin' It Real 5.12a ★★★
Twenty feet left of *Squirrelworker* is a nice face climb with hard crimping and an adventurous slab finish.
70 ft. 7 bolts. *Jim Patton, Dustin Stephens, 2014.*

58 Squirrelworker 5.11a ★★★
Do some bulge wrestling to reach the easier face above.
70 ft. 7 bolts. *Dustin Stephens, Scott Curran, 2012.*

59 Peaches and Cream 5.10b ★★★
This crack climb begins with a low roof.
60 ft. *Mike Conley, Ron Snider, 2009.*

60 J-Rat's Back 5.12a ★★★★
The best route in this section. Climb slotted pockets to a distinct crux section after clipping the fourth bolt. Continue a short stretch of overhanging pockets just before the chain
70 ft. 10 bolts. *Dario Ventura, 2007.*

61 Mike Teavee 5.12a ★★★
Fifteen feet right of *J-Rat's Back*. Climb a few bolts to reach tough crux guarding the prominent flake feature, which lea to easier climbing for the rest of the route.
70 ft. 10 bolts. *Kenny Barker, 2007.*

J-Rat's Back

54 Chocolate River 5.9 ★★
Just right of *Augustus Gloop*. Begin with a reachy mantel, then climb a technical, slabby face and finish over a bulge.
50 ft. 5 bolts. *Sam Cervantes, Dave Strawser, 2009.*

55 Meh 5.9+ ★★★
The mixed line just right of *Chocolate River* has been described as "awkward."
50 ft. 4 bolts. *Christian LeBlanc, Karen Clark, 2009.*

Patxi Usobiaga relies on *Pure Imagination*, 5.14c (page 330). Photo: Javier Pérez López-Triviño.

Violet Beauregarde 5.12a ★★

ghtmost line on the vertical wall. Begin on the left edge of a
w hueco. The first bolt is extremely high.
) ft. 10 bolts. *Nate Auk, 2007.*

Easy Pickins 5.8 ★★★

ke on the corner right of *Violet Beauregarde*, which begins
th some chimney-shuffling to reach worthy rock and big
lds. Named after the ripe blackberries just outside the
imney during summer.
5 ft. *Dustin Stephens, Scott Curran, Daniel Hermanns, 2012.*

Willy Wonka 5.11a ★★★

nd this slab line 50 feet right of the previous lines, just off
e main trail. Shorties will have a tough time with the start.
otoe up the slab past several distinct cruxes.
) ft. 8 bolts. *Karen Clark, Joel Handley, Kipp Trummel, 2008.*

Fickelgruber 5.8 ★★★

the right of *Willie Wonka*, climb the obvious chimney and
fwidth. Pull a roof to get 30 feet of hand crack to a ledge.
) ft. *Greg Humburg, Don McGlone, 2009.*

Turd Mountain 5.11d ★★★★

out 20 feet left of *Andy Man Can*, this mountain is a mix of
ybacking and crimping.
) ft. 8 bolts. *Dustin Stephens, 2014.*

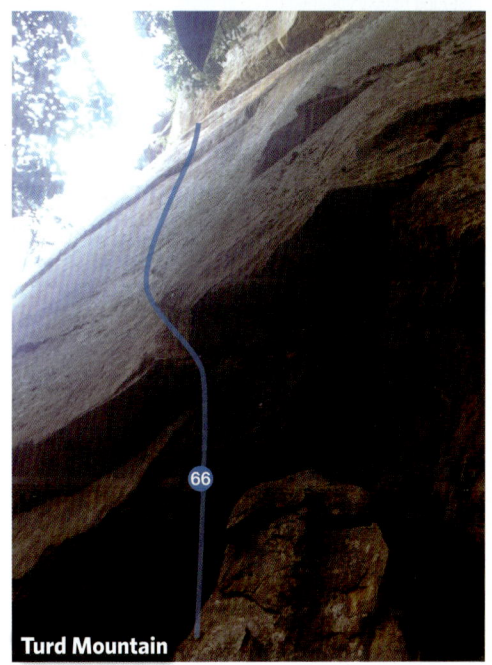

Turd Mountain

MOTHERLODE REGION

Scarlet Scorchdropper

Oompa Loomp

67 The Andy Man Can 5.10d ★★★
Walk right from *Willy Wonka* to locate this crack, situated up and left above a large ledge. Continue through the thin-hands crack in a steep dihedral to a sit-down rest in a large hueco. From the hueco, continue up an offwidth, making use of good face holds to the top.
65 ft. Andy Davis, Rachel Melville, 2007.

68 Scarlet Scorchdropper 5.11c ★★★★
Begin on the same ledge as *The Andy Man Can*. Balancey and technical face climbing with some exciting layback moves. May feel stiff for the grade.
60 ft. 6 bolts. Symon Ardila, Dustin Stephens, 2012.

69 Veruca Salt 5.12a ★★★
Start right of *Scarlet Scorchdropper*, on the same high ledge. Battle duel arêtes and shoot for a jug. Crux out onto the face, then continue up and left around the arête to the chains.
55 ft. 6 bolts. Kipp Trummel, 2008.

70 The Giant Peach 5.11b ★★★
The tall orange face between *Glass Elevator* and *Veruca Salt*. Crimp up to the ledge, take a nap, then launch up the pumpy headwall. Extend or back-clean the first bolt off the ledge to minimize rope drag on the upper wall.
75 ft. 8 bolts. Dustin Stephens, Dan Beck, 2013.

71 The Glass Elevator 5.10d ★★★★
Right of the previous routes is a featured wall hosting four bolted lines. This one is the leftmost. Great movement through small crimps that deliver a decent pump.
65 ft. 6 bolts. Nick Redinger, 2007.

72 Oompa 5.10a ★★★★
Second line from the left. Match and cross through an excellent line of sequential pockets and edges. A great line, but doesn't deliver the pump you'll get from *Loompa*.
55 ft. 6 bolts. Kenny Barker, Julie Smith, 2008.

73 Loompa 5.10c ★★★★★
One of the better 5.10 lines in the Red. Pump up the overhanging wall on incuts and pockets to reach a crux just where you don't want it. Dive for a gigantic horn and chill to the chains.
55 ft. 6 bolts. Kenny Barker, Julie Smith, 2008.

74 Gobstopper 5.12c ★★★
Right of *Loompa* is another bolted line, which begins with a few bolts worth of slightly sandy holds but quickly becomes excellent, with a difficult boulder problem midway. After the fourth bolt, shift to the right side of the arête.
90 ft. 9 bolts. Ricky Parks, Dustin Stephens, 2012.

75 Charlie 5.13b ★★★★
Just around the corner from *Gobstopper* is this striking dihedral, which received a strong attempt by Lynn Hill during the Petzl RocTrip in 2007. After her attempt, the FA team all sent on preplaced gear the same day. The route has since been done several times with gear placed on lead.
75 ft. 1 bolt.
Steve McClure, Mike Doyle, Daniel DuLac, Sonnie Trotter, 2007.

Ashley Schenck, *Loompa*, 5.10c (opposite). Photo: John Wesely.

Pure Imagination

76 Pure Imagination 5.14c ★★★★
Begin just right of *Charlie* on the large boulder. Jonathan's excellent description follows: "After some easy initial climbing, the route fires directly into a very serious boulder problem on thin, very sharp edges, finishing with a wild, all-points-off sideways dyno to a resting jug. From here the route carries on with difficult lock-offs on crimps and pockets to surprisingly frequent, albeit worsening, rests. Toward the top lies the longest section of uninterrupted hard climbing, which finishes with a reachy, shouldery lock-off (redpoint crux). There is a solid rest at the final bolt before you climb a series of pockets and long moves guarding the chains." If that's not enough beta for you, then search for the many videos.

Adam Taylor has bolted a direct start that joins the original route at the overlap. This open project, *Wonka Vision*, adds numerous double-digit boulder problems that will likely put the route in the 5.15 range.

75 ft. 9 bolts. Jonathan Siegrist, 2010. Equipper: Kenny Barker.

77 Chocolate Factory 77 Open Project
The first of two impossible-looking projects between *Pure Imagination* and *Golden Ticket*, bolted by Adam Ondra.

78 Chocolate Factory 78 Open Project
Also bolted by Adam Ondra.

79 The Golden Ticket 5.14c ★★★★★
Fifty feet right of *Pure Imagination* is this striking line, which served many during the 2007 Petzl RocTrip. Climb the slightly overhanging face, passing accuracy stabs and near-double-digit boulder problems, to a brutal showdown at the chains.

75 ft. 9 bolts. Adam Taylor, 2009. Equipper: Kenny Barker.

The Golden Ticket

80 Taffy Puller Open Project
Right of the previous line is a prow-like feature hosting two lines. This is the leftmost, and angles right to take on a short and steep arête, then finishes on a more vertical face.

70 ft. 10 bolts.

81 The Syndicate Open Project
This also takes on the prow feature. Begin beneath the prow then launch up to the right edge of a steep V-shaped hueco. Finish on a long and more vertical face.

65 ft. 8 bolts.

82 Gene Wilder 5.12d ★★★★★
Powerful moves on pockets, then technical face climbing.

75 ft. 8 bolts. Adam Taylor, 2012. Equipper: Dustin Stephens.

83 Strongyloides 5.10a ★★★
Squirm your way into the bowels of this very overhanging crack that offers unique and absorbing moves—beware the calf pump. There is some lichen, but very solid rock makes up for it. Belay your second on top and rap to prevent the rope from sucking your big cams back into the gaping maw when lowering off the lead. Typically wet in spring. Pro to 4 inches, #5 optional.

80 ft. Dustin Stephens, Scott Hammon, 2012.

CHOCOLATE FACTORY

Gene Wilder 82

Robotic Thumb 85

Bathed in Light 5.12a ★★

...om the previous routes, head right along the cliff for a bit. ...rn a corner to find this route, up a gently overhanging face ...d arête.
... ft. 5 bolts. Andrew Wheatley, 2012. Equipper: Wes Allen.

Robotic Thumb 5.10b ★★★★

...irty feet right of *Bathed in Light* and left of a crack is this ...joyable moderate on good sandstone. A nice addition to a ...ff that already contains two of the best 10's in the Red.
... ft. 6 bolts. Andrew and Mike Wheatley, 2012.

Gilgamesh 5.12b ★★★★

...alk 30 feet right from the previous lines down to a wall ...arked by two obvious dinosaur-spine features on the upper ...adwall. This is the better of the two lines and begins with ...me tough moves to reach a ledge 25 feet up. Pull up onto ...e overhanging headwall for great movement on the spine, ...hich fades into a steep and difficult finish.
... ft. 8 bolts. Jimmy Farrell, Andrew Gearing, Dustin ...ephens, 2012.

Enkidu 5.11c ★★★★

...xt route right of *Gilgamesh*. Begin with 20 feet of moderate ...mbing to reach a large hueco. Exit out left and up onto ...e overhanging gold face with a less prominent spine than ...lgamesh yet still great climbing. It's the Red, so again ...pect a tough move going for the chains.
... ft. 8 bolts. Jimmy Farrell, Andrew Gearing, Dustin ...ephens, 2012.

Gilgamesh 86 87

88 Mr. P 5.10b ★★

Twenty-five feet right of *Enkidu* is this route on poor rock. It may have cleaned up a bit, but don't expect a gem.
60 ft. 7 bolts. Michael Albers, 2012.

331

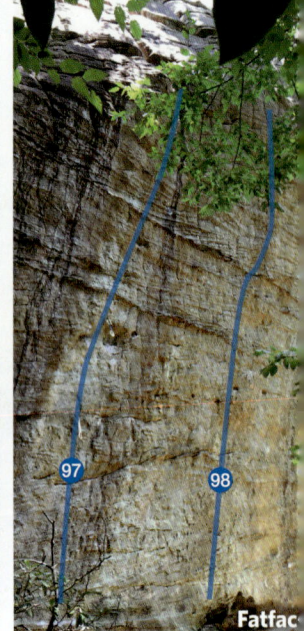

89 Storm Gutter 5.8+ ★★
Using many face holds, climb the crack left of *Breakin' the Law*, finding protection in horizontals. Finish at a pine tree.
95 ft. Dustin Stephens, Dan Beck, 2013.

90 Breakin' the Law 5.10b ★★★★
Starting on a ledge, tackle a roof move to gain access to sweet pockets.
50 ft. 6 bolts. Will Sweeney, Quinn Hill, 2013.

91 Dew Point 5.11b ★★★★
Between *Breakin' the Law* and *Theobroma* is this thin crack system. An offset cam or a good spot protects the start, then climb past long reaches between good holds.
55 ft. Dan Beck, Dustin Stephens, 2013.

92 Theobroma 5.10d ★★★★
Ten feet right of *Dew Point*, this fun route follows pockets to a ledge rest and jugs on the upper wall.
75 ft. 8 bolts. Dustin Stephens, Art Cammers, 2014.

93 Babinski Sign 5.10d ★★★
The arête with a large tree leaning against it. Begin left of the arête, then switch to the right side after the hueco for sidepulls and highsteps to the chains.
90 ft. 10 bolts. Dustin Stephens, Jeremy Kiner, 2012.

94 Crimp My Ride 5.12a ★★
Just right of and around the corner from *Babinski Sign* is a vertical wall with this so-so edging route on the left side. Climb small edges into pockets to reach a no-hands rest on ledge. Make the clip, then take on a difficult crux.
70 ft. 7 bolts. Mike Conley, Ron Snider, 2009.

95 Limbic System 5.11c ★★★★
Start from cheater stones 25 feet right of *Crimp My Ride*. Full-value climbing and high clips will keep you on your toes.
85 ft. 9 bolts. Dustin Stephens, Byron Hempel, 2014.

96 Squeeze Me Macaroni 5.9+ ★★★
The huge corner left of the cave routes. Bring big gear.
80 ft. Carlos Flores, 2012.

97 Fatface 5.13a ★★★
The left of two bolted routes right of the *Squeeze Me* corner.
50 ft. Kyle Fisher, 2012. Equipper: Kevin Wilkinson.

98 Loverface 5.13c ★★★★
Sustained boulder problems that get harder and harder. Cop shake before the showdown at the chains.
50 ft. 5 bolts. Kyle Fisher, 2013. Equipper: Dustin Stephens.

k Summers on *Swedish Fish,* 5.12a (page 335). Photo: John Wesely.

CHOCOLATE FACTORY RIGHT

to routes 1 to 81

Buttercup

Divine Punishment

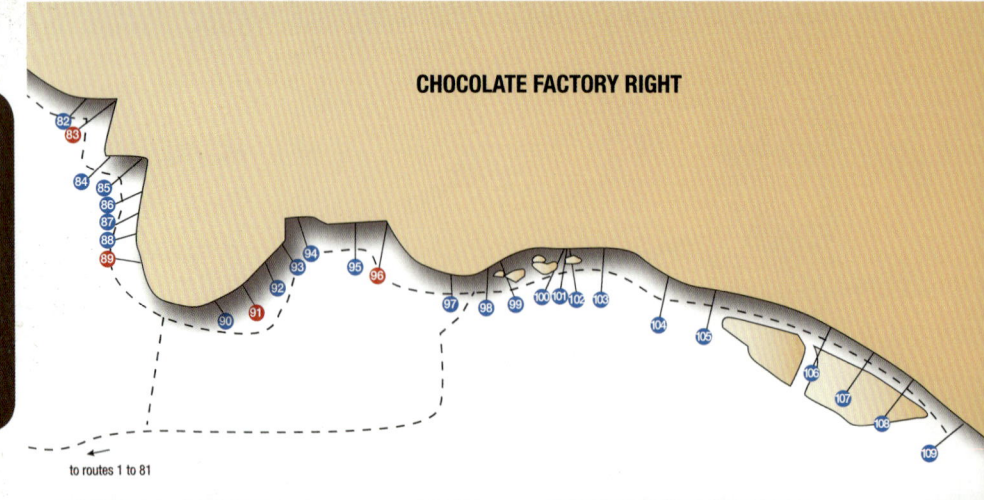

99 Buttercup 5.13c ★★★★★
A gem. Bouldery, long, pumpy, and technical.
75 ft. Kevin Wilkinson, Blake Bowling, 2012.

100 Another Blake Route 5.12d ★★★
This and the next two routes share a start. For this one, break left to skirt the right edge of a gigantic hueco 25 feet up.
75 ft. 8 bolts. Blake Bowling, 2011.

101 Molten 5.13b ★★★
Same start as for *ABR*, but head up and right on the center line of bolts. Powerful moves with good rests along the way.
80 ft. Kevin Wilkinson, 2012.

102 Divine Punishment 5.13b ★★★★
Start as for the previous lines but immediately break hard right. A difficult start leads to sustained pumping up the steep face.
95 ft. Adam Taylor, 2012. Equipper: Dario Ventura.

103 Silky Smooth 5.13c ★★★★
Thirty feet right of the previous lines is another steep route beginning with a jump to a large mouth 10 feet up. Move straight up the overhanging, featured face to the chains.
75 ft. 10 bolts. Unknown. Equipper: Kevin Wilkinson.

...lake Bowling is *Silky Smooth*, 5.13c (opposite). Photo: Edwin Teran.

Atomic Fireballs 5.13d ★★★★
This is the last route before heading around the cave to *Death by Chocolate*. Big moves on crimps and pinches just to get to the high spice.
…5 ft. 9 bolts. Adam Taylor, 2013. Equipper: Kevin Wilkinson.

Death by Chocolate 5.13a ★★★★
Named after Blake Bowling pulled a hold off into his face, got knocked out, and took a very long upside-down fall. He woke up being lowered to the ground while bleeding from the forehead and nose. The route has since cleaned up. Long and pumpy, with enough cruxes to keep it interesting.
…0 ft. Kevin Wilkinson, 2012.

Bittersweet 5.13c ★★★★
The next line right of *Death by Chocolate* starts behind a large boulder. A technical route that offers a few powerful moves and long reaches.
…evin Wilkinson, 2012.

Leche del Toro 5.13b ★
Not every route can be four stars. Bouldery and techy with some … uh … reinforcement.
…0 ft. 13 bolts. Adam Taylor, 2013.

Chocolate Factory 108 Project
This is between *Leche* and *Swedish Fish*.

109 Swedish Fish 5.12a ★★★★★
The rightmost line on the wall, and one of the best of the grade. It has everything you want in a 12 at the Red.
100 ft. 14 bolts. Andrew Wheatley, 2012.

335

SOUTHERN OUTLYING CLIFFS

This short chapter features two small cliffs in the southwest section of the RRG, but not part of either the PMRP or Motherlode area. Mount Olive Rock lie west off KY 52 past Lago Linda's, while th Oasis is a few miles west of Torrent Falls.

MOUNT OLIVE ROCK

37.646
-83.797

4 routes

.14
.13
.12
.11
.10
.9
.8
.7
≤.6

Although this small roadside area has only four routes, all are worth doing, especially if you want to escape the crowds. *South Side of the Sky* is a must-do for any crack climber. Save it for a wet day: due to the massive capstone roof, it never sees a drop of rain.

Approach: This crag sits beyond the turno from KY 498 to the Motherlode. Drive two mile down KY 498 past the Motherlode turnoff a T-intersection. Turn right on KY 52 and driv 2.8 miles to a small pulloff on the right betwee guardrails. Walk down the road 150 feet and loc for an obvious left-facing dihedral on the cliff your left. This is *South Side of the Sky*.

Conditions: Beware of poison ivy.

❶ South Central 5.11a ★★
Climb the line of obvious pockets around the corner 20 feet right of *South Side of the Sky* to chain anchors.
50 ft. 6 bolts. Chris Snyder, 1996

❷ South Side of the Sky 5.11a ★★★★★
Climb the obvious, thin, left-facing dihedral to anchors unde the roof. Watch for poison ivy around the anchors.
60 ft. Martin Hackworth, Ron Martin, 1986

❸ Sprout's Climb 5.10c ★★★
This route ascends the dihedral 50 feet left of *South Side of t. Sky*. Climb the dihedral, then continue out the roof. Pull aroun the lip, then continue up to the anchors above *Palm Friction*.
50 ft. Tom Fyffe, Matt Flach, 1997

❹ Palm Friction 5.10a ★★
Climb the face 15 feet left of *Sprout's Climb*. Be careful of t long runout between the second and third bolts. The climbi is relatively easy in that section, but the fall would be close to a grounder.
65 ft. 6 bolts. Kellyn Gorder, Barry Brolley, 1997

South Side of the Sky ❷

THE OASIS

37.7269
-83.7192

15 min / 5 min

5 routes
.14
.13
.12
.11
.10
.9
.8
.7
≤.6

This small, obscure sport crag offers a few worthwhile lines. *Paddy O'Keefe's Walking Shoes* is the best, with precise pocket stabbing on bullet sandstone, finishing with fun moves on an overhanging runout. With slopey, powerful moves, *Finnegan's Ladder* was for many years known as "the Red's Shortest Climb," but now you can find many shorties in Muir Valley.

Approach: From Miguel's Pizza, drive about seven miles south on KY 11 to the town of Zachariah, just before the Lee County line. Turn right onto 1036 and drive 2.0 miles. Just after a fenced-in oil-drilling yard, you'll see Big Bend Road. Drive past this for 0.1 miles until you see the Sun Oil parking lot to your right. Depending on the condition of the road and the quality of your 4WD vehicle, you can either park here or head down the steep gravel road that descends from the parking lot. Walk or drive this road 0.4 miles until you see an obvious cliff to your right. Head up a swampy drainage to the wall.

Conditions: This wall bakes in the sun after 2 PM, so avoid it in summer. The quality of rock on the middle two routes is poor, but better on the sides.

Tiger Swallowtail. Photo: Matt Looby.

① **Finnegan's Ladder** 5.11b ★★★★
Walk to the left side of the wall to locate this short but powerful line. Climb the face via pinches and slopers to reach anchors 25 feet up. Quite good, albeit really short.
25 ft. 3 bolts. *Mike Riegert, 1998*

② **Buzz** 5.11b ★★
Move back right and over the swampy drainage to the next bolted line on the middle section of the cliff. Climb the steep face via pockets and edges with a big move before the anchors.
50 ft. 5 bolts. *Neal Strickland, 1998*

③ **Hum** 5.11c ★★★
Step right a few feet to the next line, which climbs similarly. Beware of bats and wasps in the huecos and on ledges.
50 ft. 5 bolts. *Mike Riegert, 1998*

④ **Paddy O'Keefe's Walking Shoes** 5.11d ★★★★
This route alone will make your visit worthwhile. Walk right about 30 feet to the next line, which begins with an obvious section of pockets. Boulder through the pockets, then pull up onto the face. Creep over to a steep section, then gun for the anchors.
50 ft. 5 bolts. *Mike Riegert, Neal Strickland, 1998*

⑤ **Manzanita** 5.12b ★
Just right of the previous line is this long endurance route. Climb to the anchors, being careful of loose rock along the way. The more this cleans up the better it is getting.
85 ft. 9 bolts. *Mike Riegert, 1998*

OUTLYING CLIFFS

Be a climber.

Where you find joy: **pursue it.**
Where you see others finding joy: **encourage it.**
Whatever makes you a climber: **do it.**

These are words. See our actions at beaclimber.com

TRANGO

GRADED LIST OF SPORT CLIMBS

Projects

☐ Hammerhead	★★★★	64
☐ Iron Mike	★★★★	249
☐ What About Bob 17	★★★★	239
☐ Bottles Up	★★★	76
☐ Crossroads Crack	★★★	165
☐ G.I. Joe	★★★	299
☐ Hirsute	★★★	238
☐ LOMM	★★★	179
☐ Marley 44	★★★	272
☐ Marley 46	★★★	273
☐ Marley 51	★★★	273
☐ Reasonable Doubt	★★★	64
☐ Room With a View	★★★	299
☐ Running in Place	★★★	238
☐ Seam Project	★★★	246
☐ Slackjaw Willie	★★★	64
☐ Van der Waals Goo	★★★	96
☐ Velo 13	★★★	195
☐ Marley 50	★★	273
☐ Three-Toed Sloth	★★	95
☐ Avast Ye		196
☐ Bear's Den 29		298
☐ Bear's Den 30		298
☐ Black Hoof		114
☐ Chocolate Factory 13		320
☐ Chocolate Factory 44		324
☐ Chocolate Factory 5		319
☐ Chocolate Factory 77		330
☐ Chocolate Factory 78		330
☐ Closed Project		218
☐ Dagon		139
☐ Dustopian Left		139
☐ Fall of the Anticlimber		306
☐ Gallery 35		218
☐ Gold Star Project		167
☐ Ivory Tower 4		131
☐ Ivory Tower 5		131
☐ Ivory Tower 7		131
☐ Keelhaul		196
☐ Marley 52		273
☐ Megacave 1		228
☐ Megacave 2		228
☐ Megacave 3		228
☐ Megacave 5		228
☐ Megacave 7		229
☐ New Zoo 31		64
☐ Poop Deck		196
☐ Quaffed Up		79

☐ Taffy Puller		330
☐ Tectonic 5		134
☐ The Galaxy Project		283
☐ The Odyssey		231
☐ The Sharma Project		286
☐ The Syndicate		330
☐ Velo 11		194
☐ Weak Sauce		214
☐ Zoo 7		61

5.14d

☐ Southern Smoke Direct	★★★★★	269
☐ Your Heaven, My Hell	★★★★	269

5.14c

☐ Fifty Words for Pump	★★★★★	269
☐ Lucifer	★★★★★	234
☐ Southern Smoke	★★★★★	269
☐ The Golden Ticket	★★★★★	330
☐ Twenty-Four Karats	★★★★★	167
☐ Pure Imagination	★★★★	330

5.14b

☐ The Death Star	★★★★	184
☐ The Shocker	★★★★	214
☐ Zookeeper	★★★★	61
☐ Mr. Sandy		306

5.14a

☐ God's Own Stone	★★★★★	167
☐ Omaha Beach	★★★★★	313
☐ Thanatopsis	★★★★★	307
☐ Transworld Depravity	★★★★★	310
☐ 100 Ounces of Gold	★★★★	167
☐ Bearly There	★★★★	302
☐ Cherry Red	★★★★	120
☐ The Nothing	★★★	283

5.13d

☐ Swingline	★★★★★	187
☐ True Love	★★★★★	168
☐ Ultra Perm	★★★★★	269
☐ Last of the Bohicans	★★★★	311
☐ Super Charger	★★★★	281
☐ Thug Life	★★★★	284
☐ White Man's Shuffle	★★★★	309
☐ Sugar Magnolia	★★★	265

5.13c

☐ Black Gold	★★★★★	167
☐ Buttercup	★★★★★	334
☐ Kaleidoscope	★★★★★	284
☐ The Madness	★★★★★	313
☐ Angry Birds	★★★★	284
☐ Eternal Fire	★★★★	319

☐ Jethro Bodean	★★★★	64
☐ Loverface	★★★★	332
☐ Pushin' Up Daisies	★★★★	313
☐ Slow Stepper	★★★★	64
☐ White Man's Overbite	★★★★	309

5.13b

☐ Cat's Demise	★★★★★	320
☐ Cut Throat	★★★★★	307
☐ Dracula '04	★★★★★	234
☐ Elephant Man	★★★★★	187
☐ Flour Power	★★★★★	311
☐ Golden Boy	★★★★★	167
☐ The Return of Darth Moll	★★★★★	184
☐ BOHICA	★★★★	310
☐ Dirty, Smelly Hippie	★★★★	281
☐ Drunken Master	★★★★	77
☐ Falls City	★★★★	75
☐ Golden Touch	★★★★	305
☐ No Redemption	★★★★	265
☐ Paradise Regained	★★★★	236
☐ Pay the Devil	★★★★	198
☐ Shiva	★★★★	93
☐ Skywalker	★★★★	179
☐ Squirrels Gone Wild	★★★★	299
☐ Straight Outta Campton	★★★★	187
☐ Swine Flew	★★★★	250
☐ Take That, Katie Brown	★★★★	307
☐ The Castle Has Fallen	★★★★	234
☐ Absolute Zero	★★★	282
☐ Big Burley	★★★	184
☐ Dead but Dreaming	★★★	139
☐ Gecko Circus	★★★	169
☐ Jedi Mind Trick	★★★	184
☐ JFR	★★★	228
☐ Non Starter	★★★	187
☐ Paranoia	★★★	68
☐ Song of Solomon	★★★	131
☐ Speedy Gonzales	★★★	62
☐ The Wheel of Time	★★★	49
☐ Bourbon Barrel Shot Gun	★★	77
☐ Buck Eye	★★	313
☐ El Encuentro	★★	272
☐ MILF Money	★★	266
☐ Quantum Narcissist	★★	189

5.13a

☐ Convicted	★★★★★	315
☐ Evil Emperor	★★★★★	183
☐ Paradise Lost	★★★★★	236
☐ Prometheus Unbound	★★★★★	121

SPORT GRADED LIST

Route	Rating	Page
☐ Rock the Casbah	★★★★★	130
☐ Rules of Engagement	★★★★★	299
☐ Snooker	★★★★★	309
☐ The Force	★★★★★	184
☐ Beer Belly	★★★★	281
☐ Better Eat Yo' Wheatlies	★★★★	179
☐ Brilliant Orange	★★★★	168
☐ Bundle of Joy	★★★★	106
☐ Forty Ounces of Justice	★★★★	313
☐ Geronimo	★★★★	130
☐ Hoofmaker	★★★★	314
☐ Kya	★★★★	114
☐ Medicine Man	★★★★	179
☐ Name Dropper	★★★★	120
☐ Skin Boat	★★★★	314
☐ Spank	★★★★	282
☐ Zendebad	★★★★	102
☐ Zero Dark Fiddy	★★★★	296
☐ A Farewell to Arms	★★★	92
☐ All That Twitters	★★★	299
☐ Amyloid Plaque	★★★	289
☐ Calm Like a Bomb	★★★	216
☐ Chunnel	★★★	58
☐ Easy Rider	★★★	284
☐ El Patron	★★★	129
☐ Fatface	★★★	332
☐ Pimp Juice	★★★	284
☐ Red-Eye Flight	★★★	273
☐ Second Nature	★★★	188
☐ Slampiece BAM!	★★★	266
☐ Taste the Raibow	★★★	227
☐ Blue Jacket	★★	114
☐ Blue Sunday	★★	120
☐ Starfish and Coffee	★★	92
☐ Bareback	★	321
☐ Cosmic Sausage	★	309

5.13
Route	Rating	Page
☐ Davy Jones' Locker Direct	★★★	196
☐ The Tribute	★★	217

5.12+
Route	Rating	Page
☐ Unknown 12	★★	323

5.12d
Route	Rating	Page
☐ 8 Ball	★★★★★	307
☐ Dog Bites & Fist Fights	★★★★★	179
☐ Gene Wilder	★★★★★	330
☐ Jesus Wept	★★★★★	121
☐ Team Wilson	★★★★★	314
☐ Triple Sec	★★★★★	121
☐ Code Red	★★★★	240
☐ Darkness Falls	★★★★	79
☐ Fiat Lux	★★★★	179
☐ Harvest	★★★★	314
☐ Leave It to Beavis	★★★★	313

Route	Rating	Page
☐ Peace Frog	★★★★	120
☐ Racer X	★★★★	69
☐ Shanghai	★★★★	184
☐ Subman	★★★★	314
☐ Tapeworm	★★★★	93
☐ Tuna Town	★★★★	314
☐ Tuskan Raider	★★★★	187
☐ Wicked Games	★★★★	52
☐ Zen and the Art of Masturbation	★★★★	214
☐ Arachnophobia	★★★	286
☐ Better Than Homemade	★★★	77
☐ Brokeback Finger	★★★	298
☐ Crime Time	★★★	314
☐ Cruxifixion	★★★	123
☐ Dustopian	★★★	139
☐ Inches and Fractions	★★★	298
☐ Itchy and Scratchy	★★★	298
☐ Mind Meld	★★★	184
☐ Phantom Menace	★★★	187
☐ Reticent	★★★	270
☐ Skinny Love	★★★	269
☐ Slam Dunk	★★★	229
☐ The Flux Capacitor	★★★	314
☐ Tie One On	★★★	75
☐ Urban Voodoo	★★★	104
☐ American Graffiti	★★	214
☐ Hoosier Boys	★	120
☐ Pile Driver	★	227
☐ Mad Porter's Disease		74

5.12c
Route	Rating	Page
☐ Cell Block Six	★★★★★	93
☐ Demon Seed	★★★★★	265
☐ Hellraiser	★★★★★	236
☐ Malice	★★★★★	324
☐ Reload	★★★★★	90
☐ Stain	★★★★★	305
☐ Steelworker	★★★★★	69
☐ Wild Gift	★★★★★	57
☐ Afros, Macks, and Zodiacs	★★★★	203
☐ Astrodog	★★★★	131
☐ Banksy	★★★★	213
☐ Belly of the Beast	★★★★	230
☐ Blank Canvas	★★★★	213
☐ Blood Bath	★★★★	270
☐ Blowin' Loadz	★★★★	179
☐ Bush League	★★★★	179
☐ Eager Beaver	★★★★	64
☐ Earth-Bound Misfit	★★★★	249
☐ False Positive	★★★★	307
☐ Hang Over	★★★★	78
☐ Heart-Shaped Box	★★★★	306
☐ Herd Mentality	★★★★	176
☐ Honey Badger	★★★★	63

Route	Rating	Page
☐ Iron Lung	★★★★	8
☐ Mirage	★★★★	10
☐ Mosaic	★★★★	21
☐ One Love	★★★★	27
☐ Resurrection	★★★★	31
☐ Science Friction	★★★★	5
☐ Space Junk	★★★★	17
☐ Stomp U Out	★★★★	16
☐ The Crucible	★★★★	9
☐ The Dainty Butterfly	★★★★	32
☐ The Departure	★★★★	18
☐ The Hunt for Red's October	★★★★	10
☐ The Pessimist	★★★★	12
☐ The Return of Frank Byron	★★★★	20
☐ Ticks and Beer	★★★★	30
☐ Vortex	★★★★	9
☐ Water Music	★★★★	12
☐ Where's the Beef?	★★★★	27
☐ Wookie Love Nest	★★★★	18
☐ 2-Fold	★★★	32
☐ Dirty Sanchez	★★★	18
☐ Drop the Hammer	★★★	11
☐ Fungus Among Us	★★★	27
☐ Gobstopper	★★★	32
☐ Gorilla	★★★	9
☐ Hell or High Water	★★★	30
☐ Hot for Teacher	★★★	30
☐ Into the Mystic	★★★	6
☐ Irony of Twisted Fate	★★★	6
☐ Mr. Roarke	★★★	16
☐ Rostam	★★★	10
☐ Silent Killer	★★★	13
☐ So Long Mr. Petey	★★★	10
☐ Stone Pipe	★★★	26
☐ The Reacharound	★★★	30
☐ To Julie, With Love	★★★	20
☐ Two Cups of Silly	★★★	7
☐ Contact High	★★	26
☐ Granny Panties	★★	26
☐ Thunder	★★	21
☐ Psychopathy	★	17
☐ Torrential	★	6
☐ Twinkie's Little Sister	★	31
☐ Hydro Shock		6
☐ Impossible Choss		6
☐ Throne of Lies		28

5.12b
Route	Rating	Page
☐ Abiyoyo	★★★★★	10
☐ Sail	★★★★★	19
☐ Samurai	★★★★★	25
☐ Swahili Slang	★★★★★	30
☐ Ale-8-One	★★★★	3
☐ American Dream	★★★★	18

SPORT GRADED LIST

Route	Stars	Page
☐ Bear Belly	★★★★	300
☐ Big Money Grip	★★★★	68
☐ Blue Collar	★★★★	123
☐ Blue-Eyed HonkeyJesus	★★★★	176
☐ Brownian Motion	★★★★	179
☐ Buff the Wood	★★★★	305
☐ Bullfighter	★★★★	90
☐ Colt 45	★★★★	259
☐ Cosmic Trigger	★★★★	125
☐ Deep Six	★★★★	50
☐ Duputyren's Release	★★★★	240
☐ False Idol	★★★★	227
☐ Far From God	★★★★	227
☐ Fresh Baked	★★★★	181
☐ Galunlati	★★★★	106
☐ Gilgamesh	★★★★	331
☐ Guernica	★★★★	218
☐ Iniquity	★★★★	93
☐ Jersey Connection	★★★★	54
☐ Loaded for Bear	★★★★	300
☐ Mis-Conception	★★★★	249
☐ Pimptastic	★★★★	203
☐ Rocket Dog	★★★★	315
☐ Signed in Blood	★★★★	163
☐ Sparkling Jackass	★★★★	62
☐ Super Best Friends	★★★★	105
☐ Technical Difficulties	★★★★	274
☐ Tic-Tac-Toe	★★★★	56
☐ Unbearable	★★★★	301
☐ Yoko Ono	★★★★	205
☐ AfroSquad	★★★	203
☐ Babyface	★★★	92
☐ Ball and Chain	★★★	134
☐ Barbed Wire	★★★	250
☐ Bleak December	★★★	320
☐ Bleed Like Me	★★★	220
☐ Cindy Groms	★★★	298
☐ Cold Hard Bitch	★★★	256
☐ Cottonmouth	★★★	134
☐ Davy Jones' Locker	★★★	197
☐ Eye of the Tigger	★★★	298
☐ Flesh Wound	★★★	90
☐ Gild the Lily	★★★	238
☐ Godbolt	★★★	298
☐ High Life	★★★	78
☐ Hippy Wick	★★★	273
☐ Imagine There's No Heaven	★★★	227
☐ Kentucky Grape Vine	★★★	320
☐ Knees and Toes	★★★	281
☐ Liquid Courage	★★★	78
☐ Peel It Back	★★★	274
☐ Pimpto-Bismol	★★★	203
☐ Purdy Mouth	★★★	306

Route	Stars	Page
☐ Sidewinder	★★★	62
☐ So Low	★★★	307
☐ Storming the Beech	★★★	198
☐ Stretcherous	★★★	119
☐ Strevels Gets in Shape	★★★	56
☐ Summer Solstice	★★★	195
☐ Summer Sunshine	★★★	106
☐ Sun's Out, Guns Out	★★★	168
☐ Techno Destructo	★★★	307
☐ The Low Easy One	★★★	315
☐ The Sauce	★★★	313
☐ The Stallion	★★★	131
☐ The Verdict	★★★	315
☐ Tumble Dry Low	★★★	239
☐ Watching the World Burn	★★★	139
☐ Whipper Snapper	★★★	280
☐ Headwall	★★	53
☐ In Red We Trust	★★	295
☐ Irreverent C	★★	227
☐ Knot Sure	★★	218
☐ Outbreak	★★	210
☐ Perros Grande	★★	139
☐ Sarahinity	★★	320
☐ Seeker	★★	50
☐ The Chronic	★★	305
☐ Zone of Silence	★★	170
☐ Aviary	★	62
☐ Beer Trailer	★	76
☐ DreadLocked	★	263
☐ Manzanita	★	337
☐ Sister Catherine the Conqueror	★	259
☐ Damascus		167
5.12a		
☐ Bare Metal Teen	★★★★★	68
☐ Check Your Grip	★★★★★	280
☐ Dogleg	★★★★★	265
☐ Hippocrite	★★★★★	62
☐ Ro Shampo	★★★★★	56
☐ 72-Hour Energy	★★★★	296
☐ Afternoon Buzz	★★★★	78
☐ Break the Scene	★★★★	217
☐ Chainsaw Massacre	★★★★	315
☐ Cheetah	★★★★	129
☐ Child of the Earth	★★★★	88
☐ Continental	★★★★	150
☐ Delicatessen	★★★★	105
☐ Fatman	★★★★	322
☐ Glide	★★★★	95
☐ Gluttony	★★★★	234
☐ Golden Brown	★★★★	179
☐ Golden Road	★★★★	86
☐ Golden Shower	★★★★	170
☐ Grippy Green	★★★★	184

Route	Stars	Page
☐ GSW	★★★★	240
☐ Hakuna Matata	★★★★	279
☐ Hood Luck	★★★★	163
☐ Icebreaker	★★★★	319
☐ J-Rat's Back	★★★★	326
☐ Jingus Khan	★★★★	165
☐ Kick Me in the Jimmie	★★★★	315
☐ Little Teapot	★★★★	230
☐ Lobster Claw	★★★★	243
☐ Magnum Opus	★★★★	104
☐ Massive Attack	★★★★	211
☐ Morning Wood	★★★★	75
☐ Naked	★★★★	322
☐ Naked Lunch	★★★★	279
☐ Pine	★★★★	57
☐ Primus Noctum	★★★★	280
☐ Ring of Fire	★★★★	128
☐ Routeburglar	★★★★	299
☐ Scar Tissue	★★★★	61
☐ Specific Gravity	★★★★	76
☐ Starry Night	★★★★	212
☐ Stay the Hand	★★★★	54
☐ Supafly	★★★★	176
☐ Suppress the Rage	★★★★	152
☐ Swallow the Hollow	★★★★	165
☐ Tacit	★★★★	270
☐ There's a Bad Moon...	★★★★	205
☐ Trouble in Paradise	★★★★	97
☐ Us and Them	★★★★	71
☐ Way Up Yonder	★★★★	57
☐ Wearing Out My Welcome	★★★★	245
☐ Wet Your Whistle	★★★★	78
☐ Wildfire	★★★★	210
☐ A Cat Amongst the Pigeons	★★★	194
☐ Apadana	★★★	102
☐ Archangel	★★★	265
☐ Ball Scratcher	★★★	306
☐ Barren Gold	★★★	296
☐ Beef Stick	★★★	109
☐ Bettavul Pipeline	★★★	272
☐ Burlier's Bane	★★★	315
☐ Butane Junky	★★★	322
☐ Cork Eye	★★★	243
☐ Crimps and Bloods	★★★	279
☐ Dagobah	★★★	182
☐ Das Krue	★★★	289
☐ Death Wish	★★★	280
☐ Dr. Synchro	★★★	240
☐ Espresso	★★★	152
☐ Evening Wood	★★★	75
☐ Extra Backup	★★★	279
☐ Eyeball Chaw	★★★	272
☐ Flying Serpents	★★★	97

Route	Stars	Page
Freakin' Deacon	★★★	91
Gold Nugget	★★★	170
Green Machine	★★★	273
Helluva Caucasian	★★★	256
Hookah	★★★	324
Ivory Poacher	★★★	273
Keepin' It Real	★★★	326
King Cobra	★★★	259
Labor Day Weekend	★★★	222
Legalize It	★★★	160
Lolita	★★★	101
Mama Benson	★★★	184
Marmight	★★★	204
Mike Teavee	★★★	326
OG Pimp Juice	★★★	203
Ohio Arts	★★★	113
Posse Whipped	★★★	118
Praestantissimum	★★★	187
Praying Mantis	★★★	162
Route 22	★★★	266
Sam Krieg Will Bolt Anything	★★★	315
Sendex 147	★★★	63
Shootin' Hot Hugs	★★★	319
Sluts Are Cool	★★★	75
Snozzberries	★★★	322
Sons of Perdition	★★★	63
Tabernacle	★★★	124
Techulicous	★★★	184
The Fray Train	★★★	79
The Juice	★★★	324
Unknown 12	★★★	48
Veruca Salt	★★★	328
Yosemite Sam	★★★	250
Bathed in Light	★★	331
Crimp My Ride	★★	332
Double Stuff	★★	108
Go Home Yankee	★★	245
Paladine	★★	102
The Bulge	★★	47
The Frayed Ends of Sanity	★★	50
Violet Beauregarde	★★	327
Jeff's Boneyard Project	★	95
Scrambled Porn	★	316
Black Plague		167
Bow to Stern		197
Crumblies		230
Sam and Terry's Line		66

5.12

Route	Stars	Page
Far Side TR	★★★	188

5.12-

Route	Stars	Page
Beechcomber	★★★	197

5.11+

Route	Stars	Page
Mentor	★★	263

5.11d

Route	Stars	Page
Don't Call It a Comeback	★★★★★	205
The Return of Chris Snyder	★★★★★	57
Action Potential	★★★★	65
All In	★★★★	306
Birth of a Legend	★★★★	205
Black Pearl	★★★★	198
Buddha Hole	★★★★	176
Ethics Police	★★★★	174
Everything That Rises ...	★★★★	100
Evil Eye	★★★★	162
Foot Jive	★★★★	163
Gold Rush	★★★★	216
Guilty Pleasure	★★★★	276
Head and Shoulders	★★★★	281
Hemisfear	★★★★	53
Hippie Speed Ball	★★★★	162
Horn	★★★★	270
June Bug	★★★★	165
Manifest Destiny	★★★★	104
Night Foxx	★★★★	144
Paddy O'Keefe's Walking Shoes	★★★★	337
Papa Love Jugs	★★★★	188
Recoil	★★★★	69
Red Shift	★★★★	169
Seek the Truth	★★★★	73
Tecumseh's Curse	★★★★	114
Tree Hugger	★★★★	93
Turd Mountain	★★★★	327
Velvet	★★★★	270
Velvet Revolution	★★★★	152
Welcomed Guest	★★★★	245
Wobbler	★★★★	323
You Take Sally	★★★★	258
All Gold Everything	★★★	170
Amish Whoopie Cushion	★★★	163
ATM	★★★	189
Avalanche Run	★★★	210
Bear Down	★★★	300
Beer-Thirty	★★★	78
Bromance	★★★	301
Brouwer Power	★★★	176
Climb Aboard	★★★	196
Collision Damage	★★★	230
Coming-Out Party	★★★	227
Crack the Whip	★★★	225
Deep Fried	★★★	181
Double Century	★★★	195
Earthsurfer	★★★	115
East of Eden	★★★	101
Flush	★★★	270
Fresh Off the Bone	★★★	254
Goblins in My Mind	★★★	65
Grumpalump	★★★	32
Highway Turtle	★★★	17
Immaculate Deception	★★★	12
Levitation	★★★	27
My Name is Earl	★★★	24
No Fluff	★★★	16
Outlaw Justice	★★★	25
Pongosapien	★★★	23
Rug Muncher	★★★	30
Scissors	★★★	5
Search and Seizure	★★★	20
Shadow Enhancement	★★★	29
Sheet Rock	★★★	14
Sport for Brains	★★★	7
Stalker	★★★	32
Stella	★★★	31
Sweet Tater	★★★	9
Team Wilander	★★★	24
The Agile Process	★★★	13
The Handout	★★★	14
The Happy Fisherman	★★★	11
The Stranger	★★★	10
Tongue-Punch	★★★	18
Wake and Bake	★★★	16
Who Is Who?	★★★	22
Slut Men	★★	27
The Adventure	★★	5
The Last Slow Draw	★★	9
Who Knows?	★★	22
Wreaking Havoc	★★	5
Beeper		26
Hoosier Buddies		7
My How Things Have Changed		7
Onaconaronni		7
Sand		5
The Business		28

5.11c

Route	Stars	Page
Banshee	★★★★★	10
Crown of Thorns	★★★★★	17
No Place Like Home	★★★★★	4
10-Pound Tumor	★★★★	20
Arêterection	★★★★	12
Bangers and Mash	★★★★	9
Battery Life	★★★★	10
Breakneck Speed	★★★★	19
Bring Up the Bodies	★★★★	23
Centerfire	★★★★	
Crimpin' Ain't Easy	★★★★	
Crosley	★★★★	20
Disappearer	★★★★	5
Enkidu	★★★★	31
Explanatory Gap	★★★★	17
Limbic System	★★★★	

SPORT GRADED LIST

Route	Stars	Page
Lip Service	★★★★	109
Noo-tha	★★★★	114
October Sky	★★★★	163
Out for Justice	★★★★	50
Psyberpunk	★★★★	125
Pyrite	★★★★	173
Sacred Stones	★★★★	88
Scarlet Scorchdropper	★★★★	328
Severn Bore	★★★★	164
Smokin' on Kesha	★★★★	177
Special Boy	★★★★	232
Spicer	★★★★	301
Spirit Fingers	★★★★	280
The Unbearable Lightness...	★★★★	100
All the Pretty Horses	★★★	100
Apotheosis Denied	★★★	117
Arête-Headed Stranger	★★★	302
BabaBooey	★★★	63
Batten Down the Hatches	★★★	198
Bessie	★★★	257
Big Sinkin' Breakdown	★★★	280
Bowling Pain	★★★	241
Breathe Right	★★★	306
Cannabis Love Generator	★★★	162
Chucklehead	★★★	259
Conscription	★★★	210
Count Dookku	★★★	184
Crucify Me	★★★	226
Different Strokes	★★★	214
Flying Monkeys	★★★	46
Giblets	★★★	287
Happy Feet	★★★	163
Here Comes Palin	★★★	302
Hum	★★★	337
Jolly Roger	★★★	198
Korsakoff Syndrome	★★★	78
Levi Yoder	★★★	300
Lynx Jinx	★★★	61
Mas Choss	★★★	266
Midlife Crisis	★★★	119
Misfire	★★★	69
Much Ado About Nothing	★★★	98
One-Zero-Six	★★★	181
Oz	★★★	46
Parasite	★★★	118
PBR Street Gang	★★★	78
Picador	★★★	90
Sam's Boy Toy	★★★	295
Sex Show	★★★	71
Situational Awareness	★★★	67
Stirrin' the Grits	★★★	232
Teeter Totter	★★★	225
The Fury	★★★	101
The Love Song of J. Alfred...	★★★	101
Tight Lipped 2	★★★	254
Ultrathon	★★★	272
Undesirable	★★★	317
Who Pooped in the Park?	★★★	100
A Confederacy of Dunces	★★	101
Dark City	★★	67
David and Goliath	★★	170
Digitalgia	★★	188
Down by Law	★★	50
Hagis, Neeps and Tatties	★★	97
Mentee	★★	263
One-Eyed Willy Up the Back	★★	305
Red Tag Rape	★★	164
Stephanie's Cabaret	★★	222
Subtle Thievery	★★	210
The Sound	★★	101
Which Is Which?	★★	226
G'sUs		73
Hoosierheights.com		96
Livin' in the UK		74

5.11b

Route	Stars	Page
Amarillo Sunset	★★★★★	250
Yellow Brick Road	★★★★★	47
Believer	★★★★	232
Boarding Pass	★★★★	196
Cabin Boy Fever	★★★★	198
Capture the Flag	★★★★	225
Citizen's Arête	★★★★	226
Climactic Crush	★★★★	319
Consenting Adult	★★★★	125
Donor	★★★★	221
Endangered Species	★★★★	129
Fear or Common Sense	★★★★	150
Finnegan's Ladder	★★★★	337
Geezers Go Sport	★★★★	61
Hip to the Jive	★★★★	322
Hippopotomoose	★★★★	62
Jingus	★★★★	230
Like a Turtle	★★★★	231
Lollipop Kids	★★★★	46
Nanotechnology	★★★★	231
Pinkalicious	★★★★	295
Random Precision	★★★★	214
Receiver	★★★★	69
She Might Be a Liar	★★★★	258
Skunk Love	★★★★	232
Tequila Sunrise	★★★★	250
Toxicodendron	★★★★	320
Tug-o-War	★★★★	128
Tweaked Unit	★★★★	245
Weed Eater	★★★★	151
A Portrait of the Artist ...	★★★	100
Animal Husbandry	★★★	61
Buccaneer	★★★	113
Buddhalicious	★★★	86
Cannonball	★★★	61
Chickenboy	★★★	174
Clair Obscur	★★★	213
Del Boy	★★★	71
Fake ID	★★★	75
Hematopoiesis	★★★	97
Leftomaniac	★★★	306
Let's Boogie	★★★	221
Mellow Yellow	★★★	93
Mentor Powers	★★★	119
Mona Lisa Overdrive	★★★	174
Mooch	★★★	300
Murder at Frozen Head	★★★	287
Night Moves	★★★	109
No Country for Old Men	★★★	100
On Beyond Zebra!	★★★	61
Predator	★★★	111
Prey	★★★	111
Psychopomp	★★★	292
Resuscitation of a Hanged...	★★★	100
Same Way	★★★	220
Smear Tactics	★★★	144
Social Stigma	★★★	118
Strip the Willows	★★★	88
The Country Boy	★★★	160
The Giant Peach	★★★	328
The Hanging Tree	★★★	286
The Peyote Pup	★★★	63
Trad Sucker	★★★	305
Trust in Jesus	★★★	306
Twisted	★★★	305
Two Rons Don't Make a Right	★★★	301
Unknown Road	★★★	94
Ursa Minor	★★★	302
Yadda Yadda Yadda	★★★	281
About Five Ten	★★	67
Amelia's Birthday	★★	170
Buzz	★★	337
Devil Made Me Do It	★★	294
Flavor of the Week	★★	96
Jack Move	★★	223
Laura	★★	306
Ode to Poopie Head	★★	73
Red Rover	★★	224
Smack Dab	★★	213
Sunday Night Cockfights	★★	321
Tea at the Palaz of Hoon	★★	101
The Muir the Merrier	★★	119
Whippoorwill	★★	164
Young Jedi	★★	183

INDICES

Route	Stars	Page
☐ Gym Jones Approved	★	95
☐ Baer Necessity		124
☐ Burnout		229
☐ Ferdowsi		102
☐ Spinal Tap		321

5.11a

Route	Stars	Page
☐ Air-Ride Equipped	★★★★	104
☐ Balance Beam	★★★★	225
☐ Bandolier	★★★★	69
☐ Barrel Full of Monkeys	★★★★	62
☐ Bathtub Mary	★★★★	90
☐ Edge-a-Sketch	★★★★	113
☐ I'll Take Sue	★★★★	258
☐ Momma Cindy	★★★★	113
☐ Monkey in the Middle	★★★★	61
☐ Optical Rectitus	★★★★	239
☐ Return to Balance	★★★★	88
☐ Size Doesn't Matter	★★★★	258
☐ Toker	★★★★	263
☐ Two Women Alone	★★★★	231
☐ Whip-Stocking	★★★★	280
☐ 100 Years of Solitude	★★★	100
☐ Aural Pleasure	★★★	245
☐ Autograph	★★★	223
☐ Brothel Doc	★★★	241
☐ Brushfire Fairytales	★★★	141
☐ Burning Bush	★★★	136
☐ Captain Blondie Sinks the Ship	★★★	96
☐ Chica Loca	★★★	177
☐ Clay City Exit	★★★	292
☐ Creeping Elegance	★★★	142
☐ Dime a Dozen	★★★	134
☐ Drip Wire	★★★	240
☐ Edgehog	★★★	59
☐ Elevation	★★★	272
☐ For Your Health	★★★	318
☐ Green Horn	★★★	174
☐ Hot Drama Teacher	★★★	256
☐ Injured Reserve	★★★	306
☐ Johnny B. Good	★★★	218
☐ Johnny on Roofies	★★★	221
☐ Jungle Trundler	★★★	148
☐ Junior's Gesture	★★★	287
☐ Morning Sun	★★★	111
☐ One Side Makes You Taller	★★★	324
☐ Radical Evolution	★★★	111
☐ Rising	★★★	148
☐ Romance Explosion	★★★	64
☐ Sandy Malone	★★★	177
☐ Scalawagarus	★★★	181
☐ Skin the Cat	★★★	61
☐ Snake Charmer	★★★	64
☐ Snapper	★★★	316

Route	Stars	Page
☐ Squirrelworker	★★★	326
☐ Team Tough on Tour	★★★	326
☐ The Ankle Brute	★★★	209
☐ The Dangling Participle	★★★	289
☐ The Dude Abides	★★★	255
☐ The Preacher's Daughter	★★★	218
☐ Tourette Syndrome	★★★	242
☐ Ursa Major	★★★	302
☐ Willy Wonka	★★★	327
☐ All Hands on Deck	★★	197
☐ American Psycho	★★	101
☐ Ben	★★	306
☐ Mint Julip	★★	139
☐ MumMum	★★	86
☐ No Love for Charlie	★★	223
☐ Rectal Exorcism	★★	73
☐ South Central	★★	336
☐ Steal the Bacon	★★	224
☐ Tao Bato	★★	97
☐ Unworthy	★★	317
☐ Cordillera Rojo	★	140
☐ Hopscotch	★	223
☐ Hot Fudge Sunday		95
☐ Trundling Trolls		87

5.11

Route	Stars	Page
☐ French Fighter		189
☐ NAMBLA RAMBLA		189
☐ Nose Ring		189

5.10d

Route	Stars	Page
☐ Breakfast Burrito	★★★★★	280
☐ Fire and Brimstone	★★★★★	279
☐ Barn Dance	★★★★	187
☐ Critters on the Cliff	★★★★	149
☐ Fairweather Friend	★★★★	163
☐ Girls Gone Wild ... WOO!	★★★★	226
☐ Hatfield	★★★★	242
☐ K.S.B.	★★★★	249
☐ Karmic Retribution	★★★★	125
☐ Normalised Bramapithecus	★★★★	222
☐ Pulling Pockets	★★★★	54
☐ Return of Manimal	★★★★	149
☐ Ruby Slippers	★★★★	46
☐ The Glass Elevator	★★★★	328
☐ Theobroma	★★★★	332
☐ Armadillo	★★★	59
☐ Armed Insurrection	★★★	96
☐ Babinski Sign	★★★	332
☐ Barenjager	★★★	141
☐ Castoff	★★★	196
☐ Circa Man	★★★	50
☐ Cruisin' for a Bruisin'	★★★	115
☐ Dain Bramage	★★★	212
☐ Dragonslayer	★★★	54

Route	Stars	Page
☐ Family Values	★★★	6
☐ Fever Pitch	★★★	23
☐ Generosity	★★★	22
☐ Gnome Wrecker	★★★	12
☐ Happy Trails	★★★	21
☐ Helping Hands	★★★	22
☐ It's Alive	★★★	6
☐ Jailbird	★★★	5
☐ Just Duet	★★★	5
☐ Low-Hanging Fruit	★★★	29
☐ Makin' Bacon	★★★	11
☐ Melancholy Mechanics	★★★	12
☐ Muffin Top	★★★	23
☐ Nameless	★★★	18
☐ Naughty Neighbors	★★★	12
☐ Off the Couch	★★★	29
☐ Pocket Pussy	★★★	7
☐ Pooh and Piglet, Too	★★★	29
☐ Pork and Bondage	★★★	7
☐ Rasta	★★★	27
☐ Sacriledge	★★★	9
☐ Scrumbulglazer	★★★	12
☐ Shaved Squirrel	★★★	22
☐ Subject to Change	★★★	18
☐ Super Pinch	★★★	17
☐ Take the Scary Out of Life	★★★	23
☐ Tanduay Time	★★★	9
☐ Tong Shing	★★★	22
☐ Touch of Grey	★★★	11
☐ Yell Fire!	★★★	16
☐ All Draws & No Brains	★★	21
☐ Pickpocket	★★	17
☐ Universal Gravitation	★★	11
☐ Bottle Infrontome	★	21
☐ Mantel Peace	★	11
☐ The Golden Box	★	8

5.10c

Route	Stars	Page
☐ Lightning Rod Arête	★★★★★	19
☐ Loompa	★★★★★	32
☐ Baby Blue Eyes	★★★★	25
☐ Brohemian Rhapsody	★★★★	20
☐ Brohymn	★★★★	20
☐ Crazyfingers	★★★★	5
☐ Curbside No Traction	★★★★	20
☐ Delayed Gratification	★★★★	24
☐ Diamond in the Rough	★★★★	4
☐ Golden Snow Cone	★★★★	29
☐ Kentucky Flu	★★★★	23
☐ No Sleep Till Campton	★★★★	24
☐ Old English	★★★★	25
☐ Out of the Dark	★★★★	11
☐ Preemptive Strike	★★★★	11
☐ Real Girls Don't Pumptrack	★★★★	19

SPORT GRADED LIST

Route	Stars	Page
Short by a Foot	****	212
Some Humans Ain't Human	****	152
That's What She Said	****	258
The Century	****	195
Thunderclinger	****	87
Annie the Annihilator	***	119
Augenblick	***	128
Buttsweat and Tears	***	176
Dingo the Gringo	***	152
Don't Take Yer Guns to Town	***	148
Fifth-Bolt Faith	***	134
Flying the Bird	***	256
Ghost in the Machine	***	210
Heard It on NPR	***	140
Hey There, Fancy Pants	***	148
Hurt	***	220
McCoy	***	242
N4	***	160
One Brick Shy	***	61
Pinkies Extended	***	220
Poopie Head	***	73
Sabertooth	***	138
Sojourner Truth	***	289
Stool Sample	***	73
Sunbeam	***	110
The G-Man	***	248
Unbridled	***	317
Upworthy	***	231
Workin' for the Weekend	***	149
A Wave New World	**	280
Banjolero	**	165
Bridge Suite	**	201
Frontal Lobotomy	**	213
Last Resort	**	67
Return to Sender	**	287
Single Finger Salute	**	210
Special K	**	117
The Second Labor of Hercules	**	210
The Speed of Enzo	**	240

5.10b

Route	Stars	Page
A Brief History of Climb	****	218
Boltergeist	****	116
Breakin' the Law	****	332
Deeper is Better	****	281
Gettin' Lucky in Kentucky	****	134
Machete	****	151
Nice to Know You	****	222
Robotic Thumb	****	331
The Juggernaut	****	319
Thrillbillies	****	88
A1A	***	164
Action Over Apathy	***	209
Apoplectic Chick From Missouri	***	223
Beta Spewer	***	144
Beware the Bear	***	117
Crude Awakening	***	213
DaVinci's Left Ear	***	213
Dirty Bird	***	65
Good Gravy	***	259
Harshin' My Mellow	***	286
Imminent Demise	***	152
Jungle Gym	***	224
Little Viper	***	148
Lone Coyote	***	65
Loosen Up	***	50
Make a Wish	***	280
Mancala	***	136
Murano	***	218
No Brain, No Pain	***	212
Put Me in the Zoo	***	59
Reanimator	***	67
Sam	***	98
Serpentine	***	133
Slick and the 9mm	***	276
The King Lives On ...	***	217
When Rats Attack	***	256
You Can Tune a Piano...	***	58
Bombardier	**	87
C Quest R	**	300
Family Tradition	**	221
Lucy Goosey	**	96
Mr. P	**	331
Retirement Day	**	87
Significant Other	**	248
Steel Reserve	**	152
Surfin' the Whale's Back	**	95
The Short, Happy Life ...	**	100
Virgin Bolter Tag Team	**	151
Weathertop Stings	**	239
Buenos Hermanos	*	246
Motor Booty Pimp Affair	*	258
Snarf Victory	*	321
Here Comes the Beep Beep		65
Peer Review		173

5.10a

Route	Stars	Page
Bad Company	****	124
Bitter Ray of Sunshine	****	113
Brown-Eyed Girl	****	257
EGBG	****	319
Monkey Bars	****	225
My Mind Escapes Me	****	230
Oompa	****	328
Plate Tectonics	****	134
Pottsville Escarpment	****	286
Rat Stew	****	149
59-Inch Drill Bitch	***	136
A.W.O.L.	***	54
Bethel	***	136
Black Powder	***	109
Botanical Gardens	***	64
Brambly Downslide	***	176
Chimp	***	59
Dynabolt Gold	***	113
Fadda	***	53
Kentucky Pinstripe	***	49
Monobrow	***	243
Moonshine	***	110
Moots Madness	***	115
Rest Assured	***	67
Spinner	***	136
STD	***	245
Street Fight	***	227
Sugar Rush	***	325
The Decline of Western ...	***	174
The Gimp	***	236
Thru Space and Time	***	223
Tire Swing	***	225
Ultegra	***	193
Waterfall Ballet	***	114
Watering Hole	***	138
Wonkaholic	***	322
Bulldozer	**	249
Crescent Moon	**	142
Farley's Folley	**	222
King Pin	**	152
Padawan	**	184
Palm Friction	**	336
Raindancer	**	255
redriveroutdoors.com	**	147
Spyder's Hangout	**	230
Stem Cell	**	239
Sudoku	**	209
Waltz the Deal	**	209
Jumbo Shrimp	*	237
Throbbing Emotions	*	321
Where's JJ?	*	262

5.10

Route	Stars	Page
The Cream Machine	***	306

5.9+

Route	Stars	Page
Kampsight	****	57
Lanterne Rouge	****	194
Darwin Loves You	***	221
Netizen Hacktivist	***	125
Tar Baby	***	292
Wadcutter	***	70
Altered Scale	**	57
Jump for Joy	**	53
Mercenary of the Mandarin...	**	144
Stay Off the Radio, Jeff!	**	147

5.9

☐ Miranda Rayne	****	248
☐ Augustus Gloop	***	325
☐ Backstabber	***	111
☐ Cindarella	***	96
☐ Dyn-o-mite	***	108
☐ Flutterby Blue	***	147
☐ Grandpa Joe	***	321
☐ Gunner	***	65
☐ Kokopelli's Dream	***	152
☐ Manteleer	***	86
☐ On the Prowl	***	173
☐ One-Armed Bandit	***	96
☐ Ridin' the Short Buzz	***	256
☐ Ryanosaurus	***	138
☐ Slide	***	225
☐ Small Fry	***	184
☐ Tall Cool One	***	134
☐ Tourist Trap	***	67
☐ Trouble Clef	***	57
☐ Chocolate River	**	326
☐ Crazy Eyes	**	181
☐ Crimpy and the Brain	**	212
☐ Dance of the Druids	**	117
☐ Jet Lag	**	223
☐ Live Music Is Better	**	205
☐ Love Potion #9	**	160
☐ Low Exposure	**	143
☐ Neanderfall	**	138
☐ Norway on My Mind	**	172
☐ Rumspringa	**	300
☐ Stealing Melinda	**	94
☐ Sunny the Boxer	**	172
☐ Two Chicken Butts	**	137
☐ Hijacked Project	*	95
☐ Threat Level Blue	*	239
☐ Days of Thunder		243
☐ Listerine Girl		227
☐ Waiting on JJ		263
☐ Where's My Chisel?		110

5.9-

☐ Send Me on My Way	***	149

5.8+

☐ Dura-Ace	****	193
☐ Prehistoric Extermination	****	138
☐ First Time	***	222
☐ Crescendo	**	142
☐ Rorschach Inkblot Test	**	242

5.8

☐ 27 Years of Climbing	*****	218
☐ Boilerplate	****	165
☐ All Cows Eat Grass	***	58
☐ Audie	***	248
☐ Built for Life	***	145
☐ Casey	***	98
☐ Gandee Candy	***	298
☐ Kiss the Manta Ray	***	198
☐ Rikki Tikki Tavi	***	98
☐ Brolo El Cunado	**	255
☐ Cordelia	**	71
☐ Deeznuts	**	165
☐ Dream of a Bee	**	70
☐ Face Up to That Arête	**	118
☐ Ledgends of Limonite	**	112
☐ Mona Lisa Crack	**	145
☐ Ohio Climbing	**	149
☐ Panda Bear	**	98
☐ Parks and Rec.	**	145
☐ Redeye Brew	**	147
☐ Thanks Holly	**	136
☐ Valor Over Discretion	**	54
☐ Coprolite	*	138
☐ International Route of...	*	115
☐ Shawty	*	143
☐ Abby Gabby Doo		96

5.8-

☐ Irish Mud	**	145

5.7

☐ C Sharp or B Flat	***	58
☐ Glory and Consequence	***	112
☐ Ledger Line	***	58
☐ The Bee's Business	***	147
☐ The Offering	***	148
☐ 7-11	**	173
☐ A-Beano	**	148
☐ Ai Bang Mai Fa Kin Ni	**	144
☐ CH4	**	148
☐ Fear of Commitment	**	145
☐ Harvey	**	98
☐ Pee-Wee	**	248
☐ The Archeologist	**	145
☐ Trundling Kentucky	**	148
☐ Slabalito	*	143
☐ Hired Guns		74
☐ Pocahontas Path		254

5.6

☐ Eureka	****	48
☐ Capstan	***	198
☐ Dragon's Mouth	**	142
☐ La Escalada	**	113
☐ Swap Meet	**	222

5.5

☐ Lowered Expectations	**	223
☐ Lucky Duck Soup	**	172
☐ Who Pooped the Playground?	**	146
☐ Yu Stin Ki Pu	**	143
☐ Basilisk	*	1
☐ Mary Pop-Parazzi	*	2
☐ Physically Strong, Mentally...		

5.4

☐ School of Rock	***	1
☐ T's Knobs	***	1
☐ Acrophobiacs Anonymous	**	1
☐ Dripity Dew Da	**	1
☐ Grandma's Rocker	**	1
☐ Porch Potato	**	1

5.3

☐ Child's Play	***	1

GRADED LIST OF TRAD CLIMBS

5.13b		
Charlie	****	328

5.12c		
All That Glitters	*****	216
Moment of Truth	****	265
On Beyond Velodrome	****	194

5.12b		
Jackie the Stripper	***	246
Flying J	**	128

5.12a		
Buddha Slept	****	123
Dreamthiever	****	126
Flash Point	****	89
Home Is Where the Heart Is	****	53
12-Ounce Curl	***	79
Ballnuts & Brassies...	***	324
Four Out the Door	***	79
Pistol Gripped	***	250

5.12		
Dog Wars	****	150

5.11+		
Sticks and Stones	***	141
Stucconu	***	214

5.11d		
Through the Looking Glass	****	324
Chain Mail	**	49
Milkin' the Chicken	*	53

5.11c		
Renegade	****	97
Back in the Days of Bold	***	237
Fallen Angel	***	232
Marriage Counseling	***	259
The First Fast Draw	*	95

5.11b		
Windy Corner	*****	66
Dew Point	****	332
Harder Than Your Husband	***	54
In a Pinch	***	126
Lord of the Ring	***	281
My Quads Are Too Big	***	195
Psychochicken	***	174
Perfidious Deciduous	**	120
Linkage Disequilibrium		289

5.11a		
South Side of the Sky	*****	336
Ascentuality	****	129
Gotta Get Away	****	203
Rebar	****	172
Synchronicity	****	54

The Man Behind the Curtain	****	45
Beastly Traverse	***	144
Dark Matter	***	169
Farewell Drive with a Spit...	****	239
Kentucky Waterfall	***	126
Redneck Jedi	***	183
Scantily Trad	***	64
Spread Eagle	***	230
Bear's Den Project 6	**	294
Kindred Spirits	**	241
Neither	**	68
Three Wasted Bolts	**	306
The Proverbial Donkey	*	234
Shotgun Funeral		229

5.11		
Hand and Fingers	****	204
A Spot of Bother	***	195
Critical Crystal	***	44
Uncharted Waters	**	197

5.11-		
Trailer Trashed	***	79

5.10+		
Do the Hemlock Rock	****	205
Conquistador of the Crumbly	*	123
Psycho Billy Cadillac	*	128

5.10d		
Treetop Terror	****	129
Falkor	***	258
Imperial Stout	***	77
Spring Jammers and...	***	176
Summer Shandy	***	77
The Andy Man Can	***	328
Uncle Ferdouz	***	274
Chickenhawk	**	224
The Climbing Corpse Cometh	**	246
Thunda Bunda	*	258

5.10c		
Mantel Route	*****	52
It's a Trap!	****	182
Riptide Ride	****	172
The Podium	****	194
All Mixed Up	***	116
Bourbon and Bluegrass	***	117
Bushwhacked	***	116
Hoot and Holler	***	116
R. Kell Ethics	***	319
Scarecrow	***	47
Sprout's Climb	***	336
Exit Stage Left	**	44

Fubar	**	172
Honduran Rum	*	256
Psycho Killer	*	54

5.10b		
Smoothie Nut	****	169
Tradisfaction	****	126
Wonderland	****	324
A Briefer History of Climb	***	218
BDSM	***	144
Delirium Tremens	***	78
End of the Innocence	***	324
Hot Pursuit	***	170
Mist of Funk	***	232
No Bones About It	***	128
Peaches and Cream	***	326
Stormtrooper	***	183
T N T	***	47
The Fangs and the Furious	***	65
The Spice of Life	***	254
Thin Skin	***	213
All That Quivers	**	217
Buffalo Crickets	**	249
Enganche	**	151
Frozen Bananas	**	134
Holly Golightly	**	56
Sexy Sadie	**	258
Spider Crux	**	140
Pumped Puppies		45

5.10a		
The Haas Memorial Route	****	222
Hard Left	***	53
Runnin' Down a Dream	***	53
Strongyloides	***	330
The Rusty Philosopher	***	165
Wet Willy	***	295
Green Tea	**	172
One-Cheek Wonder	**	111
Son of a Wanted Man	**	95
Battle of the Bulge	*	54
Let's Get Drunk and Think...	*	257
Notso Borneo		201
Stabbed in the Back	*	316
The Seventh Circle of Dante	*	237
Dirty Girl		231

5.10		
Brass Gunkie	***	240
Bumpin' With Bulldog	***	65
Primordial Dissonance	***	111
Jungle Direct	**	286

TRAD GRADED LIST

Route	Rating	Page
Revenge of the Sith	**	111
The Wondrous Boat Ride	*	323

5.9+

Route	Rating	Page
Andromeda Strain	****	52
Broken Chicken Wing	****	172
The Rube Goldberg Experiment	****	272
Deep in Dis Bear	***	292
Loan Shark	***	274
Meh	***	326
Mini Me	***	151
Squeeze Me Macaroni	***	332
Epic Indicator	**	242
Erik's Second 5.6	**	169
Excellent, Slithers	**	133
Howard Roark	**	48
Peach Pit	**	324
Three Amigos	**	111
Nettles	*	44
Spiny Norman	*	46
Not Named		170

5.9

Route	Rating	Page
A Happy Ending	***	142
Adventures of the Leper Nurse	***	240
Ear Infection	***	108
Eddie Merckx Gets a Perm	***	194
Friable	***	46
Hotdog in a Hallway	***	276
Little T-Bone	***	113
Sharp	***	45
The Mad Hatter's Tea Party	***	323
Tickets to the Shitshow	***	275
Unfastidious Moth	***	320
Walk the Line	***	128
Weapons of Mass Deception	***	112
Yakuza	***	176
Captain Turtlehead	**	286
Chicken Little Loves Abubu	**	91
Crescenta	**	306
Cultural Wasteland	**	239
Darkside of the Flume	**	214
Down the Rabbit Hole	**	324
George of the Jungle	**	287
Gluteus	**	238
Magic Medicine	**	75
Trad Is His Son	**	246
Camel-Toe Jockey	*	57
Maximus	*	238
Overdrive	*	306
Retroflex		74

5.9-

Route	Rating	Page
Live Action	***	59
Erik's First 5.6	**	169
Sierra's Travels	*	140

5.8+

Route	Rating	Page
The Shining	****	47
Bearly Legal	***	294
Buried Alive	***	64
Dirty Old Men	***	123
Ear Drops	***	108
Epigyne Crack	***	181
Harley	***	65
The Right Bauer	***	164
Anger Management	**	221
Butterfly Gangbang	**	232
End of Days	**	289
Old School	**	117
Quaquaversal Crack	**	125
Storm Gutter	**	332
From the Ashes	*	170

5.8

Route	Rating	Page
Cheaper Than a Movie	*****	257
First Fall	****	123
Five-Finger Discount	****	53
Indecision	****	126
Whiteout	****	45
Be My Yoko Ono	***	257
Burcham's Folly	***	68
Dead Man Chest Hair	***	198
Easy Pickins	***	327
Fickelgruber	***	327
Get on the Good Foot	***	149
Jake Flake	***	49
Mini Keg	***	75
Off With Batman	***	48
Oink! Oink!	***	95
Old People Are Awesome	***	193
Put the Best Foot Forward	***	148
Quicksilver	***	90
Smell the Glove	***	220
Tony's Happy Christmas...	***	266
24-Hour Bug	**	98
A Chip Off the Old Sturnum	**	221
Baccaus Goes Climbing	**	152
Born Again Christian	**	116
Darling Dirtbag	**	254
Kiss It All Better	**	245
Stuck Buckeye	**	239
Summer Breeze	**	250
The Wal-Martification...	**	221
Tomthievery	**	147
Environmental Imperialism	*	129
Hole	*	238
If Trango Could Whistle	*	223
Mental Affair	*	137
Owgli Mowgli	*	118
Quicky	*	254

Route	Rating	Page
Tobacco Crack Ho	*	2
And They Called It a Route		2
Catholics' Traverse		1
Come to Me, Marie		2
LIDAR		1
Roof Crack		1
The Universe Next Door		1

5.8-

Route	Rating	Page
Four Shower Tokens ...	**	2
Sweet Jane	**	1

5.7

Route	Rating	Page
Roadside Attraction	*****	
Call of the Wild	****	1
Casual Viewing	****	
Alternative Medicines	***	2
ED	***	1
Father and Son	***	
Gettin' Ziggy With It	***	2
Go West	***	
I Didn't Know This Was the End	***	
Laying Pipe Under the Bridge	***	2
Octopus Tag	***	2
Shock and Awe	***	1
Tradmill	***	1
Vision	***	
Continental Drift	**	1
Crack 'n Up	**	1
Immodium AD	**	1
Old School Chocolate	**	3
Paraplegic Power	**	1
Short and Sweet	**	1
Slow Jack	**	1
Wrong Turn	**	1
Brain Stem	*	1
Climbing With Crowbars	*	1
Cybersex	*	1
Dirt in Eye	*	1
Krypton	*	1
Pain Is a Spice	*	1
Rinse and Repeat	*	2
Smoke Screen	*	1
Sorostitute	*	2
Strawberry Shortcake	*	
May as Well		2
Should've Known Better		
South Fork Cemetery		
Stefanie Bauer Route		
Winona		

5.6

Route	Rating	Page
Motha	***	
Wild Turkey Crossing	***	2
A Prayer for Owen Meany	**	
Don't Do It	**	

348

Worn Anchors? Rusty Bolts?

BAD BOLTS.COM

where worn and rusty nuts go

www.badbolts.com – online database for reporting and repairing bad bolts

TRAD GRADED LIST

☐ Friction Slab	★★	44	☐ Spoke Junkies	★	193
☐ Looking Through the Devil's...	★★	232	**5.4**		
☐ Mud on the Rug	★★	286	☐ Can of Biscuits	★★★	65
☐ Return to Zoe	★★	223	☐ Chester Fried Chicken	★★	172
☐ The Cheerleader Catch	★★	243	☐ Fat Man's Misery	★★	234
☐ The P. Heist Rockway...	★★	148	☐ Futuristic Testpiece	★★	170
☐ Buckwheat's Climb...	★	164	☐ The Perfect Pint	★★	172
☐ Dementia	★	289	☐ Turkey Crossing	★★	164
☐ Lula Mae	★	94	☐ Trekker of the Treacherous		110
☐ The Friend Zone	★	254	**5.3**		
☐ The Giver	★	100	☐ Dragon's Tail	★★	142
☐ Pine Needle Shuffle		147	☐ Gumby Land	★	58
5.5			**5.2**		
☐ Cromper's Mom	★★★	275	☐ Hmmm	★	70
☐ Velveteen	★★★	151	☐ Slither and Squeeze	★	143
☐ Sweet and Sour	★★	144	**5.1**		
☐ Father's Day	★	45	☐ Kate's First Trad Lead	★	143
☐ Flee From Fixer	★	223	☐ Mossy Mayhem		110
☐ Hiking Boot Highway	★	86			

349

INDEX

7-11	173
10-Pound Tumor	205
100 Ounces of Gold	167
100 Years of Solitude	100
12-Ounce Curl	79
2-Fold	320
24-Hour Bug	98
27 Years of Climbing	218
5.10 WALL, ROADSIDE	**53**
5.10 WALL, TORRENT FALLS	**67**
5.11 WALL	**69**
5.12 WALL, ROADSIDE	**56**
5.12 WALL, TORRENT FALLS	**68**
59-Inch Drill Bitch	136
72-Hour Energy	296
8 Ball	307

A

A Brief History of Climb	218
A Briefer History of Climb	218
A Cat Amongst the Pigeons	194
A Chip Off the Old Sturnum	221
A Confederacy of Dunces	101
A Farewell to Arms	92
A Happy Ending	142
A Portrait of the Artist as a Young Man	100
A Prayer for Owen Meany	100
A Spot of Bother	195
A Wave New World	280
A-Beano	148
A.W.O.L.	54
A1A	164
Abby Gabby Doo	96
Abiyoyo	107
About Five Ten	67
Absolute Zero	282
Acrophobiacs Anonymous	143
Action Over Apathy	209
Action Potential	65
Adventure, The	56
Adventures of the Leper Nurse	240
Afros, Macks, and Zodiacs	203
AfroSquad	203
Afternoon Buzz	78
Agile Process, The	131
Ai Bang Mai Fa Kin Ni	144
Air-Ride Equipped	104
Ale-8-One	315
All Cows Eat Grass	58
All Draws & No Brains	212
All Gold Everything	170
All Hands on Deck	197
All In	306
All Mixed Up	116
All That Glitters	216
All That Quivers	217
All That Twitters	299
All the Pretty Horses	100
Altered Scale	57
Alternative Medicines	240
Amarillo Sunset	250
Amelia's Birthday	170
American Dream	184
American Graffiti	214
American Psycho	101
Amish Whoopie Cushion	163
Amyloid Plaque	289
And They Called It a Route	246
Andromeda Strain	52
Andy Man Can, The	328
Anger Management	221
Angry Birds	284
ANIMAL CRACKERS	**98**
Animal Husbandry	61
Ankle Brute, The	209
Annie the Annihilator	119
Apadana	102
Apoplectic Chick From Missouri	223
Apotheosis Denied	117
Arachnophobia	286
Archangel	265
Archeologist, The	145
Arête-Headed Stranger	302
Arêterection	129
Armadillo	59
Armed Insurrection	96
ARSENAL, THE	**90**
Ascentuality	129
Astrodog	131
ATM	189
Audie	248
Augenblick	128
Augustus Gloop	325
Aural Pleasure	245
Autograph	223
Avalanche Run	210
Avast Ye	196
Aviary	62

B

BabaBooey	63
Babinski Sign	332
Baby Blue Eyes	257
Babyface	92
Baccaus Goes Climbing	152
Back in the Days of Bold	237
Backstabber	111
Bad Company	124
Baer Necessity	12
Balance Beam	22
BALD ROCK FORK	**25**
Ball and Chain	13
Ball Scratcher	30
Ballnuts & Brassies or Busted Ankles	32
Bandolier	6
Bangers and Mash	9
Banjolero	16
Banksy	21
Banshee	10
Barbed Wire	25
Bare Metal Teen	6
Bareback	32
Barenjager	14
Barn Dance	18
Barrel Full of Monkeys	6
Barren Gold	29
Basilisk	13
Bathed in Light	33
Bathtub Mary	9
Batten Down the Hatches	19
Battery Life	10
Battle of the Bulge	5
BDSM	14
Be My Yoko Ono	25
Bear Belly	30
Bear Down	30
Bear's Den 29	29
Bear's Den 30	29
Bear's Den Project 6	29
BEAR'S DEN	**29**
Bearly Legal	29
Bearly There	30
Beastly Traverse	14
Bee's Business, The	14
Beechcomber	19
Beef Stick	10
Beeper	26
Beer Belly	28
Beer Trailer	7
BEER TRAILER CRAG	**7**
Beer-Thirty	7
Believer	23
Belly of the Beast	23
Ben	30
Bessie	25
Beta Spewer	14
Bethel	13
Bettavul Pipeline	27
Better Eat Yo' Wheatleys	17
Better Than Homemade	7
Beware the Bear	11
BIBLIOTHEK	**9**

350

Entry	Page
ig Burley	184
ig Money Grip	68
ig Sinkin' Breakdown	280
IRD CAGE	63
irth of a Legend	205
itter Ray of Sunshine	113
lack Gold	167
lack Hoof	114
lack Pearl	198
lack Plague	167
lack Powder	109
lank Canvas	213
leak December	320
leed Like Me	220
lood Bath	270
lowin' Loadz	179
lue Collar	123
lue Jacket	114
lue Sunday	120
lue-Eyed Honkey Jesus	176
oarding Pass	196
OB MARLEY CRAG	262
OHICA	310
oilerplate	165
oltergeist	116
ombardier	87
ONEYARD, THE	94
orn Again Christian	116
otanical Gardens	64
ottle Infrontome	212
ottles Up	76
ourbon and Bluegrass	117
ourbon Barrel Shot Gun	77
ow to Stern	197
OWLING ALLEY	152
owling Pain	241
rain Stem	137
rambly Downslide	176
rass Gunkie	240
reak the Scene	217
reakfast Burrito	280
reakin' the Law	332
reakneck Speed	197
reathe Right	306
ridge Suite	201
RIGHT SIDE	177
rilliant Orange	168
ring Up the Bodies	231
ohemian Rhapsody	201
rohymn	201
rokeback Finger	298
roken Chicken Wing	172
rolo El Cunado	255
romance	301
RONAUGH WALL	230
rothel Doc	241
rouwer Power	176
rown-Eyed Girl	257
rownian Motion	179
BRUISE BROTHERS WALL	147
Brushfire Fairytales	141
Buccaneer	113
Buck Eye	313
Buckeye Buttress	305
Buckwheat's Climb for Stef	164
Buddha Hole	176
Buddha Slept	123
Buddhalicious	86
Buenos Hermanos	246
Buff the Wood	305
Buffalo Crickets	249
Built for Life	145
Bulge, The	47
Bulldozer	249
Bullfighter	90
Bumpin' With Bulldog	65
Bundle of Joy	106
Burcham's Folly	68
Buried Alive	64
Burlier's Bane	315
Burning Bush	136
Burnout	229
Bush League	179
Bushwhacked	116
Business, The	284
Butane Junky	322
Buttercup	334
Butterfly Gangbang	232
Buttsweat and Tears	176
Buzz	337

C

Entry	Page
C Quest R	300
C Sharp or B Flat	58
Cabin Boy Fever	198
Call of the Wild	117
Calm Like a Bomb	216
Camel-Toe Jockey	57
Can of Biscuits	65
Cannabis Love Generator	162
Cannonball	61
Capstan	198
Captain Blondie Sinks the Ship	96
Captain Turtlehead	286
Capture the Flag	225
Casey	98
Castle Has Fallen, The	234
Castoff	196
Casual Viewing	50
Cat's Demise	320
Catholics' Traverse	182
Cell Block Six	93
Centerfire	69
Century, The	195
CH4	148
Chain Mail	49
Chainsaw Massacre	315
Charlie	328
Cheaper Than a Movie	257
Check Your Grip	280
Cheerleader Catch, The	243
Cheetah	129
Cherry Red	120
Chester Fried Chicken	172
CHICA BONITA WALL	254
Chica Loca	177
Chicken Little Loves Abubu	91
Chickenboy	174
Chickenhawk	224
Child of the Earth	88
Child's Play	146
Chimp	59
CHOCOLATE FACTORY	318
Chocolate Factory 13	320
Chocolate Factory 44	324
Chocolate Factory 5	319
Chocolate Factory 77	330
Chocolate Factory 78	330
Chocolate River	326
Chronic, The	305
Chucklehead	259
Chunnel	58
Cindarella	96
Cindy Groms	298
Circa Man	50
Citizen's Arête	226
Clair Obscur	213
Clay City Exit	292
Climactic Crush	319
Climb Aboard	196
Climbing Corpse Cometh, The	246
Climbing With Crowbars	136
COAL BANK HOLLOW	157
Code Red	240
Cold Hard Bitch	256
Collision Damage	230
Colt 45	259
Come to Me, Marie	223
Coming-Out Party	227
Conquistador of the Crumbly	123
Conscription	210
Consenting Adult	125
Contact High	265
Continental	150
Continental Drift	134
Convicted	315
Coprolite	138
Cordelia	71
Cordillera Rojo	140
Cork Eye	243
Cosmic Sausage	309
Cosmic Trigger	125
Cottonmouth	134
Count Dookku	184
Country Boy, The	160
COYOTE CLIFF	86
COURTESY WALL	245

INDEX

351

Crack 'n Up	125	
Crack the Whip	225	
Crazy Eyes	181	
Crazyfingers	54	
Cream Machine, The	306	
Creeping Elegance	142	
Crescendo	142	
Crescent Moon	142	
Crescenta	306	
Crime Time	314	
Crimp My Ride	332	
Crimpin' Ain't Easy	65	
Crimps and Bloods	279	
Crimpy and the Brain	212	
Critical Crystal	44	
Critters on the Cliff	149	
Cromper's Mom	275	
Crosley	263	
Crossroads	160	
Crossroads Crack	165	
Crown of Thorns	179	
Crucible, The	92	
Crucify Me	226	
Crude Awakening	213	
Cruisin' for a Bruisin'	115	
Crumblies	230	
Cruxifixion	123	
Cultural Wasteland	239	
CURBSIDE	**209**	
Curbside No Traction	209	
Cut Throat	307	
CUT TREE WALL	**301**	
Cybersex	125	

D

Dagobah	182	
Dagon	139	
Dain Bramage	212	
Dainty Butterfly, The	320	
Damascus	167	
Dance of the Druids	117	
Dangling Participle, The	289	
Dark City	67	
Dark Matter	169	
DARK SIDE, THE	**182**	
Darkness Falls	79	
Darkside of the Flume	214	
Darling Dirtbag	254	
Darwin Loves You	221	
Das Krue	289	
David and Goliath	170	
DaVinci's Left Ear	213	
Davy Jones' Locker	197	
Davy Jones' Locker Direct	196	
Days of Thunder	243	
Dead but Dreaming	139	
Dead Man Chest Hair	198	
Deadwood, The	198	
Death Star, The	184	

Death Wish	280	
Decline of Western Civilization, The	174	
Deep Fried	181	
Deep in Dis Bear	292	
Deep Six	50	
Deeper is Better	281	
Deeznuts	165	
Del Boy	71	
Delayed Gratification	242	
Delicatessen	105	
Delirium Tremens	78	
Dementia	289	
Demon Seed	265	
Departure, The	182	
Devil Made Me Do It	294	
Dew Point	332	
Diamond in the Rough	46	
Different Strokes	214	
Digitalgia	188	
Dime a Dozen	134	
Dingo the Gringo	152	
Dirt in Eye	147	
Dirty Bird	65	
Dirty Girl	231	
Dirty Old Men	123	
Dirty Sanchez	188	
Dirty, Smelly Hippie	281	
Disappearer	50	
Do the Hemlock Rock	205	
Dog Bites & Fist Fights	179	
Dog Wars	150	
Dogleg	265	
Don't Call It a Comeback	205	
Don't Do It	294	
Don't Take Yer Guns to Town	148	
Donor	221	
Double Century	195	
Double Stuff	108	
Down by Law	50	
Down the Rabbit Hole	324	
Dr. Synchro	240	
Dracula '04	234	
Dragon's Mouth	142	
Dragon's Tail	142	
Dragonslayer	54	
DreadLocked	263	
Dream of a Bee	70	
Dreamthiever	126	
Drip Wire	240	
Dripity Dew Da	139	
DRIVE-BY CRAG	**276**	
Drop the Hammer	118	
Drunken Master	77	
Dude Abides, The	255	
Duputyren's Release	240	
Dura-Ace	193	
Dustopian	139	
Dustopian Left	139	
Dyn-o-mite	108	

Dynabolt Gold	113	

E

Eager Beaver	64	
Ear Drops	108	
Ear Infection	108	
Earth-Bound Misfit	249	
Earthsurfer	115	
East of Eden	101	
Easy Pickins	327	
Easy Rider	284	
ED	128	
Eddie Merckx Gets a Perm	194	
Edge-a-Sketch	113	
Edgehog	59	
EGBG	319	
El Encuentro	272	
El Patron	129	
Elephant Man	187	
Elevation	272	
EMERALD CITY	**45**	
End of Days	289	
End of the Innocence	324	
Endangered Species	129	
Enganche	151	
Enkidu	331	
Environmental Imperialism	129	
Epic Indicator	242	
Epigyne Crack	181	
Erik's First 5.6	169	
Erik's Second 5.6	169	
Espresso	152	
Eternal Fire	319	
Ethics Police	174	
Eureka	48	
Evening Wood	75	
Everything That Rises Must Converge	100	
Evil Emperor	183	
Evil Eye	162	
Excellent, Slithers	133	
Exit Stage Left	44	
Explanatory Gap	170	
Extra Backup	279	
Eye of the Tigger	294	
Eyeball Chaw	272	

F

Face Up to That Arête	113	
Fadda	5	
Fairweather Friend	163	
Fake ID	78	
Falkor	254	
Fall of the Anticlimber	300	
Fallen Angel	231	
Falls City	7	
False Idol	22	
False Positive	30	
Family Tradition	22	
Family Values	6	

352

angs and the Furious, The 65
ar From God 227
AR SIDE **188**
ar Side TR 188
arewell Drive with a Spit in the Eye 239
arley's Folley 222
at Man's Misery 234
atface 332
ather and Son 49
ather's Day 45
atman 322
ear of Commitment 145
ear or Common Sense 150
erdowsi 102
ever Pitch 230
at Lux 179
ckelgruber 327
fth-Bolt Faith 134
fty Words for Pump 269
nnegan's Ladder 337
re and Brimstone 279
rst Fall 123
rst Fast Draw, The 95
rst Time 222
ve-Finger Discount 53
ash Point 89
AT HOLLOW **190**
avor of the Week 96
ee From Fixer 223
esh Wound 90
our Power 311
ush 270
utterby Blue 147
ux Capacitor, The 314
ying J 128
ying Monkeys 46
ying Serpents 97
ying the Bird 256
ot Jive 163
r Your Health 318
rce, The 184
rty Ounces of Justice 313
ur Out the Door 79
ur Shower Tokens ... .222
ay Train, The 79
ayed Ends of Sanity, The 50
eakin' Deacon 91
ench Fighter 189
esh Baked 181
esh Off the Bone 254
able 46
ICTION SLAB **44**
ction Slab 44
end Zone, The 254
om the Ashes 170
ONT PORCH **139**
ontal Lobotomy 213
ozen Bananas 134
bar 172

G
Fungus Among Us 273
Fury, The 101
Futuristic Testpiece 170

G
G-Man, The 248
G.I. Joe 299
G'sUs 73
Galaxy Project, The 283
GALLERY, THE **212**
Gallery 35 218
Galunlati 106
Gandee Candy 298
Gecko Circus 169
Geezers Go Sport 61
Gene Wilder 330
Generosity 222
George of the Jungle 287
Geronimo 130
Get on the Good Foot 149
GETAWAY, THE **201**
Gettin' Lucky in Kentucky 134
Gettin' Ziggy With It 263
Ghost in the Machine 210
Giant Peach, The 328
Giblets 287
Gild the Lily 238
Gilgamesh 331
Gimp, The 236
Girls Gone Wild ... WOO! 226
Giver, The 100
Glass Elevator, The 328
Glide 95
GLOBAL VILLAGE **48**
Glory and Consequence 112
Gluteus 238
Gluttony 234
GMC WALL **307**
Gnome Wrecker 129
Go Home Yankee 245
Go West 88
Goblins in My Mind 65
Gobstopper 328
God's Own Stone 167
Godbolt 298
GOLD COAST **167**
Gold Nugget 170
Gold Rush 216
Gold Star Project 167
Golden Box, The 87
Golden Boy 167
Golden Brown 179
Golden Road 86
Golden Shower 170
Golden Snow Cone 296
Golden Ticket, The 330
Golden Touch 305
Good Gravy 259
Gorilla 95

Gotta Get Away 203
Grandma's Rocker 139
Grandpa Joe 321
Granny Panties 266
GREAT ARCH, THE **108**
GREAT WALL, THE **112**
Green Horn 174
Green Machine 273
Green Tea 172
Grey Matter 137
Grippy Green 184
Grumpalump 322
GSW 240
Guernica 218
GUIDE WALL **145**
Guilty Pleasure 276
Gumby Land 58
Gunner 65
Gym Jones Approved 95

H
Haas Memorial Route, The 222
Hagis, Neeps and Tatties 97
Hakuna Matata 279
Hammerhead 64
Hand and Fingers 204
Handout, The 142
Hang Over 78
Hanging Tree, The 286
Happy Feet 163
Happy Fisherman, The 119
Happy Trails 217
Hard Left 53
Harder Than Your Husband 54
Harley 65
Harshin' My Mellow 286
Harvest 314
Harvey 98
Hatfield 242
Head and Shoulders 281
Headwall 53
Heard It on NPR 140
Heart-Shaped Box 306
Hell or High Water 309
Hellraiser 236
Helluva Caucasian 256
Helping Hands 222
Hematopoiesis 97
Hemisfear 53
Herd Mentality 176
Here Comes Palin 302
Here Comes the Beep Beep 65
Hey There, Fancy Pants 148
HIDEOUT, THE **115**
High Life 78
Highway Turtle 170
Hijacked Project 95
Hiking Boot Highway 86
Hip to the Jive 322

353

Hippie Speed Ball	162	
Hippocrite	62	
Hippopotomoose	62	
Hippy Wick	273	
Hired Guns	74	
Hirsute	238	
Hmmm	70	
Hole	238	
Holly Golightly	56	
Home Is Where the Heart Is	53	
Honduran Rum	256	
Honey Badger	63	
Hood Luck	163	
Hoofmaker	314	
Hookah	324	
Hoosier Boys	120	
Hoosier Buddies	74	
Hoosierheights.com	96	
Hoot and Holler	116	
Hopscotch	223	
Horn	270	
Hot Drama Teacher	256	
Hot for Teacher	309	
Hot Fudge Sunday	95	
Hot Pursuit	170	
Hotdog in a Hallway	276	
Howard Roark	48	
Hum	337	
Hunt for Red's October, The	109	
Hurt	220	
Hydro Shock	68	

I

I Didn't Know This Was the End	58
I'll Take Sue	258
Icebreaker	319
If Trango Could Whistle	223
Imagine There's No Heaven	227
Immaculate Deception	123
Imminent Demise	152
Immodium AD	148
Imperial Stout	77
Impossible Choss	66
In a Pinch	126
In Red We Trust	295
Inches and Fractions	298
Indecision	126
INDY WALL	**118**
Iniquity	93
Injured Reserve	306
INNER SANCTUM	**124**
International Route of Pancakes	115
Into the Mystic	68
Irish Mud	145
Iron Lung	89
Iron Mike	249
Irony of Twisted Fate	62
Irreverent C	227
It's a Trap!	182

It's Alive	67
Itchy and Scratchy	298
Ivory Poacher	273
IVORY TOWER	**131**
Ivory Tower 4	131
Ivory Tower 5	131
Ivory Tower 7	131

J

J-Rat's Back	326
Jack Move	223
Jackie the Stripper	246
Jailbird	59
Jake Flake	49
Jedi Mind Trick	184
Jeff's Boneyard Project	95
Jersey Connection	54
Jesus Wept	121
Jet Lag	223
Jethro Bodean	64
JFR	228
Jingus	230
Jingus Khan	165
Johnny B. Good	218
Johnny on Roofies	221
JOHNNY'S WALL	**136**
Jolly Roger	198
Juggernaut, The	319
Juice, The	324
Jumbo Shrimp	237
Jump for Joy	53
June Bug	165
Jungle Direct	286
Jungle Gym	224
Jungle Trundler	148
Junior's Gesture	287
Just Duet	57

K

K.S.B.	249
Kaleidoscope	284
Kampsight	57
Karmic Retribution	125
Kate's First Trad Lead	143
Keelhaul	196
Keepin' It Real	326
Kentucky Flu	239
Kentucky Grape Vine	320
Kentucky Pinstripe	49
Kentucky Waterfall	126
Kick Me in the Jimmie	315
Kindred Spirits	241
King Cobra	259
King Lives On, The	217
King Pin	152
Kiss It All Better	245
Kiss the Manta Ray	198
Knees and Toes	281
Knot Sure	218

Kokopelli's Dream	152
Korsakoff Syndrome	78
Krypton	193
Kya	114

L

La Escalada	113
Labor Day Weekend	222
LADY SLIPPER	**45**
LAND BEFORE TIME WALL	**138**
Lanterne Rouge	194
Last of the Bohicans	311
Last Resort	6
Last Slow Draw, The	95
Laura	306
Laying Pipe Under the Bridge	254
Leave It to Beavis	313
Ledgends of Limonite	11
Ledger Line	58
LEFT FIELD	**222**
Leftomaniac	306
Legalize It	160
Let's Boogie	221
Let's Get Drunk and Think About It	257
Levi Yoder	306
Levitation	272
LIDAR	133
Lightning Rod Arête	193
Like a Turtle	23
Limbic System	333
Linkage Disequilibrium	281
Lip Service	109
Liquid Courage	74
Listerine Girl	22
Little T-Bone	11
Little Teapot	238
Little Viper	14
Live Action	5
Live Music Is Better	20
Livin' in the UK	7
Loaded for Bear	30
Loan Shark	27
Lobster Claw	24
Lolita	10
Lollipop Kids	4
LOMM	17
Lone Coyote	6
Looking Through the Devil's Window	23
Loompa	32
Loosen Up	5
Lord of the Ring	28
Love Potion #9	16
Love Song of J. Alfred Prufrock, The	10
Loverface	33
Low Easy One, The	31
Low Exposure	14
Low-Hanging Fruit	29
Lowered Expectations	22
Lucifer	23

Lucky Duck Soup 172	Mini Me 151	Night Foxx 144
Lucy Goosey 96	Mint Julip 139	Night Moves 109
Lula Mae 94	Mirage 106	No Bones About It 128
Lynx Jinx 61	Miranda Rayne 248	No Brain, No Pain..........................212
	Mis-Conception 249	No Country for Old Men 100
M	Misfire 69	No Fluff..168
Machete 151	Mist of Funk..................................232	No Love for Charlie 223
Mad Hatter's Tea Party, The 323	Moment of Truth 265	No Place Like Home........................45
Mad Porter's Disease 74	Momma Cindy 113	No Redemption 265
MADNESS CAVE 309	Mona Lisa Crack............................145	No Sleep Till Campton...................240
Madness, The 313	Mona Lisa Overdrive 174	Non Starter 187
Magic Medicine 75	Monkey Bars..................................225	Noo-tha 114
Magnum Opus 104	Monkey in the Middle 61	Normalised Bramapithecus............222
Make a Wish..................................280	Monobrow 243	**NORTH 40 ....250**
Makin' Bacon.................................118	Mooch 300	Norway on My Mind......................172
Malice 324	Moonshine 110	Nose Ring 189
Mama Benson 184	Moots Madness 115	Not Named 170
Man Behind the Curtain, The 45	Morning Sun 111	Nothing, The 283
Mancala..136	Morning Wood 75	Notso Borneo.................................201
Manifest Destiny 104	Mosaic...216	
Mantel Peace 117	Mossy Mayhem 110	**O**
Mantel Route 52	Motha 53	**OASIS, THE 337**
Manteleer 86	**MOTHERLODE REGION...................290**	October Sky 163
Manzanita......................................337	**MOTHERLODE, THE.........................304**	Octopus Tag 225
Marley 44 272	Motor Booty Pimp Affair 258	Ode to Poopie Head 73
Marley 46 273	**MOUNT OLIVE ROCK 336**	Odyssey, The 231
Marley 50 273	Mr. P 331	Off the Couch................................296
Marley 51 273	Mr. Roarke.....................................168	Off With Batman..............................48
Marley 52 273	Mr. Sandy 306	Offering, The 148
Marmight 204	Much Ado About Nothing 98	OG Pimp Juice 203
Marriage Counseling......................259	Mud on the Rug 286	Ohio Arts..113
Mary Pop-Parazzi..........................254	Muffin Top.....................................230	Ohio Climbing................................149
Mas Choss.....................................266	Muir the Merrier, The 119	Oink! Oink!......................................95
Massive Attack 211	**MUIR VALLEY 80**	Old English 259
Maximus...238	MumMum 86	Old People Are Awesome 193
May as Well 243	Murano..218	Old School 117
McCoy 242	Murder at Frozen Head 287	Old School Chocolate....................322
Medicine Man 179	My How Things Have Changed.......74	Omaha Beach 313
MEGACAVE 228	My Mind Escapes Me 230	On Beyond Velodrome...................194
Megacave 1 228	My Name is Earl 248	On Beyond Zebra!............................61
Megacave 2 228	My Quads Are Too Big 195	On the Prowl..................................173
Megacave 3 228		Onaconaronni 73
Megacave 5 228	**N**	One Brick Shy..................................61
Megacave 7 229	N4 160	One Love 273
Meh 326	Naked...322	One Side Makes You Taller 324
Melancholy Mechanics 128	Naked Lunch 279	One-Armed Bandit 96
Mellow Yellow 93	NAMBLA RAMBLA 189	One-Cheek Wonder 111
Mental Affair 137	Name Dropper 120	One-Eyed Willy Up the Back.........305
Mentee 263	Nameless 188	One-Zero-Six 181
Mentor 263	Nanotechnology 231	Oompa 328
Mentor Powers 119	**NATURAL BRIDGE 40**	Optical Rectitus 239
Mercenary of the Mandarin Chicken 144	Naughty Neighbors 124	Out for Justice 50
Midlife Crisis 119	Neanderfall 138	Out of the Dark 110
MIDNIGHT SURF 92	Neither 68	Outbreak..210
Mike Teavee 326	Netizen Hacktivist 125	Outlaw Justice 250
MILF Money 266	Nettles 44	Overdrive 306
Milkin' the Chicken 53	**NEW ZOO 62**	Owgli Mowgli 118
Mind Meld 184	New Zoo 31 64	Oz 46
Mini Keg 75	Nice to Know You 222	

P

Entry	Page
P. Heist Rockway to Heaven, The	148
Padawan	184
Paddy O'Keefe's Walking Shoes	337
Pain Is a Spice	50
Paladine	102
Palm Friction	336
Panda Bear	98
Papa Love Jugs	188
Paradise Lost	236
Paradise Regained	236
Paranoia	68
Paraplegic Power	136
Parasite	118
Parks and Rec	145
Pay the Devil	198
PBR Street Gang	78
Peace Frog	120
Peach Pit	324
Peaches and Cream	326
Pee-Wee	248
Peel It Back	274
Peer Review	173
PMRP	**154**
Perfect Pint, The	172
Perfidious Deciduous	120
Perros Grande	139
PERSEPOLIS	**102**
Pessimist, The	129
Peyote Pup, The	63
Phantom Menace	187
Physically Strong, Mentally Awake	74
Picador	90
Pickpocket	179
Pile Driver	227
Pimp Juice	284
Pimptastic	203
Pimpto-Bismol	203
Pine	57
Pine Needle Shuffle	147
Pinkalicious	295
Pinkies Extended	220
Pistol Gripped	250
Plate Tectonics	134
PLAYGROUND, THE	**224**
Pocahontas Path	254
Pocket Pussy	71
Podium, The	194
Pongosapien	238
Pooh and Piglet, Too	298
Poop Deck	196
Poopie Head	73
Porch Potato	139
Pork and Bondage	71
Posse Whipped	118
Pottsville Escarpment	286
PRACTICE WALL	**142**
Praestantissimum	187
Praying Mantis	162
Preacher's Daughter, The	218
Predator	111
Preemptive Strike	116
Prehistoric Extermination	138
Prey	111
Primordial Dissonance	111
Primus Noctum	280
PROJECT WALL	**302**
Prometheus Unbound	121
Proverbial Donkey, The	234
Psyberpunk	125
Psycho Billy Cadillac	128
Psycho Killer	54
Psychochicken	174
Psychopathy	174
Psychopomp	292
Pulling Pockets	54
Pumped Puppies	45
Purdy Mouth	306
Pure Imagination	330
PURGATORY	**232**
Pushin' Up Daisies	313
Put Me in the Zoo	59
Put the Best Foot Forward	148
Pyrite	173

Q

Entry	Page
Quaffed Up	79
Quantum Narcissist	189
Quaquaversal Crack	125
Quicksilver	90
Quicky	254

R

Entry	Page
R. Kell Ethics	319
Racer X	69
Radical Evolution	111
Raindancer	255
Random Precision	214
Rasta	272
RASTA WALL	**272**
Rat Stew	149
Reacharound, The	305
Real Girls Don't Pumptrack	195
Reanimator	67
Reasonable Doubt	64
Rebar	172
Receiver	69
RECESS ROCK	**146**
Recoil	69
Rectal Exorcism	73
Red Rover	224
Red Shift	169
Red Tag Rape	164
Red-Eye Flight	273
Redeye Brew	147
Redneck Jedi	183
redriveroutdoors.com	147
Reload	90
Renegade	97
Rest Assured	67
Resurrection	314
Resuscitation of a Hanged Man	100
Reticent	270
Retirement Day	87
Retroflex	74
Return of Chris Snyder, The	57
Return of Darth Moll, The	184
Return of Frank Byron, The	209
Return of Manimal	149
Return to Balance	88
Return to Sender	287
Return to Zoe	223
Revenge of the Sith	111
Ridin' the Short Buzz	256
Right Bauer, The	164
Rikki Tikki Tavi	98
Ring of Fire	128
Rinse and Repeat	255
Riptide Ride	172
Rising	148
RIVAL WALL	**242**
Ro Shampo	56
Roadside Attraction	53
ROADSIDE CRAG	**52**
Robotic Thumb	331
Rock the Casbah	130
Rocket Dog	315
Romance Explosion	64
Roof Crack	115
Room With a View	299
Rorschach Inkblot Test	242
Rostam	102
Route 22	266
Routeburglar	299
Rube Goldberg Experiment, The	272
Ruby Slippers	46
Rug Muncher	306
Rules of Engagement	299
Rumspringa	300
Runnin' Down a Dream	53
Running in Place	238
Rusty Philosopher, The	165
Ryanosaurus	138

S

Entry	Page
Sabertooth	138
Sacred Stones	88
Sacriledge	90
Sail	198
Sam	98
Sam and Terry's Line	66
Sam Krieg Will Bolt Anything	315
Sam's Boy Toy	299
Same Way	220
Samurai	250
SANCTUARY, THE	**120**
Sand	57
Sandy Malone	177

arahinity 320	Skinny Love 269	Spiny Norman 46
auce, The...313	Skunk Love 232	Spirit Fingers 280
calawagarus 181	Skywalker...179	Spoke Junkies 193
cantily Trad 64	**SLAB CITY 88**	Sport for Brains 73
car Tissue 61	Slabalito 143	Spread Eagle 230
carecrow 47	Slackjaw Willie...................................64	Spring Jammers and Widget Blocks ...176
carlet Scorchdropper 328	Slam Dunk 229	Sprout's Climb 336
chool of Rock..................................146	Slampiece BAM!..............................266	Spyder's Hangout.............................230
cience Friction 53	Slick and the 9mm...........................276	Squeeze Me Macaroni.....................332
cissors...56	Slide 225	Squirrels Gone Wild.........................299
crambled Porn 316	Slither and Squeeze........................143	Squirrelworker..................................326
crumbulglazer 128	Slow Jack...172	Stabbed in the Back........................316
eam Project 246	Slow Stepper 64	**STADIUM, THE 126**
earch and Seizure 204	Slut Men...276	Stain...305
econd Labor of Hercules, The........210	Sluts Are Cool 75	Stalker..323
econd Nature 188	Smack Dab 213	Stallion, The.....................................131
EE ROCKS 44	Small Fry 184	Starfish and Coffee 92
eek the Truth 73	Smear Tactics..................................144	Starry Night 212
eeker...50	Smell the Glove...............................220	Stay Off the Radio, Jeff! 147
end Me on My Way 149	Smoke Screen 66	Stay the Hand 54
endex 147 63	Smokin' on Kesha 177	STD 245
erpentine 133	Smoothie Nut...................................169	Steal the Bacon 224
eventh Circle of Dante, The 237	Snake Charmer 64	Stealing Melinda 94
evern Bore 164	Snapper..316	Steel Reserve 152
ex Show 71	Snarf Victory....................................321	Steelworker..69
exy Sadie..258	Snooker..309	Stefanie Bauer Route 164
hadow Enhancement 296	Snozzberries....................................322	Stella..316
HADY GROVE 226	So Long Mr. Petey...........................104	Stem Cell 239
hanghai 184	So Low...307	Stephanie's Cabaret 222
harma Project, The.........................286	Social Stigma 118	Sticks and Stones 141
harp...45	Sojourner Truth 289	Stirrin' the Grits 232
haved Squirrel 227	**SOLAR COLLECTOR 174**	Stomp U Out 163
HAWNEE SHELTER 114	**SOLARIUM, THE 104**	Stone Pipe 266
hawty...143	Some Humans Ain't Human 152	Stool Sample 73
he Might Be a Liar 258	Son of a Wanted Man 95	Storm Gutter....................................332
heet Rock 144	Song of Solomon 131	Storming the Beech 198
hining, The.......................................47	Sons of Perdition 63	Stormtrooper 183
HIPYARD, THE 196	**SORE HEEL HOLLOW...................206**	Straight Outta Campton 187
HIRE, THE..248	Sorostitute 259	Stranger, The 100
hiva 93	Sound, The 101	Strawberry Shortcake 58
hock and Awe 116	**SOUTH CENTRAL 336**	Street Fight......................................227
hocker, The.....................................214	South Fork Cemetery 44	Stretcherous 119
hootin' Hot Hugs 319	South Side of the Sky.....................336	Strevels Gets in Shape 56
hort and Sweet 143	**SOUTHERN OUTLYING CLIFFS 336**	Strip the Willows 88
hort by a Foot 212	Southern Smoke 269	**STRONGHOLD WALL....................130**
hort, Happy Life of FM, The 100	Southern Smoke Direct 269	Strongyloides..................................330
hotgun Funeral 229	Space Junk......................................176	Stucconu 214
hould've Known Better...................173	Spank...282	Stuck Buckeye.................................239
idewinder..62	Sparkling Jackass.............................62	Subject to Change 188
ierra's Travels 140	Special Boy......................................232	Subman 314
igned in Blood................................163	Special K..117	Subtle Thievery 210
gnificant Other 248	Specific Gravity.................................76	Sudoku 209
lent Killer 139	Speed of Enzo, The 240	Sugar Magnolia 265
ngle Finger Salute 210	Speedy Gonzales..............................62	Sugar Rush 325
ster Catherine the Conqueror 259	Spice of Life, The 254	Summer Breeze 250
tuational Awareness........................67	Spicer...301	Summer Shandy 77
ze Doesn't Matter 258	Spider Crux.....................................140	Summer Solstice 195
kin Boat...314	Spinal Tap 321	Summer Sunshine 106
kin the Cat 61	Spinner 136	Sun's Out, Guns Out.......................168

Entry	Page
Sunbeam	110
SUNBEAM BUTTRESS	**110**
Sunday Night Cockfights	321
Sunny the Boxer	172
SUNNYSIDE	**150**
Supafly	176
Super Best Friends	105
Super Charger	281
Super Pinch	174
Suppress the Rage	152
Surfin' the Whale's Back	95
Swahili Slang	307
Swallow the Hollow	165
Swap Meet	222
Sweet and Sour	144
Sweet Jane	147
Sweet Tater	97
Swine Flew	250
Swingline	187
Synchronicity	54
Syndicate, The	330

T

Entry	Page
T N T	47
T's Knobs	146
Tabernacle	124
Tacit	270
Taffy Puller	330
Take That, Katie Brown	307
Take the Scary Out of Life	231
Tall Cool One	134
Tanduay Time	97
Tao Bato	97
Tapeworm	93
Tar Baby	292
Taste the Raibow	227
Tea at the Palaz of Hoon	101
Team Tough on Tour	326
Team Wilander	249
Team Wilson	314
Technical Difficulties	274
Techno Destructo	307
Techulicous	184
Tectonic 5	134
TECTONIC WALL	**133**
Tecumseh's Curse	114
Teeter Totter	225
Tequila Sunrise	250
Thanatopsis	307
Thanks Holly	136
That's What She Said	258
Theobroma	332
There's a Bad Moon on the Rise	205
Thin Skin	213
Threat Level Blue	239
Three Amigos	111
Three Wasted Bolts	306
Three-Toed Sloth	95
Thrillbillies	88

Entry	Page
Throbbing Emotions	321
Throne of Lies	281
Through the Looking Glass	324
THROWBACK CRAG	**204**
Thru Space and Time	223
Thug Life	284
Thunda Bunda	258
Thunder	211
Thunderclinger	87
Tic-Tac-Toe	56
Tickets to the Shitshow	275
Ticks and Beer	301
Tie One On	75
Tight Lipped 2	254
Tire Swing	225
To Julie, With Love	205
Tobacco Crack Ho	239
Toker	263
Tomthievery	147
Tong Shing	221
Tongue-Punch	181
Tony's Happy Christmas Crack	266
TORRENT FALLS	**66**
Torrential	68
Touch of Grey	112
Tourette Syndrome	242
Tourist Trap	67
Toxicodendron	320
Trad Is His Son	246
Trad Sucker	305
Tradisfaction	126
Tradmill	141
Trailer Trashed	79
Transworld Depravity	310
Tree Hugger	93
Treetop Terror	129
Trekker of the Treacherous	110
Tribute, The	217
Triple Sec	121
Trouble Clef	57
Trouble in Paradise	97
True Love	168
Trundling Kentucky	148
Trundling Trolls	87
Trust in Jesus	306
Tug-o-War	128
Tumble Dry Low	239
Tuna Town	314
Turd Mountain	327
Turkey Crossing	164
Tuskan Raider	187
Tweaked Unit	245
TWELVE WALL	**300**
Twenty-Four Karats	167
Twinkie's Little Sister	318
Twisted	305
Two Chicken Butts	137
Two Cups of Silly	75
Two Rons Don't Make a Right	301

Entry	Page
Two Women Alone	231

U

Entry	Page
Ultegra	193
Ultra Perm	269
Ultrathon	272
Unbearable	301
Unbearable Lightness of Being, The	100
Unbridled	317
Uncharted Waters	197
Uncle Ferdouz	274
UNDERTOW WALL	**313**
Undesirable	317
Unfastidious Moth	320
Universal Gravitation	111
Universe Next Door, The	124
Unknown	320
Unknown	323
Unknown 12	48
Unknown 12	323
Unknown Road	94
UNLODE, THE	**317**
Unworthy	317
Upworthy	231
Urban Voodoo	104
Ursa Major	302
Ursa Minor	302
Us and Them	71

V

Entry	Page
Valor Over Discretion	54
Van der Waals Goo	96
Velo 11	194
Velo 13	195
VELO CRAG	**193**
Velvet	270
Velvet Revolution	152
Velveteen	151
Verdict, The	315
Veruca Salt	328
Violet Beauregarde	327
Virgin Bolter Tag Team	151
Vision	49
VOLUNTEER WALL	**220**
Vortex	93

W

Entry	Page
Wadcutter	70
Waiting on JJ	263
Wake and Bake	160
Wal-Martification of Trad, The	221
Walk the Line	125
Waltz the Deal	209
WARM-UP WALL	**300**
WASHBOARD WALL	**145**
Watching the World Burn	139
Water Music	129
Waterfall Ballet	114
Watering Hole	138

358

ay Up Yonder...................................57	White Man's Shuffle........................309	**Y**
eak Sauce.......................................214	Whiteout..45	Yadda Yadda Yadda 281
eapons of Mass Deception............112	Who Is Who?.....................................226	Yakuza...176
earing Out My Welcome.................245	Who Knows?......................................226	Yell Fire!..164
eathertop Stings 239	Who Pooped in the Park? 100	Yellow Brick Road 47
eed Eater 151	Who Pooped the Playground?...........146	Yoko Ono 205
elcomed Guest...............................245	Wicked Games....................................52	Yosemite Sam...................................250
et Willy..295	Wild Gift..57	You Can Tune a Piano, but 58
et Your Whistle..................................78	Wild Turkey Crossing........................296	You Take Sally...................................258
HAT ABOUT BOB WALL................238	Wildfire..210	Young Jedi..183
hat About Bob 17 49	Willy Wonka.......................................327	Your Heaven, My Hell 269
heel of Time, The 49	Windy Corner......................................66	Yu Stin Ki Pu 143
hen Rats Attack 256	Winona 95	**Z**
here's JJ?..262	Wobbler...323	Zen and the Art of Masturbation.......214
here's My Chisel? 110	Wonderland 324	Zendebad 102
here's the Beef?..............................270	Wondrous Boat Ride, The 323	Zero Dark Fiddy 296
hich Is Which? 226	Wonkaholic.......................................322	Zone of Silence................................170
hip-Stocking....................................280	Wookie Love Nest 183	Zoo 7 61
hipper Snapper 280	Workin' for the Weekend..................149	**ZOO, THE..59**
hippoorwill......................................164	Wreaking Havoc..................................50	Zookeeper 61
hite Man's Overbite........................309	Wrong Turn 164	

STILL NEED MORE ROUTES?!

heck out these guides: *Red River Gorge North* (750+ routes), the essential companion to *RRG outh*, including all the crags north of the Mountain Parkway; and *Miller Fork* a guide to this ewly developed area (400+ routes) on the east side of Route 11 not far from the Motherlode.

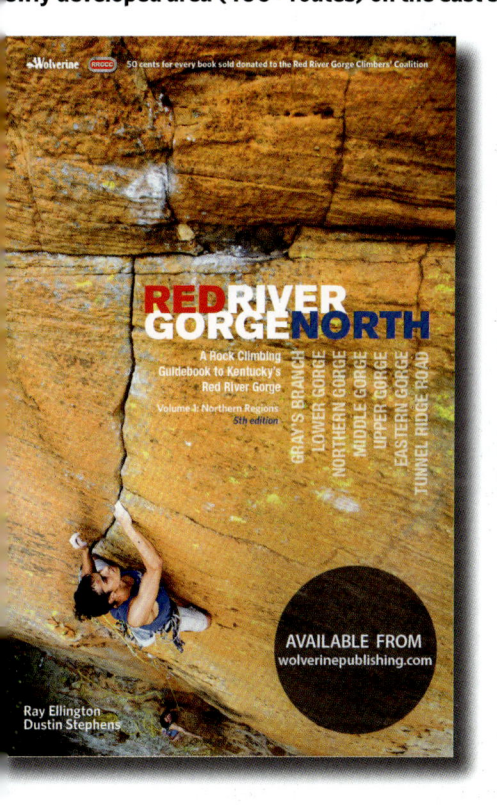

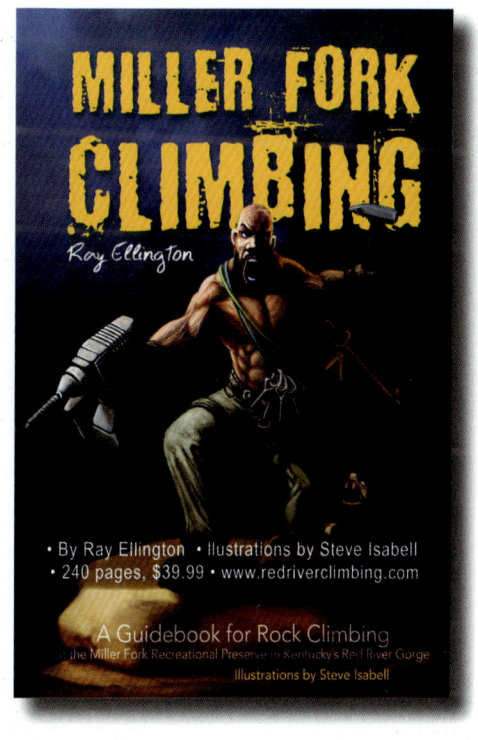

359

ABOUT THE AUTHORS

RAY ELLINGTON has been climbing in the Red River Gorge for over 25 years, has done four previous editions of this guidebook, and is tired of talking about himself for this page. He lives in Lexington, Kentucky, with his wife and climbing partner, Michelle, and dogs Nala and Maggie, works as an IT Security Architect, and runs his website www.redriverclimbing.com.

BLAKE BOWLING lives and climbs in the Red River Gorge. He spends his time developing new routes, working for the American Alpine Club, and maintaining his website BadBolts.com, a nationwide bolt database where rock climbers can report bolts and anchors that need attention. He also is AMGA certified, and works closely with the Red River Gorge Climbers Coalition and the Access Fund to promote safe climbing and protect access for all climbers. Over the past 25 years Blake has ticked over 1700 routes in the Red, holding the top position in the rankings on redriverclimbing.com. Epic 14-hour solo adventure races, high-angle swiftwater and cave rescue, and van life are not foreign to him, but writing in the third person is. You can find Blake in and around the Red River Gorge, adding to his massive tick-list, dusting off boulders, and replacing crappy climbing anchors.